THE IV LAYER APPROACH TO BECOMING
THE STRONGEST VERSION OF YOURSELF

ELLIOTT HULSE
WITH CHRIS BARNARD

THE IV LAYER APPROACH TO BECOMING THE STRONGEST VERSION OF YOURSELF

Copyright © 2015 by Elliott Hulse

All rights reserved.
Published in the United States by Strength Camp Media Inc.
a division of Strength Camp II Inc.
3608 Morris St. N St Petersburg FL 33713
www.strengthcamp.com

No part of this book may be reproduced in any form or by any means without the prior written consent of the Publisher, excepting brief quotes in reviews.

Book design and cover by Derek Brigham | www.dbrigham.com | bigd@dbrigham.com

Photography by Daniel Garry.

All registered trademarks in this book are property of their respective owners.

IBSN 978-0-692-59351-6

DISCLAIMER: The authors and publisher of this material are not responsible in any manner whatsoever for any injury that may occur through following the instructions contained in this material. The activities, physical and otherwise, described herein for informational purposes only, may be too strenuous or dangerous for some people and the reader(s)
should consult a physician before engaging in them.

First Edition

Special Thanks to

Cole Lutz

Mark Novak

Teiko Reindorf

Stephanie Lee

Derek Brigham

– ALL MY BLESSINGS –

As *The Tree of Knowledge* gave birth to human consciousness,

We each offer our blessings to humanity by the health and goodness of our soil and root systems.

Regardless, all humans are bound to both liberation by light, and affixation by the density of our darkness.

There is no way to resist this dilemma; to embrace it is Divine.

All of my mother's hopes, dreams, loves, fears, anxieties, desires, choices, experiences, circumstances and DNA.

Whatever her judgment, or the judgement of others,

It was her composition that provided the soil from which my physical, mental, and emotional being sprung forth.

I love you mom for being you; and for being more than enough to nourish and nurture myself and my siblings.

Your being is the life-giving compost responsible for this book, Strength Camp, my YouTube videos, blog posts, and the millions of people who have been attracted to the fruits of my toil.

Mother, you and I are one thing.

All seeds carry the blueprint which its progeny patterns itself.

Love and physical nourishment spark the flame of creation;

But energy, ideas, symbols, and its patterns bend the seedling towards light, and prune the shoots that were led astray.

Father, I honor you for taking my mother as the Earth to which you lay seed to my physical, mental, emotional, and spiritual awakening.

In this life, I've patterned my purpose, knowledge, love, and integrity after you.

Thank you for the opportunity to live as an extension of your character and being.

All that I am, all that I've done, and all that I have yet to accomplish carries the stamp of your devotion to my mother, compassion towards my siblings, your practical wisdom, and generativity.

You've always demanded that I grow up to be "better than you."

Father, you and I are one thing.

We all come into this world of boundaries, physically obliged to our flesh and emotionally compelled by our ego.

Awakening to one's Self requires nothing less than the systematic deconstruction of these perceived boundaries.

Nowhere is our ability to safely navigate the dissolution of these walls more possible than through relationship to our physical, mental, and spiritual counterpart.

Colleen, my Anima, my beloved life partner, teacher, and best friend;

You are the mirror through which I may perceive the best and worst in myself.

Since youth, you have known the strongest version of me, and have been relentless in your patience and support of my mission.

My devotion to yourself, Isabelle, Emerson, Simone, and Benjamin is infinite and everloving.

l do all that I do, first and foremost, for you.

Best Friend, you and I are one thing.

A Spark ignites a burning brush fire, but the chemical composition of trees is what consumes an entire forest.

Alchemy is required for transforming what is raw into what is consumable.

Ideas and action spark momentum, but a willing body of life is required to sustained combustion.

Through your pouring forth of competence and good care to my customers, clients, friends, and fans...

Through your hard work and devotion in supporting Strength Camp Gym towards its new life...

Through your willingness to learn, grow, and become everything you're capable of...

Chris Barnard, you gracefully wear your destiny as the roaring Alchemical Flame Of Creation.

I am grateful for your contribution to this book, to Strength Camp, and to my life.

Alchemist, you and I are one thing.

Uncle Elroy, Auntie, Eric, Ellis, Stacey, Ryan Magin, Danny Magic, Shan-dog, Paul Chek, Robert Glazer, Dave Ruel, Matt Gallant, Mike Westerdal, my mentors (large and small), my family (named and not), my friends (proponents and detractors), fans (curious and devoted), my demons, my angels...

And Cole Lutz and Mark Novak for your loving contributions to this book...

We Are One God.

Thank you, Creator.

With open and penetrating love,

Elliott Hulse

Elliott I Hulse

Fall 2015

— Contents —

All My Blessings	iii
Preface by Chris	1
Letter from Elliott	11

Introduction

King's Character, Core Values, and Mission	15
Four Layers of Strength Overview	29

Section I: Neuromuscular Strength

1.1 Introduction to Strength Camp Training	31
1.2 Structure	
Lesson I - Four Power Centers & Structural Integrity	51
Lesson II - Posture, Primal Patterns, & Movement Units	75
1.3 Strength	
Lesson I - Types of Strength & Training Maxes	111
Lesson II - Periodization, Hypertrophy, & Nervous System	133
1.4 Speed	
Lesson I - Motor Units, & Rate Coding	173
Lesson II - Force/Velocity Curve, Rate of Force Development, & Plyometrics	183
1.5 Silence: Deload, Balancing Your Nervous System, & Recovery Methods	197
1.6 Mechanics: Strength Camp Periodization & Movements	209

Section II: Physiological Strength

2.1	Nutrition: Biochemical Individuality, Macro Typing, Meal Prep, & Fine Tuning	273
2.2	Digestion: Healthy Digestion, Enzymes, & Probiotics	295
2.3	Hydration: Water & Bath & Body Products	305
2.4	Biological Rhythms: Daily Rhythms, Annual Rhythms, & Seasons of Life	315

Section III: Energetic Strength

3.1	Your Body is Your Brain: The Three Brains, Electromagnetic Heart, & Chakra System	335
3.2	Bioenergetic Breathing: The Bow, Bioenergetic Stool, & Open Front Breathing	367
3.3	Meditation: Active Meditation, Bioenergetic Catharsis, & Anabolic Bioenergetics	381
3.4	The Psyche: The Quest of Meaning & Development of the Psyche	405
3.5	Archetypes of Wholeness: King, Warrior, Magician, & Lover	421
3.6	The Inner Journey: Dancing the Four Quarters, Eating Your Shadow, & Finding the Center	443

Section IV: Life Mastery

4.1	Your Vision: Establishing Your Vision & Core Values	459
4.2	Setting the Intention: Visualization & Affirmation	479
4.3	The Hero's Journey	489
4.4	Initiation: The Outer Journey, Ritual Process, & Initiation in the Modern Era	509
4.5	Grow Stronger and Empower Others	519

References	527

– Preface –

He was raised in a blue-collar home, where he was taught to always be a provider, not a taker; and to stay true to the hardworking, honest, and humble path.

For years, this upbringing had suppressed the big dreams and ideas that he had. A lack of self worth weighed heavily on him from an adolescence steeped him in a society and culture that encouraged mediocrity. In fact, they made mediocrity a standard to strive for and be comfortable with.

This culture had made him a slave for such a long time that he learned to accept his place in life as final, perhaps unchangeable. Fear of dead ends drove him into a corner. With no one to guide him, it seemed as though the corner was where he'd have remained, anxious, unsatisfied, scared. Still, he found himself constantly pondering about how he would escape the mental shackles that had enslaved his mind and his life.

Eventually, he grew older; experienced more; became wiser. Somehow he stumbled upon an awareness of the fact that the feelings of inadequacy that he felt in himself were just that: feelings. The fear that he felt gripping his chest whenever he thought of chasing his dreams was merely a construct of his own mind. It was not real. These fears had trapped him in his past and locked him in place, preventing him from moving forward and realizing the dreams that he had held within.

Through time, he identified and began to take control of these concepts that did not serve him but rather had held him back from his journey. This period started out as a small spark of hope within his heart. He didn't realize it at the time, but the lessons he was learning from watching those around him and on the football field had started a fire burning. No one could notice it. Not even he could, but he began to subconsciously believe that he was more than what his life had been. This was the first step on his journey, on his mission.

The spark was cultivated through mentorship, until it grew and grew, slowly being fed by thought and focused action.

He knew that something was happening, and he knew that in order to build the fire he needed to feed it with those around him and with the environment in which he had placed himself. These were essential steps: he took control of his surroundings, and he had to detach himself from the people, ideas, beliefs that were not serving his mission. It was from that place that he set forth into the unknown.

He made a commitment to associate only with those who supported his yet unrealized goals. He made a commitment to only be in places that allowed him to share his gifts with others and to build his innate talents. Over time, that small spark transformed into a roaring fire, a fire that became the call to action he'd always desired and the journey he'd deserved--that we all deserve.

As his excitement grew, he felt the darkness of his prior self-doubt and fear of unworthiness creep into the pit of his stomach and tighten like a vice around his chest.

What would people say? What would his parents think? What happens if it didn't work out? What if he failed?

Forget all that!

The blazing fire of courage and purpose leapt forth and engulfed these ideas, burning them up.

Preface

He set forth.

At this moment his journey has been in progress for years. He finds new comfort in uncertainty. He has become comfortable with being uncomfortable. He is finally walking his own path and discovering his own truth. Only now is he starting to realize how amazing he, and everyone, really is. He sees his true reflection but not as the unworthy man the world had previously cast him as.

This is just the beginning, as he now carries a fierce determination and the discipline to continue on this journey with those who stand around and with him. This is just the beginning to the journey of his Becoming a Stronger Version of Himself.

This book, perhaps, is the beginning of you Becoming the Strongest Version of Yourself.

Maybe you have felt that spark that he once felt. Maybe this is the calling all of us need to find; to take what is ours and set forth on this endless journey, with the hope of approaching inner mastery and peace. His goal was to express love freely and live without doubt or fear. His goal remains the same.

This is me. This is you. This is us.

This book's intention is not to provide a operations manual, or a step-by-step process, but rather to open and enrich your mind through ideas of setting forth on this journey for yourself. This book is simply a spark. You must fan the flames and feed the fire. You must diligently work through each aspect of yourself to become strength. Strength in body. Strength in mind.

My name is Chris Barnard, and I sit here today, writing this to you with the hopes of reaching you in whatever stage of your own personal development you may be in. I hope to share with you, through my ideas and my experiences, the joys of personal growth that must be fostered through courage and commitment.

To me the Modern King represents our ability to master our own personal and shared struggles and successes. Just as Kings of the past had to rule their Kingdom through the use of laws, displays of power, and sometimes going to war, we have to rule our lives through developing good daily habits, setting goals, constantly learning, and disciplining ourselves mentally and physically.

Becoming a King does not mean that you are better than anyone else. It means that you are a King of your own domain which is your own body and mind. Becoming a King represents understanding and mastering one's own consciousness, as well as choosing the path to become continuously better each and every day. Kings realize that the little things are the big things and that the only way to have an impact on others is to first grow stronger as an individual.

We want this book to open your own mind into exploring ways to help you become better. We aim to do this through sharing with you the lessons that we have learned through our own personal experiences. These are lessons that have helped us Become Stronger Versions of Ourselves. These are lessons that will in turn help you.

Allow myself and Elliott to open your mind and body, as we come from a place of love and an authentic desire to watch you find and heed your own call-to-action in life, and finally, conquer the limitations the world may have put in front of you. Limitations that are not real. Limitations that are meant to be shattered. Realize that those obstacles are there to help you grow into the man or woman you are meant to be. Without those obstacles there would be no growth.

Watching people grow stronger every day has been one of the ultimate blessings I've been able to have from my place in helping Strength Camp grow into the community it is today.

Strength Camp started as an idea in a park. This idea spoke to the soul of the attendees and later transcended the particular exercises for that day and the people performing them. It became a call-to-adventure that spoke to many young men and women who wanted more in life and strived to not settle for mediocrity. It became a call-to-action to better oneself.

It became a mission of ours to forge anyone and everyone into Becoming the Strongest Version of Themselves by empowering them to feel strong in their bodies and strong in their minds.

We are not here to tell you exactly what to do to get there. There is no one way. This book, however, is a blueprint of ideas that have supported us to become the Strongest Version of Ourselves. Use them how you will.

My Strength Story

Growing up in South Florida, football was my life. I made the majority of my best memories in pads on the football field. My football team that started off as friends and teammates ended up being family. For the span of almost a decade, from little league through high school, we practiced together, played together, won together, and lost together. It was on the dusty football field under the scorching Florida sun amongst a squad of young men that I learned many of the life lessons that have made me the man I am today.

However the football field was not the only place that I was educated. I was a skinny kid and I knew that if I really wanted to stand out on the field I would have to start weight training. The reason I knew this was because my friend Kenny told me that if I wanted to get bigger and stronger I should train with him and his dad. Now Kenny's dad wasn't just an average dad who liked to hit the gym every now and then. Kenny's dad was a straight up southern badass. He had recently been released from prison for being a suspected mob enforcer. The man was a monster and that was evident when he trained.

I remember it like it was yesterday. Me and my scraggly group of friends trailing in Big Kenny's wake as he shouldered through the doors of the old hardcore bodybuilding gym on the rough side of town. The front of the gym was actually kind of nice with some new machines and treadmills. Kenny's dad had other plans and we marched right past those and he led us into the back of the gym into what looked like a metal chamber.

There were no mirrors, no shiny machines, no piles of plush towels, not one set of dumbbells that was not dented and bent. There was simply an iron cage, a bar, and some rusty iron plates. We started training. For the next 2 hours Big Kenny punished each of us ordering us to do rep after rep of the most basic movements. I remember feeling the sweat pouring off my face, and my knees starting to give, and my stomach getting queasy as we moved from squats to bench press to deadlifts.

My friends Chad, Kenny, and Jon were a bit older than me and were throwing around more weight than I could. I started to feel a cold feeling of inadequacy creep into my gut and I vowed that I would not be the weakest for long. I came up with a master plan that included benching damn near everyday, consuming information from the latest muscle magazines, choking down all the protein bars that I could find, and training any chance that I got.

I thought that if I could just get a bigger chest and bigger arms like the guy in the magazines that I would be the strongest guy in the gym and on the field. The truth is the more I did bodybuilding routines the more my performance declined. The best thing I gained from three years of chasing my tail with dead end workouts and misinformation was a relentless passion to becoming bigger, stronger, and faster. I learned how to dedicate myself to a task and to see it through to the end. And I learned the importance of training with intensity.

After highschool I linked back up with Big Kenny to train. This is when I was truly introduced to powerlifting. We trained every Monday, Wednesday and Friday without fail. We would also Squat, Bench, and Deadlift without fail. I was really skeptical at first because I was used to training specific body parts and doing isolated movements. Big Kenny's workouts went against everything I had read in the magazines, but

PREFACE

despite my apprehensions I decided to turn my brain off, put my faith in him and train the only way I knew how; hard. How could I not? He was a gorilla in the weightroom and I had barely put 10lbs of muscle on my frame in three years.

After 6 months of loading more and more weight on the bar I had transformed from a scrawny little kid to a yoked man child. It was through this experience that I learned the power of using compound movements, simple periodization, and intense focus.

A few years later I would have another experience that would change how I trained forever. At the time I had moved on from high school ball and was having an amazing season playing H Back at a Junior College out in Arizona. I was away from home for the first time, had a few offers from D1 Schools, I was on top of the world and truly felt like a ball player. Midway through the season I caught a high screen pass from our quarterback and before my feet could hit the ground I was cracked by a well-timed linebacker. He drove me shoulder first into the ground and I felt a spasm of pain as I lay on the ground. I was able to play the next play but quickly realized I needed to come off the field as I felt my collar bone protruding underneath my shoulder pads.

That night after the game I went to the ER and I recall the doctor telling me that I may never play football again. I spaced out as the doctor explained to me exactly what had happened. A flood of memories came over me from the extreme practices I had gone through with my football team to the hours and hours I had spent in the gym training my heart out with Big Kenny. I thought of my family and how much it meant to me to make them proud and in that moment I made a choice to come back better than ever. I would not let this injury hold me down.

Over the next few days I went on the internet to search out some Strength and Conditioning coaches in my area back home in Florida. I came across a guy named Elliott Hulse. Something was telling me that this was the guy that I had to go see. Despite the fact that he was an hour away I hopped in my car with my friend Byron and drove south to meet him.

The rest of my story is history as Byron and I trained with Elliott for the next year. He introduced us to a style of training that helped myself and Byron shatter all of our performance goals. The workouts consisted of sprinting, jumping, strongman and bodybuilding performed in a stimulating and intense environment. We came to work everyday and got better everyday.

My dream was always to play at the U. Or the University of Miami for those of you who don't know. And after training at Strength Camp with Elliott I felt that I had what it took to make it. I ended up getting picked up to play linebacker by the D-Line coach. I was almost on the team, I just had to make it through the paperwork process. My dreams were finally coming true. Unfortunately at the last minute there was a complicated process to transfer from my junior college to the NCAA and I was deemed ineligible due to some transfer issues that would actually end up being cleared up midway through the season. However I sat out just long enough for things not to swing my way that season.

I felt like my heart had been ripped out. I had worked so hard for something that I felt was my destiny and I had it taken away by some stupid paperwork out of my control. I was bitter for a number of years because of that but as the years have gone by I have come to see that this was a blessing in disguise for me. I ended up getting my degree in Applied Kinesiology and Physiology from the University of Miami and I have had the opportunity to first take over coaching at Strength Camp and now go into business with Elliott.

Throughout my journey playing football at Junior College and trying to walk on at Miami, Elliott was always there pushing me to break free from mediocrity and work hard for what I wanted my life to become.

When I started working with him I saw something in him that I wanted. I wanted to be strong and confident. I wanted to be purposeful in my life and directing my energy towards something greater than my own self interest.

Preface

His influence and mentorship is something that I can never thank him enough for as it pushed me to new heights and allowed me to believe in myself and my abilities. There is no doubt in my mind that without it I would not be where I am today.

Our relationship has constantly been evolving, from coach and athlete, to manager and intern, to business partners and confidants. It is this evolution that has allowed us to be successful and constantly push the boundaries of what is possible for us as individuals.

Elliott is not always an easy guy to be around. I mean this in the best way possible. He demands so much of himself. He is constantly seeking new ways to grow and understand himself. Because of this when you spend time with him you can't help but start to demand more of yourself. You can't help but get out of the comfort zone that you may be slipping into.

The energy that he carries has influenced myself to such a degree that it has spilt over into my relationships with my friends, family, coworkers, and athletes. Don't make the mistake of choosing friends that make you comfortable and do not challenge you. Through Elliott's example I have learned this and no longer value that which does not help me progress as a son, brother, friend, coach, business owner, and athlete.

Because of his influence I was able to pursue my passion of helping young athletes not only reach their dreams of playing at a higher level, but more than that I am able to instill good values and principles in them. My mission is to build strong men and women, not just strong athletes. I am able to do this everyday and I hope to do the same for you. My journey through life continues and I always strive to humble myself and learn more everyday. I hope that you can learn from my mistakes and successes in the same way that I have.

I'd like to say thanks to my family (Mom, Pops, Heather, Josh, Jason, and all extended family). I do this for you, and I love you guys with all I have. To my mentor, friend, and brother, Elliott: I appreciate your guidance through the years. To the Four Horsemen and all of my other friends: I appreciate the support and encouragement you give me to pursue my dreams. Much love to our team here at Strength Camp: Danny, Shannon, and Teiko. Special thanks to Mark Novak for his contributions to the book, as well as his intelligent insight and his help organizing my ideas.

Chris Barnard

Letter from Elliott

Dear friend,

Thank you for investing in my book.

It is with my sincere appreciation that I bring you **KING**, a book that covers many aspects of my personal growth, as well as the growth of my hundreds of clients and millions of YouTube fans.

In life--and in fitness--our greatest ally on the journey of Growing Stronger is balance.

A fitness program that lacks balance among strength training, flexibility, diet, and recovery will always yield sub-par results.

And so, too, will a life that fails to balance wisdom, discipline, relationships, and the bestowment of hope unto others.

To be a King, you must tend to your physical and mental health, as well as to the balanced Kingly character that you wish to exemplify.

In this book, I will show you my personal roadmap for having become a Stronger Version of Myself. It includes the application of my *Four Layers Of Strength* model for Growing Stronger. In section one "Neuromuscular Strength", you will hear from my friend, partner, and COO of Strength Camp Inc. Chris Barnard.

Chris will share our philosophy as it relates to physical strength and performance training. We take a holistic approach to fitness training, so even if you're not interested in training with weights, you will want to read this chapter to better understand many of my concepts in the following chapters--particularly Energetic Strength and Life Mastery.

The remainder of the book that covers Physiological Strength, Energetic Strength, and Life Mastery has been written by yours truly.

In the following section, I will share the philosophy behind my approach, as well as the **Strength Camp Core Values** and **Strength Camp Mission**.

I am humbled and honored to be a part of your life's journey to becoming the Strongest Version of Yourself, and above all, a balanced King of your own world.

Blessings To You On Your Path,

Elliott Hulse

Elliott Hulse

P.S. For your information, Strength Camp is my fitness training community located in St. Petersburg, Florida. You can learn more about it at our website: StrengthCamp.com.

INTRODUCTION

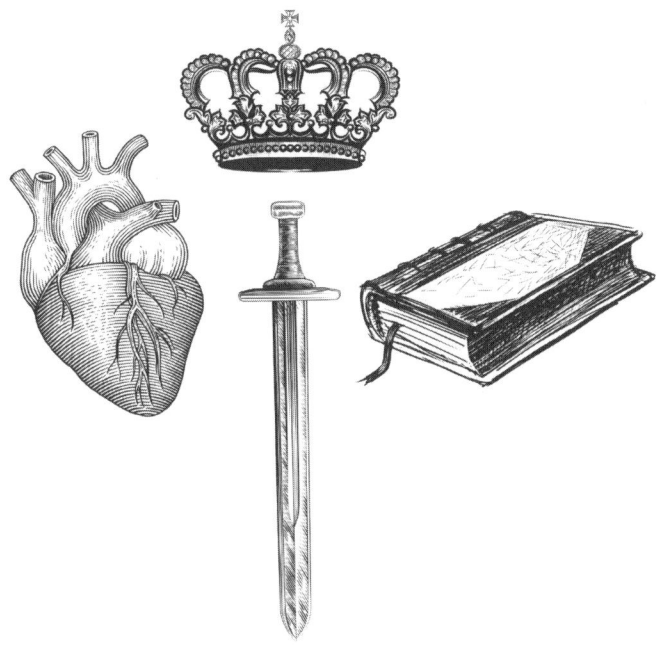

– King's Character –
Core Values
and Mission

The character of any individual or organization is defined by their deeply held **core values**.

The core values of an organization are evidenced by how the people in an organization treat one another and their clients. But more important than core values (and the virtues they embody) is the <u>reason why</u> these core values exist.

They exist because someone has to step up to exemplify these core values, and teach them to the organization. Not surprisingly, the person that holds the greatest responsibility for protecting an organization's core values is their leader.

As founder of Strength Camp, that responsibility ultimately rests on me.

The ***Strength Camp Core Values*** have grown out of my personal experiences as a team sports athlete, a professional Strongman, a strength coach, a father, a husband and a businessman.

The Strength Camp Core Values follow an archetypal theme, or themes following patterns, that we also recognize in religion, poetry, mythology, personal growth methods, and life philosophies of all sorts.

Within each of us is a tendency toward gaining **knowledge**, having a **purpose**, enjoying compassionate **intimacy**, and having the awareness of a **legacy** that we want to leave behind.

Everywhere we look we can see these themes taking shape, whether in ourselves or in others.

These four virtues of knowledge, purpose, intimacy, and legacy make up merely a fraction of our core values and all other qualities that they embody. I will share these core values with you in just a moment, but the most important thing here is that we must find and create a balance between these core values.

Before we get to that, I want to first share with you a bit more about myself.

I've Alway Had a Purposeful Warrior's Mindset

I was a football player in high school and college. **After college, I applied to join the U.S Marines, ranked as an officer.**

As I was packing my bags to take off for Officer Candidate School, I received word that my ship-out date had been delayed. After being delayed twice, I decided to **continue in my vocational work as a personal trainer.**

As a personal trainer and strength coach, I had the opportunity to keep my *Warrior's Mindset* alive, not only vicariously through the athletes that I trained but also through **my competing in the brutal sport of Strongman.**

Using this very same *Warrior's Mindset*, **I battled my way to the top of my vocation and industry**, while raising a family of six.

So if there is anyone who knows how to live a modern-day, civilized Warrior's life, it's your old friend *E Hulse* here, as I've done a lot of slashing, succeeding, and conquering.

Yet...

I Also Know What It Feels Like to Be a Failure

I felt like a failure when my football coach told me I was **too stupid to play** offense.

I felt like a failure when the people I called "friends" betrayed me, and I ended up in jail.

I felt like a failure when a girl, whom I'd secretly admired for months and brought flowers to, **laughed at me and called me ugly**.

Experiences, especially painful ones, shape our character. Every time we are judged, punished, or rejected, a part of our true character gets cast into the shadows of our consciousness.

These unresolved "shadow" issues keep us unbalanced. I'll explain in more detail what these shadow issues are, but for now, they may keep you from speaking up when you've been wronged; they may cause you to fear failure; and they may even keep you from ever enjoying intimate and loving relationships with others.

They become our character.

My own character has been greatly shaped by the experiences I've just shared with you but also perhaps by countless other experiences. Some of my experiences can be consciously recalled, whereas others rule me at the subconscious level.

Right now, you are also being greatly influenced by the experiences you've had in this lifetime... and perhaps by even countless other lifetimes.

Your Character Is Your Destiny

Now join me for a moment in this train of thought, as it follows a lot of the ideas and philosophies that I will soon share with you throughout this book.

Just like how an actor or actress dresses up for a role in a movie, you and I, too, wear a "costume," our physical bodies, to play our own characters in life.

Our characters can be revealed in the way we carry ourselves and even in our posture, for example. Even these subtle shifts in body language can further be heavily affected by how we feel about ourselves at any given moment.

In later chapters of this book, I will introduce you to some of the latest research on trauma psychology, the field in psychology that attempts to understand the impact of traumatic events on a person's psyche. Many prominent scientists and therapists have shown that the ramifications of the pain we've experienced (mostly in early-life) can manifest themselves in our physical bodies.

Think of it this way: your physical body must change--grow stronger, in this case--to meet the demands of your exercise program, but it must also change to meet the emotional demands of your own life.

However, in many cases, these demands cause us to reject or ignore critical parts of our nature in favor of self-preservation.

A good example of what I mean is to look at the different behaviors of two young men:

One young man grows up in a house with an abusive father. The boy may decide that he must be the "hero" of his home to protect his mother and siblings from the tyrant father. Further, this boy chooses that in order to overcome his father's aggression he must "stand tall" and "keep his chest up."

Another young man growing up in a similar environment may decide that it is best to keep quiet and remain unseen by the father, in order to avoid his attacks. For naming's sake, we'll call him the "coward."

Both the "hero" and the "coward" create psychological defences to protect themselves in these scenarios, but their physical bodies also begin to personify a "big-chested hero" or a "coward with his tail between his legs", respectively.

The hero may find that it becomes difficult to breathe when his father is present. He has trouble breathing perhaps because he is physically holding his belly in and his chest high. He doesn't realize it yet, but this manner of breathing is physically impeding him.

Likewise, the coward takes shallower breaths to avoid being noticed by the raging father. Unfortunately, this manner of breathing also becomes a physical impediment for him.

The young men in both examples are suffering, albeit a little differently: one from being overly stimulated, whereas the other is under-stimulated. These muscular holding patterns (that is, a high chest versus a caved chest and depressed posture) not only disrupt the boys' ability to breathe fully and deeply, but they also have a deeper psychological and physiological impact on their health and character.

If either of these boys grows up playing the character of "hero" or "coward", he may subconsciously overcompensate with one of our core values, at the diminishment of the others.

When core values are unbalanced, this can manifest in the young person's personal life and in their physical bodies. Similar to how the young man has paved his destiny and character, we might even say that **we are being our destiny** right now.

The road to changing our character, to becoming the Strongest Version of Ourselves and living out an enjoyable destiny, has two paths: of soul and of body.

We must travel both paths in order to work on both our mental character (soul) and our physical character (body), and ultimately, to Grow Stronger.

This book reflects the duality of my approach to achieving the Strongest Version of myself. By having read this far, you've already begun to move the wheels of your own destiny and shape your character through learning the importance of the core values discussed within this chapter.

The remainder of the book will focus on developing the physical character, the body, through exercise, diet, and a better understanding of our physiology and psyche.

Transformation of mind and body begins to take place when we choose our core values.

As we continue through this book, we will travel back and forth between ideas and the application of exercises that aim to transform both our minds and our bodies, **so that we may become Stronger Versions of Ourselves.**

THE FOUR STRENGTH CAMP CORE VALUES

Each of our four Strength Camp Core Values relates to a type of spiritual energy, which Carl Jung, the father of analytical psychology, called archetypes.

An archetype is simply a pattern.

According to Jung, there are very measurable patterns within the human experience. Some of these patterns are much more grand in scale, like the rise and fall of world empires, while some are less visible and seemingly insignificant, like your daily rituals.

According to Neo-Jungian Professor, Robert Moore, PhD, **there are FOUR very distinct patterns within human behaviour.**

These four archetypes work together to make a person whole. We each have some portion of each archetype.

#1 - **The Warrior aspect:** The disciplined, purposeful, decisive, and devoted parts of you.

#2 - **The Magician aspect:** The knowledgeable, objective, competent, and wise parts of you.

#3 - **The Lover aspect:** The sensual, compassionate, vulnerable, and intimate parts of you.

#4 - **The King (or Queen) aspect:** The generous, authentic, integrous, and legacy part of you.

Balancing the Four Strength Camp Core Values

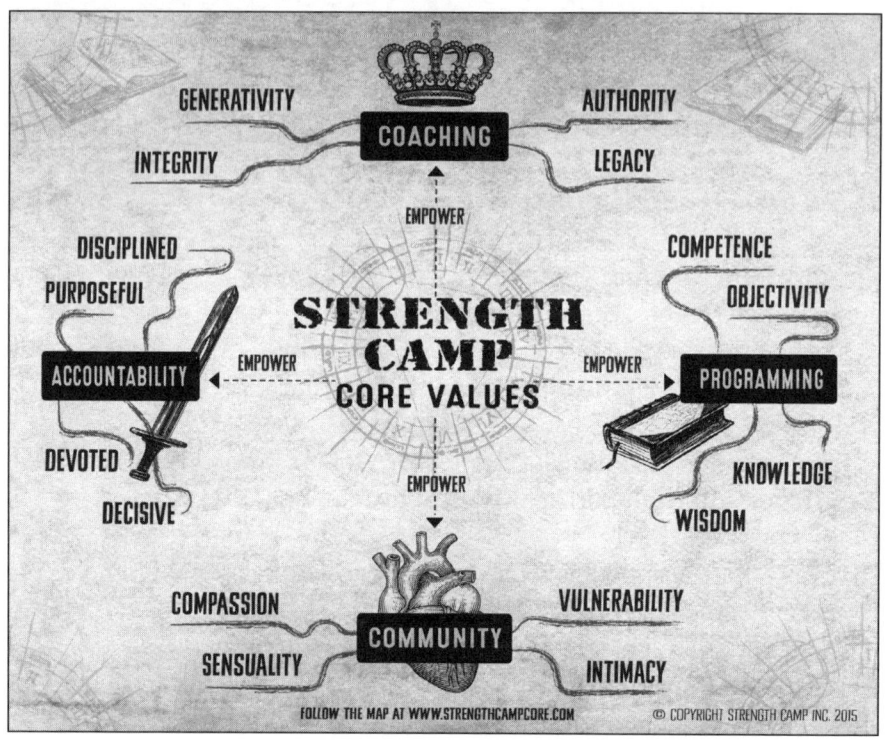

As I mentioned earlier, A Warrior's Mindset had always come easily to me. But it has taken me many years to mend the wounds of my Lover or Magician aspects.

Things might be a little different for you, **but the fact remains that we're all doing our best to live a joyful and BALANCED life.**

When consciously choosing our core values, we strive to create a balance of *Warrior, Magician, Lover, and King*.

CORE VALUES OF A KING

Core Value #1. ACCOUNTABILITY (Warrior) - Accountability represents the Warrior aspect of our system. The virtues associated with this aspect are: Discipline, Decisiveness, Purpose, and Devotion.

Core Value #2. PROGRAMMING (Magician) - Programming represents the Magician aspect of our system. The virtues associated with this aspect are: Competency, Objectivity, Knowledge, and Wisdom.

Core Value # 3. COMMUNITY (Lover) - Community represents the Lover aspect of our system. The virtues associated with this aspect are: Sensuality, Compassion, Vulnerability, and Intimacy.

Core Value # 4. COACHING (King or Queen) - Coaching represents the King aspect of our system. The virtues associated with this aspect are: Generativity, Integrity, Authority, and Legacy.

ACCOUNTABILITY VIRTUES

Devotion: We are about being DEVOTED to a higher sense of Self, or whatever you perceive to be a *Stronger Version of Yourself*. There is no requirement to devote yourself to anyone, or anything else, but your own ideal Self.

This might sound selfish to some, but later on, I will discuss how "I-Love" is the prerequisite for "We and All-Love."

Purpose: We are about having a PURPOSE toward that which we direct our efforts for *growing stronger*. Our reason for becoming a Stronger Version of Ourselves must be bigger than ourselves.

Purpose is your *Why*, the underlying reason for your being a Strength Camp member. Ask yourself honestly: why become a stronger you?

Decisiveness: We are about being DECISIVE when choosing what is right for you. Oftentimes, you may wait for the stars to align or for someone else's permission before choosing.

You have a primal sense about what is right and good for you at any given moment. Choose to take decisive action on what you believe in.

Discipline: We are about having the DISCIPLINE to do what you have to do, whether you feel like it or not. When you choose who you want to become, and what you need to do to get there, you just do it.

Nothing worthwhile is ever built without a healthy dose of self-detachment, or being able to step away from situations that may hinder you. Discipline yourself and work every day on the things that are necessary for growing stronger.

Programming Virtues

Knowledge: We are about exploring a wide spectrum of ideas, philosophies, and scientific concepts, with the aim of applying what is good and useful to our lives and the lives of others.

When we are aware of our ignorance and make efforts to gain knowledge, we are actively growing stronger.

Competence: We are about gaining mastery in areas of knowledge that are interesting and useful to you. Mastery requires that you can competently apply your acquired knowledge.

Competence comes from the experiences of having applied knowledge, and is required for living an effective life.

Objectivity: We are about being open-minded to new ways of thinking, training, and being. We remain objective by taking an "outsider's view" of our ideas, beliefs, biases, and feelings.

Objectivity releases us from our personal shackles, and gives us a more holistic perspective on the people and circumstances that life presents us.

Wisdom: We are about giving ourselves, as well as the people in our lives, the time necessary to learn and grow. Some things can only be learned through experience, and with experience comes wisdom.

Wisdom requires patience, which in turn, may be the guiding principle in nature. As famous American poet and philosopher Ralph Waldo Emerson puts it, *"Adopt the pace of Nature, her virtue is patience."*

COMMUNITY VIRTUES

Sensuality: We are about being deeply in touch with your senses. By listening to the subtle language of our bodies and minds, we are more grounded in our choices and behaviour.

When we hear, trust, and act based upon the primal wisdom of our bodies, we are being guided by "the Holy Spirit."

Human beings have more than just the five senses of seeing, smelling, hearing, touching, and tasting; we also have reasoning, will, memory, perception, imagination, and intuition, all of which should be given ample consideration.

Vulnerability: We are about being honest with ourselves so that we may ultimately have the strength to be honest with others. Instead of protecting ourselves by willfully remaining ignorant about our real hopes, dreams, fears, and general feelings, we can observe ourselves and make peace with our frailty as humans.

When we are honest with ourselves, we are confident enough to allow ourselves to be vulnerable with others, without fear of rejection.

There is great strength in allowing yourself to be vulnerable.

Compassion: We are about realizing our own imperfections so that we may have compassion for others. Human beings are social by nature. We are deeply dependant on one another.

Compassion allows us to forgive ourselves, forgive others, and allow for warming intimacy.

With compassion, we can all be more accepting, knowing that there is a soft spot in ourselves, as well as a soft spot in others.

That we are to love others, just as we love ourselves.

Intimacy: We are about community. For any healthy community to survive, there must be a healthy amount of intimacy. We develop intimate bonds--either consciously or subconsciously--with all of the people in our world.

We all want a safe environment in which we can be ourselves and enjoy one another.

COACHING VIRTUES

Integrity: We are about aligning our actions with our deepest held beliefs. When we are clear about our Core Values and allow them to guide the choices we make, we become mentally and physically aligned.

Integrity is about a common thread between our thoughts, words, actions, habits, and characters.

Authority: We are about writing the book on our own lives. By assuming authorship, we are the authority of our own experiences. It is after self-authorship, knowing our own experiences and circumstances, that authority amongst men begins.

When we take responsibility for the people and circumstances that we have written into our lives, we are more likely to draw the very best of those people and circumstances toward ourselves.

Generativity: We are about "paying it forward", the idea of repaying a good deed by helping others. In life, we will have received support from everyone, including our mothers who brought us into this world or perhaps a stranger who saved your life.

We ascend in life through the altruisms and blessings of others, and it is our human responsibility to pass on these blessings to others--to pay it forward. Everything--from a firm pat on the back to saving someone's life--generates hope for the future of our human family.

Generativity means sowing positive seeds in the hope for a fruitful future, even long after you've passed away.

Legacy: We are about realizing that the world doesn't end at our front door. We are all part of an awesome Universe, so vast and indescribable.

Yet the ripples we create from our actions can effect change. Your Legacy is measured by both the quality and quantity of ripples that you're sending out at this very moment.

We are life, and life is happening to us.

These four Core Values, along with their connective virtues, are our tools for reconstructing our characters into the Strongest Version of Ourselves.

As the Strongest Version Of Ourselves, it is our main mission in life to *empower one another*.

Hence, the mission of this program is to:

Become the Strongest Version of Ourselves, and to empower one another.

BECOME THE *Strongest* VERSION OF *Yourself*

STRENGTHCAMP.COM

Four Layers of Strength Overview

As in my ***Four Layers Of Strength*** ebook, this book, too, is comprised of four major sections, each containing several subsections and designed to be actionable for you. Each section relates to one of the Strength Camp Core Values, as well as one of the Four Layers Of Strength.

If you're unfamiliar with them, here are our Four Layers Of Strength:

Layer One -
<u>Neuromuscular Strength</u> (Core Value: Accountability)

In Layer One, we associate neuromuscular strength with our core value of accountability. This represents the devotion, the discipline, and the purposeful attitude which we must garner in order to follow our training programs with unyielding consistency.

The section Neuromuscular Strength was written by my friend and COO at Strength Camp, Chris Barnard. In this section, Chris will introduce you to our four-part training model that consists of: Structure, Strength, Speed, and Silence.

Layer Two -
<u>Physiological Strength</u> (Core Value: Programming)

Layer Two speaks to our core value of programming because it embodies the competence, the wisdom from our own experiences, and objectivity needed to make good choices for your health.

The section on Physiological Strength, as well as all of the remaining sections, was written by me, Elliott Hulse. In this section, I will introduce you to the best practices for diet, lifestyle, and honoring your biological rhythms.

Layer Three -
__Energetic Strength__ (Core Value: Community)

This Layer Of Strength ties into the core value of community. It represents the sensuality that we require to be physically, mentally, and emotionally in tune with ourselves. Along with sensuality, it represents the compassion for others which we develop through an honest exploration of ourselves.

In this section, I will introduce you to concepts that help you become more in tune with yourself, such meditation, bioenergetics, your personal search for meaning, and a journey into the psyche.

Layer Four -
__Life Mastery Strength__ (Core Value: Coaching)

Finally, Layer Four has to do with the core value of coaching, through which we shift our perspective from self-love to love for others. When we generously share our knowledge, experiences, and goodwill with others, we all become coaches.

In the section entitled Life Mastery, I will introduce you to ideas around "empowering others" in order to stand with integrity, be an authority, and sow productive seeds for future generations.

Section I
Neuromuscular Strength

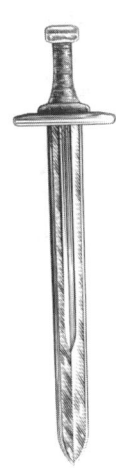

Introduction to Strength Camp Training

Training and Adaptation

When you train, the ultimate goal is to progress. Progress can take on many forms: going from "scrawny to brawny", learning how to manage emotions in times of stress, or developing the mindset of a champion. But in the following chapter, we will be more primarily focused on physical, or strength, progression.

Let's make this clear from the get-go: for any physical progress to be occurring, you must focus on the application to and management of stress on the body. Stress comes in two forms: physical and physiological. Physical stress includes: injuries, physical activity, infections, various types of physical trauma, and disease. Physiological stress can involve work, family and personal relationships, school, witnessing traumatic events, and major life events.

This means that the physical stress we apply to the body in the form of resistance training—and the subsequent adaptations that occur—is the most important way to measure our individual progress. As we put our body through intense training, it interprets the stimuli as signals to constantly adapt, to grow, and to recover. This is how we humans continue to grow.

If you have a specific physical goal that you want to achieve, you must embrace stress and apply it to your body in a progressive manner, over a long period of time.

GENERAL ADAPTIVE SYNDROME

In 1936, an Austrian-Canadian scientist, Hans Seyle, introduced to the world something called general adaptation syndrome, or GAS. In short, GAS describes the body's short- and long-term reactions to stress. He theorized (and subsequently based his research on) that stress caused most diseases because of its role in creating negative chemical changes within the body. During his research, his experiments showed the effects of stress on the body. When you extrapolate this data on disease, they can explain how to train—to apply stress to the body—to elicit favorable adaptations.

An example would be bigger muscles and greater strength to adapt to increasing loads on the body during training.

Seyle discovered that the body always reacted with a "biological pattern". When it's stressed, the body releases chemicals to restore itself to its previous comfort level. The aforementioned body's "comfort zone" is also known as homeostasis, the body's self-regulatory system that makes sure everything is "in balance" to survive. It is an important concept to understand.

Han's Seyle (source: http://www.selyeinstitute.org/)

You have undoubtedly heard about the body's reaction to a threat, known as your "fight or flight" response. It's so you can react to a threat very quickly. For example, if a bear appears before you, your survival vitally depends on a quick reaction, lest you end up as his lunch. These hormonal responses also allow you to react to stress and recover from stress, as your body attempts to return to that comfort zone, or homeostasis.

Don't misunderstand. Stress is not necessarily a bad thing. Stress is simply a stimulus that the body receives and reacts to. Seyle once said, "Stress is the spice of life...complete freedom from stress is death."

We need stress to spur us on the path to greater growth. It releases the chemicals in our bodies that can lead to more strength, more speed, and even more compassion for our fellow man. Without stress--as Seyle has told us--we would die.

In order to become the Strongest Version of Ourselves, we need to be able to force our bodies out of homeostasis by applying specific amounts of stress over a long period of time. It is a delicate balance, for if you apply too much stress—your body will not be able to recover. Apply too little, and your body will not change at all.

Stress can be your friend, if used correctly. It is all about how you react and recover.

To better understand the importance of stress, you must first understand the three basic stages that the body must undergo in response to stress: Alarm, Resistance, and Exhaustion.

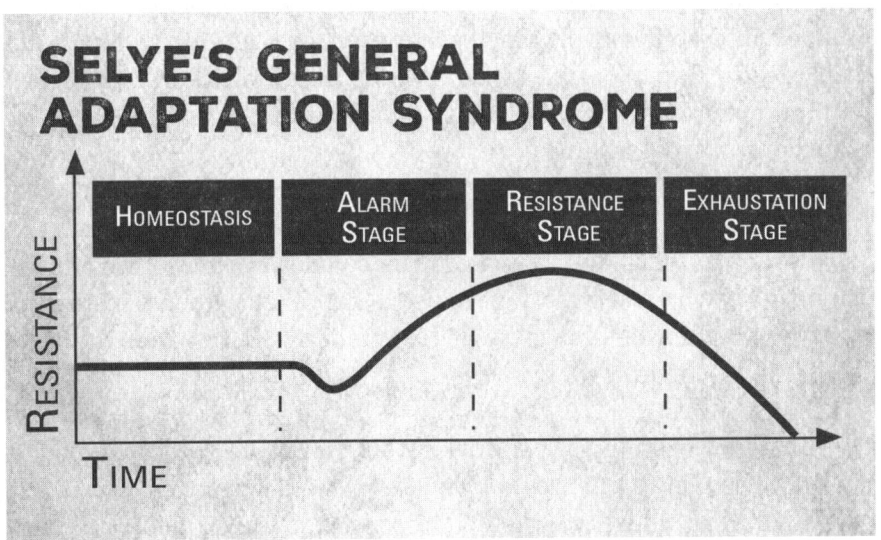

ALARM STAGE

The Alarm stage involves your body's rapidly activating the sympathetic nervous system and adrenal glands, while almost simultaneously dumping cortisol, adrenaline, and non-adrenaline into your bloodstream. All of these hormones are known as "stress hormones", and are released in order to give you the energy you need to either fight or flee.

These things—collectively part of your "fight or flight" response—happen very quickly. I am sure you have felt it before. Perhaps someone just cut you off in traffic, forcing you to slam on your brakes and swerve out of the way; or when the local bully approaches and you must defend yourself; or while you're playing a sport, you make some moves to escape a would-be tackler.

All of these situations usually involve you not remembering how you reacted, or why you reacted the way you did. It most likely felt involuntary, and essentially, it is.

Once your sympathetic nervous system kicks in, your heart rate goes up while blood is diverted from your digestive organs and gets pumped into your muscles instead to prepare them for action. Your body is going into full battle mode, so being able to fight off an attacker with pumped muscles and a hyper-focused brain is more important than digesting your last meal.

It's full-on battle mode! All non-essential tasks go on the backburner to focus everything on "the soldiers" going to war. As an aside, this is why it is important to use dynamic movements instead of passive stretching before we train; the latter can actually keep the body in "digestion" mode.

This is all well and good, but a problem occurs when your body does not use the energy provided by these stress hormones. Too much adrenaline can cause your blood pressure to spike, and can even lead to stroke or heart attack. Too much cortisol can cause various cardiovascular problems, ulcers, strokes, excess belly fat, high blood sugar levels, sleep issues, and so on.

During the Alarm stage, you may also experience feelings like anger, anxiety, fear, and/or panic. Your body needs these hormones and feelings in order to react in enough time to keep you alive. So, in this sense, these stress hormones are not bad. In fact, they are necessary for your survival.

Athletes that are hungry and driven to succeed are the ones that also happen to usually be the greatest. They are, in the words of Ray Lewis, "pissed off for greatness." Anger is not a bad feeling. Fear will not kill you. They can, in fact, lead to great feats of strength and athletic prowess. Both feelings just need to be harnessed and used correctly.

Remember what Seyle said: "There is no life without stress."

Resistance Stage

Once your body has inundated you with stress hormones—and you have successfully fought off the threat, or ran away from it—your body moves into the Resistance stage.

The stress hormones that previously filled your body will be reduced, and you will be left with lower levels of energy and a lessened ability to fight off another immediate threat.

This is the phase that kicks in if our body remains in a stressful state for a longer period of time, and it is in this phase that stress becomes unhealthy. Maintaining a level of high stress is not conducive to optimal health.

People in the Resistance stage will be very psychologically taxed, and often attempt to return themselves to homeostasis by: denying the situation that they are in, calming themselves down with drugs or alcohol, and repressing their emotions. None of these solutions are ideal for stress management. Plus, they rarely lead to any type of long-term resolution.

Physiologically, the body will begin to release hormones that cause the breakdown of fat to be used as an energy source. As long as there is enough fat on the body, the body can stay in the Resistance phase for months. Someone who has become lost in the wilderness, without any food, can survive for a long time because of this mechanism in the Resistance phase.

The body is built to survive. In the Resistance phase, survival is its primary concern. It is not interested in growing stronger or building muscle, both of which require a lot of energy. Rather, it is interested in feeding on its own energy stores in order to survive for as long as possible. Once again, it is not necessarily a bad response to stress, but it is one that we want to avoid, unless we are in an actual life-threatening situation.

If you remain in the Resistance phase for too long without adequate rest or recovery, your chances of getting sick tremendously increase. You will also enter the final phase of your stress response.

EXHAUSTION STAGE

The Exhaustion stage is exactly what it sounds like.

Your body is physically and psychologically exhausted. It can no longer put up a fight. When people say they are "burnt out", it is usually means they are in the Exhaustion stage of stress. At this point, your body is very susceptible to infection and disease, as all of its resources have been mobilized in the Alarm stage and used up in the Resistance stage.

If this continues, memory and brain function in general will be impaired. Depression will begin to set in. High blood pressure, heart disease, and other stress-induced illnesses will begin to take over the body.

Introduction to Strength Camp Training

In real life, an example of this could be a person who has an extremely stressful job and a stressful home life. If he is not able to deal with the stress or remove it altogether, there's a real possibility he could end up with high blood pressure, or worse, a heart attack. To make things worse, very stressful lives are usually accompanied by eating foods that are also stressful to the body's digestive system, as well as indulging in excessive amounts of alcohol and doing very little physical activity.

This combination of lifestyle habits and stressful psychological situations can be very dangerous, if you are not equipped to handle stress in a constructive manner. Meditation, training, and deep breathing are all methods that I have used to deal with stress. I've found that the better I get at dealing with stress—rather than resisting it or pretending that it is not there—the stronger I become.

Once again, I want to reiterate that stress is not a bad thing.

We need it to grow and to enjoy our lives. Playing sports is stressful, yet enjoyable at the same time. Getting promoted at work is a stress—but the good kind of stress. Starting a business and wanting it to succeed so that you can help others is a stress, but again, it's a good one if handled correctly.

Seyle once said, "Stress is not even necessarily bad for you; it is also the spice of life, for any emotion, any activity, causes stress."

I say these things because we need to understand how stress affects us to learn how to recover properly from our training and from our lives in general. The world is full of stress, but the stress itself can turn negative or positive based on how we react to it.

We can easily apply this exact model to training:

1. Training session (Alarm)
2. Recovery (Resistance)
3. Overtraining or under recovery (Exhaustion)

When we train, we are providing the body with stimuli that will force it to recover and adapt to repeated bouts of that stress. If we do not allow the body to recover properly, we will experience overtraining, or 'burnout', due to the body's inability to recover from constant stress. As athletes, we want to balance the right amount of stress with proper recovery and progressive programming to ensure we do not overtrain, or exhaust the body.

SUPERCOMPENSATION

When stress has been properly applied to the body, and is then given the adequate time and resources to recover, we are able to apply more intense stimulation to the body. This is the sweet spot we athletes desire. Known as supercompensation, this refers to the body's ability to recover from a training session and come back stronger than before.

Think of our body's state of homeostasis as a wooden fence. When we apply stress to that fence by smashing it with a sledgehammer, it is obviously going to break down.

However, we are breaking it down so that we can build it back up with bricks and mortar--much stronger building blocks for a stronger foundation. It will take careful planning, sweat, and multiple resources, but it will definitely be stronger than it was before.

Our new state of homeostasis is like that brick wall: stronger and more resistant to future sledgehammer attacks.

Supercompensation then is the body's ability to have a higher capacity for performance after having recovered from a previous training session.

Imagine yourself as an untrained individual, who begins doing push-ups for the first time. In your first training session, you perform three sets of as many push-ups as you can with one minute of rest between each set. Once this training session ends, your body begins to recover as you eat protein-rich foods, hydrate, and sleep, going through the Resistance stage.

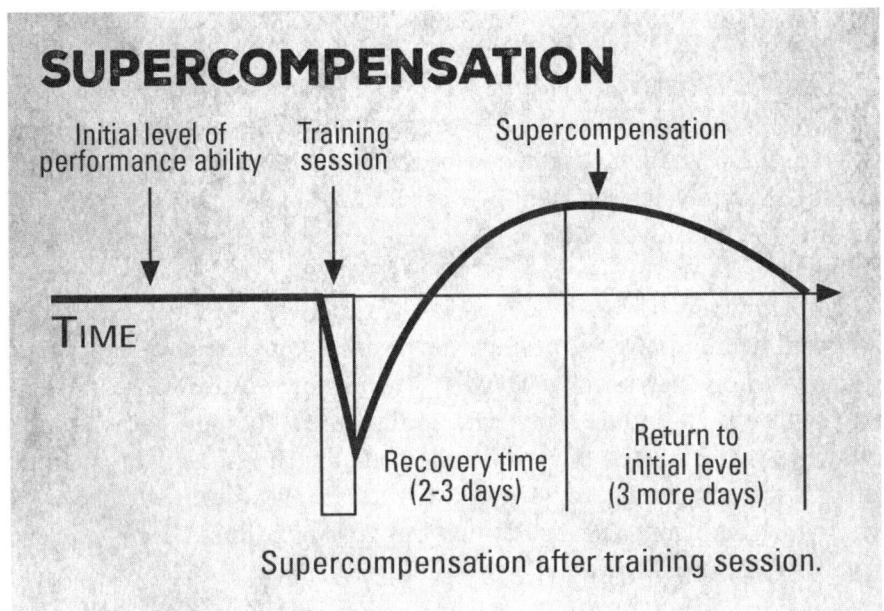

Supercompensation after training session.

The amazing human body begins to prepare for the next training session so that it can adapt to the stress a little bit more easily. So, during the next session of push-ups, you will notice that you can perform a few more reps than the previous week. If you are able to perform more, you are experiencing the benefits of supercompensation (and progress!).

The body is a beautiful machine, right?

As you can see in the figure, it is very important to understand that if we do not utilize supercompensation properly, our bodies will return us to our original, untrained state. This is because it feels that it may not need to complete the costly biological functions necessary to complete more push-ups in the future.

Supercompensation is a powerful concept that can even be applied in real life. It is the basis for periodization--or a well-planned training program, essentially--and can be used to get you or your athletes extremely strong in a smart, progressive manner.

Overtraining

Now, the opposite of supercompensation is overtraining. Overtraining can be experienced when we over-stimulate the body with stress—be it physical or mental—over and over again, before the body has a chance to fully recover.

This typically occurs over a period of time without letting the body recover. Going back to the push-up example: you might experience the effects of overtraining if you try to perform multiple sets every day, neglecting to nourish, hydrate, and rest the body properly. By not allowing recovery, the body no longer adapts, reaches a plateau, and then eventually begins to burn out. Overtraining would only occur in very rare cases from doing push-ups, but I use it to illustrate my point—you guys can understand the bigger picture.

Symptoms of overtraining depend on the athlete but can include: excessive damage to tissue—which can lead to an increased risk of injury and nagging muscular soreness; elevated cortisol levels; and nervous system burnout, which can manifest in the body as unremitting fatigue, depression, and vulnerability to illness because of a compromised immune system.

While overtraining should be avoided, the fear of overtraining should not be an excuse to avoid training with intensity or consistency. Your body can do amazing things and is extremely adaptable, as long as it is given adequate fuel and time to relax.

To further understand this overtraining, we must also know to balance Seyle's Exhaustion stage, or in the context of our training, overtraining.

First, we now know that overtraining is like a "burnout", or when your training exceeds your capacity to recover.

When your strength, hypertrophy or weight loss progress plateaus, overtraining could be a cause. Before you look at overtraining, there

Introduction to Strength Camp Training

are other areas of your lifestyle to examine first. Perhaps your diet is lacking in the micro- and macronutrients that your body requires to recover and rebuild. It could also be a lack of quality sleep and times of relaxation. It could even be due to the monotony of your training program, or not enough time between training sessions.

Put simply: overtraining is the physiological response that happens when the body has exceeded its capacity to recover from the amount of stress we place on it. But remember that you make it work hard for you, and so you must work hard to nourish it, take care of it, and train in a way to minimize the chances of overtraining.

Deloading

Over time, your nervous system will become overloaded by training stress, and your strength gains will begin to plateau. This is commonly a time when people begin to give up on their training, thinking that inferior genetics, poor biomechanics, or a lack of willpower and/or consistency are the problem.

It's none of these; the usual problem is that you are not giving your body the time it needs to recover and come back stronger!

A simple tactic to combat this is through a process called deloading. Deloading is a programmed rest period at a certain time in an athlete's training schedule. In other words, it is a "planned" rest.

Deloads allow tissue to repair; the nervous system to recover; and hormones to regulate themselves. As we have seen, overtraining has been shown to reduce performance, decrease your capacity for work, alter the psychology of the athlete, and increase fatigue when resistance training.

This brief deload period, typically lasting 5-10 days, promotes recovery and allows you to properly implement higher intensities during your working phases. Just think of the supercompensation curve on a monthly basis, rather than weekly, for your training. It is essential to program deloads into your training to ensure constant progression (and to avoid over-stimulating your body).

When Elliott coached me for college ball, I had trouble grasping these particular words of his: "The hardest thing for an athlete to do is rest." This makes so much sense now. As athletes, we tend to fatigue ourselves, but fatigue is our body's way of saying it needs to deload. But instead of listening, we typically push a little more, thinking we can overcome the fatigue.

It just doesn't work that way. A deload can also give you the time to recover mentally. After all, it can be stressful to constantly get under a heavy bar and try to hit personal records (PRs) week after week, month after month.

I've found that when my athletes deload and aren't allowed to touch heavy weights for a week, they are hungrier than ever to attack heavy weights again the following week, and train with a renewed intensity and focus.

However, the deload is not a time to simply come into the gym and do whatever you want. You should be focused on technique, or spend time on mobilization and stabilization sequences. I like to use my deloads to pinpoint and address some weaknesses during that time. For example spending more time on strengthening my thoracic spine stabilization or working in some extra loaded carries for core strength. I also use the time to refocus on my goals and determine whether I'm on the right track or not.

Understanding this model, we understand the general process that our bodies must go through when actively training. We perform a training session, applying stress to the body. Then, our bodies begin to adapt and go through a process of recovery to internally balance the stress. Finally, our bodies supercompensate and naturally grows stronger for the next time we experience that similar stimuli.

So, training is essentially a constant effort to increase the amount of stress we can apply to the body and giving it the ideal environment in which to recover. As we train for a particular goal, it is important to intelligently program our workouts, so that each workout is consistently increasing intensity, volume, frequency, or load. At the same time, the program needs to include time to let the body recover and strengthen weaknesses.

We will be delving into those topics as we move through this chapter.

STRUCTURE, STRENGTH, SPEED, SILENCE

Strength Camp's method of training has always been built around four pillars: Structure, Strength, Speed, and Silence.

Through these four phases, we are able to successfully build strong, athletic, and durable bodies.

Working out is the easy part. What I mean is that I see many people who just go to their local commercial gym, hop on the treadmill for a few minutes, and then go through the motions with free weights. Maybe do a few sets of bench presses, curls, and lateral raises; then call it a day.

The problem with this is that you are just working out. There is no progression. There are no goals to aim for or guide your progress.

At Strength Camp, I preach that everyone needs to bring one hour of focus to the gym. We are not here to simply work out. We are here to train.

Training implies that we have goals that we are focused on, that we are striving for progression, and that we are committed to tracking our results. Progress is ensured by following a program that is not just spat out that day. Progress is ensured by consistently following a program with intensity, over a long period of time.

Structure, Strength, Speed and Silence are the framework that can be applied to a wide variety of athletic pursuits: from Olympic Lifting and Strongman to training to be a better ballerina. For instance, building structural integrity, improving posture, making sure that all your joints are aligned, and increasing stabilization of the core muscles always come before developing brute strength and blazing speed.

I have taken countless athletes through this path of progression, and they always achieve the results that they are looking for—as long as they are consistent with their training.

STRUCTURE

Structure is the initial phase of training and perhaps is the most important.

Building structure is correcting common muscular imbalances and setting a strong foundation upon which you can continue to build. We will discuss muscular imbalances in more detail later on in the Structure section, but essentially, they occur when opposing muscles become too tight or weak, and lead to the body's being unable to perform in an efficient manner. Muscular imbalances can lead to poor posture, injury, chronic pain, and other ailments. Our entire intention with correcting imbalances is to not only perform at a higher level, but to prevent injury.

To correct these imbalances, we apply stimulus to the body in the form of mobilization and activation. We will usually focus on mobilizing a joint, lengthening tight muscles, or activating and strengthening weak muscles.

By balancing the body with a comprehensive mobility and stability program, we can allow the body to move more efficiently, and increase an athlete's performance as a result. As our body begins to balance and adapt to new movements, we can begin to increase our work capacity as well.

Introduction to Strength Camp Training

Work capacity is simply your ability to perform work. In effect, the more work you can do over a period of time, the higher your work capacity. In the Structure phase, we want to increase our work capacity so that we sustain higher levels of training for longer periods of time.

Developing work capacity does not need to be complicated. In fact, those with the most variation in their work capacity training tend to end up being scrawny and weak. It sounds counterintuitive, but for now, just focus on the basics like sprints, sled pushes and pulls, and complexes with barbells, dumbbells, or kettlebells.

STRENGTH

Strength is our body's ability to overcome resistance. Life is about overcoming resistance. Whether we are carrying groceries up a flight of stairs, juking on the football field, or shouldering a wounded buddy on the battlefield—strength is a requirement.

An individual's potential strength can be directly correlated to the foundation that they've built from the Structure phase. You often hear stories of men who work on farms, or in mines or any other hard labor-type jobs, and end up being some seriously strong dudes in the gym. This is because of the solid foundation—work capacity, strength, and functional movement—that they have built for themselves before they started "working out". If you are serious about getting strong, then you need to build a strong foundation.

As we train to gain strength, we essentially stand to gain a higher quality of life. When you are stronger, all of a sudden you're beating those guys who used to manhandle you; your kids seem lighter when you pick them up; and you no longer need two or three trips back to the car to get all the groceries.

Through proper programming, correct tempos, intensity, rest, and recovery—we can increase our ability to move greater loads. Lifting heavy weights for low reps is the usual formula for increasing strength.

However, this is not the only, nor the best, way to increase maximal strength.

Muscle growth must also be induced, as an increase in muscle mass will directly increase one's strength. The process of muscle growth is also known as hypertrophy. Muscular hypertrophy is induced in a number of ways: through an increase in volume during your workout, the amount of tension that the muscle experiences, and the total time under tension.

Speed, acceleration, and lateral quickness are vital in most sports. After all, if you are the biggest guy on the field but can't move well or quickly enough, then you won't be of much use. The key for the athlete is to increase strength and muscle mass while still being agile and speedy.

Speed

It's not enough to be strong in only a few planes of motion. The Speed phase is all about expressing structure and strength in a dynamic manner. It's important for athletes who want to hit peak condition for competition, or someone who simply wants to improve their athleticism.

We as athletes and humans need to be able to move through space in a coordinated manner, which should be helped, not hindered by strength training.

Speed is the direct result of building a foundation, strengthening it, and then allowing the body to perform with explosive power. It is during this phase that we want to increase the intensity, speed, and complexity, while also integrating movements that teach the athlete to move dynamically and with confidence.

Introduction to Strength Camp Training

Silence

From what you have read so far, it seems as if building your body always involves hard work. And this is partially true.

However, there is another component to training that takes on a very different nature. We call it Silence. Yes, it is important to push your body to its limit so that you can grow stronger, but what happens when you've already pushed your body to its limit? More importantly, are you giving it the adequate time and resources necessary to recover? Or are you constantly redlining it and hoping for never-ending growth?

That's teetering on the edge of overtraining. It's true that your body needs stimulation and stress, in the forms of resistance training, plyometrics, and heavy conditioning, in order to adapt to greater challenges and to grow faster, stronger, and more athletic—but it also needs to restore energy levels, balance hormones, and rebuild broken down tissue.

The Silence phase is all about removing stressful stimulation from the body. When I am training hard, I am also focusing on my recovery just as hard. For me and my athletes, this means a focus on activities that will stimulate the parasympathetic nervous system: yoga, foam rolling, stretching, meditation, and other forms of active recovery.

Sometimes, especially after a extremely taxing competition or a long stretch of hard training, it is advisable to take a week, a few weeks, or even a month off from resistance training entirely, in order to allow the body to repair itself. This does not mean that you are doing nothing. On the contrary, some form of movement should always be a part of your daily practice—whether this means going for a hike, swimming, or practicing Tai Chi.

Silence can, and should, be included in your daily routine. For me, this means going for a walk every morning while listening to an audiobook. It is simple and does not take too long, but it allows me to have a moment of calm in my day. The best part is that this calming mindset stays with me and helps me, as I tackle all the challenges that I face as an athlete, a coach, and a businessman.

STRUCTURE–LESSON I: FOUR POWER CENTERS & STRUCTURAL INTEGRITY

> "Don't wait for extraordinary opportunities. Seize common occasions and make them great. Weak men wait for opportunities; strong men make them."
>
> —*Orison Swett Marden*

TRUST THE PROCESS.

CASE STUDY: Danny's Comeback

Trust is something that is earned. It is not freely given.

Nowadays it seems like athletes have a very hard time finding a program or a coach whom they can trust. A lack of trust leads to the athlete's not always following the coach's direction--perhaps they change exercises, cut reps short, nd basically half-ass their time in the gym. These type of athletes will always take credit when they do well, but lay the blame on the coach or the program when their expectations fall short.

The internet is partly to blame. The amount of free and unlimited access to information we now have gives rise to so many contradictory theories on training--from how frequently you should train, to how heavy you should lift, to when you should be eating. As a result, people are stuck, unable to make a decisive step in any direction.

However, Danny wasn't that way.

Danny was a high school wrestler. He came to me with very little hope left. He had been badly injured from wrestling: a badly cracked L3 vertebrae and a number of muscular imbalances. Beyond having been physically injured, his confidence was shattered, as doctors and physical therapists told him that he was unlikely to ever wrestle again.

On the surface, it seemed Danny would be a difficult athlete to coach, and in many ways, he was. But only because of his extreme physical limitations and propensity for injury. However, his trust in me was unwavering, and he, like most wrestlers, had a "no quitting" attitude. I knew that as his coach I would do whatever it took to get him back on the mat. I knew he trusted me enough to do exactly what I said, as well.

This brings me to this crucial point: It is vital that you, as an athlete, find a program and/or a coach that you trust. Oftentimes, this simply means choosing any program and following it *consistently*. Trust that if you put in the work, you will get results. Trust that it's not about having a perfect program, but about following your program perfectly.

The number one advice I offer to up-and-coming coaches is to really care about your athletes and clients. It doesn't matter how much knowledge you have, what degrees you have, or what certifications you have completed. Those are a dime-a-dozen and take a backseat to your compassion for your clients.

As a coach, If you don't care about your athletes' performance in their sports, or even as people, then you're not worth much as a coach and mentor, plain and simple. After all, if you don't care, why would you expect them to care? And if they don't care, why would they put in the effort and sacrifice to do the work necessary to succeed?

I cared about Danny. That's where it started. I already knew his strengths from watching a number of his matches. He certainly had the technique and speed on the mat. Next came identifying his weaknesses--overall tightness, core stability, and brute strength--and attacking them by building his upper and lower body movements while strengthening his core.

I first focused on mobilizing his hips. They were brutally tight from spending so much time in an uneven wrestling stance. From there, I consistently worked with him on core stabilization, with specific movements that allowed him to transfer energy efficiently through his upper and lower body.

Danny ended up doing some crazy weighted pull-ups and even benched a solid 225 pounds for 5 reps, while weighing only 132 pounds--that's crazy! For his lower body, I had to work with Danny's compromised spine; so in order to avoid loading it too much, we worked on belt squats and heavy unilateral movements with dumbbells. His legs had gotten so strong that the belt we used couldn't fit anymore weight!

Throughout his training, he completed gruelling, interval style swimming sessions on his own during "off days". He committed to doing mobility work before and after sessions--which isn't always fun, but he knew it was necessary. He pushed himself even without other athletes or me around--a testament to his will to succeed. He was a warrior.

Eventually, we got his core balance up to par, eliminated his back pain, and more importantly, had him conditioned and ready to wrestle in the City Championships, the biggest midseason tournament for him.

The day came. The pressure--for both of us--was immense, but I knew his heart, and I knew how much he had put himself into his training. I was nervous to see all the work we had done together be put to the test, but I was also confident that Danny would be better than ever.

Even more satisfying was how his entire Latin family had greeted and showed me their love and appreciation in a way that only Latin people can. Their warm reception made me realized just how much of an influence I'd had over this young man. And I couldn't be more proud.

At first, Danny breezed through his first few matches; few opponents were able to match his finesse. But the time finally came to test his might against a really good and strong opponent.

His entire family and I were behind him--hell, we were the loudest people in the place! Emotions rode high because everyone knew about the work, sweat, and time he went through to even be able to step on the mat again, let alone compete for first place.

Danny's opponent was no joke. Most wrestlers were physically intimidating, and this one looked the part. He was packed full of shredded muscle, and he didn't care about the Danny's comeback; he wanted to win. Danny started the match with slight hesitation. Noting this, his opponent took it to him for most of the time. However, Danny had managed to keep it tied until the last minute in the last round.

He deftly got himself into a position in which he could roll his opponent over and pin him, but he would need all his strength to do so. They sat there, locked up for what seemed like the whole minute, and he slowly wore out the kid with his strength and pure will.

Danny held on just long enough to feel the other guy give in just a percent, and then he slammed the guy on his back. In the next instant, I saw the ref pound the mat. Victory--Danny's well-fought victory--was had. We all jumped up, going crazy, and meanwhile, I saw the tears of joy running down his face.

In that moment, I was reminded about why I coach: I coach to build connections with people; I coach to show people the true potential that they possess. The way to do this is to get them to trust you. And the way to get them to trust you is to truly care about them.

From here on out, Danny was on a tear, beating the record for the most wins in school history and making it to the state finals, where he lost to the eventual state champ. All this was possible because Danny didn't just show up to every session--he gave his all every session; he did the homework I gave him; and he trusted me fully to help him recover.

He absolutely trusted the process, and as a result, he was rewarded.

Danny's Program

In order for you to gain a deeper understanding of the type of training Danny was doing, I have included one day of his training plan. The reason that I did not include a week or a month is that this is not the kind of program that you can just print out, do yourself, and then get the results that you want. Danny's training required me to be constantly re-adjusting the intensity, volume, and types of exercises that he would be doing.

If I had just written out a whole training cycle for him and just let him follow it by himself at some random gym, he would have end up hurting himself. My role as Danny's coach was to hold him back, yet know when to push him. Mainly, I had to let him know that he was not going to hurt himself doing certain movements, and showed him the protocol for prehabilitation, or a proactive way to reduce chance of injury, that he needed to do to stay healthy.

Pre-Warm-up (Hip Mobility)

Danny's warm-up always included a variety of hip stretches. The general consensus is that static stretching before training is not ideal because it eliminates the stretch-reflex component of muscular strength. In addition, the slowed breathing patterns stimulate the parasympathetic nervous system that promotes rest and digestion. However, when you are dealing with a client or athlete who is chronically tight in their hips to the point of injury, it is vital that you try to relax those tonic muscles.

Dynamic Warmup

All Strength Camp athletes and clients perform the same dynamic warm-up. It involves progressively more challenging and dynamic movements, from a simple walking lunge to backpedaling 10 yards and then sprinting forward. At this time it was important to really get his blood flowing and increase his heart rate, as it would not be a good idea to allow him to train cold.

Post-Warm-up (Midline Stability)

Midline stability, in this sense, is essentially core strength. This simply means how stable a position you can create and maintain in your midline through the duration of a movement. Think of keeping a flat back during a deadlift, or not overextending your back as you might do in a shoulder press. It is important to develop strength in this area of your body, as it is the base upon which all other movements are built.

For Danny, this part of the workout was treated as an extended warm-up. Traditionally, training midline stability is saved for the end of the workout. But for Danny, this was a priority. We had to make sure that the muscles supporting his core were firing and ready to stabilize his limbs.

You will notice that the movements that Danny did here all involved stabilizing his core while moving his limbs around. This is important, as wrestling is an unpredictable and dynamic sport in which combatants need to be able to remain stable in a variety of positions, while grappling with external forces caused by an unpredictable opponent.

Static holds are also great, and we utilized them extensively in Danny's training. But on this day, my focus was to teach him how to remain stable while moving his arms and legs against external forces. Simple exercises like bird dogs, dead bugs, ab wheel rollouts (when ready), and other exercises forced him to remain steady, resisting flexion, and stable in his core.

We used integrated movements, such as a reverse lunge with a twist. Integrated movements are essential for teaching both athletes and folks in the general population how to transfer force from the upper body to the lower body, or vice versa, while still remaining stable and aligned in the midsection.

Power

Danny is a tremendously strong athlete, but he had to learn how to use that strength to his advantage. At this point of his training session, he would be fully warmed up and have his midline activated. He would now be able to use his strength in a variety of explosive and plyometric movements. This is done before strength training so that the body is not fatigued. I want my athletes to be explosive when they are training to be explosive, plain and simple. They should not be fatigued when it comes time for plyometrics. Every rep should look the same, and be powerful and dynamic. If this is not the case, then they are no longer training power--they are simply doing sloppy conditioning work.

Strength

Due to Danny's spinal injury, it was impossible to load his spine. Squats and deadlifts were out of the question. This meant that I had to get creative with how to increase his strength without these classic strength-promoting exercises. The solution: pairing belt squats with unilateral exercises, such as front foot elevated reverse lunges. When we did this, Danny was able to increase his strength while sparing strain on his back.

Training the posterior chain (back, glutes, hamstrings) was also important for Danny, as he was very weak in this area. Sometimes trainers and athletes make the mistake of assuming that tightness in an area is associated with being too strong there. This is not true. Muscles can be tonic and very weak at the same time.

This was the case with Danny and his posterior chain. All these muscle groups needed to be strengthened in order to protect his back from the beating he took on the mat (or rather the beating he gave to other people). We incorporated power movements in med ball slams, for example, and plyometric movements, with a focus on being powerful and explosive on every rep.

Danny shows that it is possible to maintain, and even increase, the strength of athletes who are injured. This takes a thorough assessment and careful consideration of how loads are applied to the body.

For his conditioning, Danny worked in the pool--he would either tread water or swim laps, both done in an interval style. Once again, the swimming allowed his back to remain unloaded. It would have been foolish to push him in the gym, as conditioning often requires a high volume of work, which would've been too rough on Danny's compromised back and hips. After all, I knew he had already taken enough abuse during training and in competition, so I'd jump at any opportunity to reduce the amount of wear and tear on his body.

Finally, Danny's training required constant communication between the two of us, as well as with other coaches. Do not assume that you alone know everything (especially in regards to rehabilitation, in this case). Seek out a respected professional in your area and ask their opinion. Find a coach who knows his stuff and get him to perform an assessment on you. It is worth the time and the money.

DANNY'S SAMPLE PROGRAM

CORRECTIVE STRETCHES

1. Band Hip Flexor Stretch (Lead Leg Emphasis) - 2 x 20 seconds each

2. Band Waiter's Bow - 2 x 20 seconds each

3. Hip Circle to Pigeon Pose Pause - 2 x 10 each

DYNAMIC WARM UP

CORE STABILITY

1.A. Plank Bird Dogs - 3 x 20

1.B. Plank Banded Rows - 3 x 10 each arm

1.C. Swiss Ball Stir the Pot - 3 x 5 each way

1.D. Reverse Lunge with Med Ball Twist - 3 x 6 each way

POWER

1. Resisted SL Broad Jump (land 2, mimic shoot) - 6 x 1 each

2. Alternating Split Lunge Jump with Med Ball Twist - 3 x 6

3. Box Jump (Pause at Bottom for 2 seconds) - 5 x 1

STRENGTH

1. Elevated Belt Squats - 10, 10, 6, 4, 4, 3, 2

2. DB Supinated Elevated Reverse Lunge - 5 x 6 each leg

3.A. Swiss Ball Thrust to Leg Curl - 3 x 15

3.B. Med Ball Slam - 3 x 20 seconds

3.C. Front Load Lateral Lunge - 3 x 8 each leg

POOL SESSION (INTENSE)

1. Tread Water (to belly button) - 2-3 x 10 sec. on 10 sec. off for 4.5 minutes

Four Power Centers

There are four power centers, or key areas, of the body. All four power centers are intrinsically related. This means that if one is out of balance, then the rest of them will be affected. When they are strong and in balance, they can lead to massive potential for strength and power. [1]

Think of an Olympic lifter hitting a clean and jerk PR. If you've never seen a world-class lifter, go on YouTube and look some up. They make massive weights look as light as a feather because their bodies are perfectly balanced, and they are able to express strength and power in a dynamic fashion.

In essence, when you have some type of pain or an muscular imbalance that needs to be alleviated, it is usually--if not always--related to one of the power centers. As we develop stronger structural integrity, these are the centers that allow us to continue to grow stronger and build true power, athleticism, and dynamic expression in our body.

THE FOUR POWER CENTERS ARE AS FOLLOWS:
1. Navigational Center
2. Extensor Center
3. Core
4. Base

In the same way the four layers of strength build upon one another, the four power centers are so closely connected that weakness in one impacts all of the rest. For example, an imbalance in your base could also cause an imbalance in your extensor center.

---

1. Lee Paramore, Power Posture: *The Foundations of Strength,* Apple Publishing: 2001

NAVIGATIONAL CENTER

The navigational center is the main center through which all other power centers align themselves. If your navigational center is off, you can be sure that your extensor center, core, and base are off as well. As such, you can imagine that it causes the most problems in other areas of the body.

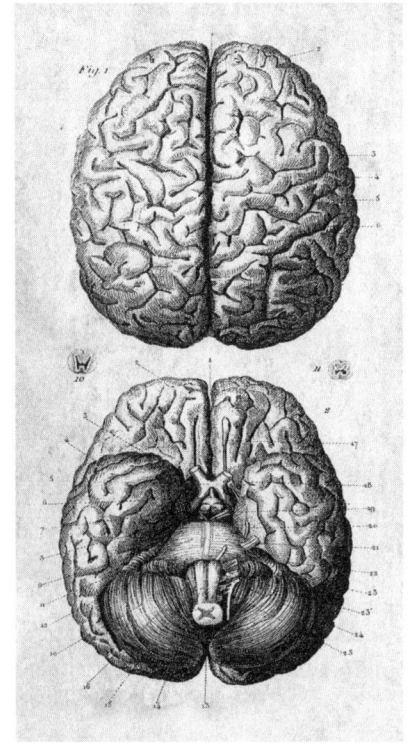

Think of the navigational center as the pilot of a plane. He's in the cockpit, making crucial decisions: how fast the plane is flying, if and when it descends or ascends, when they need to stop to refuel--all the while making announcements to the passengers. Your navigational center is analogous to this pilot. It controls everything: your thoughts, your breathing, how you recover from tripping on the sidewalk, or how you balance on one leg, to name a few.

The navigational center resides in your head and neck.

We want to be very mindful about the performance of our eyes, ears, nose, and mouth (such as with breathing and chewing). It may sound strange, but imbalances and problems in these areas can have a huge effect on the rest of the body.

There was a client of mine who had this problem. He had terrible low back pain that did not allow him to squat or lunge without being in tremendous pain the following few days. He wanted to lose weight, yet not being able to move without pain obviously was not helping him reach his goals.

I knew that there had to be a reason for his pain. And I found out why: his hips, core, and low back were twisted, or rotated. Usually, I would've stopped here and attempted to use only corrective stretching for his hips and core stabilization techniques to try to alleviate the imbalance and pain.

However, soon I noticed that every time he had a conversation with me he'd tilted his head to one side. When I described an exercise or told him what I'd done over the weekend, sure enough, he'd always cocked his head to one side. I figured that there was something wrong with his ears. He later revealed that he'd had an ear infection as a child and lost some hearing in his right ear, which put him in the habit of tilting his good ear toward the talker in order to hear what was being said. It seemed to me at the time that this would not have become an issue during training.

But let's think about this: in the early days of man, we know that seeing, chewing, hearing, and smelling all primarily contributed to his survival.

If he can't see and react quickly to a lion's sneaking up on him, he's going to be dead pretty quickly. To put it in the context of modern times: if he can't see and react quickly to a linebacker's looking to knock him on his ass, he's going to be riding the bench pretty quickly.

Based on this evolutionary drive to survive, your body will sacrifice everything for your ability to hear, see, and breathe.

In my client's case, his body had undergone a natural navigational shift. This meant that he was twisted in a particular way after years of leaning to one side in order to hear better. This led to his shoulders' being out of line, the imbalance of which continued to travel down his body to his hips and left him with back pain and an inability to move well.

We all deal with structural imbalances at various levels. None of us are perfect, but the main point is that the pain in your knee, or the lack of strength in your midline or lats, can usually be traced back to your navigational center. Again, it is the source of many problems. Survival is its only concern, after all.

If you want to learn more about this process, I invite you to find The Survival Totem Pole by Paul Chek. Paul includes a really incredible diagram that describes this process. In a nutshell: at the top of the totem pole is your breathing. If you stop breathing, nothing else below will function properly. Down at the bottom are your knees, ankles, and hips, which are usually the main joints that end up feeling all the pain because of your dysfunctional navigational center.

In essence, the site of pain is not always the source of the pain.

THE EXTENSOR CENTER

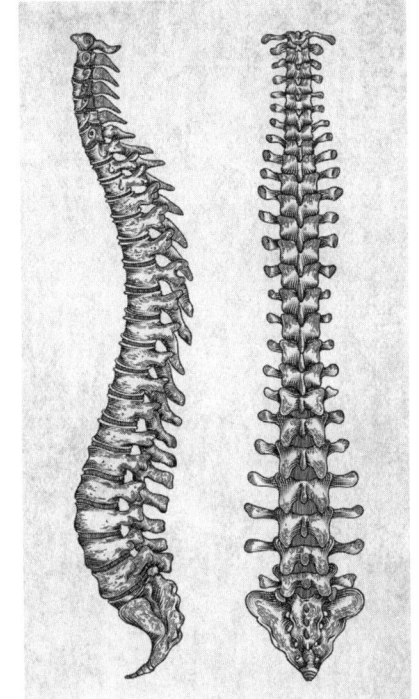

When talking about the extensor center, the most important thing to understand and create within our bodies is the thoracic extension. You've probably heard Elliott mention it a thousand times--and for good reason. The ability to move your thoracic spine within its full range of motion is one of the keys to unlocking your athletic and strength potential. It's that important.

The thoracic area of the spine goes from T1, T12, and is more generally the area that is right between the shoulder blades and the heart (T5-T6).

Many of the athletes whom I've worked with tended to have weak upper backs and anterior shoulders that were overdeveloped and very tonic, or tight. These issues can lead to instability during overhead movements, breathing issues, and core instability. Basically, they rob the athletes of their true power.

Healthy upper back muscles should behave like postural muscles, which means that they should be able to hold your body in the same position while being under load and keeping a stable core. In addition, you should be able to breathe fully and deeply. Unfortunately, most athletes tend to grow weak in their postural muscles due to sitting at work or in class all day.

Then, as these athletes start going to the gym, they tend to stick to and overdo it on the exercises that they are strongest in--usually pressing movements--and neglect other exercises that they need to be doing, like pulling and other corrective exercises. After this goes on for some time, his muscles in the front of the body become overdeveloped, and he ends up in a slouched posture--perhaps without even realizing it.

A dysfunctional posture is a result of repeating poor habits in your training and in your life outside of the gym.

The main problem is that no one really teaches you how to use your body. It's as if you learn to move well by instinct your entire life: you start off crawling; you learn how to walk; then you're off running---but you're kind of on your own after that. In today's society, you sit at a desk all day, do homework at a desk, watch TV or play video games while sitting, and then sleep in a strange position with your neck twisted and your back extended all night.

By the time you're 20, your posture has become less-than-ideal. If you follow this pattern for 20 more years, you can only imagine the consequences. Basically, your body is tremendously adaptable and works itself into the positions that you most often use (sitting, in this case). When you translate this to training, your imbalances, such as a very tight thoracic spine, makes it hard to progress very much over time.

There's hope yet, but correcting posture is not something you can do for a few minutes before or after you train only three times a week. You need to work hard on loosening tight muscles just as hard as you do with your normal strength training. If you are slumped over a desk all day and then try to overhead squat that night, don't expect to get a personal record or feel very strong in that movement.

Be patient with your progress, become conscious of your posture throughout the day, and stay consistent with both training and corrective exercises. Years of bad patterns are not going to be changed in a single night, but if you focus on slowly making progress over time, you will surely make improvements.

There will be setbacks, but don't give up!

CORE

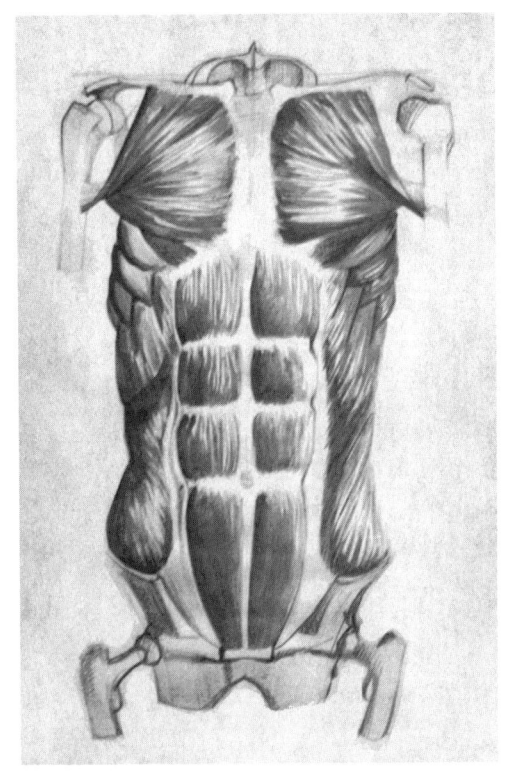

The core power center consists of the "inner unit" and the "outer unit".

The inner unit consists of: the transversus abdominis, the internal obliques, the diaphragm, the pelvic floor muscles, the multifidus, and the lumbar portions of the longissimus and Iliocostalis.

The muscles of the inner unit function as stabilizers for the torso, spine, and sacroiliac joint. Their role is to stabilize before movement occurs. So, before your arms and legs even move, these muscles should already be firing and locked in place. They need to have good muscular endurance, as they need to be activating when you're walking, sitting, or squatting a heavy weight.

The transversus abdominus is vital for stabilizing your body throughout a full range of movement.

For example, when you are squatting, you only want your hips, knees, and ankles to be flexing and extending. Your entire back should maintain the same angle and position for the entirety of the movement and sets. In fact, each and every rep should be identical to the first.

In order to create this type of stability, you need to be able to create strong intra-abdominal pressure--which is done by taking in a deep breath, filling your belly fully of air, and "pressing" into this air with your core to stabilize during the movement. This is essentially emulating the pressure as though you were wearing weight belt around your midline.

Without going too heavily into concepts like intra-abdominal pressure and the hydraulic amplifier mechanism, it is important to know that the inner unit is responsible for your being able to lift heavy weights.

Without a strong inner unit, you will not be strong. And without mobility, you will not be able to utilize your strong inner unit. It is that simple. Work on mobility first, and then stabilize.

Do not be fooled into thinking that strong abs mean a strong core. No, if you have abs, you simply have a low body fat percentage.

On the other hand, the "outer unit" consists of the rectus abdominus and the outer obliques..

These are the muscles that people see when you take your shirt off. And as a result, they tend to be the muscles that get trained the most.

This is not to say that you should not train them--you just probably shouldn't train them as much.

Pay close attention to how all of those core muscles interact because together they form the foundation of core stability. When you punch harder, throw harder, or do whatever it is that you want to perform through your upper body, it happens via a ground-reaction force, wherein that force is transferred to the hips and right through your core. In order to transfer the most power, you need a core that is extremely stable.

This is not something that crunches will help you with.

Rather, learning how to move dynamically while keeping a braced core will.

First, deal with your mobility restrictions and stabilize your inner unit. In so doing these, the outer unit will usually look after itself.

BASE

The base is what you stand upon. And as we have learned, this base can be highly affected by what's going on above it.

The navigational center, the extensor center, and your core all play a role in the function or dysfunction of your base, which includes the hips, knees, and ankles.

If you've got a forward-leaning head and rounded upper back, chances are your hips are probably tipped forward as well. This means you'll have weak hips, knee pain, and tight ankles.

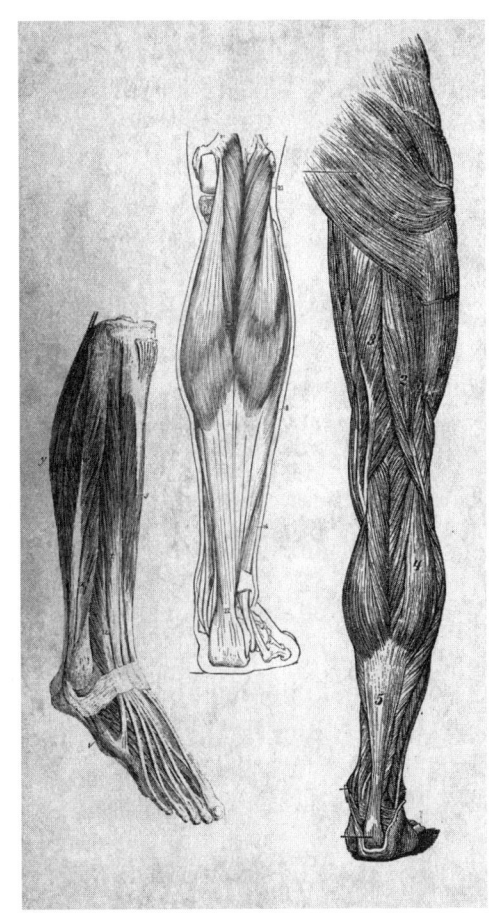

I know because I've dealt with this in hundreds of clients and in myself as well. Years of football, Strongman, bad squatting patterns, and overuse have left me with extremely tight hips, which can eventually lead to problems in my knees and ankles. I'm constantly working through my own corrective exercises and stretches to keep my legs strong and healthy.

My own experience with correcting this imbalance has taught me what it takes to develop a good strong base.

One way is to simply be aware of how you carry yourself, or basically having a sense of body awareness. It is something that not a lot of people think about, but it is very important to building a strong base.

Movement seems natural at first. You've learned how to move unconsciously. You watched how your parents carry themselves and probably mimicked them. Humans, especially children, are very adept at mirroring the behaviour of those around them. In fact, you have neurons that fire in the same way, whether you're doing something or observing someone else doing something.

In other words, if your parents have poor posture and movement patterns, then you probably are going to end up with similar patterns if you don't learn a better way from someone else.

For most people, building better patterns should be preceded by increasing the mobility of ankles and hips while also stabilizing their knees.

This can be done by using corrective stretches and exercises, in conjunction with just challenging your body to move through various planes of motion. Explore the limits of your body and find out how to push those limits. It will take time, but it will be worth it, as creating a strong base is vital to becoming the Strongest Version of Yourself.

STRUCTURAL INTEGRITY

Structural integrity is all about laying down a solid foundation.

If the foundation (i.e. the platform upon which a building is built) isn't strong and stable, then the building will naturally crumble.

Our mission is to become the Strongest Versions of Ourselves—not pile muscle onto an imbalanced, structurally-unsound frame. This is why we begin building strength from the ground up—by developing structural integrity. We are always talking about the importance of developing structural integrity, core strength, thoracic extension, and posture. Our aim is to build strength that lasts.

Because without developing strength, mobility, and stability in those areas, our bodies will inevitably fall apart under a great enough load. Weak structural integrity can lead to injury. It happened to me when I hurt my shoulder.

I'll soon share how imbalances in the other four layers of strength can negatively impact structural integrity, and vice versa, but allow me to first explain where my passion for structural integrity comes from.

I have always been a good athlete. Ever since I was young, I'd been playing with older kids and winning, though not usually on pure athletic talent but on sheer will and a willingness to put my body in dangerous situations.

I started playing football at a very young age, so the injuries began soon enough. I already had shoulder surgery when I was just out of high school; I tore my hamstring weeks before my first NFL combine, and I had always fought to keep good thoracic extension. Working at a desk all day tends to do that to you--I'm sure many of you can relate.

While I was born with some of these imbalances (to a certain extent), I've also brought further injuries upon myself through years of physical wear and tear.

Now chances are that—like me—you are structurally-imbalanced, too. We're all sort of screwed-up in our own unique ways. These imbalances can be brought on by poor movement patterns from childhood, old injuries, or just from genetics.

The important thing to ask now is: what can we do about it?

I believe it is vital that we remain aware of our unique imbalances and be in touch with our bodies enough so that we are able to detect new imbalances when they arise. This way we can implement the necessary tools to correct and prevent them.

One way that would help is to view your exercise program as a form of customized "medicine" that aids in alleviating your imbalances. You are not training to destroy your body. You are training to build a solid base upon which you can build strength and power.

This goes as much for your daily habits and activities—how you sit, how you sleep, how you get from home to work or school—as it does for your training routine.

If I were to continue beating the crap out of myself with Strongman exercises and football, I would continue to breakdown. It is vital that I take care of myself and focus on structural integrity *before* strength and power. There is no way around it.

When you lack structural integrity, there is usually a misalignment of your joints. This means your joints don't sit in their instantaneous axis of rotation, or in more simple terms, their more "optimal" position. Of course, every joint is very different. I'm referring to a very rudimentary model of a ball-and-socket joint. Basically, if the muscles surrounding the joint are all in balance--meaning there aren't too many weaknesses or tightnesses yanking them out of position--they should sit in very stable and mobile positions.

That is, your shoulders, your hips, your elbows, and your neck all need to be aligned properly for you to have a structurally sound body.

When healthy, our joints should move very smoothly, allowing us to carry ourselves through a full range of motion and expression of power. But they can eventually grow more dysfunctional as we find ourselves injured, overusing, or abusing our joints. In turn, this can lead to muscles on one side of a joint becoming more developed and their pulling your joints out of their axis of rotation.

When this occurs, problems manifest themselves as bursitis, or joint inflammation, which means that you will be in pain when you do certain movements, or even sometimes when you are at rest. Remember that pain is not just in the body; it can affect many different parts of your life: from how you perform at your sport, to how able you are to play with your kids, to how productive you are at your job.

Structural integrity goes beyond the gym or athletic performance.

If you begin training with misaligned joints and poor posture, you should focus first on proper movement. Most people go to the gym and do the exact opposite of what they need. They might do single-joint exercises, such as bicep curls. But flexion at the arm from bicep curls is unnatural. Instead it is: very distal to your core, an accessory movement to pulling, and more importantly, not a primal movement pattern.

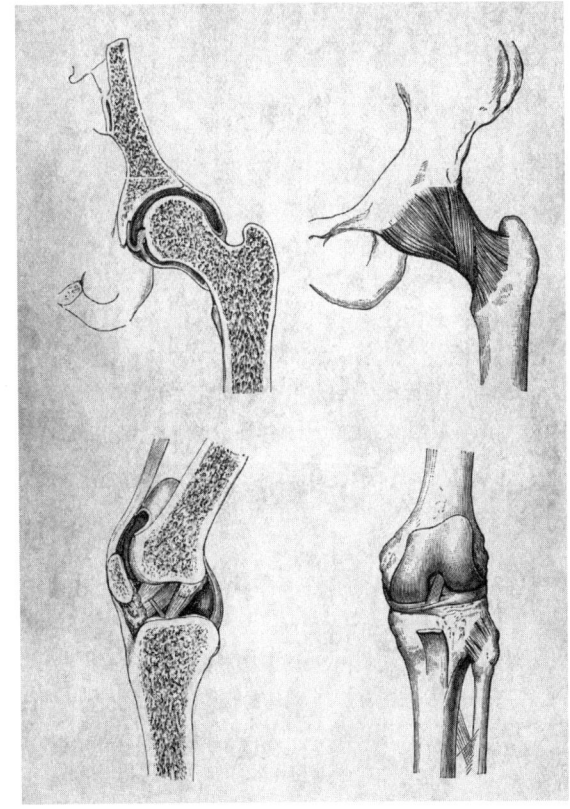

Now I'm not saying strong arms aren't valuable because you should absolutely have strong arms for added strength and athleticism--but they are far from being the first thing you should focus on. Rather than depending on strong arms for flexion and to pick things up, we humans are meant to deadlift. We gather things together with our hands and arms, then we use our back and our core simultaneously in order to lift the weight off the ground.

Isolation exercises--that is, movements that work a specific muscle--should be coupled with compound movements (such as the deadlift) and midline stability work. There's a proper sequence that must occur when the prime movers and the stabilizing muscles work together to lift something off the ground, squat with a load, push something away, or pull something toward you.

A proper sequence means that you're moving through various primal patterns efficiently and effectively. If your prime movers move without your stabilizers, then you are limiting your strength potential and asking for injury. Put simply, proper sequencing contributes heavily to better performance.

Really, it boils down to these questions: how are you performing? In the gym? In your sport? And in life? And if you're not performing at the level you should be, or if you're injured, your performance is going to go down the drain.

So, do not neglect training the stabilizers. When people tell me that they only squat, deadlift, bench press, and do pull-ups, this tells me that they aren't very strong, and if they are, they probably are going to get injured.

The reason is that even a big squat doesn't mean you're activating the right muscles. It doesn't mean that your glutes and other external rotators are properly firing. It doesn't mean that you are working proper thoracic extension or building up your core. You might have huge quads and no hamstrings.

That's just a recipe for an overdeveloped lower back and a lack of midline stability. In addition to the squat or any other compound movement, you need to perform the proper accessory movements to work on your individual weaknesses and build a structurally sound body.

For squats, these might be glute bridges, hamstring curls, and lat pulldowns. They might not be as "complex" as a squat movement, but in their simplicity underlies a tremendous benefit.

As Elliott often says, your body is your mind. So, if you have poor alignment, it is likely that your muscles are misfiring and essentially not activating correctly. You might be experiencing other issues, too, such as not breathing or moving well, let alone overhead pressing correctly.

And my final point: if you're physical structure is unstable, it will affect how you access the psychological fortitude, the strength, and emotional power necessary to navigate your life in a resourceful way. For if you cannot empower yourself, you will not be less able and effectively to empower others.

The whole body--of mind and of physical body--is connected.

STRUCTURE–LESSON II: POSTURE, PRIMAL PATTERNS, & MOVEMENT UNITS

"I FEAR NOT THE MAN WHO HAS PRACTICED 10,000 KICKS ONCE, BUT I FEAR THE MAN WHO HAS PRACTICED ONE KICK 10,000 TIMES."

—Bruce Lee

MOBILIZE, STABILIZE, DOMINATE.

CASE STUDY: Josh's Comeback

Bruce Lee once said, "I fear not the man who has practiced 10,000 kicks once, but I fear the man who has practiced one kick 10,000 times."

My client Josh was definitely an athlete who had practiced his kick--or rather breaststroke, in this case--10,000 times. His diligent practice transformed him into a nationally ranked swimmer, but it also left him unable to swim.

But what you have to understand about Josh is that he is a highly specialized athlete. Josh is in the pool for gruelling swim practices every day, twice a day. He is intensely focused and no stranger to pushing the limits of his physical capabilities. He's the type of athlete whom I constantly have to rein in during training--I don't have to push Josh; he pushes himself. In this day and age of crazy showboating, boasting on social media, and brash arrogance, Josh trains and competes without much fanfare. He just wins.

Josh's specialization and willingness to push himself to the limit allowed him to excel at his chosen sport. Yet it also almost crippled him.

When Josh came to me, the situation seemed dire. His medical reports revealed that he had a posterior disc herniation, which I knew was caused by his kyphotic posture (think shoulders slouched and neck protruding forward) and from constantly tucking in his pelvis posteriorly during the breaststroke.

This kept Josh from swimming, but for Josh, not swimming meant giving up on the chance to get a scholarship and go to college.

I knew it was on me to get Josh back in the pool, but I also knew it was the repetitive movement of his swimming stroke that injured him and kept him in constant pain. However, his swim coach seemed to pin the problem on Josh's training outside of the pool. He wanted Josh to stay in the pool, push through the pain, and stop training with me.

I had to stick to my guns, sit Josh down with his parents, and convince them that the best thing for their son was to stop swimming until the regional tournament. This meant staying out of the pool for a few months, which seemed like an eternity in high school sports.

This conversation was not just about getting an athlete back to doing what he loved. This was about his future. Once again, it came down to how much I cared about my athletes and my clients. I truly cared about Josh and wanted him to have the opportunity to go to the school of his choice, and to live the life he deserved. His parents sensed that I just wanted the best for their son--in the same way that they did. At the end of our meeting, we agreed that Josh would stop swimming for three months and would exclusively train with me.

For an athlete like Josh, the hardest thing to accept isn't to train hard every day, miss out on time with friends and family, eat a strict plan, or spend hours working on their skills. No, the hardest things for them to do are to step back, take a break, and actually work on weaknesses.

That's expected. We live among a fitness culture that is obsessed with pushing through pain, and stepping on the gas until your tires, so to speak, are nothing but melted rubber. And by melted rubber, I mean that you have perhaps just torn the labrum in your shoulder and need invasive surgery. Pushing yourself to the limit day after day may seem hardcore and cool, but personally, I want to be strong and athletic when I am 60 years old--not just when I'm in my 20s.

So, train smart and with the right intensity. There are rules and principles to follow if you want to avoid wrecking yourself.

Believe me, I know that training hard is important, and many sports require a very high volume of work and training. The important thing, however, is to remember that our aim in the gym is to create a strong, yet durable athlete.

Essentially, you get better at your particular sport or job by performing that particular sport or job. But you do resistance training to create a body that is strong and durable. This would imply that a part of your training time be spent on correcting inevitable muscular imbalances and posture via isolation work, midline stability drills, and mobilization techniques.

Listen to your body. If something hurts, actually listen and deal with it. It's not going to get better on its own.

If you know that you have a weakness, slow down and deal with it. And not just with a few exercises here and there at the end of your workout--make it a priority.

Building muscle, as well as durability, is an important component of Strength Camp's philosophy. As I mentioned, our aim is to build strong and durable athletes in the gym, no matter if the athlete is an elite swimmer or a middle-aged guy just trying to lose 50 pounds. Part of being strong and durable are to ensure that your muscles serve you well and are functional, even when you're doing compound movements in the gym.

So, when I was faced with the task of "rebuilding" Josh, my first inclination was to build a healthy, pain-free body. Most coaches might try to pile on volume and try to get him really strong really fast, but that is flat-out wrong. My focus was to build him a body that could endure the rigors of his sport, and then we would worry about performance later.

I would suggest that you do the same thing with your training. Take a minute. Be honest with yourself. Assess your weaknesses, or get someone else qualified to do so, and then make correcting them a priority.

Here is how I got Josh back in the pool and a Division One Scholarship.

Josh's Program

Josh's program evolved drastically, as he progressed past his injury. Soft-tissue work, however, never changed during his training. Much of the soft-tissue work went beyond my scope of practice, so Josh consulted a soft tissue specialist (Dr. Matthew Maggio of Peak Performance) a few times a week.

Corrective Stretch and Soft Tissue Work

One thing to keep in mind: it is always a good idea to find a respected and experienced professional who can help you with your imbalances and mobility restrictions, in spite of your knowledge on soft-tissue work.

The expertise found in most massage therapists, physical therapists, and any other professionals in similar fields can be very valuable to you for eliminating pain and preventing injury. Just make sure that they are either athletes themselves or have successfully worked with athletes in the past.

Mobilize and Stabilize

Josh's protocol had much emphasis on mobility and stability. We went through various movements that emphasized control of the midline while simultaneously challenging him through full range of motion movements. The wall press (for scapular mobility) drill is a great example of this. We wanted to address his lack of midline control, which he could get away with while in the pool; but with a wall press, we trained him to stay tight while being able to extend his arms overhead.

Opening up his hips was another main point of focus. You will notice that I included more hip mobility and stability drills after his general warm-up to address this. As a side note, your warm-up is not done simply to "warm up your body." Its focus is to mobilize and stabilize your body for the specific movements and planned intensities for that day, and it should be designed as such.

POWER

As a swimmer, it was vital that we maintained his power. This was his greatest strength, and it needed to be accounted for. In this particular training session, the focus was on building power in his pull movement, which for swimmers is obviously very important, as well as in his start off the blocks--again very important for swimmers.

Despite the fact that Josh wasn't cleared to go into the pool, I made sure that once he had been he would not have lost any of his power.

STRENGTH

The strength portion of Josh's training plan for this day includes even more corrective work. It may seem strange to include corrective work in a strength phase, but remember the focus for Josh was building a strong base and becoming stronger without injuring himself, or plateauing. So, exercises like hip circle squats and band snatches addressed two of his greatest weaknesses: hip and shoulder stability.

Besides, it is sometimes important to give an athlete time to grow stronger and to not push him or her along too quickly. This is a constant danger for coaches, as they often want to get results fast; it is also a constant danger for athletes who sometimes push themselves too hard without even realizing it. It is essential building a strong and durable body takes the first priority in order to minimize injury.

JOSH'S SAMPLE PROGRAM

CORRECTIVE STRETCHES + SOFT TISSUE

1. Foam Roll (Piriformis, IT, TFL, Hip Flexors, Adductors, Thoracic, Lats, Pec)
   5 minutes

2. Static Stretch (90/90, Waiter's Bow, Couch, Levator Scap, Pec Minor, Lats)
   5 minutes

DYNAMIC WARM UP
MOBILIZE + STABILIZE

1.A. Wall Press (Scap Mob) - 4 x 6

1.B. Y - Cuffs - 4 x 20

2.A. Fire Hydrants with Pause - 2 x 10 each leg

2.B. Hip Circles with Pause - 2 x 10 each leg

POWER

1.A. Lat Band Pull Downs - 5 x 10 seconds as fast as possible

1.B. Block Start Broad Jumps off Reaction - 5 x 3

STRENGTH

1. DB Neutral Grip Incline Press - 5 x 5

2. Front Load Decel Step Ups (3-5 second eccentric) - 5 x 5 each leg

3.A. Band Snatches - 3 x 20

3.B. Hip Circle Goblet Squat - 3 x 10

3.C. Seal Walks - 3 x 20 yds

SOFT TISSUE WORK

1. See Dr. Maggio for Soft Tissue work on hips

Yanda Method

Dr. Vladimir Yanda is perhaps the most cited authority on muscular imbalances. He has published 16 books and more than 200 papers on proper muscular function and muscular imbalances. Dr. Yanda was able to distill the research of many other scientists, as he could speak five languages and was a voracious reader of all things related to muscular function and biomechanics. His identification and classification of Upper and Lower Cross syndromes and reciprocal inhibition have changed the way I assess and coach all of my athletes.

Now, to understand what these concepts mean, we first need to know--in very basic terms--what is happening when a muscle is being "fired". Simply put, a muscle is made up of fibers. These fibers contract and relax based on signals sent from our central nervous system (CNS). Your nerves transmit signals from your brain to specific muscle fibers and causes them to fire, allowing you to move according to your sport (e.g. lifting weights, running, jumping, and so on).

When these imbalances are not addressed through a specially programmed mobilization and stabilization protocol, the CNS is ultimately left to its own devices to create alternate movement patterns that can usually lead to injury. My goal when working with athletes and all Strength Camp members is to ensure that we address both Upper and Lower Cross syndromes before introducing complex movement patterns or pushing harder in those movements.

Upper Cross syndrome refers to the muscular imbalance in the neck and shoulder region. This is most common in people who work at a desk all day, are on their phones often, driving every day, or who just slouch in general. The muscles that tend to be tight are: the upper trapezius, levator scapulae, sternocleidomastoid, pectoralis major and minor, anterior deltoid, and latissimus dorsi.

Muscle tightness in these areas is accompanied by inhibition and weakness in the serratus anterior, middle and lower traps, rhomboids,

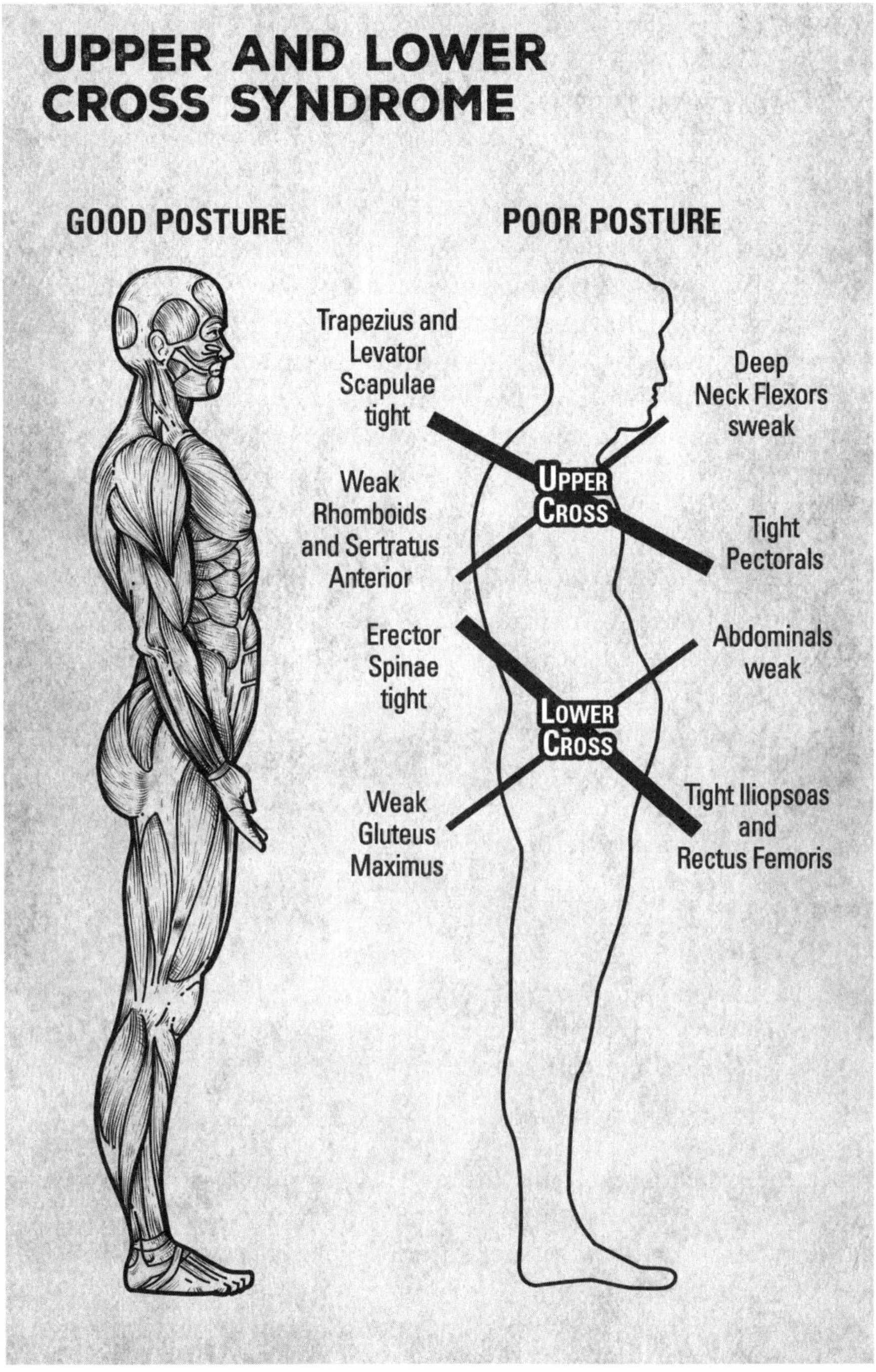

UPPER AND LOWER CROSS SYNDROME

GOOD POSTURE

POOR POSTURE

Trapezius and Levator Scapulae tight

Deep Neck Flexors sweak

UPPER CROSS

Weak Rhomboids and Sertratus Anterior

Tight Pectorals

Erector Spinae tight

Abdominals weak

LOWER CROSS

Weak Gluteus Maximus

Tight Iliopsoas and Rectus Femoris

and the cervical flexors. The results of this type of imbalance are kyphosis of the spine, forward head posture, and winged scapulae. All of this typically causes one or both sides of shoulder to be in a compromised position, resulting in a loss of power, efficient movement, and increased risk of injury.

In the next section, I will expand on addressing Upper Cross. (To be sure, it is a complex problem, but it is best treated with simple straightforward methods.) For now, the gist of it is that I prefer trying a variety of mobility and activation drills and seeing which ones work. Generally, weak, elongated muscles must be stabilized and strengthened, whereas chronically tonic and shortened muscles must be relaxed and lengthened.

This simple formula can effectively begin a treatment for someone with Upper and Lower Cross syndrome. Note that joint mobility, stability, and integrity must also be taken into account, but they are extensive and complex discussions that deserve an extensive explanation.

Lower Cross syndrome, on the other hand, is commonly identified by facilitated thoracolumbar extensors, rectus femoris, and iliopsoas muscle groups. In this syndrome, the glute muscles, medius, maximus, and minimus, along with the abdominals (particularly the transversus abdominus) tend to be inhibited and weak.

Typically, when one group of muscles contracts, the muscles on the opposite side should relax. This is known as reciprocal inhibition. For example, when you fire your glutes, your hip flexors should relax. If they cannot fully relax, then the contraction is inhibited.

A simple way to help my athletes sprint faster and jump higher is by statically stretching their hip flexors. This not only allows for a greater range of motion in the hip, but more importantly, it also allows the glutes to fully contract and generate more explosive power.

Before we continue, there are a few other concepts in muscle anatomy that you should understand.

Opposing Muscles, Antagonists, and Agonists

Opposing muscles are groups of muscles that work together to allow you to effectively perform physical movements. One group is called agonist (also known as the prime mover); the other antagonist.

The prime mover, or agonist, is named thusly because it does most of the work during a movement. An example of a prime mover would be the bicep muscle during the concentric portion (shortening the muscle) of a bicep curl. The antagonist muscle's role is to oppose and control the movement of the agonist. In the bicep curl example, the antagonist would be the triceps.

A muscle's classification as an agonist or an antagonist depends on the movement that is being performed. For example, during a squat the glutes and quadriceps would be classified as agonists, while the hamstrings and hip flexors would be antagonists. However, these roles are reversed when performing a hamstring curl.

It is important that the relative strength of opposing muscles complement each other. You will not be able to run, jump, or lift to your full capabilities if your opposing muscles have serious strength imbalances.

Imagine that you have two guys in a row boat. Each will control an oar and mindlessly row as hard as they can at all times. One guy is an Olympic-level rower while the other is a professional video game player, who has never even rowed a boat before. What do you think will happen? I imagine the boat would end up either going in circles or crashing onto the shore.

In this metaphor, a boat that is powered by two equally strong individuals will travel in a straight line and actually get somewhere.

Balance is key in order to unlock our true genetic potential. Our bodies are meant to be balanced.

When we are in a balanced anatomical state, our muscles apply the right amount of synchronized force to keep the skeletal and muscular system aligned. When any of these opposing muscles become too "tight" or too "weak", the result is imbalances that can often lead to injury and a decrease in performance.

A common muscular imbalance is in the movements of hip flexion and extension. To flex your hip, your hip flexors (iliopsoas) must contract. To extend the hip, your glutes must contract. But when the hip flexors become overly tight from sitting all day and the glutes become inhibited and weak from underuse, the hips would be unable to fully extend. This, in turn, results in the glutes and hamstrings being less effective, since their contraction requires full hip extension.

Clearly, muscular imbalances fall into a cycle of tightness to weakness, and weakness to further tightness.

Josh's back pain and disc herniation were not from excessive tightness in his back. They were caused by tightness in his hips and the dominance of his anterior chain. This is an important point to understand: the site of pain is not always the root cause of the pain; merely a symptom in most cases.

To reiterate once again: strength is built upon a strong foundation, which can be constructed from proper core stability, thoracic extension, and posture. Here are some exercises and stretches that we use to accomplish that:

Primal Patterns

The primal patterns are seven movement patterns that are necessary for basic human survival. They include: squat, bend, lunge, push, pull, twist, and gait.[1] Essentially, if you cannot do these movements properly, then you're not functioning at an optimal level and are prone to injury.

1. Paul Chek, *How to Eat, Move, and Be Healthy,* San Diego, CA. C.H.E.K. Institute: 2004

Posture, Primal Patterns, & Movement Units

You already know that becoming the Strongest Version of Yourself requires movement, which is one reason why we train.

The primal patterns were first introduced to me by Elliott when I first started training at the original Strength Camp. Before then, I had been mainly doing bodybuilding-style workouts at my local gym. Most of my workouts were split into body parts, and I did very few integrated movements outside of playing football. Although I did get big and strong, I remained weak where it counted.

I could bench press a ton of weight and had a big chest, but my strength in the gym didn't seem to carry over to the football field. I realized that I'd been missing the integration of these primal patterns into my training.

Now, when I create exercise programs for any of my athletes, the programs embody my belief that everyone must be able to meet (or exceed) a baseline proficiency in primal patterns. Being able to perform these movements is like a diagnostic test to assess level of mobility, stability, and structural integrity before they move into training that requires speed and intensity.

Squat

People often think that strong folks on the internet got that strong in a matter of months. No, every strong man or woman I know has been training for years. Longevity is key for building serious strength, so keep that in mind the next time your back rounds over trying to hit another back squat 1-rep max.

The best advice for squats: start slow. But that doesn't mean squatting with one plate. It is sometimes necessary to break your movements into smaller parts in order to teach the body how to move correctly. That could mean working according to and improving baseline levels of mobility and stability, such as holding the bottom position of the squat for minutes, or working on paused dumbbell Goblet squats for a few weeks or even months.

If you remember from earlier about opposing muscle groups and muscular balance, you may need to perform hip extension and knee flexion exercises like Swiss ball hamstring curls, one-legged Romanian deadlifts, and glute bridges to build up your glutes and hamstrings, which will help you squat better.

Keep in mind: just doing a squat doesn't automatically mean your body is using the correct muscles or movement pattern. So it's important to get it right, since the squat pattern that you do most often will be ingrained into your system, and will be activated while under a great deal of stress. That's why it's important that the culmination of your training reps does not result in an injury-promoting squat.

Make sure that you build the movement correctly before trying to lift heavy-ass weight. You'll thank me in 10 years.

On a similar note, many new trainees gravitate toward a 5x5-style strength program. While this is definitely a great, if not the best, program for building basic strength, it is not the best starting point for new trainees. As I mentioned, you must first train proper movement patterns before loading the bar. Only after you can perform bodyweight squats and goblet squats correctly that you should move on to the barbell. Even then, I recommend front squats for a while before jumping into back squats.

Front squats are more technical, so I am a big fan of getting my athletes to perform front squats instead of back squats right off-the-bat. When doing a front squat they are forced into thoracic extension, forced to keep an upright torso, and by extension, forced to create stability through the midline, as well as breathe correctly.

This is not to say that back squats are inherently bad, but they do allow you to get away with sloppier movement patterns while having a load directly on your spine. This can create muscular imbalances and structural problems. For this reason, we want to make sure that both front and back squats, along with variations like Goblet and overhead squats, are included in our programs.

BEND

The bend is one of the most integral patterns to learn correctly if you want to get big, strong, fast, and athletic. The most powerful muscles in your body are centered around your hips, which are utilized during the bend pattern such as that in the deadlift. For this reason, it should be your priority to build strong and mobile hips.

One of the most renowned speed coaches in America, Barry Ross, almost exclusively uses the deadlift to turn above average sprinters into Olympic gold medalists--and he doesn't even use full reps! He has athletes pull the bar to just below their knees and then drop the bar. This partial rep has enough of an effect on the nervous system to create some serious power!

That alone demonstrates the power of the bend pattern.

The bend pattern is often associated with having a strong posterior chain. The posterior chain consists of mainly the muscles, ligaments, and tendons on the back side of the body (e.g. the glutes, hamstrings, erector spinae group, and trapezius muscles).

While having a strong back definitely correlates with strength, another great benefit of the bend pattern is how it teaches you, if done correctly, to build and maintain midline stability.

Your back is the framework that allows your powerful hips to do their job. Your back is usually the first to fail when you pull something heavy off the ground. It is your responsibility to recognize this in yourself and fix the problem. As you've read earlier, many problems begin from the ground up, and they do not originate at the point of failure nor at the point of pain.

I am always yelling at my athletes to keep a flat back, even the ones that have been training with me for years. The reason is that as soon as an athlete gets put under a certain amount of stress they start reverting back to old, ingrained movement patterns, which usually involve rounding their backs and breathing into their chests.

Still, there's a time to be calculated and conservative with your form, and there's a time to compete and push your body to its limit. If you want to win, form sometimes has to go out the window.

I say this because, after competing in Strongman and football for many years, I know that the real world is unpredictable. You won't always be able to perfectly set up for a deadlift, or pick up every object you encounter from a perfect point of leverage. You will be forced into "bad" positions, have your back wrenched, rounded, slammed into the ground, and yet still be expected to get up for the next play or round.

So, I am not advocating *always* having a flat back. I do, however, emphasize that they remain tight. You've all seen Elliott and myself lift stones, flip tires, and lift other odd objects. Our backs aren't always flat when we do this. However, you will notice that our backs never change position once they are rounded--they're still tight. We know when it is safe to push the limits and when it is advisable to be cautious.

Understandably, this can cause some confusion about the "dangers" of rounded backs. Experienced Strongmen (and Strongwomen), such as Elliot and myself, are able to create stability even in our rounded back position, and in so doing, lift awkward objects safely. This can be learned only by first learning how to lift with a strong and flat back. A strong and flat back is always the prefered starting point. Don't take this as a free pass to continue ripping deadlifts off the ground with a back that twists and changes position seven times from the ground to lockout.

Take your time to learn how to build strength by emphasizing a flat back. Building strength is not a race. Not everyone is ready to train with odd or heavy objects. Like I said, it requires a certain amount of strength and stable midline to safely lift with a rounded back.

Creating that stable midline isn't just based on your ability to hold a plank for a whole minute. It depends on your movement patterns, and on the stability and mobility of all your prime movers. If you have any mobility restrictions in any of your prime movers, you typically won't be able to properly stabilize your midline, eventually leading to pain-- usually, in your low back.

Start with bodyweight movements if you have to. All of my athletes start out by learning bodyweight movements first. It would be egotistical for myself as a coach to get them flipping tires and loading sandbags before they're ready. Safety is of the utmost priority because you can't get stronger physically if you are injured.

If you want to do Strongman like exercises with odd objects, make sure you or your athletes have a good base of strength. And even then, only use these objects for a short period of time (usually around three weeks) before deloading and going back to utilizing strict form.

At Strength Camp, we will always be advocates of building structural integrity in all our athletes, but we also know that competing requires the use of unorthodox techniques. When that time comes, you need to be mentally prepared to push yourself to the limit and get yourself into some positions that may look strange and dangerous.

LUNGE

Lunge forward. Lunge backward. Lunge to the side. Lunge with a barbell on your back. Lunge for the length of a football field. Basically, any time that is spent on strengthening one leg is time spent on making yourself stronger. And not just stronger in terms of raw strength, but also in terms of overall balance and coordination.

I have trained many athletes who've told me that they "just don't have good balance." What they don't realize is that "balance" is a skill-- the same way that playing the piano is a skill and that "strength" is a skill. If you have bad balance, it's more than likely that you just haven't practiced it enough--as you would a skill in order to be proficient.

POSTURE, PRIMAL PATTERNS, & MOVEMENT UNITS

Lunging is a great way to teach your body how to balance. In fact, the lunge and the other primal movements are invaluable exercises to implement in anyone's training program.

Lunging properly teaches you how to decelerate on one leg properly. In many cases, I find myself cringing when I see young and old athletes jump for the first time. The problem usually comes from not knowing how to decelerate properly on one, or even two, legs.

So before you throw a bar on your back and go for a mile of walking lunges, or try to test out your max box jump, make sure that you can first perform stationary lunges, forward lunges, and reverse lunges. You may be surprised to find that you lack unilateral stability, especially if you slow down your tempo during the movement.

Take your time. Lunges are not an exercise to try to load up with weight. They should be used to build unilateral strength, but are also valuable in recognizing and correcting imbalances.

If you think about it, the vast majority of athletic movements that we perform are done on one leg (e.g. jumping, kicking, and sprinting). A soccer player sprinting down the field, for example, must suddenly plant down one leg to fire a missile into the back of the net; or a tennis player who moves laterally at high speed and then must suddenly cut back the opposite way.

Unfortunately, you can't build proper mobility and stability in the playing field. Training mobility, stability, and strength on one leg are essential in the gym.

Many injuries are caused by overusing bilateral exercises. There are deep stabilizing muscles that may not be activated in a squat, for example. Most of the time you won't even notice this imbalance until it becomes blatantly obvious or you've injured yourself. That's why it is very important that you utilize unilateral exercises in order to strengthen and mobilize each leg separately, and avoid annoying injuries.

Add unilateral exercises either before or after you perform a bilateral exercise to increase your core strength and challenge yourself mentally. (I hate nothing more than seeing that I programmed 4 sets of 12 bulgarian split squats for myself in an upcoming training session.)

Although you can heavily load many unilateral exercises, most of them put you in positions that decrease the compression on your spine to give your back a "break". (If you have back pain, try out a few of the exercises that I recommend later on and see how you feel in a month.)

Be sure to lunge well and lunge often to build strong legs and develop the balance necessary to also be powerful in your sport-specific movements.

Push

Push-ups and bench presses are two of the most common exercises that people would first try out. While these are great exercises, the pressing motion itself is definitely overused to the detriment of its complementary motion: pulling. For example, most people end up doing way more push-ups than they do inverted rows.

Excessive pressing without enough pulling leads to what we talked about in the previous chapter: Upper Cross syndrome, a type of posture that is indicated by a forward-leaning head and slouched shoulders. This type of posture can have a very dangerous effect on our shoulder health, as well as compromise many other movement patterns.

These days, with awareness of Upper Cross syndrome and the overall popularity of "functional" training, the bench press has been deemed not to be a functional movement and used only by those who train to look good. It's also a sure way to eventually tear your rotator cuff. As a result, many people look down on it. This is not because the bench press is a "bad" movement. It is because those trying to perform it don't know how to do it properly.

I still love to bench, but people must realize that pushing is a movement that needs to be trained. The primary issue is that most people don't press correctly due to the severity of their Upper Cross syndrome, and as a result, are unable to stabilize their shoulders, leading to injury.

There's no avoiding it: you need a strong chest and a solid pressing motion to fully realize your strength potential. You need a strong chest in the same way that you need a strong core, strong arms, or strong legs.

Don't be afraid to bench. It is an integral way to build strength in your chest and create a shoulder that is stable and durable. You need to make sure that you are performing it correctly, with various grip widths and from many different angles.

Your shoulder is built for mobility, so stretching won't make it any more stable or durable. Relearning proper pushing mechanics is a great place to start. From there, you can move on to pulling and pressing from a variety of angles.

There are a number of exercises that I use with my athletes on a daily basis to ensure their shoulder health. I have outlined them in the mechanics section, so skip ahead if you want to see some ideas to implement into your warm-up.

Pull

There's a quote that hangs on the wall of Strength Camp. It reads: "Backs are to weightlifters what biceps are to bodybuilders." I see it every day, and I live it in my training. This is not to say that I don't want 20" biceps--oh, I do--but building a strong back is more important to me and has always been a focus of my training.

A strong back helps solves issues that you may have with plateaus and muscular imbalances. Plus, exercises like deadlifts and heavy rows that are essential to building a strong back forces you to get outside your comfort zone and train like a beast.

To start with, you should be pulling twice as often as you are pushing. This means that for every time you do 3 sets of bench presses you should be doing 6 sets of a pulling motion.

We want to pay close attention to the ratio of push to pull when designing a program. I've seen way too many young men and women, who have been following a program that heavily skews this ratio, come into my gym with necks that protrude way too forward and shoulders that slope in.

You can avoid many of these issues by following (or designing) a program that fits into the 1:2 push-pull model.

And to be clear, just doing pull-ups is not good enough. Most people tend to incorrectly overuse their forearms, biceps, and shoulders for the movement, anyway. You need to be doing pulling motions that recruit your rhomboids, middle and lower traps, and lats. These are the muscles that help stabilize your scapula, of which doing pull-ups usually doesn't help.

As another general rule, try to make sure that your pulling motions are done with a supinated grip, as well as with a tempo that accentuates a pause at the end range of the movement. I say supinated because most of our time in the gym is spent in a pronated grip. Think of how you bench press, deadlift, and perform pull-ups. Putting yourself in a supinated position ensures that you are keeping your shoulders externally rotated and are working the proper muscles.

As you can see, there are some really common mistakes that you could be making when you pull. Always make sure to check out the mechanics section if you want to see some great cues that you can use when you pull.

TWIST

The twist is perhaps the most underused yet important movement pattern in a training setting. It integrates the strength and power of the upper and lower body.

From a golfer smashing a drive down the fairway to an MMA fighter smashing his opponent with a right hook, pretty much every sport requires a twist movement in some form.

You don't have to be 6'5" to throw over 90 miles per hour, you just have to have a bulletproof core and know how to twist efficiently and with explosiveness. Merely, it is the efficient transfer of energy, from the lower body through the midline, that separates those who are powerful from those who simply are not.

With the twist, we're working through the transverse plane of motion, and can either move from the upper body or the lower body. In other words, there are some exercises during which we twist mainly at the rib cage--shoulders twisting from side-to-side and hips staying square. Then, there are other exercises during which the upper body stays firm but the lower body twists. Both variations require different types of strength and different mechanics, but both are very important in developing your twist pattern.

I'm bewildered by how twisting and moving in the transverse plane of motion are very underutilized in many popular forms of training. By overusing movements in the sagittal plane (such as when squatting and lunging), athletes often become very tight when it comes time to twist. Without being used to twisting, any sudden movements or trying to pick something up from a less-than-ideal position usually results in an injury.

Later on, when we get into integrated exercises, you'll see how the twist is often coupled with your push, your pull, and your squat. There are actually many different things that we can do to integrate twisting into our routine. By doing so, we support the stability, explosive strength, and capacity of our abdominals.

Gait

Gait is the most used but least thought about primal pattern.

Everytime you walk you are training your gait. Anytime you sprint after a bus you are training your gait. Anytime you go for a jog with your dog you are training your gait. Anytime a running back cuts past a defender and spins around another he is training his gait. You get the picture.

Bottom-line: any locomotion is training your gait. Even various crawling patterns, such as bear crawls, crab walks, and lizard crawls fall under this category.

I love utilizing these unorthodox forms of movements with my athletes, as they force the athletes to think about how they are moving instead of mindlessly performing another sprint. They're also forced to use muscles that they don't normally use. Plus, they're often very challenging and fun--most of the time.

Posture, Primal Patterns, & Movement Units

Most people learn their forms of gait by mimicking their parents and siblings, and eventually, their bodies adapt to move in the most efficient way possible. This does not mean the best way. As we learned in the section on structural integrity, the body will find ways to move, even if it has to deal with misaligned joints and lingering injuries.

Be conscious of the way that you walk, jog, and sprint. Are your feet pointed outward or forward? When you run, do you crash down on your heels or land with a spring on your toes as a sprinter does? Do you slouch or walk tall with a proud chest?

In effect, how you walk can affect how you perform in all the other primal patterns. If you walk while slouched over, then you probably won't be that great at pulling or pushing. If you walk with your toes pointed out and with a little hip extension, then you probably won't be that great at squatting or deadlifting.

All the primal patterns work together to move your body through space, so to neglect one or to think that weakness in one doesn't matter is to neglect them all.

Movement Units

The previous discussion on primal movements has already shown the importance of primal movements and how they are all interconnected. In other words, the body must move as a unit. But this does not just mean squatting, deadlifting, pressing, and pulling. If you are simply doing all of these patterns independently of one another, then you aren't really training for movement in real life; you are simply training to get better in the gym.

I know many people follow a 5x5-style program when they are just starting out on their fitness journey. That's great. However, the 5x5 methodology does not take into account how the human body truly functions, and as a result, these trainees usually end up being stiff, riddled with muscular imbalances, and injured.

You must take into consideration whether the program has actual value on the field or in your day-to-day life. If the exercises within the program don't translate to success in your sport or to overall healthy movement when they matter the most, then what's the point of training?

In order to build a body that is both functional and durable, you should be aware of two things: main movement units and sling systems.

When most people go to the gym, they focus on the outer unit, or the muscles that you see on the outside of your body. Muscles that you can touch and admire in the mirror, like your pecs or quads, are considered superficial muscles and part of the outer unit.

If shaped properly, these muscles certainly look aesthetically pleasing if you're lean. I've met plenty of 40- or 50-year-old ex-bodybuilders who are in tremendous pain but look really "jacked" on the outer unit. He's spent years creating a deep imbalance between the muscles of his inner unit, which we'll describe in a moment, and his outer unit.

Of course, these outer unit muscles are important, as they are prime movers of the body. You need them to perform big powerful movements called gross movement patterns. Movements like pulling a heavy deadlift off the ground or sprinting up a hill are considered gross movement patterns.

These powerful movements are supported by various sling systems of the body, and this is where things can get a bit complicated. What is important to understand is that most of the time a combination of sling systems are being used. They do not often work independently of one another. Look over the following diagrams to get a better idea of how your body manages to maintain stability in a variety of different positions:

Anterior Oblique System
The anterior oblique system consists of the relationship between the external and internal oblique and the adductors of the opposite leg, as well as the anterior abdominal fascia between the two sides.

Posterior Oblique System
The posterior oblique system consists of the latissimus dorsi and the gluteus maximus on the opposite side.

Deep Longitudinal System
The deep longitudinal system consists of the spinal erectors and the bicep femoris (hamstrings).

Lateral System
The lateral system consists of the adductors and the opposite gluteus medius and minimus.

When implemented into your training, the sling systems can possibly detect, assess, and correct imbalances. They are also necessary to build the foundation for gross movement patterns.[2]

---

2. Diane Lee, *The Pelvic Girdle: An Approach to the Examination and Treatment of the Lumbopelvic Hip Region,* Philadelphia, PA: 2004

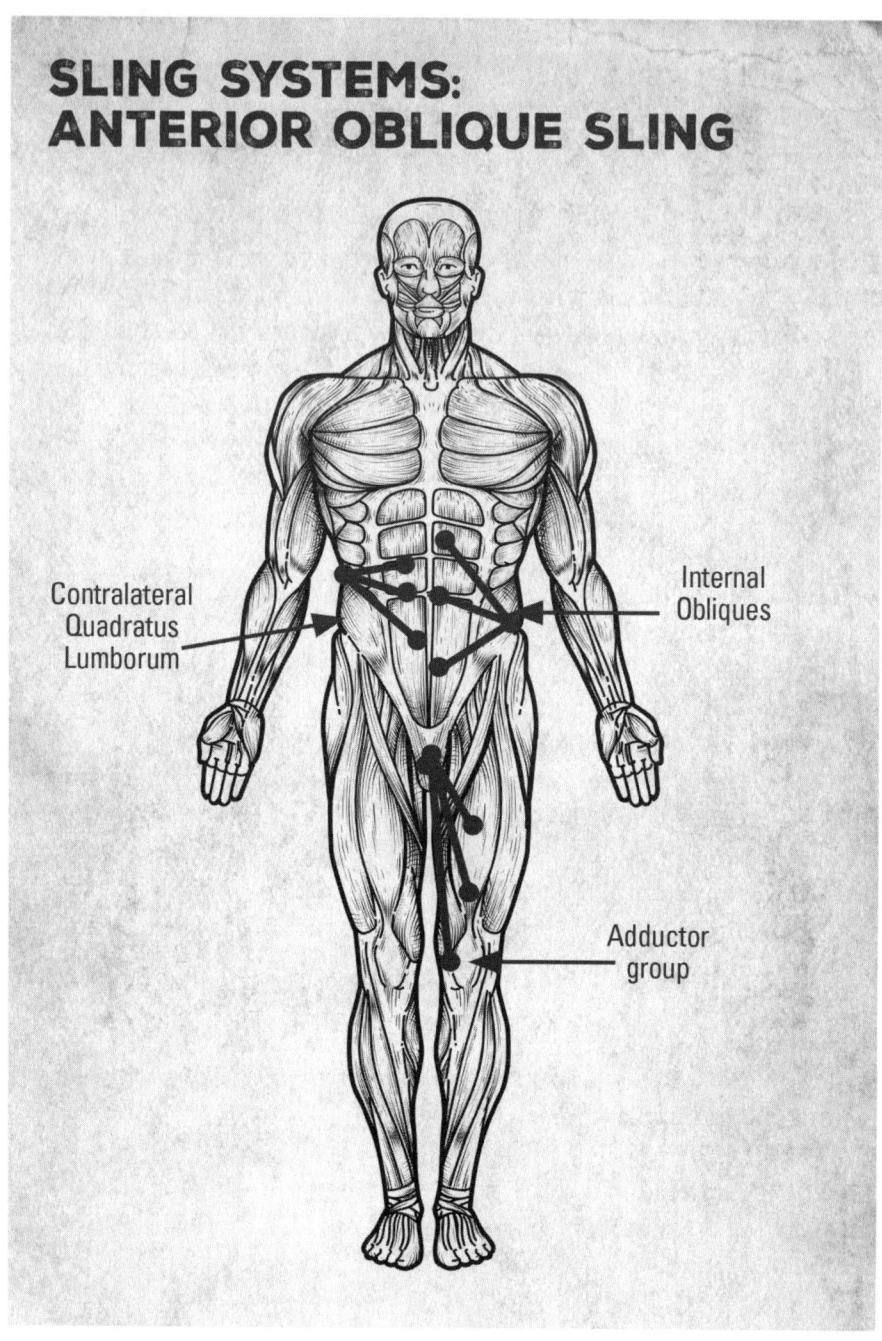

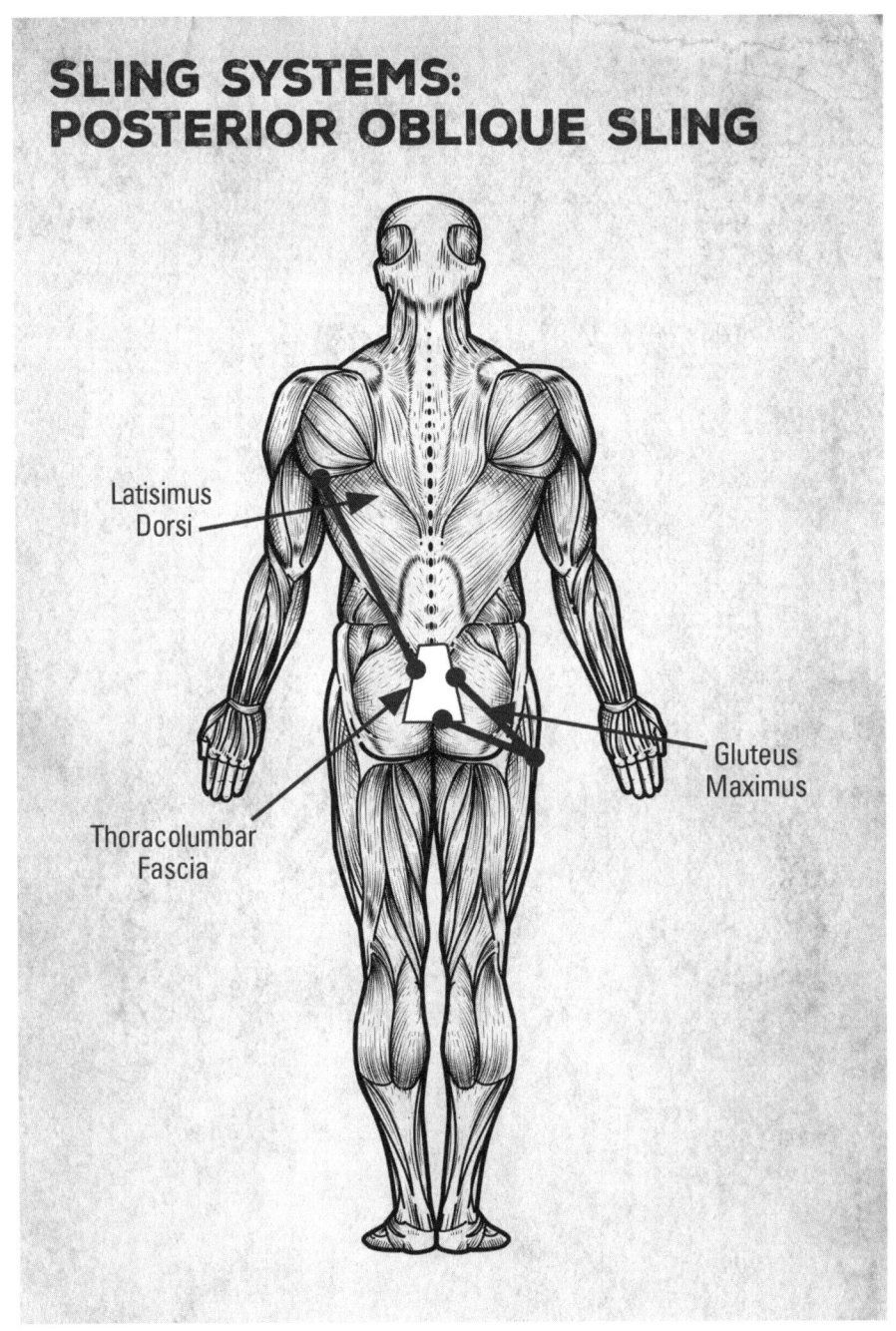

SLING SYSTEMS: DEEP LONGITUDINAL SLING

- Contralateral Erector Spinae group
- Sacrotuberous ligament
- Biceps Femoris
- Peroneus Longus
- Portion of Tibialis Anterior

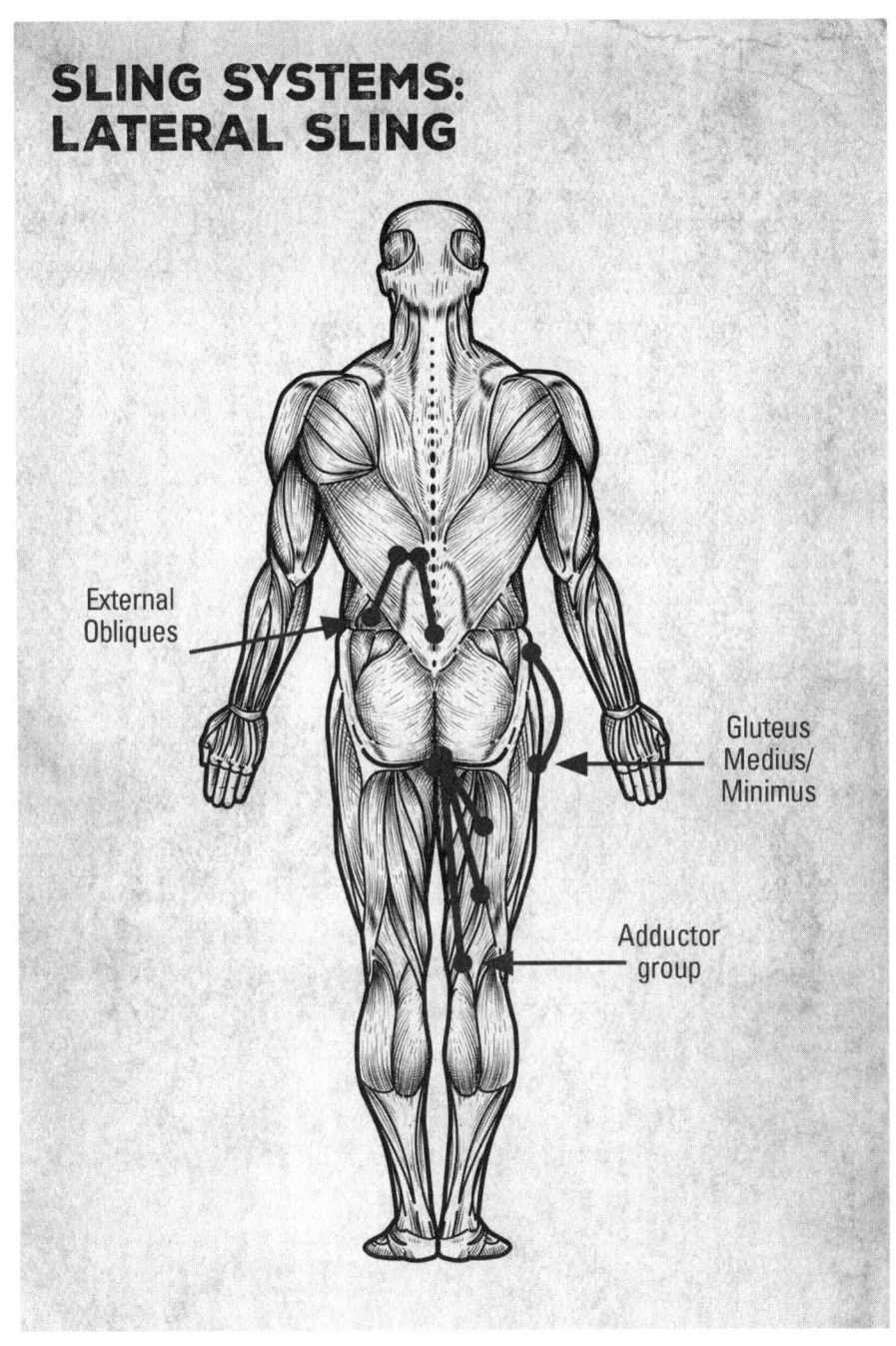

Here is where the inner unit comes in. Charles Poliquin once said that by building a big, strong, powerful outer unit, or superficial muscles, without building the inner unit is like putting a cannon on a canoe--you'll blow a hole right through the canoe and sink it.

And that's exactly what happens with a lot of athletes: their outer units are far too much for their inner unit, causing many common injuries.

The inner unit is deep--deep within the shoulders, neck and pelvis--and is made up of muscles that are closest to the spine and most proximal to your core. That means the further away you get from your spine, skull, and hip--the further away you're getting from the inner unit and the various muscles that support it. They're not the "sexy" muscles; they're the muscles that have strange names. But they build a foundation for big, powerful movements.[3]

Core stability is often emphasized for a number of reasons. First, the area lacks a solid foundation of bone. Contrast our shoulders and our navigational system, which are set atop a rigid rib cage; and our pelvis and femur support our hips and legs with sound structural integrity.

Unlike those, our core has nothing but organs, but much of our movement originate from this area. In fact, Dr. Serge Gracovetsky, a Nuclear Physicist and one of the leading mathematical researchers on the spine, calls the core the "spinal engine." Walking does not originate from your legs. It originates from the sling systems of your core.

We need an inner unit that can support a strong outer unit and initiate powerful gross movement patterns. In other words, we need a powerful engine. And to build it, we need integrated movements to develop strength in the inner unit.

---

3. Paul Chek, *How to Eat Move and Be Healthy,* San Diego, CA: C.H.E.K Institute, 2004.

In Josh's case, he had a very strong outer unit that allowed him to perform powerful gross movement patterns. This made it possible for him to be a great swimmer, but as we have learned, Josh was simply a canoe with a cannon strapped to it. And so, it was clear and vital that we needed to develop Josh's inner unit. (Take a look at his program above to see how it was done.)

When people think of developing the core, they think of superficial ab exercises, like crunches and planks. There's more to it than that. With Josh, I had to teach him how to stabilize in different positions, through different patterns, and with a variety of loads. This is important as most athletic movements require core strength as you move, not when you are stationary. The reason is that movement is not as linear or structured as it commonly is seen in the gym.

In the end, movement is not as simple as you once thought. If you want to move and perform optimally, you must be very conscious of how you move and address issues of imbalance. Challenge yourself through many different ranges of motion, from different stances, with different and odd objects, and simply by freely moving your body.

King

Strength–Lesson 1: Types of Strength & Training Maxes

> "Surround Yourself With Those On the Same Mission As Yourself."

Types of Strength and Training Maxes

Surround yourself with those on the same mission as you.

That may be the most important piece of advice, as it is echoed by many top athletes, businessmen, artists, and other successful people.

Sure, being independent is great and an essential part of your journey. But the great Stephen Covey wrote, "Dependent people need others to get what they want. Independent people can get what they want through their own efforts. Interdependent people combine their own efforts with the efforts of others to achieve their greatest success."

In other words, you become like those with whom you surround yourself. You alone have the power to pick and choose your company. You don't have to be around people who drag you down, give off negative energy, and distract you from your true goals. You can choose your environment and let it unconsciously change you into the person that you desire to become. The people who make up that environment are equally as vitally important.

This became apparent to me in the two separate times that I'd trained for the NFL Regional Combine.

The first time, I trained alone. I didn't have any distractions. I had all the equipment I needed. I had a great program that I trusted, and had enough time to follow it exactly. As a result, I got strong--really strong. At one point, I was squatting over 500 pounds and had gained about 40 pounds of muscle. I felt so prepared physically.

Now you're probably expecting me to say that I killed it. But I didn't. In fact, I didn't hit any of the numbers that I'd made in the gym. I came out flat. The competitive atmosphere was something that I hadn't experienced for some time. All of a sudden, I didn't feel the beast from the gym. My bubble of solitude left me feeling small, weak, slow, and uncomfortable. I felt out of my element. Needless to say, the Combine was a flop.

I won't lie. I was discouraged for a while. After all, I had just poured my heart and soul into something and ended up failing--or at least what I thought was a failure. I knew that I had the talent, the passion, and the mindset. I just didn't perform when it counted most.

That was a pretty low time for me, but I knew something needed to change in my training for the next time. That something was environment. I knew my program, my ability to push myself, and even my diet were all on point, but when I'd switched over to a sports performance gym and trained with other hungry college football players, it made all the difference.

At my first training session, I'd instantly noticed a change in my intensity: I pushed myself harder than before. As the new guy, I felt I had to prove myself and my abilities, which made me train with a focus that is hard to replicate in the comfort of your old, familiar surroundings.

As a result, I was able to achieve numbers in training that I have never before seen. At 230 pounds, I achieved the farthest broad jump (10'7") and highest vertical jump (39.5") out of all the aspiring NFL athletes. Further, I hit 31 reps at 225 pounds and a 40-yard dash in 4.54 seconds. I say these things not to brag, but to emphasize that these numbers became possible because I'd surrounded myself with other high-caliber athletes. My competitive nature certainly helped, too.

I also fondly remember the times when Elliott and I had trained together for Strongman. We competed on every rep. Competition for us meant that we'd only made each other better. So, I suggest that you seek out those who have similar goals to you. Find people who are stronger than you and more knowledgeable than you to help propel you toward your goals.

Be willing to fail. Be willing to be the weakest guy in the room, because if you can stick it out, you'll eventually be among the strongest.

Don't work out. Train!

> "Strength does not come from winning. Your struggles develop your strengths. When you go through hardships and decide not to surrender, that is strength."
>
> —Arnold Schwarzenegger

I know a lot of people who "work out". I also know a lot of people who get mediocre results. They say, "I just can't [insert goal here]." And it's true; they can't. There can be a number of factors that contribute to their lack of results, but in my experience, it is usually that they are working out and not training.

They may sound like the same thing, but there are big distinctions between the two.

In order for me to express my thoughts on those distinctions, I feel it necessary to first share my experiences with training for Strongman. Let me also state that I am currently not a high-level Strongman, but I have been fortunate enough to support Elliott, who is. As his training partner, he and I have gone through some of the toughest training sessions I've ever experienced. (It is my opinion that they're the most grueling sessions known to man.)

During this training, you put your body in all sorts of injury-prone positions: your forearms get torn up on almost every implement; your back gets bruised from shouldering the yoke; your legs often turn to jelly after pushing the sled until you puke; and your body often feels like a sore sack of pain all over. If it doesn't seem safe, it's because it isn't.

Most of the techniques involved in Strongman involve cues like "just lift it" and "lift that shit!" You need to have a high baseline of strength to even begin training for Strongman. Put simply, the demands Strongman training place on the body will crush a weaker person. Not only is it physically grueling, the training can be mind-numbing.

It will crush your spirit. You will train often. You will train alone. In all of this, there is no great monetary gain to be had. There is little to no public recognition outside of the Strongman community. There is seemingly no reason to subject your body and your mind to such a tedious and damaging grind.

Even getting out of bed the morning after a tough training session--and they are all tough--is agonizing. Your entire body is screaming at you to stay in bed and recover, but you have kids to get to school, a business to run, and a myriad of other responsibilities to look after.

Does this sound like what most people do when they work out?

Probably not.

People who work out give up at the first sign of distress or discomfort.

As soon as they hit a wall, they stop. It gets hard, so they stop. It gets painful, so they stop. It gets uncomfortable, so they stop.

Training is all about facing these walls. These walls symbolize our adaptations as athletes. They are there to test us--physically, mentally, and spiritually. They are there to see who has what it takes to either get over the wall or run through it head first.

It's easy to avoid training when you're sore, tired, hungover, or seemingly don't have the time. But what you need to understand is that your brain is not on your side. Your brain doesn't want you to reach your goals. Your brain wants you to be comfortable and safe. So, if you want to really train, get comfortable with being uncomfortable. It is the only way to make real progress.

Therein lies the distinction between someone who is successful and someone who just can't hack it.

All the good athletes I know are physically gifted, yes, but what separates the good athletes from the great ones is work ethic. That's it. It's the same work ethic that separates a good writer from a great one; a good musician from the great; or a good businessman from the great. And so on.

It is the willingness to embrace the grind of training day in and day out.

This love of work is what differentiates "working out" and training.

When you **train**, you embrace the process. Even if that process is difficult. You are working toward something that may have no extrinsic reward, but you still do it because that means the world to you. That is no exaggeration. I will elaborate on it later, but I can honestly learn more about a person by watching them train than I can from talking to them for a few hours.

Talent is overrated. If you think that you are talented and that talent alone will carry you through life, then sooner or later you are going to have a rude awakening. There are literally thousands of people on this planet that are more talented than you. Your only hope is to work harder than them for a longer time.

Work harder and longer. Be stubborn. Hone your craft day in and day out, whether you feel like it or not. Eventually, you will get good--really good if you do it long enough.

So, don't just work out. Train!

Training means going to the gym, even when you don't want to. Training means working on your weaknesses, even when you don't want to admit them. Training means giving up certain habits that hinder your progress, and adopting those that benefit your craft. Training means competing against yourself or others. Training means shutting your brain off when you train and just moving the weight.

When you train, you aren't going to question your motives; you aren't going to ask "why" in the middle of a set. You are just going to do it. You will learn "why" later.

By contrast, working out means that it can wait 'til later. Working out means barely breaking a sweat. Working out means being on your phone and talking with friends. Working out means having high expectations, not putting in the work, and then being upset with reality. Working out means not going to the gym when you don't feel like it.

Make no mistake you can train or work out in any environment. Change your mindset, and you change your training and your results.

Compete and Set Goals

To start training and make "working out" a thing of the past, set goals and compete.

Setting goals for your training is one of the most valuable steps you can take toward success. The mere act of writing down what you want to achieve instantly elevates you beyond working out and into the realm of training.

I recommend signing up for some type of competitive event. That could mean Olympic weightlifting, Strongman, powerlifting, bodybuilding, and various races like Tough Mudder or a 5k. Just committing to go on a difficult hiking trip can be a great option.

Once you've signed up, paid the entrance fee, and have the date marked on your calendar, you've begun training. You now have a reason to train. You are now an athlete. So train like one.

In high school and college, I trained for football. After that, I trained for Strongman and the NFL combine. I always had a reason to get my ass to the gym, even on days when I didn't feel like training.

There were times when I'd questioned myself about why I was doing something, but I just did the work. That's what training is all about: having every reason in the world not to do another set, not to go to the gym, and not to sleep enough--but doing them anyway.

Bottom-line: if you really want to make progress and improve your athletic performance and your life, set big goals. Take a moment of mindfulness to think about what you really want to achieve and write it down in a place that you can see every day. Set goals that fire you up, even if they seem crazy at the time. Set crazy goals that you can tell your grandkids about with pride. Because we already know that it is a proper work ethic that will get you there, not some type of innate talent.

Once you've set a big goal, you can break them down into smaller, more achievable milestones to keep consistent.

LITTLE THINGS ARE THE BIG THINGS

To preface this section, I want to tell you about John Wooden. He was the basketball coach at UCLA from 1948-1975. During his 12-season tenure, his team won ten national championships--seven in a row at one point. It was an astounding feat, as no other coach had ever won more than two championships in a row.

John Wooden had rightfully earned his nickname as the "Wizard of Westwood". He seemed to have had a magical effect on all the young men whom he taught at UCLA. But it wasn't because of his ability to motivate his players or a particular skill set that was far superior to other coaches. He'd simply possessed a great attention to detail on the little things, as well as a sincere concern for the young men whom he coached, including one named Kareem Abdul Jabbar.

I remember hearing one story in which Kareem Abdul Jabbar, one of the greatest NCAA and NBA basketball players of all time, arrived in California from Manhattan for his first day of practice with John Wooden and the UCLA Bruins.

Types of Strength & Training Maxes

If you're unfamiliar with Kareem Abdul Jabbar, he went on to become the all time leading scorer in the NBA. Even having entered the NCAA with the Bruins, he had high hopes for his career. And he expected John Wooden to push him in a way that other coaches had in the past; subjecting him to mind-bending drills and winning strategies.

At Kareem's first practice, it became clear that John would not be that kind of coach. John immediately got all of his players to sit down in a circle and to remove their shoes and socks. Obviously, his players were baffled by his request, but John merely responded with:

"I'm going to teach all of you how to put on your socks so that you don't get a blister. I'm going to teach all of you how to tie your shoes so that they don't come undone."

Yes, John Wooden, who was named the Coach of the Century by ESPN, started out every year with every new player by teaching them how to properly put on their shoes and socks.

Remember, the little things are the big things. Even when you are working with a high level athlete or even when you have achieved a high level of success yourself.

Putting on socks and tying shoes were of no lesser importance to John Wooden than running a full court press correctly, or learning how to shoot a jump shot off the dribble. Everything was valuable, and it was John's recognition of this fact that allowed him to build each player from the ground up, leaving no room for bad habits.

Bruce Barton, a U.S. Congressman from the late 1930s, once said: "Sometimes when I consider what tremendous consequences come from little things. I am tempted to think there are no little things."

In training, small things include: visualizing your training beforehand, putting on your shoes and socks properly, treating your warm-up with respect, attacking PRs with intensity, recording your every detail of your workout each and every time, not skipping out on your stretching, eating meals that fit your training, getting to bed on time, and then getting up and doing them all again the next day, even if you don't feel like it.

If you learn these and put them into practice, your training will change immensely.

Ignoring the small things is the biggest mistake that I see young men and women committing nowadays. They just jump right into training with no regard for building a strong base. They want to squat and bench press with heavy weights before they can perform a good bodyweight squat or a push-up. They want to do the Olympic lifts without putting effort into increasing their mobility, or even mastering the basics of the sport.

And eventually, these people plateau. Once they hit a plateau, they decide that jumping to a new and exciting program is the best way to make progress. This usually goes on for years until they get injured, get frustrated with a lack of progress, get too busy to train, or usually, it's a combination of all three.

This behavior of hopping from one program to another is a direct result of not realizing that the little things are the big things. Be diligent with your training. Build a solid base. Treat the little things like the big things, because they are the big things, and you will continue to progress for as long as you train.

Types of Strength

What does being strong mean to you?

Does it mean being able to deadlift 500 pounds? To perform a freestanding handstand push-up? To be able to run efficiently over the duration of a marathon? Or does it mean being able to run over a defender on one play and hurdle him on the next?

Types of Strength & Training Maxes

My definition of strength is not the same as that of someone who competes in powerlifting. To me, being strong means being able to display brutal strength on the main lifts while still retaining a great deal of mobility, athleticism, and explosiveness. I value building athletes who aren't only strong but also durable, explosive, and athletic. Whereas the powerlifter might be more concerned with moving the most weight possible, from point A to point B.

Still, this interpretation of strength is no less correct than my own.

The important thing to realize is that strength can mean something different to every person, yet their varying definitions could all be valid. There is no one definition of strength that is better than all of the others. CrossFitters, bodybuilders, powerlifters, Olympic lifters, Strongmen, and other strength athletes tend to bicker among themselves over whose method of training is best. It doesn't matter--no one method is best!

More important are the principles of the different methodologies: progressive overload, the training of different energy systems, hypertrophy, and so on each serve a purpose in creating and improving the ideal type of strength for that particular sport and training discipline.

However, no matter the athletic goal you have, compound movements are going to help you build strength. Famed powerlifter Mark Bell said, "No one ever regretted getting stronger." I couldn't agree more with his sentiment. Having a solid base of strength will make you better at virtually any sport. I learned this during my football days.

Early on in my football career, I did very basic bodybuilding workouts and noticed really good improvements in my muscularity really quickly. Despite that, these results didn't translate that well to the field, as I seemed to fall behind other guys in strength and agility.

It wasn't until I started training strength at Strength Camp that I'd realized my mistake in previously focusing only on building muscle and not strength. Soon, I was squatting and deadlifting heavy weight for low reps. I flipped tires like a madman, pushed heavy sleds, did all kinds of loaded carries, and performed explosive movements that focused on forceful hip extension. I trusted Elliot and followed his programming.

As my strength increased, I noticed a direct correlation to my performance on the field and in my baseline speed and agility testing. I started outperforming the same guys, who had previously outdone me. The changes to my nervous system turned me into a beast on the field. Training strength is no joke; it was one of the greatest boons to my athletic and training career.

With that in mind, size does not always correlate to greater strength. Size does definitely help to an extent, but it's not about the size of the muscle. Rather, you should be concerned with how the muscles serve you on the field.

This is where it is important to understand the difference between the two main types of strength: absolute strength and relative strength.

Absolute Strength

In simple terms, absolute strength is how much weight you can move. In slightly more complex terms, it's how much force you can produce with maximal muscular exertion in one single moment. For absolute strength, weight does matter because bigger is simply better. The more you increase your body mass, the more muscle you will be building (assuming you are consuming adequate amounts of protein and training, of course).

As you get bigger and build more muscle, you will be stronger. This is due to a number of reasons that we will get into in later chapters. For now, this concept of increased muscle means increased absolute strength. End of story. This does not necessarily mean that you will be more athletic, faster, or more explosive. It means that you will be able to exert greater force against heavier and heavier external objects.

Types of Strength & Training Maxes

You know the folks who look as if they can't tie their shoes but can pull 900 pounds for reps? That's absolute strength. Powerlifters and Strongmen often fit into the category of athletes who need to have superior absolute strength.

As a strength athlete, your focus has to be totally on building as much strength at all costs. Your only objective is to exert as much force as possible to move as much weight as possible. All other facets of strength will be ignored. This is not necessarily a bad thing. It is just something to keep in mind, because athletic capabilities are not correlated with higher absolute strength..

Therein is a key disadvantage to absolutely strength: you won't really excel in much else. Running probably won't go so well. Jumping--well, let's not picture that. Absolute strength is only one component that can help make you a star in your sport.

Still, you would benefit from building absolute strength because without a good base of raw strength, you will have a hard time building power, speed, and explusiveness. I've seen coaches take young athletes through "agility" and plyometric drills before they are stable or strong enough to confidently do basic bodyweight movements. This is counterproductive, as these young athletes do not have the requisite strength to gain any physiological benefit from plyometric or agility training.

Building absolute strength first is rarely a bad idea. As we've always said about a strong foundation, build a good strength base first with various primal, bodyweight, barbell, dumbbell, and kettlebell movements before moving on to the more sport-specific training.

Relative Strength

If you want to run faster, jump higher, and overall be a better athlete, then increasing relative strength is important. Relative strength is how much weight you can move, or how much force you can exert relative to your body weight.

Running and jumping are all about the amount of force you can put into the ground to propel you horizontally and vertically, respectively, against the forces of gravity. But it isn't only about how strong you are. If that were the case, then Olympic lifters and powerlifters would be pretty darn fast; except they're not.

Speed is dependent on how much force you can apply in relation to your body weight.[1] Stride rate and stride length are important, but both increase, anyway, as the athlete gets stronger in relation to his size.

For example, if you have one boat with a 250-horsepower motor that weighs 500 pounds and another boat with the same engine that weighs 900 pounds, the lighter boat with an equal amount of force creation potential is always going to be faster. Along the same vein, if you have two athletes racing against each other, both of whom can put the same amount of force into the ground but one is 100 pounds heavier, the lighter athlete will win every time.

This concept is very important for increasing your athletic potential. That is, you need to be strong, yes, but you also need to be strong in relation to your body weight. If you are interested in delving deeper into this concept, check out Barry Ross' book Underground Secrets to Faster Running.

Being able to express your strength by spinning, dodging, flipping, and doing handstands is a byproduct of having good relative strength. Basically, anything that you want to do that involves dynamic movement--from playing soccer to doing gymnastics--requires a great degree of relative strength.

As an athlete, you want to aim to keep your weight and strength within a very specific ratio. If you start gaining too much weight in order to gain a bit more strength, you will upset the ratio and potentially decrease your capacity to sprint, jump, and move in general.

---

1. Barry Ross, *Underground Secrets of Running*, Lulu Enterprises Incorporated, 2005

Types of Strength & Training Maxes

NFL running back, Darren Sproles, is a great example of someone with fantastic relative strength. He's only 5'6" and 190 pounds--which by NFL standards is a tiny build. However, he is one of the fastest, most powerful, and most dynamic players on the field. These are possible because Darren has otherworldly relative strength. You don't often see a person of his size that is as strong as he is, which is why you very rarely see other players of his stature starring in the NFL.

Again, the key to excelling at most sports is to build a high level of strength while keeping your weight reasonable. If you gain too much weight, your relative strength decreases and along with it, your athletic performance. As an athlete, you need to be able to move through many different planes of motion well, and still maintain your balance and stay grounded. You need to be explosive and powerful, and still be strong enough to take on your opponents. There's nothing that checks your ego quite like running into a small dude who can knock you on your ass and outrun you.

There are many ways to increase your relative strength. Gaining mastery of your body weight is a great place to start. I have trained football players who can bench press 315 for reps yet can barely do push-ups. Put simply: if you want to be a successful athlete, it is essential that you be able to control your body and have a good strength-to-weight ratio.

Another way to increase relative strength is to do plyometrics. Once I have built up an athlete's mobility and stability, I love to introduce plyometrics. These teach the athletes how to produce force quickly, control their bodies in space, and recruit the maximal amount of muscle fiber. It's also a really easy way to gauge how much relative strength someone has. If you can deadlift 550 pounds but can barely do a 30-inch box jump, then it's likely you need to reevaluate your program.

Big numbers on the main lifts look great, but when their numbers are put to the test on the field, I'll take the athlete who has the greatest relative strength any day.

TRAINING MAX VERSUS COMPETITION MAX

It's hard to describe the feeling of competition to someone who has never done it before themselves.

Competition has been ingrained in me for as long as I can remember. I was fortunate enough to compete on the football field for most of my youth, and then as a Strongman a few years back. I always had a focus and drive that not everyone could match.

For me, I'd always been focused because I thought of competition not for the sake of being better than other people, but for the sake of bringing out the best in myself, through competing against others. I knew that I could coax the Strongest Version of Myself via competitive goals that challenged me and a competitive atmosphere through which to express my hard training.

In the end, the best way to understand what goes through--or to be more precise, what doesn't go through--the minds of professional athletes as they ply their trade on the court or field is to enter competition yourself. Do what they do. Competing against others forces you to concentrate or else you will lose. Competition increases your level of skill. The more you compete in a focused manner, the better you will get, and the greater the challenges you can overcome. Simply put, competing against others is enjoyable as long as you aren't doing it in a mean-spirited manner.

Unfortunately, many people who used to compete as kids no longer compete when they enter adulthood. They may deem it unnecessary to adult life or see it as a contest to measure the biggest dick. In my mind, they're looking at competition the wrong way. Competition brings out the best in you no matter what sport you pursue. It makes you better despite whether you've just begun or have been training for years.

Even if you aren't, or don't feel ready, compete.

Even if you don't think that you are going to win, compete.

Even if you are scared, compete.

And especially if you are scared, compete!

You won't regret it. The worst thing that can happen is that you may lose. That's it. You are not going to die (although injuries could happen). Even in the face of a loss, you stand to benefit and win in other ways. Take your losses now and learn from them. It is a required part of growth. You will have time to be a winner later.

In every competition, you will run into athletes that are better than the ones at your gym. It is important that you learn from every competitor you come across. Don't view others as your enemy; they are there to teach and inspire you, as you continue to grow stronger. Acknowledge the gap between your skill and theirs, your strength and theirs, and determine what you need to do to close that gap.

Eventually, once you are able to calm your nerves and focus on the task at hand--whether that means deadlifting, snatching, sprinting 100 meters, or whatever you are doing--you will be able to put up your best numbers; ones that will crush your training numbers.

TRAINING MAX

If you have been training for some time, you undoubtedly have attempted a PR at some point. If it was not done in a competitive atmosphere, it would be known as your training max. Your training max is simply "the heaviest load which one can lift without substantial emotional excitement." This means that you will have performed this lift without a great risk or reward. If you hit it, you hit it. If you miss it, you miss it. No big deal.

---

2. Mel Siff, *Supertraining*, Denver, CO, Supertraining Institute, 200

Training maxes can change on the daily--you may feel great one day, horrible the next. Although they will vary day to day, the important thing is that you will always perceive them to be equally as difficult. That's why it's also important to consistently give your best.

Now, completing a training max does not always mean hitting a certain percentage, as prescribed percentages in a program can't take into account the stressors of life (e.g. how much you slept the night before, how much you drank, or whether things are going well in your relationships). Such factors will come into play during your training, but the most important thing is to block them out and give your best on that particular day--no matter what.

Don Miguel Ruiz once said, "Always do your best. Your best is going to change from moment to moment; it will be different when you are healthy as opposed to sick. Under any circumstance, simply do your best, and you will avoid self-judgment, self-abuse and regret."

This is what a training max really is. It is your ability to consistently train at a level that approaches or exceeds your best effort on that particular day.

The longer you are able to do this, the stronger you will become. Remember that growing stronger is a marathon, not a sprint. Success hinges on your ability to push yourself to your limits day after day, regardless of what your limits are.

Keep in mind that you are not going to discover your true limits if you don't compete, or if you allow other people to put limits on you. Take risks. Put another plate on and see what you are capable of each and every day.

COMPETITION MAX

Your competition maximum strength is "the ability of a particular group of muscles to produce a maximum voluntary contraction in response to optimal motivation against an external load."[3]

In other words, your competition max is the most you can, for example, squat in front of a big group of people right after taking three scoops of a pre-workout supplement and getting slapped in the face by your coach.

In that scenario, you will most likely squat more than if you were training at your school's gym on a Thursday afternoon, with a Katy Perry song blaring through the music speakers.

Interestingly, Mel Siff, a doctor in human physiology who popularized the research of the great Russian sports scientist Yuri Verkhoshansky in the west, found that competitive atmospheres substantially increase emotional excitement, which in turn, increases strength output by up to 35% in an untrained athlete, and up to 10% in trained athletes. So, if you are a trained athlete who can squat 550 pounds during competition, you may be able to increase your max by up to 55 pounds. That is a very substantial increase simply from external stimuli!

As an aside, think of what this means for your day to day training. Are you training in an atmosphere and with people that help you lift more, or stunt your development?

In my experience, training for Strongman seems harder than competing in Strongman.

At a Strongman show, you will only do each event one time over the course of an afternoon. There is very little volume, but each event is usually performed at maximum speed and intensity.

3. Mel Siff, *Supertraining*, Denver, CO, Supertraining Institute, 200

Elliott and I at my first Strongman show

Conversely, in training for the Strongman event, you will do each event many times in gruelling training sessions that will leave you beat-up, bloody, and covered in dirt. These sessions can last up to three hours and don't usually involve too much time spent on the elliptical.

I remember loading stones, flipping tires, and then finishing off with a prowler push until I puked on many occasions. Looking back, the way I trained was crazy. However, I was only able to recover because I got enough sleep, enough hydration, and proper nutrition. But every time I finished a Strongman event, I'd be out of commission for a week after. I simply couldn't train.

This is because the competitive environment places even higher levels of stress to your nervous system and high levels of psychological stress that take much more time than normal to recover from. So, even though it feels as if you're pushing yourself hard in your normal day to day training, a competitive atmosphere will take that training stress and multiply it by a hundred.

Recovery time from a strenuous competition could be a few days, weeks, or even up to a month if the event was extremely intense.

Clearly, we at Strength Camp are big advocates of competition. We believe that it brings out your best. But remember: competing should not be done to simply beat others or to gain some external reward. While these are reasons some people compete, they are cases of their egos' getting in the way. These people will never experience the true feeling of competition, or pushing others and yourself to get better at the same time. Mihaly Csikszentmihalyi, the world renowned psychologist and researcher on the methods of optimizing human experience, writes:

"The roots of the word 'compete' are the latin *con petire*, which meant 'to seek together.' What each person seeks is to actualize [his/her] potential, and this task is made easier when others force us to do our best."[4]

Competition is a worthy goal in and of itself. It helps you get better. It gives you something to build toward, and above all, it allows you to become a Stronger Version of Yourself faster. I highly recommend that you compete. You won't regret it.

Lose yourself in competition, get uncomfortable, and push your limits.

You will be amazed by what your body and mind are capable of.

---

4. Mihaly Csikszentmihalyi, *Flow*, Harper Perennial Modern Classics, New York, 1990

STRENGTH–LESSON II: PERIODIZATION, HYPERTROPHY, & NERVOUS SYSTEM

> "IT'S NOT THE WILL TO WIN THAT MATTERS— EVERYONE HAS THAT. IT'S THE WILL TO PREPARE TO WIN THAT MATTERS."
>
> *—Paul "Bear" Bryant*

PERIODIZE FOR SUCCESS

In some ways, your mind determines your success. Your mindset is what really matters when it comes to training, and to life.

Who is winning the battle in your mind?

Desires, feelings, and self-talk are all combatants in your mind that can keep you from reaching your goals. But they can also be used to your advantage. To be successful and get what you want, you must develop and maintain control over them. This is a lesson that I have learned over years of training, competing, coaching hundreds of athletes, and starting my own businesses.

Ask yourself: *are your thoughts and goals being influenced by friends and family who don't understand your journey? Or are you spending time in solitude to find out what your heart truly desires?*

Are you filling your mind with negative self-talk? Or are you consciously filling your mind with empowering visualizations?

Are you comparing yourself with others and magnifying your weaknesses? Or are you focusing on the variables that are in your control and maximizing your strengths?

You need to have a strong will and a positive mindset--and I don't mean that you have to be a happy-go-lucky person--but you do have to strongly believe in yourself. You must believe that you will absolutely achieve your goals.

You need to have this type of mindset because the process isn't always fun.

It really isn't. It's not always fun to sacrifice going out with friends in order to spend another night in the weight room. It's not always fun to drag yourself out of your warm bed early in the morning, only to feel aching limbs touch the cold ground.

Yet these sacrifices, the struggle, and dedication to the process never get easier.

Experienced athletes all deal with this struggle. Each and every one of them must win the battle in their mind each and every day, before they even set foot on the surface of competition. The difference between them and someone who is not successful is that the former have set in place rituals and systems that allow them to more easily tame their minds. Because they continue to win the battles in their minds--they continue to win battles in life.

The bottom-line is that you need to have a strong will to achieve your dreams--mainly because you are going to fail. A lot.

Your progress is going to stall.

You are going to get injured.

You are going to lose.

You are going to feel weak.

You need to understand that these are par for the course. Everyone goes through any combination of these things. Embrace the challenge, and find pleasure in the grind.

Tommy Kano, who was perhaps the greatest American Olympic weightlifter of all time once said, in regard to setting and achieving goals:

"It will take great desire, determination, dedication, plus discipline of the mind...Sacrifices will be required as well as patience for the progress. It means quality effort and time must be spent to achieve the goal. To succeed, you must have faith in your ability to carry your training and training plan to success. Progress will come in increments so you must keep hammering away with your goal always in sight. Your focus on your goal should be so great that you even dream it in your sleep. Only when you come to the point of believing in your ability to accomplish it will this goal be met."

That is what it takes to win.

It takes an undying belief that you will do what it takes to achieve your goals no matter how lofty they are. The battle must be fought in your mind each and every day. And the battle must be won every day.

In order to do so, excuses must be banished.

Excuses like: I'm too tall; I'm too short; I'm too slow; I'm not smart enough; I don't have enough time; or I'm too tired--I've heard them all. I've made them all to myself as well. I remember thinking at one point,

"If only I were a few inches taller, I would make a great linebacker in the NFL." I thought this for a long time until I heard another one of my taller friends say, "If I was your height, I would be fast enough to be a running back in the NFL."

Both of us wanted something that we could not have. Both of us had made excuses in our minds that were not valid. Destroy excuses. I really mean it.

Excuses will quickly demolish you in the battle of your mind. They lull you into the sense that your laziness or lack of effort is justified.

Look, here's a dose of harsh reality: none of your excuses are valid, and no one owes you anything. Once you realize this, sear it into your mind and understand it. Once you do, you can start applying this and begin to develop consistency in your training.

We all know that consistency is the best way to get strong, because everything worth having and doing takes time. Those really strong people on YouTube and Instagram that you probably look up to didn't get that way overnight. In fact, you're kidding yourself if you think that you are going to deadlift 600 pounds after a few years of training--and surprisingly, I still meet some people who think this way.

Elliott has been training since he was just a kid. At his age, he already has over 20 years of training under his belt. Don't look at the finished product and expect to look the same way in a year or two, or even three or five. Put in ten years of solid work first and then realize where you stand: you'll probably find that you are the strongest guy in the room.

It's not because ten years automatically makes you strong. It's the *consistency*.

Most people quit before they have been training for ten years. When you dedicate that many years of consistently developing any skill, you will be rewarded. Consistency, of course, means that you don't miss training sessions every week and always do your best with what you have. It's definitely not deciding to skip training just because all the variables are not perfectly in place.

If you're sick, you do your best.

If you're hungover, you do your best.

If you are injured, you do your best.

Doing your best means that even if you have 20 minutes to train, you use that time to the best of your abilities--do anything, except force your body to do things it is not capable of doing.

At this point, I've painted training to be more akin to a battle that is meant only for the most hardened, veteran warriors with Spartan-like mental fortitude. But I still advocate that the best way to train with intensity and consistency is to actually have fun.

Even the strongest guys I know aren't always doom and gloom. For the most part, they are enjoying themselves and joking around...until it's time to perform. It's as if they flip a switch and turn into a warrior with laser-like focus.

It's taken them much time to develop this skill: to go from goofing around to training with ferocity and focus. They focus when they're at the gym and do the work. They aren't on their phones; they aren't worried about who is watching them; they aren't distracted by any external variables that don't matter; they focus on one specific task and channel all of their physical and mental energy into it. Only once the task is complete that they are able to flip the switch again and recover.

Most top-level performers in the world share this ability. It is possible for average folks to learn via a few ways, but meditation and deep breathing are two methods that have taken my own training to the next level. On days that I do not complete my breathing practice I can feel a difference--my focus is not there, and I am easily distracted and aggravated.

Make sure that you add relaxation practice to your daily routine. That could mean going for a walk in the morning (which I personally do while listening to an audio book). It could mean doing yoga, or spending time in prayer before bed. Whatever it is that works for you, make sure that you find the time to do it. Your recovery and mental acuity are as much linked to your physical success as all the time during which you spend exerting energy and lifting weights.

The athletes who excel are the ones who are able to recover well and stay the most consistent, even when conditions are not perfect.

Love what you do.

Love the grind.

Love the pain.

Love the struggle.

These are important points to grasp because if you don't love what you are doing, then you will never make the sacrifices necessary to be successful.

When things start getting tough--and they will--fill yourself with positive self-talk, for you must look at these tough moments as signs of success. If you are hitting roadblocks, you are moving forward; you are getting somewhere. It is those times when the strong-willed can weather the storm and get ahead. It's only when nothing is going wrong that you should be worried.

Always ask yourself: *who will win the battle in my mind today?*

Win the battle every day.

Do your best.

Love what you do.

If you can do these three things, then your potential for victory will be unlimited.

Periodization

There is a time for everything. We must dedicate a time to balance things--whether in our lives or in training. Later on in Elliot's chapters, we will dive further into this idea of "seasonal cycles".

For now, let's use forest fires as our example. They can wreak havoc and be generally seen as "bad" for the environment. In reality, they are necessary for the survival of that particular ecosystem. The forest's ecosystem needs fires and other natural "disasters" during the heat of summer to eliminate undergrowth, re-fertilize the soil, and ultimately help certain species of trees to release their seeds. Now I don't profess to know every detail of these things, but I do know that if summer stuck around all of the time, there would be no cycle of decay and growth. Instead, it would just be decay, turning the earth into a barren wasteland.

The idea behind this whole metaphor can be applied to your training: if you are constantly pushing yourself to the limit, lifting heavy, and doing a high volume of work--basically, wreaking havoc upon your body as forest fires do to trees--with little time for recovery, your body is going to break down. As it gets bad, you plateau, regress, or even get injured.

Periodization is the way to ensure that this does not happen.

According to world-renowned sport scientist Natalia Verkhoshansky, periodization is the "long-term cyclic structuring of training and practice to maximize performance to coincide with important competitions."

In simpler terms, it is a programming design that controls tempo, volume, rest, and intensity to elicit maximal gains in strength, mobility, and athleticism. Normally, people think periodization is used for preparing an athlete for their sport's in-season or competition--but it also ensures that the athlete minimizes his risk of injury and does not get bored with their training. You'd be surprised by how often people quit due to boredom.

There are different methods and ways to implement periodization into your training.

First, break your calendar days, weeks, months, and years into training cycles, named thusly:

A **microcycle** typically includes 5-10 training sessions over the course of a week. Each microcycle needs to include at least two different types of training sessions. You can't just do the same workout five times a week and call it a microcycle. You need variation in volume, tempo, and intensity within the microcycle.

A **mesocycle** will last between 1-4 months and can be broken down into microcycles.

A **macrocycle** usually encompasses an entire competitive season (usually under a year) and can be broken down into mesocycles and further into microcycles.

There're also quadrennial cycles and a multi-year plans, which are typically much larger--the former typically helping prep for Olympic games. For our purposes, we use the macrocycle as the largest block of periodization.

Understanding these cycles are important, as each cycle should work together to reach a specific goal. If each cycle is trying to advance different types of fitness at the same time, they just end up interfering with one another, ensuring that you make little to no progress. Periodization helps you identify the big goals, and then helps you break them down into achievable steps--or your macrocycles, mesocycles, microcycles, and then individual training sessions.

Furthermore, there are many different types of periodization that are used to reduce plateaus, minimize injury, and increase training stimulation. Each has advantages and disadvantages, and one is not really any better or worse than another. Which you use simply depends on the situation and how it would be applied.

Before we dive into the different periodizations, the most important aspects to remember are still to: keep it simple, keep your progress steady, and stay consistent.

Linear Periodization

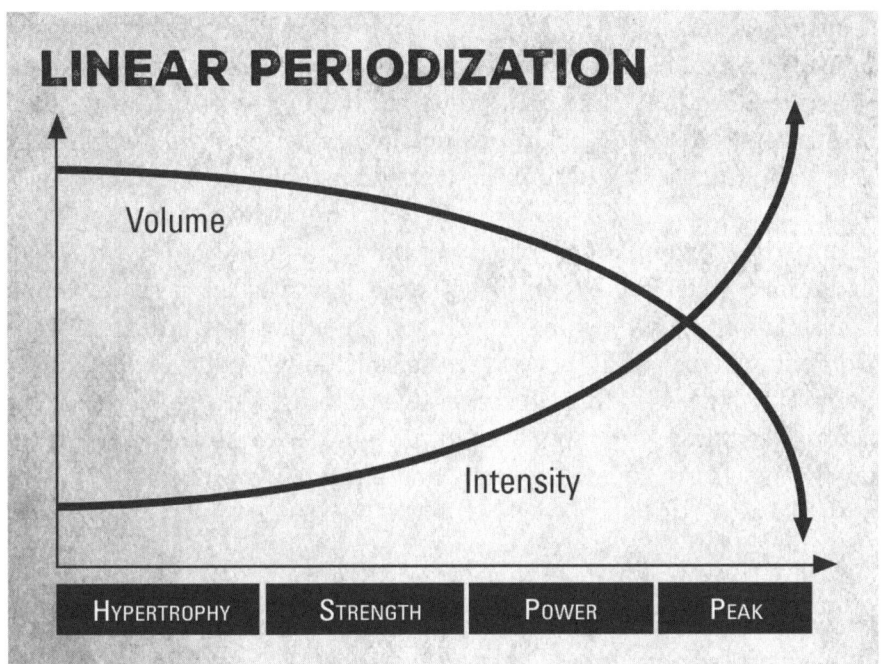

(Source: www.elitefts.com)

Linear periodization is the traditional method of periodization. It is also the most simple. All you are doing is manipulating volume, tempo, rest, and intensity over a number of mesocycles.

Usually, this means increasing the amount of weight lifted in each successive workout while simultaneously decreasing the number of reps. For example, in month one, you might be doing 3 sets of 12 reps. In month two, it would be 10 reps; month three would be 8 reps; and month four would be 6 reps.

I use linear periodization for most beginner athletes, especially if I have a good amount of time to work with them and they have never trained before. It allows the athlete to move through four mesocycle phases: general physical preparedness (GPP), special preparatory phase (SPP), competition phase (C), and transition phase (T).

The advantage of this type of linear periodization is that it does not focus on one type of skill exclusively. It allows the beginner athlete to build multiple types of fitness (strength, endurance, speed) at the same time. Most athletes simply need to increase their general physical preparedness, which determines how much work an individual can do in a specific period of time. It is vital that GPP increases before working on specific skills. This is why a simple linear periodization works best at the beginning stages of training, or when rehabbing from an injury.

A prime example of linear periodization is found in the 5x5 program, popularized by Mark Rippetoe. This program is more simple than manipulating reps or sets. All you do is increase intensity every workout--maybe add 10 pounds to the squat and deadlift and 5 pounds to the bench press with each successive training session. It is great for getting begginers strong, but once improvements cease, they must move on to a new form of programming and a more comprehensive type of periodization.

On the other hand, more advanced athletes would benefit more from meso and macrocycles that focus on the development of specific skills and types of fitness. They may also need to "peak" for specific competitions or sporting events. As such, a linear periodization would be too general for their needs.

UNDULATING PERIODIZATION

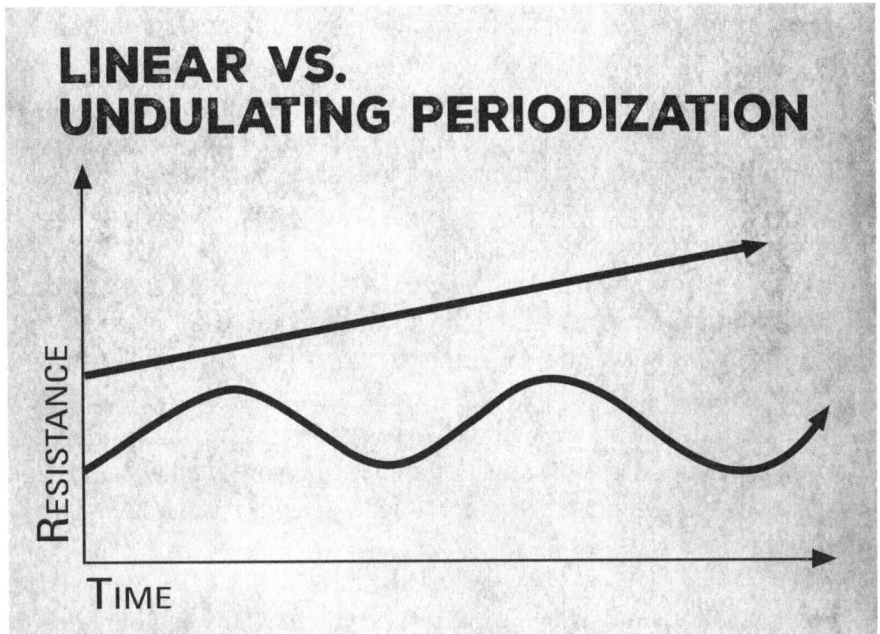

(Source: www.elitefts.com)

Undulating periodization has gained much popularity in recent years. It allows for more continual growth and recovery once people hit the training ceiling of traditional linear periodization. Undulating periodization is based on Han Seyle's general adaptation syndrome (GAS) which, if you recall, is the theory that describes the body's reaction to short- and long-term stress.

As you can probably guess, undulating periodization varies the stress on your body on either a weekly or daily basis. This forces your body to be faced with new stress constantly, and does not allow it to fully adapt to or get comfortable with your training. Keep in mind: this is not muscle confusion.

You are entering a cycle of: applying new stress, allowing for recovery, and then applying a new stress. With this simple technique, you keep your body in a state of constant growth via the manipulation of volume and intensity in your workouts.

We do this because, as you probably know, your body is very adaptable. It does not take long for you to be as stiff as a gargoyle statue if you're sitting all of the time, which would be counterproductive to being mobile and athletic. In the same way it adapts to sitting and being sedentary, it adapts fairly quickly to your training as well.

During training, it will adapt most quickly to rep ranges, yet it will adapt very slowly to the stress applied through exercise selection. This is why in the traditional linear periodization you can do the same exercises for months, increase the weight each time, and see continual progress. When most people come to me for advice, I discover that they are switching the movements too often. This is a terrible way to increase strength, as the body will have to adapt to a new movement at a lower weight, but by the time it is ready to start lifting heavier--the movements have changed again. Make sure that you stick with the basic and primal movement patterns for a long period of time (I'm talking years here, not months).

So, in a daily undulating periodization, you hit the same movements multiple times a week, whereas you would be doing a movement only once a week at most in a linear periodization. In daily undulating periodization, we usually want to manipulate the rep range. The movements should stay the same in each mesocycle, but volume and intensity need to be managed. Each movement is trained at least twice a week, but by varying the rep ranges, the body is never allowed to adapt.

If you aren't used to this style of training, hitting the same movements twice a week in undulating periodization might seem crazy to you. I mean, how can you expect to train squats twice in one week? Or bench--that's only for Mondays, right? Wouldn't you overtrain?

I call overtraining to be a load of crap.

To go off on a tangent: when someone says they're experiencing symptoms of "overtraining", they're truly just under-recovering. That means they're: not sleeping enough, being stressed out by work or relationships, not drinking enough water, getting wasted every weekend, and probably taking enough pre-workout and other stimulants to keep a horse awake for a week. Basically, don't worry about overtraining; fix your habits and worry about getting really strong instead.

Moving along: daily undulating periodization allows you to train--let's say squats--three times a week, maybe even seven, by varying the intensity and volume, which decreases the amount of fatigue on the muscles. So, instead of trying to do 5 sets of 12 on back squats once on a Monday and then being totally wrecked the rest of the week, you would be doing 3 sets of 10 reps one day; then 4 sets of 6 reps the next training session.

In essence, you could be squatting every day if you wanted to!

Squatting every day is a training methodology that has been popularized recently by the well-respected American weightlifting coach Jon Broz, as well as by athlete Corey Gregory. It may seem like crazy high volume at first, but in actuality, if you manage the intensity and the variety of the squatting movements properly, it is a great way to force your body to adapt and still give it enough time to recover and grow. It is the perfect example of daily undulating periodization, although I would not recommend this type of program for a beginner. (However, working in bodyweight squats every day is never a bad way to increase mobility and stability in a beginner.)

Another benefit to daily undulation is that, by doing the same movement at least twice a week, you can refine your movement patterns and technique. If you only were able to practice the piano once a week for 20 minutes, I imagine that you probably wouldn't be ready for a recital any time soon. If you are squatting only once a week, spending perhaps 20 minutes in total on it, you probably would not get very proficient at the movement either. When people wonder why they're hardly making progress on a particular lift when they're doing it once a week, my usual answer is: "Do it more." Period.

And it's not just me who says to do a movement more often. Pavel Tsatsouline, a great strength coach whose no-nonsense training philosophy I respect greatly, popularized kettlebell training in America and has a concept called "greasing the groove." It is the idea of performing certain key movements on a regular basis--but never to exhaustion--in order to learn the movement pattern as a skill. According to Pavel, strength is not just about muscular strength, it is a skill. In his mind, not only are you better at the movement itself, but you are stronger as well.

Let's say you were interested in increasing the number of push-ups you could do. At the time, you can do 15. Following the ideas of daily undulating periodization, you would aim for 3-4 sets of 8-9 reps a day. In this way, you are increasing the volume of work you are doing, as well as increasing your proficiency with the movement, without exhausting yourself. Over time, your body gets more skilled at the movement pattern and will get stronger for greater number of reps due to increased stress, decreased muscular exhaustion, and increased skill.

As you can see, there are many benefits to following an undulating periodization, especially if you are an intermediate or advanced lifter who has hit a strength, hypertrophic, or fat loss plateau.

Concurrent Periodization

STRENGTH CAMP MESOCYCLE

MONTHS	1				2				3			
FOCUS	STRUCTURE				STRENGTH				SPEED			
INTENSITY												
Weeks	1	2	3	4	5	6	7	8	9	10	11	12

Concurrent periodization essentially means that there is not a direct focus on developing any one ability in an athlete over a period of time. In this type of periodization, strength, hypertrophy, mobility, speed, and so on are all addressed over the period of a microcycle, wherein one is not typically emphasized over another.

We use concurrent periodization with most of the athletes at Strength Camp. Concurrent periodization allows for my athletes to make progress in a variety of different abilities while still ensuring that they do not regress in any ability. I have found that, through this style of periodization, I can make individual adjustments on the fly as I learn what each of their strengths and weaknesses are. My advice to aspiring coaches is to take a long-term approach to building athletes, ignore traditional training dogmas, and focus on their individual needs. In this way, you will do more good for them than you can imagine.

For example, if I have a wrestler who has great conditioning and can run for miles on end but whose absolute strength is terrible, then I'd focus more on strength than on conditioning. This seems intuitive, but it does not seem to be common practice with many coaches and athletes who coach themselves.

The same type of adjustment can be made depending on the time of year. As football season approaches, most athletes traditionally would stop strength training and instead focus on power. Sure, this is great if the athlete is already adequately strong. However, if the athlete is still very weak, then it would be a good idea to continue building their strength.

Each athlete, including yourself, has a particular set of needs that must be addressed in order for him to reach his athletic potential. This holds true for your own training. While a program needs to be followed over a long period time to see results, it is also important to realize that adjustments and implementation of corrective protocols must be made according to the individual's injuries and imbalances.

When I train athletes, I observe them on a day to day basis and manipulate their program to suit their training needs. Other styles of programming are fairly rigid, making adjustments, especially based on day to day observations, difficult to do. Further, program flexibility is important when dealing with larger groups of athletes at the same time. It is vital to remember that you are training individuals, not just football players, swimmers, or wrestlers.

For the athlete, concurrent periodization tends to be very engaging. After all, it changes constantly in terms of intensity, volume, and rest periods--getting bored of the programming is not really a concern. In fact, that might be one of its greatest strengths, since these days it might be hard to keep someone's attention for longer than a couple minutes!

Things aren't all rosy, however. As an athlete gets more and more specialized, things can get very complicated with concurrent periodization. Eventually, they need microcycles that reflect this specialization. Your higher level athletes, such as powerlifters, Olympic lifters, and those in other strength-based sports, need blocks of training that are implemented specifically to increase some abilities while maintaining others.

When it comes down to it, a good coach will always use different types of periodization at the same time. They don't get stuck to one method of periodization and discount all others. I myself am constantly mixing different styles of periodizations together to address weaknesses and shortcomings in my athletes. In this way, I am able to do what is best for them and not what is best for my ego. I believe training in real life is far too multifaceted to be able to neatly fit into one form of periodization.

Focus on strengthening the individual weaknesses of yourself, or your athletes if you train any, as well as maintaining and building your individual strengths. You will make much more progress than if you just fanatically follow one form of periodization without any wiggle room.

At Strength Camp, we have always used a hybrid approach to building muscle, strength, and speed. Through experimentation, we preserve exercises and methods that work, and discard ones that do not serve us or our athletes. From this, we have been able to create systems of training that we feel allow each and every member reach his athletic potential in the gym.

Do the same with your own training, and you will be well on your way to becoming the Strongest Version of Yourself.

Periodization Variables

Tempo

Tempo is essentially how fast or slow you are performing the movement, or in fancier terms, the time under tension (TUT) of the movement you are performing. Tempo has a massive impact on how effective that movement will be in helping you grow stronger.

Whether someone is a complete beginner or a highly advanced and specialized athlete, pretty much everyone can benefit from manipulating the tempos in their training. It's one of my favorite ways to increase the strength of my athletes, as well as reduce their risk of injury and increase their movement proficiency. Usually, it involves slowing the movement down and even pausing at certain points of the movement.

Now, to better understand tempo and how it affects strength, you need to understand the specific phases of a lift:

ECCENTRIC

Eccentric portion is also the "lowering" part of the lift (i.e. when you lower yourself to the ground in a squat or in a pull-up).

When focusing on the eccentric portion, we train one of the most powerful human reflexes--the stretch reflex. The stretch reflex consists of muscle spindles and the Golgi tendon organs. When trained properly, it can increase force production by adapting to the higher levels of stress associated with the slower eccentric portion.

ISOMETRIC

An isometric contraction is basically holding a static contraction (i.e. a pause at the bottom of the squat).

When focusing on the isometric portion, we are able to focus on two key components for athletes: motor unit recruitment and rate coding. The former is essentially increasing the number of muscle fibers we turn on during a movement. The latter is the rate at which those fibers fire.

The isometric phase is important to building athleticism because, the faster we can absorb force, stop the eccentric contraction, and then produce force from a dead stop, the more we are able to create an explosive movement. Think of someone running in to dunk a basketball. Do they tend to slow their stride, squat down, and then attempt to jump; or do they seem to pop off the ground?

This is how we can train that pop.

CONCENTRIC

The concentric phase usually gets all of the credit. It's the portion that actually pushes the weight off your chest or reaches that huge box jump. No one wants to know how much weight you can squat to the bottom and then drop off your back. They want to know how much weight you can squat down and up!

The concentric portion of a lift is valuable in that it measures the rate of force development in an athlete.

With the phases of contraction defined, you can better appreciate this example of tempo manipulation for a back squat: 3|2|X|2.

Looks confusing at first, but let's decipher that together.

The first number, a 3, is always going to be your eccentric portion of the lift.

The second number, a 2, represents the isometric part of the movement. In this example, you would be pausing for 2 seconds at the bottom of the squat, fighting to keep good position.

The third number, or letter X, represents the concentric portion of the lift. X typically tells you that there is no pause, so you will move the weight explosively. This is always the upward moving part of the lift. In a squat, you are rising up from the bottom; in a pull-up, you are pulling yourself to the bar; and in a push-up, you are pushing yourself off the floor.

The fourth number, a 2, represents how long you pause at the top of the movement. For a squat, this represents how long you will wait (2 seconds) before starting the next rep. For a pull-up, this would be how long you spend at the top of the movement with your chest against the bar.

So putting it all together in this example, you would be lowering for two seconds, pausing for two seconds, driving up explosively, pausing for two seconds, and then starting the next rep.

Reading tempo may seem complicated at first (especially with pull-ups and other movements that start the movement with a concentric part), but just remember that the first number always represents the eccentric part of the movement, and the third represents the concentric part of the movement. Once you know those, you can pretty well decipher the rest.

I mentioned earlier that Increasing TUT can lead to increased connective tissue strength and increased skill at the movement itself. It's not the be-all, end-all of training, but when it is implemented properly in a comprehensive training program, you can make some truly great progress.

For beginners, this is especially vital! It forces them to use lighter weights, but will increase their confidence with the movement and lead to greater mobility and stability. I have all of my beginner athletes perform weeks, sometimes months, of tempo work before they jump into attempting any type of max lift. This ensures that they have strong connective tissue, good stability, and are confident enough with the movement to move some serious weight. It may seem tedious, boring, and hurtful to the ego, but slow tempos and pause reps undoubtedly make you stronger, especially if you have never used them before.

In addition, utilizing tempo decreases the amount of stress that is placed on your body. Sounds paradoxical since I was just talking about how it can increase stress, but hear me out: when you see a guy at the gym bouncing a bar off his chest in order to do bench press, he is actually putting a tremendous amount of stress on his tendinous and ligamentous connective tissues. The muscles are almost taken out of the equation.

If that same guy were to slow down his reps drastically and allow his muscles to take the brunt of the load, as they are meant to, he would be decreasing the stress placed on his connective tissue. When you look at tempo's effect on stress reduction in this way, you can see that tempo reduces the risk of injury.

Plus, it forces you to be aware of the muscles that *should be* working. This includes engaging (and building) a very solid midline stability, or core strength. Oftentimes, I see people try to rush a lift because they lose stability; it's how rounded backs and injuries can occur. Strict tempos eliminate this possibility, as it forces you to use lower weights and focus on stability in all positions.

You're not going to notice if you're bouncing around. It is important that you are in tune with your body, how it is moving, which areas feel good, and which areas feel tight. Slow eccentrics and pauses will help you gain this awareness.

Volume

Volume is simply the amount of work you do in a given training session and can impact your training. This can be measured by looking at how many reps and sets you are performing. Higher volume training is usually done with hypertrophy in mind, whereas lower volume training (which usually correlates with higher intensity) is done with strength gains in mind.

Each type of volume will have a different effect on the body, but both still require a good amount of recovery. Higher volume training (think of German Volume Training which involves 10 sets of 10 reps of multiple exercises) tends to result in muscular fatigue and soreness. This type of training uses high volume to induce sarcoplasmic hypertrophy, which we will delve into later. Recovery typically takes a few days, so it is not the best idea to only do high-volume training all the time.

Lower volume training, on the other hand (i.e. 6 sets of 3 reps at a higher intensity), tends to be more draining on your nervous system. It still takes time to recover from this type of strength training, but you will not, for the most part, feel the same type of soreness or muscular fatigue.

Ideally, you would not be doing just one type of training. At Strength Camp, we have hybrid-style training approaches, combining high- and low-volume, compound and isolation movements, and dynamic expressions of strength through various movements. We tend to avoid becoming overly attached to one style of training to avoid imbalances and weaknesses.

Each type of volume training has its place. Using high volume with isolation movements is an amazing way to bring up lagging body parts that may be limiting your overall strength. If you have a deficiency in hamstring strength, for example, doing more squats is not going to help. You need to break the movement down, and use lower weights and higher volume to build that weak area up.

On the flip side, most people who love using high-volume training tend to overtrain their chests and neglect their backs and pulling motions. Here is when it would be great for them to use lower reps and sets with higher intensity on their pushing movements; and then use higher sets and reps to build up their pulling movements, and subsequently, their backs. By doing it this way, they simultaneously maintain the strength of their push and combat muscular imbalances like Upper Cross syndrome via the increased pulling volume. This may all seem complicated, but it can all be tracked and planned out if you are diligent about keeping a training journal, which you all should be doing anyway.

For the beginner, increasing volume can be as easy as walking for a half hour each day or doing some light stretching and mobility work. Put simply, any type of movement that you can add to your program and does not compromise your overall recovery will help you reach your goals. So, don't be afraid to move on your rest days, moving is what your body was built to do.

It is important that you be familiar with the volume you are using in your training, as too little can mean that you aren't putting enough stress on your body to elicit any type of change. Too much volume can mean that your body will have a harder time recovering from your last workout.

INTENSITY

In a very traditional weight training sense, intensity is simply the amount of weight you are moving in proportion to your body weight and to your established 1-rep max in that particular movement. According to the Merriam-Webster dictionary, intensity in physics is "the power transferred per unit area, which is transmitted through an imagined surface perpendicular to the propagation direction."

Both are useful definitions that directly correlate to training in a tangible and intangible sense. When you are deadlifting, you are transmitting force through a "surface perpendicular to the propagation direction"; you are resisting gravity, and you are creating force in order to move a certain amount of weight perpendicular to the floor.

So, in the training context, higher intensity simply means that the amount of exertion is close to that of your 1-rep max. This is where people get really caught up in percentages. By all means, I love using percentages as a guideline for the amount of weight to aim for within a particular set, but there's more to it than just basing percentages on past performance. More on that in a moment.

There are many additional ways to define intensity. In one, intensity can be defined as "the quality of being intense." Synonyms include: passion, fire, fervency, and violence. This definition is just as valid as any, but it opens up a whole new conversation regarding what intensity in training means. Additionally, increasing the intensity could also mean adding an extra set or a few extra reps, or even simply shortening rest periods. Intensity is not just how heavy you go. Clearly, there are many ways to define intensity, but we can put them all together to apply to your own training..

Let's start with a thought exercise. Which is harder to do--or more accurately, which requires more intensity: hitting a back squat at 100% of your 1RM, or 20 reps at 75% of your 1RM?

If we go purely by percentages, 100% is obviously higher than 75% so a 1RM requires more intensity, right? But if you have ever done 20 reps at 75%, you will know that it requires a very high degree of intensity, fire, and violence to complete them all. Most likely you will be yelling; you will have thoughts of giving up; and most likely, you will think that it is one of the most intense things that you have ever done.

Based on that thought, intensity refers to both physical and mental strength. Intensity is how hard you are working in relation to how hard you know that you could be working. Oftentimes, intensity is something that you have to gauge for yourself. Only you alone know how hard you are pushing yourself--and sometimes you need someone else to give you a reality check or some type of external stimulus to take your intensity up a notch. It may look like you are moving a good amount of weight with intensity, but in your mind, how hard are you working?

How challenged are you by your training? Is your training too intense, leaving you unable to walk the next day or unable to train again that week? Conversely, is your training not intense enough, allowing you to breeze through each workout but leading to no real results?

With the right intensity, you are focusing on the task at hand, giving your best and ensuring that you don't leave a rep or two in the tank when you should be going all out. Intensity is a mindset that has no room for distractions. If you spend half your workout on your phone, then I'm sorry--you aren't training with intensity.

Training with intensity does not necessarily mean going ham on everything. Approaching your warm-up sets with intensity could mean focusing all of your attention on each rep, setting up for each set like you would for a 1RM, staying tight through the movement, controlling your breathing, being aware of how you are moving, and above all, preparing yourself for the rest of your training.

On your own scale, you should be working at around 75-85% of your maximum intensity regardless of whether you are doing more high-volume work or more strength-based work. On days that you feel great, change that to 90-100% intensity. There is a time and place to crank up the intensity, and it's up to you to know your body well enough and flip that switch.

Strength training is a long-term pursuit, so be wary about burning yourself out before too long. Otherwise, you will never be able to see what you are capable of.

Don't deceive yourself, put in the right amount of intensity, and reap the rewards.

Rest Times

Rest between sets is simple, yet very important. Here's a basic guideline:

If lifting between 1-5 reps, rest 2-4 minutes. If lifting between 6-12 reps, rest 60 seconds.

Rest for Strength Focused Rep Ranges (1-5)

When you are training for strength, you want to make sure that each rep and set look like the first--with good, solid form and energetic, focused intentions. Keep in mind that your last rep doesn't have to be as fast as your first one, but it does mean that your form should remain intact. If your last rep leaves you with a rounded back or twisted in dangerous ways, then you are not getting stronger, plain and simple. Rather, you are simply reinforcing poor movement patterns under load into your brain and straining your body in an unhealthy way. Nope, you're doing it wrong.

The thing is that when you train at a high percentage of your 1RM, you are taxing your nervous system immensely. This is why you may not feel very much *muscular* fatigue between sets of strength work. So, you may be tempted to cut down on rest times because of this. That is a mistake--don't do that. Make sure that you get at least two minutes of rest in-between each set. In fact, the more, the better, but try not to exceed four minutes, as you don't want your body to cool down (plus, you want to maintain your momentum).

With enough rest in-between each set, you can recover fully and hit each rep perfectly. That is the idea. Save the broken down form for when you want to build some mental strength using bodyweight movements that will not result in a herniated disc or a blown-up shoulder.

Rest for Hypertrophy Focused Rep Ranges (8-12)

In the next section, you will soon learn the ins and outs of myofibrillar and sarcoplasmic hypertrophy. When it comes to building muscle, we want to focus on sarcoplasmic hypertrophy, as it will yield the most gains in terms of size. Maintaining TUT, especially on the eccentric, while working with increasingly more fatigued muscles will allow you to build the most size. Rest periods for this type of sarcoplasmic hypertrophy should be between 60-90 seconds. Rest periods are kept short in order to prevent your muscles from fully recovering from the set before.

Do not wait too long in-between sets. Your nervous system is not being taxed to the same degree as strength-based training, and as such, needs much less time to recover. When training with higher reps, your goal should not be to lift as much weight as possible. You can continue to push lighter weights for more reps with little rest. Focus on maintaining tempo and range of motion while limiting your rest to the allotted time period.

Unlike Strength training, your focus should be to push your muscles as far as they can go and never leaving a rep in the tank.

When it comes to rest, keep your rest periods simple and appropriate for the type of training that you are doing. If you aren't seeing the results that you would like, my recommendation is to try not spending five minutes in-between sets of shoulder raises and seeing if anything changes.

Hypertrophy

Hypertrophy is the process of building bigger muscle, more size.

Focusing on building muscle does not always mean that you are a bodybuilder. Building muscle does not always mean that you aren't training functional fitness. Building muscle does not always mean that you are vain or self-absorbed. Simply, building muscle may mean that you are trying to fix weak points, increase athletic potential, and grow stronger.

Growing stronger is what Strength Camp is all about. Growing stronger is what my life is all about. From the football field, to the weight room, to competing as a Strongman, to starting my own business as a college student, I have always been growing stronger in one way or another. So whenever I wanted to grow stronger in the gym I knew that I had to build stronger muscles and get bigger. Now I don't mean that the only way to grow stronger is to get bigger, but hey, it never hurts.

Just look at the strongest men and women across the competitive field of powerlifting, Olympic lifting, and Strongman. They are all big people. Even elite Olympic lifters in lower weight classes are ripped and muscular enough to appear to be bodybuilders. More muscle simply lend themselves greater strength.

Actually, I should say being more powerful and versatile, in general.

When was the last time you saw a skinny sprinter? Or a skinny running back? Or a skinny CrossFit Games champion? All three of these athletes require great deals of strength *and* athleticism. If you aren't "big", you probably aren't "strong".

Of course, size is only one aspect of strength. Your body needs to be balanced; you need to be able to move all of your joints freely; and your muscles need to be able to be effectively charged by your brain and nervous system. If you are big but can't move or express your strength properly, then what is the point?

I believe that simply looking a certain way brings very fleeting and shallow satisfaction. Being able to fully participate in any challenge or activity that comes your way is much more satisfying.

Essentially, what I'm getting at is that you don't want to overindulge in either type of training. If you are just training for strength, you could probably add in some muscle-building training and get great benefits. Likewise, if all you do is train for muscle growth, then you could definitely benefit from strength training.

A hybrid approach to building muscle and strength will help you be much better off. With that being said, there are two types of muscle that your body can build.

The two different types of muscular growth are known as sarcoplasmic hypertrophy and myofibrillar hypertrophy. These concepts were first introduced to the Western world by Mel Siff, and further supported by Pavel Tsatsouline and Charles Poliquin. These coaches and authors are well-respected in the world of strength and conditioning, and they all credit this theory to the legendary Russian sports scientist Vladimir Zatsiorsky.

As a caveat, there is not much hard scientific evidence to support the idea that you can grow two different types of muscle fiber--both usually end up being built simultaneously. But if you train in a certain manner that allegedly supports the growth of one of these types of muscle, then you could end up manipulating your aesthetics and looking a certain way.

Moreover, as with many aspects of fitness, genetics play a serious role here, as some people just have a higher genetic potential in terms of size and strength, whereas others may more easily put on size and less strength. Yet some may not have a propensity towards either. The important point to consider is that, as athletes, we want to build muscle and strength to the point that they improve our performance on the field. Otherwise, the training should be altered to address this issue.

The two types of muscular growth are known as sarcoplasmic hypertrophy and myofibrillar hypertrophy.

SARCOPLASMIC HYPERTROPHY

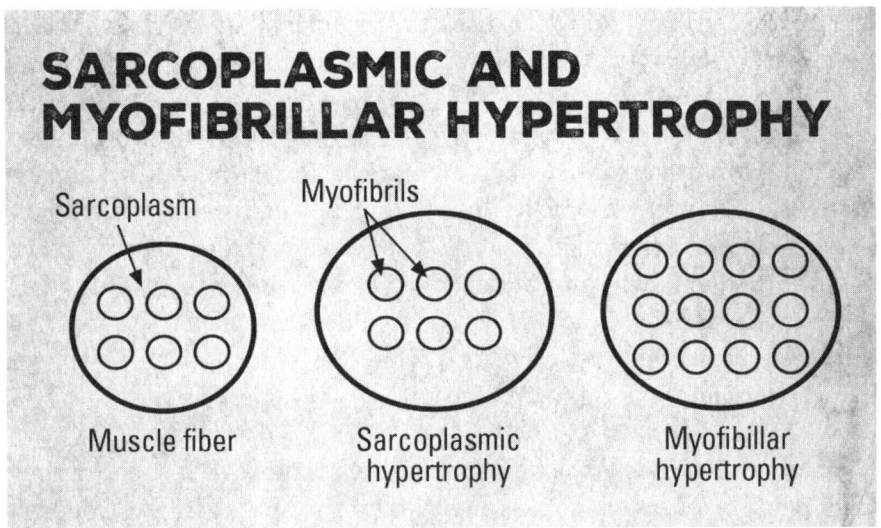

Source: "Science and Practice of Strength Training" by Vladimir Zatsiorsky

Sarcoplasmic hypertrophy is an increase in the sarcoplasm, the cytoplasm in each muscle fiber. Sarcoplasm is comparable to the cytoplasm of other cells. Essentially, the sarcoplasm is a watery solution that holds within it all the key force-generating components of the muscle fiber, including ATP, phosphagen, enzymes, and other molecules. The sarcoplasm of each muscle fiber also houses 1,000 to

2,000 myofibrils, which facilitate contraction of various proteins like actin and myosin. This is the smallest contraction of a muscle fiber, and it is in here that our strength is housed.

You can think of sarcoplasm as the box that contains a dozen donuts. The box allows for their safe transport, but it by itself does not do much in terms of helping the donuts taste great and boost your glycemic index. The donuts represent what you want, if you are interested in getting stronger--the more, the better.

Now the donut shop could increase the size of the box, but that does not mean that more donuts will be in the box. The bigger size of the box merely allows for more donuts to be potentially added, but increasing the size does not immediately correspond with there being more donuts inside. Translating this back to sarcoplasm, you want increased sarcoplasm which means an increased potential for strength.

The theory of sarcoplasmic hypertrophy says that lifting lighter weights for more reps can lead to an increase in sarcoplasm, increasing the cross-sectional size of the muscle but not increasing the amount of muscle fibers. This distinction is supposedly seen in the difference between bodybuilders and athletes in strength-based sports, such as powerlifting and Olympic lifting. Bodybuilders are usually bigger than the latter, but looking at pound-for-pound they're not typically stronger than powerlifters and Olympic lifters.[1]

In my experience, explosive strength is a skill that is supported by more muscle, although some might argue that bigger muscle doesn't always equate to bigger strength. Well, one of the main reasons that bigger guys are not always stronger on, say, a 1RM squat test is that they merely haven't trained that movement often. In other words, it comes down to their nervous system's not knowing how to utilize the muscle that they have. (It does not necessarily mean that they have a different type of muscle.)

Mel Siff, *Supertraining*, Denver, CO, Supertraining Institute, 2004

As people compete more in multiple disciplines, it becomes clear that more muscle often means more strength. The main issue is in building muscle without building the skills or trained nervous system needed to lift heavy. We all know that one person who trains only on machines and neglects squats or deadlifts. He may be huge, but he lacks the neuromuscular strength and the movement patterns to use his muscle effectively.

The old saying "You can't flex bone' holds true to this day. During the process of growing bigger, you increase the amount of sarcoplasm and number of muscle fibers, thereby growing the cross-sectional size of your muscles will grow. Bottom-line: sarcoplasmic hypertrophy is not a myth. It does occur, but it does not occur independently.

MYOFIBRILLAR HYPERTROPHY

If you want to be stronger, you need more myofibrils, which are tube-like structures that, when packed together, make up the bulk of the muscle fiber itself. The contractile proteins, actin and myosin, are found within myofibrils. Recall that actin and myosin enable contraction when prompted by the nervous system.

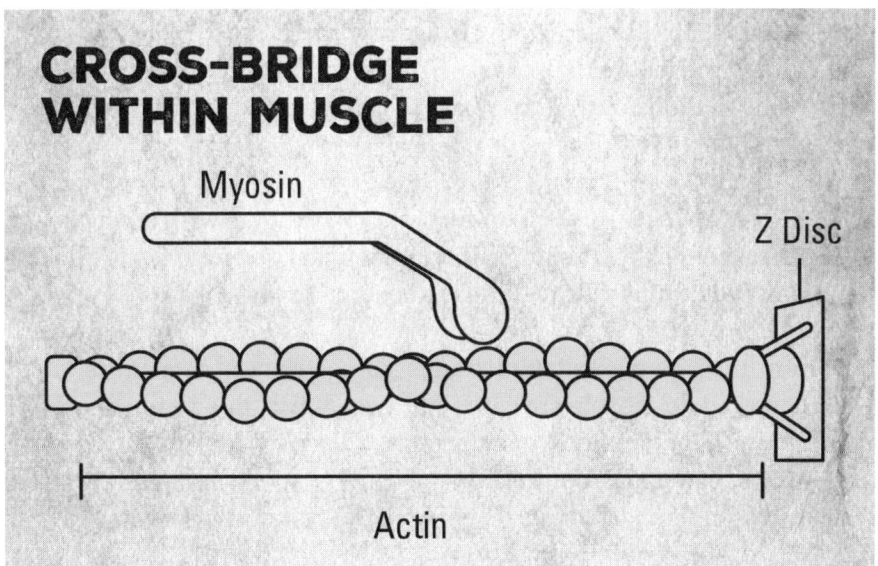

You can think of actin and myosin as Velcro. The actin would be like the loop part of the Velcro, and the myosin would be the hook. When the actin and myosin get the signal from the nervous system to contract, the myosin hook will grab onto an actin loop and pull on it. This process is repeated, causing the myosin to ratchet its way up to the degree at which the muscle needs to be contracted.

Very simply put: the more myofibrils you have, the greater contractile force you should be able to generate, which is great for lifting heavy weights.

Most of the training to increase myofibrillar hypertrophy falls into the range of 1-5 reps using 85-100% of a 1RM. This type of training should increase the density of muscle fibers due to an increased dependence on the contractile force of the myofibrils.

However, to say that increasing myofibrillar hypertrophy is the sole reason for greater contractile force would be to ignore something very important: your nervous system.

When your body is called upon to lift a heavy load, your nervous system is what allows you to recruit enough muscle fibers to get the job done. Training at rep ranges and at intensities that heavily tax the nervous system will make you stronger by increasing the neural drive that can be utilized by the muscles. Lifting at high intensities will also allow your nervous system to learn the movements in physically and mentally stressful environments.

In other words, the more comfortable you become with lifting heavy loads, the stronger you become. Remember that strength is a skill. You need experience under heavy loads to become strong.

Oftentimes, untrained individuals gain strength at a more rapid rate than they do muscle size. It is not necessarily due to the degree of myofibrillar hypertrophy. This is because they are adapting their neural systems to becoming comfortable with the movements. By simply learning the skill and allowing their nervous systems to recruit a higher percentage of their muscle fibers, they are able to increase intensity and very quickly grow stronger.

As we further learn about how to build muscle and strength, we are realizing more that sarcoplasmic hypertrophy and myofibrillar hypertrophy do not occur completely independently. Some people will build more muscle training in higher rep ranges, and some will build more muscle training in lower rep ranges but with more weight. Either one will help you grow stronger, but you are encouraged to train in both rep ranges and at a variety of percentages of your 1RM.

Otherwise, you only place limits on yourself by sticking to one type of training. Greater strength comes from focusing on learning the movements well, being mobile enough to not restrict your range of motion, and training with a high level of intensity regardless of whether you are doing 3 sets of 10 or 7 sets of 2.

Your Nervous System

Strength is a function of numerous biological components. Perhaps the most important--and the most neglected in terms of either not training it enough or beating it to the ground--component is the nervous system. By now, we understand that training the nervous system lays the groundwork for building strength, but what does that entail and what does your nervous system compose of?

We will get to how to train your nervous system later, but for now, let's focus on what the nervous system is.

The nervous system controls all movement in the body. The nervous system consists of the **central nervous system (CNS)** and the **autonomic nervous system (ANS)**. As a quick overview for your understanding, movement is initiated voluntarily or reflexively in the CNS, which sends a signal (an action potential) down your spinal cord through your nerves. The nerves themselves are connected to a motor unit which connects to the muscle fibers, thus firing that muscle to ultimately create a movement.

Simple so far? Let's break it down further.

Central Nervous System

The central nervous system is made up of the brain and the spinal cord. It is named thusly because it is the center that receives all of the information and interprets it throughout our body. Our brain is the main processing center for of the CNS and is comprised of four main components: brainstem, cerebellum, diencephalon, and cerebrum. Attached to the brain is the spinal cord, which encases the nerves that run down it. It is these nerves that innervate our muscles and ultimately control movement.

The eyes--the optic nerves--can also be considered a part of the CNS. The eyes are the only part of the CNS that is in direct contact with the environment around you. The CNS is constantly taking in stimuli from your environments, processing and acting based on this information. Obviously, its function and thus protection are vital to your survival. Your brain is encased in your skull. Your spinal cord is encased in your bony vertebrae. Both the brain and the spinal cord are covered in a membrane that offers them further protection.

Despite this protection, trauma from athletic events or contact sports can compromise an athlete's safety and normal CNS functioning. Brain injuries are a growing concern in many different contact sports because the physical effects of damage to your CNS can be very real and profound.

Autonomic Nervous System

The autonomic nervous system controls the involuntary actions of your body, those that you don't have to think about at all. Even when you're at rest, your body is never truly doing nothing. On the contrary, your body is always doing something, with or without your consent. You breathe, digest food, release certain hormones, fight against airborne viruses, repair muscle, and perform thousands of brain computations that you will never remember or even notice.

The autonomic nervous system itself can be further divided into two branches. You have the sympathetic nervous system and the parasympathetic nervous system. If imbalanced, these systems can lead to the feeling of being "burnt out". Being burnt out, or being in a state of "overtraining", is usually not a case of someone working too hard. In reality, most people don't ever work hard enough in the gym to truly overtrain. However, people often end up under-recovering. They are placing excessive stress on one part of their nervous system while not placing enough on the other.

Sympathetic Nervous System

When you are flipping a tire, stepping into the ring for your first MMA fight, or sprinting away from pursuers on the football field, you are stressing your sympathetic nervous system, or your "fight or flight" response. During this heightened period, your body is highly focused, releasing hormones and chemicals that support this state of hyperalertness. It is through the sympathetic nervous system that you can express your strength in a very aggressive manner.

It does this through a few ways: it diverts blood flow away from the digestive organs and shuttles most of your blood flow to your muscles and brain. This makes sense, since in a survival situation, digesting food is not a concern. Your body wants you to survive--giving priority to the muscles and brain is important for your survival.

In the process of everything, the sympathetic nervous system also activates your adrenal and thyroid glands, which release hormones and chemicals like adrenaline, cortisol, and dopamine. All of these are necessary for you to perform great feats of strength and endurance. At the same time, these hormones and chemicals are also associated with breakdown, or catabolism.

When the body is in a catabolic state, it is essentially breaking down big molecules into smaller ones. This is not a good state to be in if the goal is to build muscle. A balance between the two nervous systems will ensure you continue on your path to growing stronger. Be sure to stress the body through the sympathetic nervous system, and then recover through stimulating the parasympathetic nervous system.

It's possible to manually stimulate your sympathetic nervous system through your choice of music, your training environment, your training partner, and whether or not you are in a competitive situation. We talked earlier about training maxes versus competitive maxes. Recall that one reason a competitive max would be different is that your sympathetic nervous system is much more stimulated in stressful situations. The required time for recovery from such events should help you realize that being in a too heightened stressful state for too long, or chronically, can be detrimental to your health.

Still, as we've learned from Seyle's GAS theory, stress is not a bad thing. It is how we handle stress that determines whether it can be negative or positive. My advice to you would be to stimulate the sympathetic nervous system through heavy compound movements, plyometrics, and sprinting, but remember that you need time to recover. That recovery time depends on how hard you've been working; the harder your training effort, the more time needed to recover properly.

This is where the other part of the nervous system comes in.

Parasympathetic Nervous System

The parasympathetic nervous system is the yin to the yang that is the sympathetic nervous system. This system is associated with actions that allow the body to "rest and digest", or "feed and breed." This is associated with bodily functions that occur following sex, a good meal, defecation, urination, certain meditative-like activities, and so on.

PERIODIZATION, HYPERTROPHY, & NERVOUS SYSTEM

Your breathing has slowed and is under control; you are not exerting great amounts of energy; you are calm; you are not anxious or jumpy; you are in the moment and allowing your body to feel relaxed and comfortable.

This branch of the nervous system is anabolic, meaning that it promotes the building process. Strictly speaking: when you are in a parasympathetic state, your body is focused on rebuilding. Blood flow has reverted back to the digestive organs; it is releasing hormones and chemicals that will not amp you up but rather promote relaxation. It is also associated with the release of testosterone, which aside from being a hormone for many bodily functions, is essential for building muscle and increasing strength.

If you are not resting and relaxing properly, then your body will not be able to perform at a high level. This is why elite athletes have to rigorously stimulate their parasympathetic nervous system through a variety of physical therapies, stretching, lots of sleep, eating high-quality foods, yoga, and meditation. It is those athletes who attend to their parasympathetic nervous system that are able to perform at an elite level for a long time.

These elite athletes are like Ferraris. They need the best gas, the best mechanics, and the best drivers in order to work properly. When something malfunctions, it usually costs a lot of money and can usually incur more damage than a regular car because Ferraris are built for speed, not safety. Similarly, if you are planning on performing at a high level, you will need to maintain your body in the same way that you would look after a nice, expensive car.

Take an athlete like Kobe Bryant. He came into the league as a player who could mow down anyone who stood in his way en route to the rim. If he continued to play in this manner, without any regard for learning new skills or recovering properly, he would not still be in the league at his age of 37 (which in the sports world is considered ancient). Kobe has long been a proponent of the cerebral aspect of the game. Despite incurring injuries over the years, he has been able to remain relevant by his focusing on the little things, such as stretching, therapy, and meditation.

Yes, meditation. Here is what Kobe has to say on the subject:

"It's crazy to me that meditation is viewed as hokey. Just look at the people who've done phenomenal things. Do they meditate? Absolutely. I meditate every day...it sets me up for the rest of the day...it's like having an anchor."

It is clear that Kobe understands the importance of balancing the sympathetic system with the parasympathetic. Without this balance, it would be impossible for him to continue to be dominant in a league that is entered by so many more youthful, faster, and more athletic players.

How to Promote the Strength of Both

The difference between a good athlete and a great one is that the latter has learned the importance of balancing the sympathetic nervous system with the parasympathetic nervous system--just like Kobe Bryant. Keep in mind that the sympathetic and parasympathetic nervous systems cannot be stimulated or function at the same time. Their stimulation needs to be separate, and the trick is to find time for both to reach your full potential. Rest and recovery are just as important as pushing hard in the gym.

Most of us have no problem with stressing our sympathetic nervous systems. Strength training, plyometrics, sprinting and competition all easily get the job done. On top of that, most of us are stressed all the time from family situations, relationships, school, work, or even just from the massive amounts of information we take in every day from our surroundings and the media.

Unfortunately, many of us suck at massaging the parasympathetic system. For one thing, most of us don't sleep enough. Sleep is vital. Getting sleep is essential for allowing your body to repair and rejuvenate itself for your next bout of training. Try to get eight hours a night and get in a nap if you can. If you can't sleep, try napping for 30 minutes in your car on your lunch break. Your body needs this time to recover from other stresses that you put it through during the day.

Next, focus on nutrition. Make sure that you are eating nutritious whole foods, fruits and vegetables, high-quality meats, eggs, nuts, berries, and essential fats. Every single listed item should be a part of your regular diet. Your digestive system can be stressed by processed foods that are high in sugar, just like how your brain can be stressed by being on your phone all the time. So, give it food that it can easily process. If your digestive system is draining your energy, how can you expect to push heavy weights in the gym, or excel at your sport of choice?

Finally, find an activity that takes you away from your phone, computer, and any other electronics. Activities like reading, journaling, walking, doing yoga, and meditating are all easy habits to add to your daily routine. Truly, they can make a big difference toward reducing and managing the stress in your life.

It is easy to become over-stimulated by the world, so take a deep breath and go for a walk. They may seem pointless, but they may be just what you need to grow stronger.

SPEED–LESSON 1: MOTOR UNITS & RATE CODING

"To keep the body in good health is a duty... otherwise we shall not be able to keep our mind strong and clear."

— Buddha

MOVEMENT COMES FIRST

Speed is the final phase of our training progression. Our principles are based on our concepts of Structure, Strength, and Speed.

Speed comes last for a reason.

You need to have a strong base of mobility and stability.

Then you need to have an adequate level of strength.

Only then is it time for dynamic movement, or speed.

Speed does not simply mean running really fast. It is the extension of your Structure and Strength. After all, speed takes a solid, athletic foundation, and subsequently, the strength you've built and tests what you can do with them. Overall, your aim is to be big, strong, and able to move like an athlete.

At Strength Camp, we train men and women from all walks of life to be the best athletes that they can be; to be able to express their strength and mobility in a dynamic manner by being able to sprint, jump, and perform movements through all planes of motion--confidently. The Speed phase is all about confidence. For athletes, it should make them confident that they are the fastest, most explosive player on the field. They should feel unbreakable and able to take on anyone, or anything. This confidence must be developed over time.

Even for those "average folks" whom we train, we want them to feel confident about their own bodies and capabilities to be able to tackle any challenge, such as finishing Tough Mudders, playing with their kids, cutting down a tree without throwing their backs out, and playing football in the backyard. You cannot accomplish these things through sheer strength and size alone--it's not enough to "just be big." You need "speed", which is a combination of moving like an athlete, having the mental fortitude, and being focused.

Balancing Structure, Strength, and Speed is the key to remaining injury-free, enjoying your life, looking great, and feeling optimal.

Developing Speed In the General Population

Many of us participated in competitive sports as kids and perhaps into our adolescent years. But once adulthood came around, our athletic endeavors may have fallen by the wayside.

Then, it seemed that the only way to stay active was to go to the local gym and perform stale routines that may give them results for a short period of time. Unfortunately, this kind of atmosphere and lack of periodization is not mentally or physically stimulating. It seemed that we were doomed to never experience the cycle of training, shattering plateaus, and performing well that previous athletic training had offered us.

On the bright side, competition among adults (and even younger people) have found new homes in popular strength-based sports like CrossFit, Powerlifting, Olympic lifting, and Strongman. It's been amazing to see this happen!

My main complaint is that each one of these sports tend to be very linear in terms of its style of training. They all rely heavily on movements in the sagittal plane. These include: squats (all variations), deadlifts (all variations), lunges (most variations), rowing, biking, clean and jerk, snatch, and box jumps.

These are all movements that deserve recognition for the amount of athleticism that is required to perform them, but they often miss out on training the body in a variety of other planes of movement, as well as training for agility and speed.

At Strength Camp, we pride ourselves on making sure *all of our athletes* are durable, adaptable, and ready for any type of training environment. That even includes non-athletes from the general population. Each and every one of our members must first build a sufficiently strong baseline of movement (via primal movements and more).

If someone is not mobile or does not have stability in the right joints or positions, then they need to improve those aspects before they can start performing athletic movements. As a side note, however, I feel as though most people can train like an athlete from day one, as long as the conditions under which they are training are highly controlled. This could mean that instead of doing 100 snatches for conditioning work, we would have someone push a prowler. (Yes, most everyone can do this from the get-go!) This way members can safely build up their general physical preparedness and capacity for speed--in a safe environment.

As I've mentioned time and time again, speed requires a very strong base before one can attempt to do dynamic movements at a faster pace over time. Speed is nothing without proper control and practice. It's like a scenario in which someone gave me a Lamborghini and told me to drive it around a racetrack as fast as I could. That's great, but one of two things would likely happen: I would crash it; or my driving skills would be so abysmal that I end up driving around at a snail's pace, stalling every 100 feet. However, show me a Ford Focus with a driving coach and a year to practice, and I would absolutely smash my time in the Lamborghini.

It's the same thing as when you tell a beginning trainee to do something with little to no coaching. One of two things are going to happen: they are going to work hard, really exert themselves, and then blow a knee/shoulder/back out, or they are going to cruise through the movement, not really exerting themselves enough to get the results that they want or expect.

Speed is the culmination of what we teach at Strength Camp. This same foundational approach to training can be found in almost every other pursuit--from learning to play the violin to learning to read. You start with the basics, learning what a note is or the alphabet, and then you put together your piecemeal knowledge to take on more complicated steps. Only once the previous level has been mastered that you can move on to the next.

There is no benefit to skipping steps, and if you do, you will suffer the consequences. It pains me to see young men and women jump into powerlifting, Strongman, or CrossFit and just try to go as heavy as they can right off the bat. They don't realize that years of building a base through basic movement patterns and building a strong core go a long way into performing at a high level, in any discipline or sport.

Always remember, too, that building these things doesn't happen all at once. Or even in a year or two. It takes years and years of training to create the final product that you see on YouTube, in magazines, and on Instagram. Be patient. Enjoy the ride, grow stronger, and then become faster.

SCIENTIFIC CONCEPTS OF SPEED

When it comes down to it, excelling in most sports requires an athlete to create maximal force in a minimal amount of time. Of course, the athlete also needs to be skilled in terms of how they move on the field and how well they can perform the requisite skills, such as throwing, catching, passing, shooting, etc. In all cases, however, the athlete who is able to create more power in a shorter period of time has the greatest advantage.

If two soccer players are bolting after a pass down the sidelines, the faster player is going to get the ball every time. This is not rocket science. Being powerful and explosive is a requirement for the athlete looking to go to the next level; whatever that next level may be.

How many slow guys do you see playing in the NFL? Not too many. And the ones that are, I'm looking at you Peyton, are on another level when it comes to how skilled they are. It is only his off the charts skill and his ability to control the game that allows someone as slow as Peyton Manning to thrive in a league in which 'speed kills'.

So, what does it take to develop speed? And what are the underlying biological mechanisms that we need to understand?

MOTOR UNIT RECRUITMENT

The first thing you need to understand when it comes to developing power and speed is motor unit recruitment. But before that, you should know that motor units are tiny. A motor unit is composed of a motor neuron as well as the muscle fibers which it innervates. Your bicep is not a motor unit itself, but it is made up of many different motor units and the muscle fibers. Check out the diagram below to get a better idea.

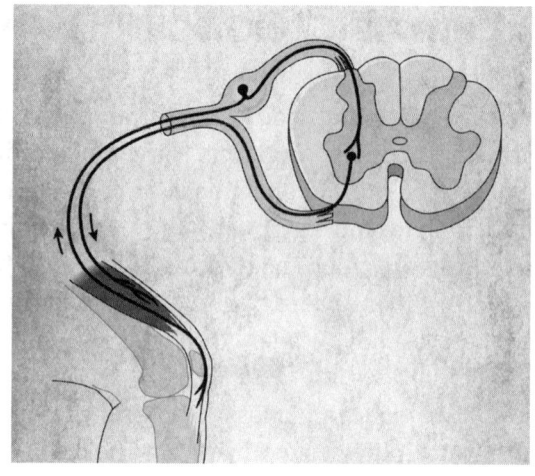

Explanation of a motor unit is best explained in another metaphor. A muscle fiber is like a lightbulb, and the motor neuron is the wire that leads to that specific bulb. You need to be able to send as much electricity to that bulb as possible to light up the room. Similarly, you need to recruit as many motor units as possible if you want to light up the scoreboard.

Typically, motor units are recruited in a certain order. It is determined by the size of the motor neuron, as well as by the number of muscle fibers that it innervates. Size also dictates which types of muscle fibers are innervated: the largest motor neurons innervate type II (fast-twitch muscle) while smaller motor neurons innervate type I muscle fibers (slow-twitch muscle).

As the force placed on the body increases more and more, larger and larger motor units are recruited. Imagine that you are reading in the dark. In this room, you have a light switch that controls the dimness of the room. In order to read the words on the page, you need to turn the light to its brightest setting and must use more electrical power--which, in this metaphor, represents the number of large motor units being recruited. The potential to light the room is ever present, but it is only when you turn the brightness way up that the potential is actualized.

In the context of exercises, you would need fewer and smaller motor units recruited for performing a bodyweight squat. Your body is not going to waste energy trying to recruit as many motor units as it can. But when it's time to do a 1RM back squat, it's all hands on deck, as your body recruits a much larger percentage of motor units.

Most people believe that in order to recruit the maximal number of motor units you need to do many, many reps and burn out sets with submaximal weights. This is wrong. When you are performing powerful and explosive movements like sprinting, jumping, flipping a tire, or leaping onto a box, you are taxing one of your energy systems--the ATP-CP system. Anything done with max effort lasting under 10 seconds is supported by the ATP-CP energy system.

Tying this whole concept together, we can surmise that in order to fully utilize the largest and most powerful muscles in our body, we need to recruit the most and largest motor units. In order to do that, we need to be performing powerful and explosive movements for under 10 seconds, not doing 100 reps of bicep curls with 5-pound dumbbells. This way, you can become the athlete who can create maximal force at a moment's notice.

RATE CODING

Okay, so we know what motor units are and how to best recruit them, but we also need to know how to recruit them in a precise and immediate manner.

This is where the concept of rate coding comes into play. First, know that motor units do not fire only at one speed. They are able to fire at different frequencies--at low and high frequencies. The higher the external load that is put on the body, the higher the frequency that is required to quickly develop the right amount of muscular tension. However, you also need to understand that the signal strength of the motor neuron will always remain the same.

The CNS cannot send stronger or weaker signals. The only way that muscular tension can be increased is by increasing the frequency at which the signal is sent. That means the motor neurons do not increase signal strength, despite the external load on the body. They simply increase the frequency at which the signals are sent.

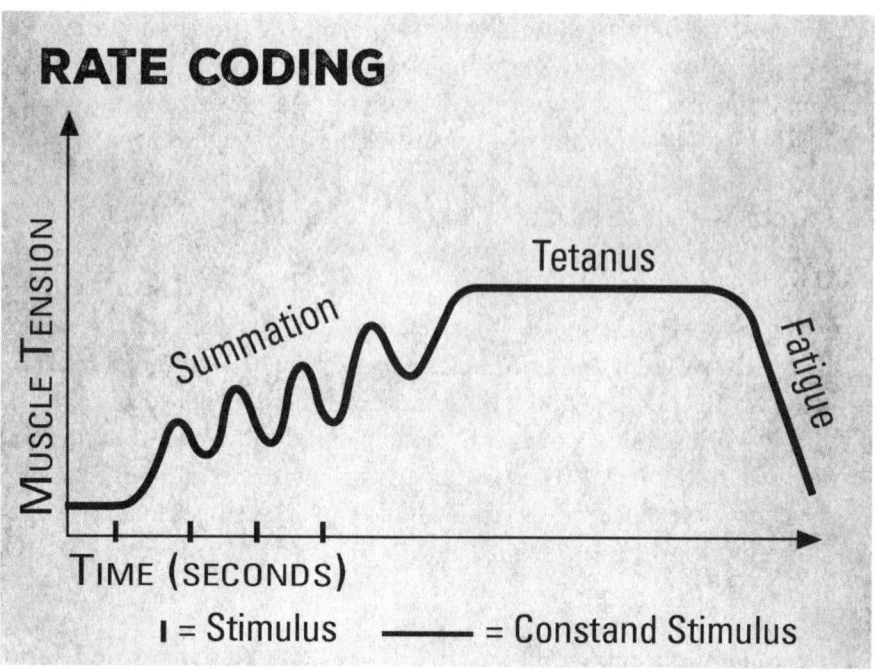

An individual signal is known as a twitch, which cannot create much force on its own. In order to create maximal muscular tension or contraction, multiple twitches are sent by the motor neuron. And as these twitches build on one another in rapid succession, force begins to build up in the muscle, producing maximal tension and leading to what is referred to as tetanus.

With this in mind, rate coding allows you to recruit more tension from individual motor units more quickly, thereby contracting more muscle simply by heightening the frequency at which the motor neuron sends signals to that particular muscle fiber. You can see now that rate coding is very tightly aligned with motor recruitment.

By changing the frequency at which it innervates motor units, the CNS can create a very low level contraction, or a high level contraction. In effect, the higher the stimulation to the muscle, the higher the frequency. When each motor unit is fired repetitively at a very rapid rate, they create enough tension to back squat double body weight, jump onto a high box, or stiff arm a defender to the ground.

But your body needs to be proficient in your movements in order for your body to be able to send high enough frequencies to stimulate your motor units and reach the highest levels of tension. This means that you need to have practiced movements over and over again. New trainees simply are not able to recruit enough muscle fibers, as their bodies have protective mechanisms in place to save them from, well, themselves. That's okay because even advanced lifters are not able to recruit 100% of their muscle fibers. (If they did, they'd end up ripping their tendons and ligaments apart.)

Rate coding allows you to move with speed and strength, but it is only through constant repetition of highly innervating movements that you are able to create frequencies high enough to achieve the type of athletic performance that you desire.

Now take the work ethic of Dimitri Klokov, an Olympic weightlifter who achieved a great deal of notoriety in fitness through his tremendous feats of strength. However, as an athlete, Klokov is extremely specialized. He can snatch, clean and jerk, and do any variations of these movements at an elite level; but he probably isn't the fastest runner, the most agile, or able to catch a pass with any type of skill. The reason he can be that great of an athlete in his sport is that he had practiced his specific movements over and over and over again.

In Bruce Lee's words: "I fear not the man who has practiced 10,000 kicks once, but I fear the man who has practiced one kick 10,000 times." Klokov is that man who has practiced one kick, or one lift rather, 10,000 times. Because of this, he is able to send signals through his motor neurons at extremely high frequencies. If you have not practiced the movement enough, then your body will be unable to create adequate muscular tension.

Rate coding is how Klokov is able to throw 400 pounds over his head. This is why drilling technique is so important. You are teaching new patterns to your nervous system, not necessarily increasing muscular size or strength. The real lesson here is to practice your skills and dynamic movements enough that they become second nature. Practice so that your CNS will know to create the high levels of muscle tension required to explosively leap, bound, sprint, and express your body in various forms of speed.

SPEED-LESSON II: FORCE/VELOCITY CURVE, RATE OF FORCE DEVELOPMENT, & PLYOMETRICS

> "IF WE COULD GIVE EVERY INDIVIDUAL THE RIGHT AMOUNT OF NOURISHMENT AND EXERCISE, NOT TOO LITTLE AND NOT TOO MUCH, WE WOULD HAVE FOUND THE SAFEST WAY TO HEALTH."
>
> *—Hippocrates*

ROAD TO A 4.5-SECOND, 40-YARD DASH AND A 42-INCH VERTICAL

There is no easy way to train speed.

I learned this through my experiences. For as long as I could remember, I wanted to play in the NFL. I wanted to be fast, and I wanted to be explosive. I remember how it felt to cut around a defender and sprint down the sideline as a kid playing in my first Pop Warner football game--it felt good. I wanted to do it again.

As I got older, I started to realize that some kids just happened to somehow be faster than everyone else. I was still pretty fast "for a white boy", but I wanted to further train my latent abilities with programming--to be even faster and more explosive. Fueled by this burning passion for speed, I'd tried every program and product that promised to make me run faster or jump higher: the weird shoes with the raised toes, agility circuits, ankle weights--you name it, I probably tried it. Of course, some methods worked better than others, but I never really got the results that I'd hoped for.

Who knew it'd be so difficult, I thought at the time.

In the end, it was only after years and years of strength training combined with athletic training with Elliott at Strength Camp that my numbers started to get better and better. I'd realized it wasn't a quick program or gimmicky products that got me a 4.5-second, 40-yard dash and 42 inches on the vertical. No, it was sheer hard work and a solid foundation of strength that I'd built over nearly 10 years.

The long nights alone training, the hour drive to Strength Camp week after week, and the times I'd chosen to stay in and study instead of partying had all contributed to my success.

There is simply no substitute for that base of structure and strength. Aside from people who are genetic freaks, that is. Some can lift crazy weights and run like cheetahs, but most of us are not like that. Most of us have to work for impressive numbers--and to be honest, I wouldn't have it any other way. I come from a blue-collar family, which instilled in me principles of hard work, dedication, consistency, and honesty that still guide my life and make me the coach and athlete that I am today.

So, when it came to getting faster and stronger, those principles drove me forward since there were no shortcuts or innate genetic gifts such as the ideal body type for lifting heavy or running fast--but I didn't give a shit. I knew that the only way I was going to be successful was to work my ass off. And that's what I did. Day after day. Week after week. Year after year.

Force/Velocity Curve, Force Development, & Plyometrics

Putting in the work when no one else is pushing you to is what it takes to be successful. That's what it takes to be fast.

After high school football games, I remember training in the weight room in my parents back room. I knew that no one else would be doing it so that had motivated me even more. I'd chosen to be exceptional. I did not wait for someone to pick me. I stepped up and chose my destiny. You can do the same.

In competition, the desire to beat other people is good motivation, but it should not be the only thing driving you. Don't you want to be the very best you at what you do? I know I do. In fact, indoctrinating myself with the belief that I was the best played an integral for me to train as hard as I did and to get as far in athletics as I did. I'd tell myself, "You're the strongest guy in the gym."

Any time I felt a flicker of doubt, any time I stepped under the bar and felt its weight grind against my back, as if to taunt me, or any time I lined up for another sprint when every cell in my body was screaming at me to have mercy--I'd still tell myself: "You're the strongest guy in the gym; you're the fastest; you're the hardest worker; you want it more."

Every day that I was on the field taking reps in practice, I told myself that I was the best linebacker on the team, even when it was clear to an outside observer that I was not. Over and over, I told myself that I could make it to the next level--that I would make it to the next level. I can. I will. Over and over. Every morning, every grueling training session, every punishing practice, and every night I told myself: I can. I will. I can. I will.

I never let up for a second. I told myself that I was the best, and slowly, I did become the best.

And you know what? This self-talk fueled me whenever my tank ran on empty. It gave me power that I would not have had otherwise. Because it's easy to let dark thoughts creep into your mind and strangle your dreams, make you lazy, and draw you to activities that do not serve you or your goals. Don't let this happen or give them room. Fill your mind with a mantra--one that reminds you of why you do what you do and who you want to become.

Someone once said: "Thought is supreme." Based on my mentality, you can see that I took this to heart, and I encourage you to as well. If you want to achieve anything in your life, visualize yourself having already achieved that thing. Constantly remind yourself of that goal and constantly fill your mind with positive imagery.

Positive self-talk is integral to your becoming the Strongest Version of Yourself. If you are letting negative thoughts enter your mind, then you are fighting a losing battle.

Part of this involves surrounding yourself with positive people. People who understand your path and your goals, and who want to support you on your journey. Positivity starts with you, and as you build the mindset of a champion these people will slowly but surely gravitate toward you. Become the type of person that you want to be--internally and externally--without concern for those who are around you. If they like who you become, great, but if not, they will drift out of your life--and that's okay. You need to consciously create your internal and external environments in order to allow your mind to be a place of motivational and dedicated focus.

Be who you want to be and tell yourself that it can happen; and that it will happen.

I can. I will. Over and over until it is so.

Developing Speed in Athletes

Athletics are not merely about who can create the most power. They are about who can create the most power in a purposeful manner. It's pointless to be the fastest guy on the field in a straight line if you can't run a route properly, or catch a ball, or spin around a defender. Jerry

Rice taught us this lesson after he ran a 4.71-second, 40-yard dash at the NFL Combine. For anyone who is unfamiliar with American Football, running 40 yards in 4.71 seconds is bad--really bad. For a wide receiver, it is unheard of because these athletes are typically the fastest and most explosive on the field.

Nevertheless, Jerry Rice went on to become the greatest wide receiver in NFL history. Jerry was neither fast nor explosive, but Jerry was able to use his precise ability to run routes and hands that could catch bricks. As a result, he caught more passes than anyone else in the history of the game.

What, then, does a relatively slow guy like Jerry Rice have to teach us about speed? That there is more to speed than just running in a straight line. While Jerry may not have been the fastest guy on the field in a straight line, he was the fastest going in and out of cuts and with his hands--off the line of scrimmage and when snatching passes out of mid air, respectively. He had practiced his routes and timing with his quarterbacks, Joe Montana and later Steve Young, countless times until enacting them became second nature.

He practiced catching pass after pass the JUGS machine, a football-throwing apparatus, and brick after brick thrown to him by his father until his hands could snatch almost any pass thrown his way, even with a faster more powerful defender draped over his back (which didn't happen often, as he had often left them scrambling to keep up with him).

They say that success leaves clues for future generations to learn from. In Jerry Rice's case, he'd left some obvious clues: you must be skilled in order to excel in your sport. It is not simply a matter of being fast and strong. You need to teach your body the required skills to the point that moving on the playing field becomes like instinct. The more that you are thinking, the slower you will be.

I often see videos of professional athletes' training in the off season, during which they are doing a ladder drill, throwing tennis balls around, or standing on a BOSU ball. I hate to think that young athletes are watching these videos and thinking that the way to get faster or stronger is to imitate these videos.

Little do they know is that these highly skilled athletes did not get to their level of calibur by dancing through a ladder. They did it through building a base of strength, practicing explosive movements ,and spending hours and hours honing their craft. Being a gym rat is great, but if you aren't spending more time on your skills, then you are only holding back your own potential.

I must admit that I am sometimes guilty of showing people the final product of an athlete, rather than the years and years of hard work that it took to create that final product. Social media has taken this to the next level. If you have YouTube and Instagram as your portals into the world of strength and conditioning, you will have a very skewed view on what it takes to get strong and fast. It isn't fast, it isn't easy--anyone who tells you otherwise is a liar.

If you're just beginning to find your stride, look to someone who has walked the path that you are currently on. You need someone who has been there and done that, someone who has made all the mistakes and learned from them; and someone who is willing to teach you from their failures and their successes. Otherwise, it's easy to get caught in the loop of expecting fast results, program hopping, and hitting plateaus.

I have to hammer home this point time and time again: these things take time, and the process is not going to be easy.

It is going to take dedication, intensity, and focus.

There are no shortcuts.

Force-Velocity Curve

Of all the scientific concepts that we have gone over so far, the force-velocity curve may be the most important in terms of understanding how to program and build strength and speed for yourself (or your athletes if you're a coach).

Force/Velocity Curve, Force Development, & Plyometrics

Thankfully, it is also one of the more simple concepts that we cover.

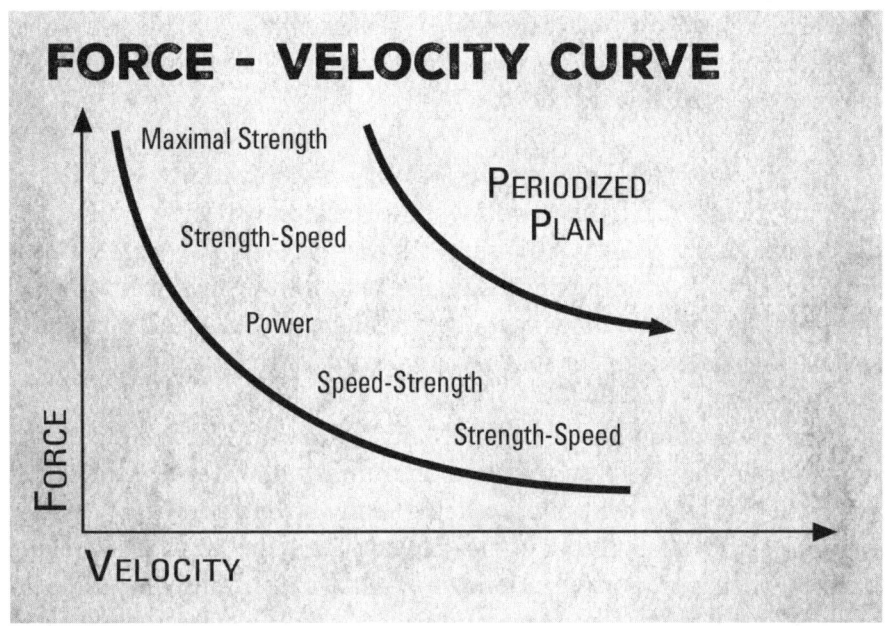

Look at the graph of the force-velocity curve. On the x-axis, we have force. On the y-axis, we have velocity. The curve swoops downwards from force to velocity in a hyperbolic fashion. What this indicates is that as force increases, velocity decreases; and as velocity increases, force decreases. When applied to training, this means that when you lift heavier weights, you will move them more slowly. When you lift lighter weights, you will move at a much higher speed.

As you move along the curve, you go from training maximal strength at the high force-low velocity side to training speed at the low force-high velocity side. Along the way, you go through phases of training 'strength-speed' (speed that is expressed under conditions of strength). In other words, you are moving a heavier weight as fast as you can. 'Power' and 'speed-strength'--the converse of strength-speed--which is strength that is expressed under conditions of speed. For this example, you could be moving lighter weights as fast as you can, as you would in a prowler push.

There's no getting around it: the force-velocity curve is important for your programming and for training athletes. After all, speed is king in athletics. If you want to win, being fast is usually a good place to start. With this in mind, the objective of our training should be to shift the curve to the right, toward speed.

As we learned in the section on periodization, concurrent periodization in particular, we focus training one specific skill at the expense of other skills. It's the same for the force-velocity curve. If you focus all of your training on maximal strength, your maximal strength will surely go up, but it does so to the detriment of your speed. Similarly, if you train specifically for speed, your maximal strength will suffer.

This is a common problem. Many people are unfamiliar with how to train for speed, so they end up training at one end of the curve exclusively. They might end up being really strong and slow, or very weak and kind of fast. What we need to do is very similar to the ideology behind concurrent periodization: we want to train multiple abilities at once. So, in using the force-velocity curve, we train all along the curve at the same time.

If I know I'll be training a particular athlete for at least a year, I generally take him through very general physical training and zero in on more and more sport-specific training as time goes on. This gives him time to develop a base and build some strength before we emphasize speed work and the specifics of his sport.

Now, most of the athletes that I work with are in high school or college. As a result, most of the training that they need is for maximal strength and power. There is little to no benefit for them to hop through agility ladders if they are not strong. The same goes for most beginner trainees--they do not have enough strength to warrant training for speed. Sure, it could be fun, but real results and real speed will not come out of sprinting across a field with a parachute trailing behind you.

That is not to say you *shouldn't* do any speed work if you want to. You can absolutely include some speed training at the start. Sprinting and jumping are great ways to teach yourself how to produce force and also to brush up on technique, but they shouldn't be the focus. That should be saved for later down the road, when you or your athletes have built an acceptable level of strength.

RATE OF FORCE DEVELOPMENT

If two athletes are equal in skill, the one who can generate the most force in the minimal amount of time will win every time. Think of two fighters going head-to-head: if one has enough power to deliver a knockout blow, I'm going to put my money on that guy every time. Similarly, baseball pitchers who can paint the corners of the strikezone and outsmart batters with off-speed pitches are good, but when there's a guy who can break 100 miles-per-hour with accuracy--now that's a real weapon. The more you think about this, the more it becomes clear that the athletes who are able to create a maximal amount of force in a minimal amount of time usually come out on top.

This ability to rapidly generate force and reach peak levels of power near instantaneously is known as rate of force development. Earlier, we learned about eccentric, isometric, and concentric movements. We bring them to the forefront again because the rate of force development occurs in the concentric phase of the lift. In a bench press: you lower the bar to your chest (eccentric), pause for a second (isometric), and then drive it up to the ceiling (concentric). You are expressing your rate of force development in the concentric phase of the bench press.

So, how do you improve your rate of force development?

You need to have a high level of strength (once again). You need to first develop a good level of strength in your main lifts. If you can't squat your body weight, then training for speed won't be as beneficial. However, once you have a good base of strength training, you have to learn how to recruit that strength in a matter of milliseconds. Olympic lifting movements, plyometrics, and balance training all can help with increasing your rate of force development.

Simply put, a guy who can back squat 450 pounds will be able to move a bar with 200 pounds on it much faster than a guy whose maximal back squat is 250 pounds. Therefore, the rate of force development is simply how fast you can call upon your base strength to perform a dynamic movement. This is why sprinters--although they aren't that big--have to put up really good numbers on their squat and deadlift. If they didn't have the base strength, they wouldn't be able to express that strength through accelerating out of the starting blocks and then flying down the track.

We talked earlier about how important developing sport-specific skills are, but at the same time, the athlete who can create the most power in the shortest amount of time often comes out on top (especially sports in which explosive power is a requirement). This is why many older players have to change their game as they get older.

Kobe Bryant, again, is a great example. If you go back to some highlight tapes of him in his first few years in the NBA, you'll see him soaring through the air to throw down some nasty dunks and running back on defense to reject opponents from lay-ups. However, as his rate of force development declined with age, he was no longer that energetic, explosive player.

He had to get more teammates involved, work on creating separation between himself and defenders in order to unleash a lethal fadeaway jump shot, and utilize his mental prowess to feed his teammates the ball as they go into advantageous positions. If Kobe had decided to stubbornly rely purely on his rate of force development and athleticism to beat defenders, he would have been out of the league years ago.

PLYOMETRICS

It seems new methods of training are constantly being touted as the next big things in developing speed, strength, or explosive power. In my experience as an athlete and as a coach, old-school methods work the best. Plyometrics is one old-school method for developing higher rate of force development in athletes.

Force/Velocity Curve, Force Development, & Plyometrics

When talking about plyometrics, it is necessary to briefly go over the history of how this method of training was developed. Back in the 1950s, the Russian coach Yuri Verkhoshansky headed the Aeronautical Engineering Institutes' track team. They were by no means a terrible team, but they were definitely not the cream of the crop in the USSR. But Verkhoshansky was not just a coach. He was a researcher and applied his same scientific methods to the training of his athletes.

One of his experiments involved depth jumps, which he used extensively with his track and field sprinters and jumpers. This training method had a profound effect on the majority of his athletes, with 12 of them from the same class receiving the prestigious title, Master of Sport. In order to be a 'Master of Sport' in the USSR, you needed to have been a national or international champion; so it was clear that Verkhoshansky was on to something.

After his success with the Aeronautical Engineering Institute, Verkhoshansky moved on to coach the Moscow United team in the mid 1960s. Verkhoshansky was put in charge of the sprinters and the jumpers, both of whom required explosive power and strength. After training with his method of plyometrics, his athletes once again experienced unprecedented success, setting many national and international records.

Verkhoshansky and his team of sprinters and jumpers dominated the international scene all through the 1960s and into the 1970s. Finally, an American track coach named Fred Wilt took notice--probably after getting sick and tired of getting his ass kicked--and started to look into exactly how the Soviets were training. What he saw was unlike anything any other country was doing at the time.

The Soviet athletes were ahead of their time. While athletes from other countries were doing static stretching before their events, the Soviet sprinters were going through intricate jumping routines to prime their nervous systems to absorb and produce force. Fred Wilt started training his athletes with the same methods as best as he could. Eventually, he started calling "his" method plyometrics, and thus, a new form of training was born in North America.

We seem to think that plyometrics, or "jump training", and dynamic warm-ups are something new, but Verkhoshansky had his athletes doing them 60 years ago. Sometimes all it takes is a look to the past in order to find the training methods of tomorrow.

Basics of Plyometrics

At this point, most people have some degree of familiarity with plyometrics. Plyometrics, or "jump training", are used to force the body to create maximal power in a minimal amount of time (which is exactly what we want). The word "plyometric" comes from the Greek root words, "to increase" and "isometric", which are actually very poor descriptors of what plyometrics aim to do. You are not aiming to increase your isometric strength; you are aiming to increase your body's ability to produce force as quickly as possible.

Think back to when we talked about motor recruitment and rate coding. Plyometrics help increase both of these things, because plyometric training places a huge focus on training the nervous system. If you are trying to move as quickly and as powerfully as possible, your CNS is forced to jump to action, fast! Over time, your nervous system will be more and more efficient at sending signals to your motor neurons, allowing you to get more explosive and more powerful-- it is rate coding at work!

In his experiments with his athletes, Verkhoshansky had them performing vertical jump tests from three different start positions: from a standstill with no countermovement, from a standstill with countermovement, and after jumping down off of a 50-centimeter box. He found that the athletes consistently jumped the highest after jumping off of the 50-centimeter box.

Source: http://www.verkhoshansky.com

What seems to happen is that the body becomes "shocked" after jumping off the box and being forced into an eccentric contraction. Then, it must absorb that force, concentrically contract, and produce yet more force. In essence, this absorption and production of force are what plyometrics is all about.

If you don't have enough strength to absorb the force, then you won't be able to produce much force either. Plyometrics should be performed in a fast and explosive manner, so if they look or feel slow, then you should probably focus on getting stronger before you devote too much time to strict plyometric training. To reiterate: build your base of strength first, then get explosive.

When you are run or jump, force can be produced in as little as 0.1-0.2 seconds. In order to train this, you need to be doing a variety plyometrics, including depth jumps. The depth jump is the best exercise when it comes to learning how to absorb the type of force required for replicating the landing and takeoff seen in sprinting and jumping.

Try the following experiment to help you understand the importance of expressing explosive power through absorbing force and then producing it. Perform a vertical jump from a standstill without bending your knees. Now try to jump into the air as high as you can with a quick bending of your knees. I guarantee that you will immediately notice a difference in your power-producing ability. It's a very simple but effective experiment in showing you the power of absorbing and then producing force.

Plyometric training also Increases the elasticity and strength of tendons. When you are playing sports, your muscles, along with your tendons, are put under a great deal of stress. Your tendons also have to stretch to absorb force and be elastic enough to not snap. Plyometric training is great because it can force you to work on your elasticity in a safe and controlled environment. Many non-contact related athletic injuries could be avoided if athletes did more plyometric work and strengthened their tendons from doing so.

Plyometrics have been proven to strengthen and even slightly increase the number of fast-twitch muscle fibers in your body, which are needed for explosive movements. Remember that you need to express strength at a moment's notice, and to do that, you need muscles that can instantly tap into your strength, too. This is the key to unlocking your athletic potential.

Once again, plyometrics are best used by the trainee who has a good base of strength, and who has demonstrated the ability to be mobile and stable enough to get into required positions. Once they are ready, the use of plyometrics will take their athletic training to the next level.

SILENCE:
Deload, Balancing Your Nervous System, & Recovery Methods

"Silence is a source of great strength."

—Lao Tzu

SILENCE

If you want to get stronger, it's important to go all out in your training. You shouldn't be holding anything back when you are in the gym. You need to be intense. You need to be focused. You need to get angry.

That is why I always tell my athletes to give me just one hour of focus, to give me 100% of their energy for that one hour. I want the stress they may be experiencing at school, at home, or in their relationships to disappear.

But once you leave the gym, the real work begins. You see, all the work in gym was breaking your body down, not building it. The building part--the recovery--comes after you step back into the real world.

Unfortunately, most people don't look at it that way. Oftentimes, the only time that we start to focus on our recovery is after we get injured. That's how I learned when I ended up needing to have shoulder surgery at a younger age. Before that, I'd previously been unconcerned with warming up or doing any type of recovery work for the muscles, ligaments, tendons and joints that served me so well. I punished my body with heavy lifting, football conditioning, and Strongman training while ignoring its need for time and to rebuild. After all, I had goals to reach. I wanted to play football at the University of Miami, and I wasn't going to let anything stand in my way. It was the mindset of a warrior.

This warrior mindset was akin to being in an army that was being led by a general who only obsessed over conquering new cities and defeating new armies; a general who was not concerned with the well-being of his warriors; and a general who did not realize that he was eventually going to run out of new cities to conquer, run out of food to feed his men, and run out of luck on the battlefield. Over time, even the most hardened warriors get broken down--whether that means physically, emotionally, or mentally.

Constantly being in attack mode can work for a time--and you may have some early victories--but Sun Tzu said, "He who knows when he can fight, and when he cannot, will be victorious." You cannot always be on the attack. An army needs time to rest, eat, let wounds heal, and take a respite from the horror of the battlefield.

Now, I am not bold enough to say that training is anything like going to war. It is not, of course, but you can draw parallels between the two situations. The philosophy behind "attack-then-rest" pertains as much to the gym as it does to the battlefield: it is imperative that you know when to work "out" and attack, and when to work "in" and recover.

Don't only be focused on going hard in the gym and beating up your body. I know that it feels right in that moment, but the truly best way to get strong is to train hard and rest just as hard. We do that by starting with the concept of deloading.

DELOAD

A deload gives your nervous system a rest. In our day-to-day lives, we are constantly being stimulated by external stressors. And as we've learned in a previous chapter, these stressors can be good or bad, mainly depending on how we react to them. Stress from training can be good, if we sleep well, hydrate, and eat adequate macronutrients to support our body's recovery. If you train hard on the other hand and ignore proper recovery procedures, not only is your training for naught but you pile on more negative stressors.

Recovery is just as important, if not more important, to your training than training itself. It is as much a part of your training as lifting weights is.

In the introduction, we learned that deload weeks have a tremendous effect on our body's ability to rebuild broken down tissue, regulate hormones, and give the nervous system time to recover. This actually has a huge impact on mental recovery as well. Grinding away under heavy weights and gruelling conditioning sessions can take a toll on your psyche. It's not easy to work hard with little to no time off day after day, week after week, and month after month (especially if progress has slowed down).

Now if you aren't training at a high percentage of your 1-rep max, or you aren't training with high volumes, then you probably don't need a deload as badly as someone who is doing those things. In fact, you might not even need a deload at all if you aren't training hard. But for those of you who train with a great deal of intensity, or coach athletes who train with intensity, the deload is absolutely vital.

The deload is a period of active rest, so it is the perfect time to experiment with new movements and exercises. This requires you to reduce the weights, as the movements are new, but it will also allow you to assess weaknesses and inject some degree of novelty to a possibly straightforward training program.

Sometimes getting away from the gym altogether after a particularly stressful competition or sporting season is another great idea. Don't go to the gym at all for a week or two, sleep as much as you can, eat lots of high-quality calories, stay active--walk, hike, stretch, work on mobility--and just let your body recover. Once you do this for a few weeks, I guarantee that you will feel great and have a renewed zeal for training. I went through it the last time I'd finished with the NFL combine, and it was just what I needed after spending years beating my body up.

This is the part of silence that many people may embrace--perhaps a bit too hard. Let me say it again: don't be afraid of training too hard, or of 'overtraining'; be afraid of not training hard enough, and also of training hard but not recovering adequately. Overtraining is not the enemy; under-recovering is.

It bears repeating because I see so many people who train for years without any intensity or consistency; and they wonder why they don't get any results. You need to apply intense stress to your body, and when you do, you also need to give it time to rebuild. A wise man once said, "No rest is worth anything, except the rest that is earned."

This could not be more true. Make sure that you are working hard enough to gain benefits in your times of silence.

Parasympathetic Nervous System

As I mentioned earlier, one of the main benefits of the deload week is to allow your nervous system to recover. But what does that actually mean, and why does our nervous system need time to "recover"?

Your nervous system, or your autonomic nervous system, controls all of the involuntary functions within your body, such as digestion, breathing, the beating of your heart, and your hormonal reaction to stressful situations. Essentially, your autonomic nervous system is working all the time; and especially so in "fight or flight" type situations (training) or in "rest and digest" situations (silence).

The autonomic nervous system is made up of two branches: sympathetic nervous system (SNS) and parasympathetic nervous system (PNS).

The sympathetic nervous system is always on high alert when you are training hard. Adrenaline, cortisol, and norepinephrine are coursing through your veins while you are pushing yourself really hard. Your body thinks that it is being forced to fight for its life and reacts as such: blood flow is diverted away from your organs and instead goes to your peripheral limbs; your blood pressure, along with your heart rate, increases; and your digestion becomes a lower priority. However, if you stay in this state too long, you won't be able to keep up with the intense demands being placed on your body. Just as the warrior that is pushed by the foolhardy general, your body eventually breaks down or your mind gives up--whichever happens first.

The parasympathetic nervous system, on the other hand, is all about resting and digesting. When your body feels at ease, it can turn on the PNS. When this happens: blood pressure and heart rate decrease; and blood flow reverts back to your digestive system, increasing your core temperature and speeding up the digestive processes. It is important to note that the PNS does not only get stimulated by laying on the couch and doing nothing. There are actually ways to actively stimulate it, so that you can accelerate recovery and generally bring a sense of mindfulness and consciousness to your day. Things like going for a walk in the woods, setting up an area for meditation in your home, or finding a space to practice yoga, tai chi, or qigong all allow your body to relax.

It's essential that you be proactive about creating an environment that is conducive to being at ease. Don't just let life happen; make sure that you have a safe place in which to relax and to be at ease every day.

Recovery Techniques

There are a number of techniques that I like to use to stimulate the PNS and aid in my recovery after every training session.

FOAM ROLLING

Foam rolling and myofascial release have been big contributors to my ability to stay healthy as I continue to train hard and train heavy.

Fascia is simply a layer of fibrous tissue that encapsulates the entire inner workings of your body, including muscles, bones, internal organs, and your spinal cord. The fascial layer is not broken up into different pieces, but is actually one continuous piece that wraps over and inside of every part of your body, from head to toe.

This is why it is important to stretch along 'fascial lines of the body' and not simply stretch your body on a muscle by muscle basis--it is all connected. Fascia affects many aspects of your mobility and stability across all your joints. If there is tightness in one area, it can ripple to multiple areas of your body at the same time. For example, it is amazing how a little bit of fascial release in the bottom of the feet, calves, and hamstrings can help with back stiffness and pain--try it!

Daily repetitive movement patterns (e.g. sitting and slouching), serious trauma, and surgery can all have a detrimental effect to the quality of your fascia. Areas that should be supple will end up tightening up in order to protect your body from further trauma. It is imperative that you improve and maintain the quality of your fascia in order to experience full range of motion in your joints without any pain. This is where foam rolling and myofascial release help.

Neither foam rolling nor myofascial release should have any detrimental effects on your fascia. While they are restorative techniques, you should experiment with them to see if they add to your recovery.

A really easy way to see if foam rolling is helping to increase a joint's range of motion or tissue quality is to do a simple test and retest. Perform a squat, a lunge, a push-up, or any complex movement. Take note of your motions, points of tension or pain, and range of motion. Now go through your foam rolling routine and retest the same movements afterward to see if there are positive or negative changes, if any.

Any significant changes could take a few weeks or even months of consistent work to notice, but you should be able to notice some minor changes almost immediately. Stick with it, especially if your test and retests are going well, and use myofascial release as a part of your cooldown routine, as well as on off days.

Myofascial release has been proven to passively elongate your fascia and the muscles that they wrap around. These points of tension are released through direct and consistent pressure administered by a therapist, or by yourself, with a foam roller, lacrosse ball, golf ball, etc.

Another thing that I love about myofascial release is that it almost automatically forces one to breathe deeply. As you will learn in the chapters on breathing, taking deep breaths is a great way to release tension in the body and to actively bring about relaxation. For this reason, foam rolling and myofascial release should be used sparingly in your warm-up routine. When you are getting to lift heavy and perform explosive movements, do you want to be breathing deeply and getting ready to rest and digest; or do you want to be increasing your heart rate and mobilizing joints through dynamic movements?

The answer should be clear to you. Unless you have some real problem areas, use foam rolling mainly for recovery, after you've trained.

MOVEMENT AS MEDICINE

Foam rolling, releasing fascia, distracting joints, flossing tissue, and a variety of other methods have grown in popularity among the fitness community. While this is not a bad thing, most people are doing it wrong: they focus on mobility without really moving.

Don't get me wrong: all of the mentioned techniques are great. I use many of them myself, but I maintain my mobility by actually *moving*. I run. I sprint. I jump. I leap. I squat. I lunge. I press. I pull. And I twist. If you aren't moving in the primal patterns or other dynamic movements, then you are not doing enough to address your mobility.

When you think about it, your ability to move is a function of many different things. Your nervous system for one. The more you perform a certain pattern correctly, the more adept your body becomes at using the muscles required to do that particular movement. However, if all you do is stretch and foam roll, your body is never having to utilize the nervous system to learn or allow itself to sink more deeply into the movements.

One main function of the nervous system is that it attempts to keep you from doing anything that hurts you. This means that your mobility restrictions will only get better by actually putting yourself into new positions consistently, thereby allowing your nervous system to release the tension that prevents you from getting into those positions in the first place. If all you do is stretch, then you are missing the point.

Keep in mind that your body is a complete unit, in which one area rarely acts independently of others. When you are squatting, your shoulder mobility can have as much of an effect on your depth as your hip mobility--as do your core strength and prior ankle or neck injuries. Neither your upper body nor lower body movement is isolated within itself. Every movement is affected by the condition of your whole body--your posture, muscular strength, tissue quality, motor patterns, joint stability, mobility, and so on. Big or small, believe me that it can make a difference.

Most people seem to think that mobility techniques are a magic pill that will help you become more mobile. They aren't. They are simply a piece of the puzzle, and a piece that is more integral than others is to simply move your body. If you sit at a desk all day, squat halfway, and simply roll out your adductors, IT bands, and quad group, you shouldn't expect to be able to go "ass-to-grass" over time.

The only way you can squat deeper is to demand that of your nervous system. Spend time in a deep squat, mobilize joints that need more mobility, stabilize weak muscles and build movement patterns that allow your nervous system to progressively get you deeper and deeper into a squat. So, try to focus more on actually moving and less time sitting. Yoga, various forms of martial arts, lightweight compound movements, or simple bodyweight movements are all great ways to increase your mobility and train you through a full range of motion.

Remember that movement is paramount.

LOW STIMULATION

Sleep is integral to your success--as an athlete and for your full enjoyment of life. Some people believe sleep is a waste of time, when they could be awake and working. However, as more and more research on the benefits of sleep can attest, sleep has paradoxically become the ultimate way to increase productivity and performance. It makes sense. Think about it: we value quality over quantity. To put it another way: are you going to get more work done in three hours of concentrated work, when you are well rested and highly creative; or are you going to get more done in six hours of work, when you are using energy drinks to stay awake and simply just trying to make it through the day?

The choice is obvious.

For optimal performance, you should be getting 8-10 hours of sleep every night. Not just on one night a week on Sundays so that you can "recover" for the week either. Make it a priority to get your sleep, and your productivity during the day will increase.

Usain Bolt, the fastest man to have ever walked the earth once said, "Sleep is extremely important to me. I need to rest and recover in order for the training I do to be absorbed by my body." This is how you should approach your sleep: see it as a part of your training. While your body sleeps, you are "absorbing" and recovering from the training that you put it through.

Furthermore, a recent Harvard Study revealed that: "In studies of humans and other animals...sleep plays a critical role in immune function, metabolism, memory, learning, and other vital functions...it is...important to get a good night's sleep after learning something new in order to process and retain the information that has been learned."

In other words, your metabolism and abilities to learn, process information, and fight off sickness all increase. It is clear that if you skimp out on sleep, you are merely placing yourself at a disadvantage to those that *are* getting enough sleep. That same Harvard study also noted, "In the long term, chronic sleep deprivation may lead to a host of health problems including obesity, diabetes, cardiovascular disease, and even early mortality."

At this point, we can all agree that sleep is vital to our physical performances in the gym and in how well we are able to perform in all facets of our lives. When asked about sleep, Arnold Schwarzenegger revealed that he only needed six hours a night, and that those who needed more should simply "sleep faster." I partially agree with that statement. I think most people should get more than six hours of sleep a night, but I do think that changes could be made to the average person's sleeping habits to make getting their sleep more efficient.

To improve sleep habits, it's important to remove distractions and set a ritual. I noticed the biggest difference when I removed my phone and other electronics from my room at night. All electronic screens emit a blue light, which slows the release of melatonin in your brain. Melatonin is a hormone that is released to induce sleep. Without it, sleep can be elusive.

Plus, when you have a phone or laptop in your room, it's easy to get caught up in texting or watching TV shows for a few hours, thereby cutting into the time you could be asleep! So, get your phone out of your room! If you can't fall asleep immediately, read a book--in particular, biographies on men and women who inspire you--or just spend some time meditating in silence.

Once you put aside your phones, you realize that you can be alone with your thoughts and concentrate on the present moment, rather than have a million thoughts racing through your mind. Bedtime is a terrible time to be thinking about things that cause you anxiety, yet for some people it seems to be the only time when these thoughts surface.

To remedy this, set up a bedtime routine for yourself. Typically, it's a routine that you follow every night to signal your mind and body for sleep. For example, you could simply turn off all your electronics, take some ZMA for better recovery, have a bath, read for 20 minutes, crawl into bed, and turn off all the lights. Keep it simple and stay consistent with it. The last thing you want to do is bombard yourself with even more blue light and information from your phone or laptop after a long day. Give your mind and body some time to unwind, spend some time in silence, and then get to bed!

Post-Training Recovery

Other methods for maximizing your recovery include contrast showers (alternating hot and cold showers), Epsom salt baths, and ice baths. All are used to increase muscle recovery and reduce soreness, swelling, and muscle inflammation. They do not have to be used after every time you train, but I find that having a freezing cold shower right after a really high-volume training session can really help with reducing delayed onset muscle soreness (DOMS). Along the same vein, when I used to play football and compete in Strongman, I loved having an Epsom salt baths once a week, as well as the night before a game or a competition, in order to relax both my muscles and mind.

My main point here is to maximize recovery by introducing different methods, like taking Epsom baths, to your daily or weekly recovery ritual. Many of the aforementioned methods are great ways to also relax your mind. That's what a lot of silence is about. Silence is making sure you give your mind and body time away from the stress and constant stimulation of the world. While we will always be bombarded by the media, advertising, social media, interactions with friends and family, reading, listening to music and the radio, and other stimuli, we must find ways to detach ourselves and bask in silence.

After all, silence is important for your recovery, and perhaps more importantly, for you to create structure in your mind and body. It is only in structure that can you find freedom. If you truly want to be the ruler of your life, make sure that you make time to be alone in silence and recovery.

MECHANICS: STRENGTH CAMP PERIODIZATION & MOVEMENTS

PROGRAM MECHANICS

The aim of this section is to help you understand how we develop the majority of our programs here at Strength Camp. These programs are based on our experiences, working with athletes and the general population over many years. Each and every time, the goal has been to help each client achieve maximum results. However, it's important to understand that these are just very general frameworks and that we constantly adjust and tailor to individual needs as time goes on.

Our training methodologies have always been focused on bringing out the inner athlete in every individual who comes into our gym. This simply means that we believe everyone should be able to move well; so first and foremost, we emphasize helping people move as they should--like athletes. Plus, athletic training is very mentally stimulating and challenging, and gets people competing and supporting one another no matter what the journey.

One thing that separates our programs from others is that we hone in on the individual and the individual's goals, while still enabling them to train in a group atmosphere. We do this by following concurrent periodization, which is built on a three-month framework of Structure, Strength, and Speed. Soon, I'll walk you through how we base programs on our main framework, yet mold them to the individual, in the section on periodization.

For now, just know that the main goal of this type of periodization is to build all of an athlete's abilities at the same time, but still emphasize one aspect in which the individual is weakest. As you can see in the graph below, we label how we progress through the first three months and what our emphasis is during each phase of training. In the first month, a client will heavily emphasize building a strong foundation from which we can start to build more specific abilities. (We have even had clients work in a Structure phase for up to 3-8 months, depending on their starting level of physical fitness.) Our next month is spent working on increasing strength, followed by speed. After completing this three-month framework, we typically analyze and reassess the client's current progress, then move them back into Structure phase.

Despite returning to the Structure phase, this does not mean that they are regressing. In fact, when they revisit Structure, they've become a completely different athlete that is able to: work on more intricate integrated movements, build more strength, get more size, and/or improve athleticism even more--depending on their goals, of course. (Note that some athletes may never go back to Structure in an off-season training scenario, but they will definitely start there.)

STRENGTH CAMP MESOCYCLE

MONTHS	1	2	3
FOCUS	STRUCTURE	STRENGTH	SPEED

In the above graph, we progressively overload (that is, to gradually add more stress to training) in each phase of Structure, Strength, and Speed. Moreover, this graph represents our base mesocycle, or the year's overall training broken into 12 weeks. Repeat this three times more throughout the year to create Strength Camp's macrocycle, a term to describe our overall training period.

This can be manipulated based on yourself (or a client) and your particular needs, but we almost always use this template as our foundation. From this, we manipulate the intensities, volume, tempo, and rest in order to increase the stress we apply to the body. (It is important to note that a very basic formula of Structure, Strength, and Speed will suffice for new trainees. There is no need to complicate things from the get-go.)

Of course, these all depend on the phase, as well as the client's needs. In reality, most people have life circumstances that don't allow them to follow a program exactly. School, work, injuries, and other variables always come into play, along with ever-changing goals and the curveballs that life throws. As a coach, I have to make sure that I am constantly helping my athletes build themselves toward their goals, yet be flexible and nimble to work around their needs.

Now, our microcycle is broken down into each week within the mesocycle and consists of balancing out primal movement patterns and a focus on either structure, strength, or speed.

STRENGTH CAMP MICROCYCLE (WEEKLY)

DAY 1	DAY 2	DAY 3	DAY 4
Structure Movements	Structure Movements	Structure Movements	Structure Movements
Strength Movements	Strength Movements	Strength Movements	Strength Movements
Speed Movements	Speed Movements	Speed Movements	Speed Movements

According to the graph, our base week consists of four days of training. We developed this by taking into consideration two things: weaving in primal movement patterns throughout a standard week and the length of time for most of our athletes to recover from each training session.

Obviously, these would differ for an off-season athlete from a rehabilitating athlete, just as a complete beginner would differ from a seasoned trainee. Based on what the athlete can handle, we would reduce or increase the number of training days. Always make sure that you understand completely where the athlete is coming from and what they can handle before you overwhelm, or worse underwhelm, them with your training schedule.

Each training day, we incorporate our Structure, Strength, Speed model. Structure begins with doing corrective stretching, a dynamic warm-up, and any other mobilizing or stabilizing exercises that we may recommend. Once the body is primed for action, we move into our Strength exercises, consisting of heavier compound movements as well as any accessory movements that support the main lifts of the training day. After this day's Strength phase, we move onto our Speed phase. Speed here is probably not what you think it is in the traditional sense. We do not necessarily do, say, sprint drills after heavy squats. Rather, speed is composed of auxiliary and supplemental exercises that are performed with recovery, hypertrophy, and/or conditioning in mind. Its purpose is to increase work capacity and keep the heart rate high with minimal rest periods.

Now, the table below demonstrates our training model for athletes. It's a little bit different from the previous one, but it'll help make more sense of what we mean by "speed."

STRENGTH CAMP ATHLETE MICROCYCLE

DAY 1 Lower Body	DAY 2 Upper Body	DAY 3 Lower Body	DAY 4 Upper Body
Structure Movements	Structure Movements	Structure Movements	Structure Movements
Speed Movements	Speed Movements	Speed Movements	Speed Movements
Strength Movements	Strength Movements	Strength Movements	Strength Movements

When we train athletes, the Speed phase comes before Strength phase to ensure that they are fresh when performing more technical movements or movements that are meant to improve their speed. We want to avoid encouraging bad movement patterns with training speed while fatigued. That's why we prefer to get fast, explosive movements done at the beginning of the training session. So, during a training session, we'd prescribe movements that are specific to an athlete's needs to be performed in a faster manner, before they move onto their strength movements.

To examine this further, the table below illustrates how we incorporate primal patterns into a microcycle. Every week, our goal is to perform each primal movement pattern at least once. However, each primal pattern must be modified to fit the phase of the program--within Structure, Strength, or Speed.

For instance, if we are in Structure phase, a squat pattern of primal movement may look like a front squat with a pause at the bottom, which helps to build solid core strength and thoracic extension. In the Strength phase, the squat pattern may be a heavy back squat for 6 sets of 3 repetitions. As you can see, same pattern; different method.

We want to ensure that our athletes work in multiple planes of motion and progress in each movement--with tempo, intensity, or integrating movement patterns.

STRENGTH CAMP MICROCYCLE WITH PRIMAL PATTERNS

DAY 1 Lower Body	DAY 2 Upper Body	DAY 3 Lower Body	DAY 4 Upper Body
Structure: Mobility & Stability	Structure: Mobility & Stability	Structure: Mobility & Stability	Structure: Mobility & Stability
Strength: Bend Pattern	Strength: Horiz Push/Pull Pattern	Strength: Squat Pattern	Strength: Vert Bend Pattern
Supplemental: Squat Pattern	Supplemental: Horizontal Push/Pull Pattern	Supplemental: Bend Pattern	Supplemental: Vertical Push/Pull Pattern
Auxillary Movements	Auxillary Movements	Auxillary Movements	Auxillary Movements

In the athlete's template, we balance the bend and squat patterns by alternating them as the emphasis for the day, twice a week. Note that we apply the same principle to push and pull movements of upper body days (Day 2 and Day 4). On Day 1, the squat is the main strength movement (i.e. heavy front squat) that is followed by a supplemental bend movement, such as single leg Romanian deadlift, good morning, or any other assistance movement that utilizes a bend pattern. (Usually, this is where we incorporate unilateral work or movements that challenge the athlete in a novel way.) We switch the emphasis on Day 3, the second lower body day, during which we use a heavy bend pattern instead and supplement that with a squat pattern.

The other primal patterns, such as lunge, gait, and twist, will typically be fit into the auxiliary movements and incorporated into our conditioning and supplemental work.

PUTTING IT ALL TOGETHER

Now that you understand the philosophies behind our programming, you can use our programs as a template, simply plug in movements, and adjust based on your needs. Here's a sample strength program that may be performed here at Strength Camp:

SAMPLE MESOCYCLE- STRENGTH PHASE

DAY 1 Monday	DAY 2 Tuesday	DAY 3 Wednesday	DAY 4 Thursday	DAY 5 Friday
1.A. Waiters Bow	1. Band Shoulder Circuit	OFF	1.A. Toe Raised Squats	1.A. B/O Plate Press
1.B. 90/90 Stretch	2. Bench Press	Foam Rolling	1.B. Groiners	1.B. T-Push Ups
2. Deadlift	3. Pull Ups	Static Stretching	2. Back Squat	2. Overhead Press
3. Goblet Squat	4.A. Face Pulls		3. Good Mornings	3. B/O Row
4.A. Step Ups	4.B. Close Grip Press		4.A. Walking Lunge	4.A. Front Plate Raise
4.B. Hamstring Curl	5.A. Barbell Curl		4.B. Lateral Lunge	4.B. ITY's
4.C. V-Ups	5.B. Tricep Extension		4.C. MB Cleans	5.A. Renegade Row
5. Sprint Conditioning	5.C. Woodchops		5. Hanging Leg Raise	5.B. Push Ups

Structure Mechanics

Push (Vertical) - Overhead Press

SETUP
- Grip the bar roughly between shoulder width and just outside of shoulder width.
- Unrack the bar and take a step back while bracing the torso. Stand with your feet shoulder width apart and maintain a neutral spine.
- Keep your forearms vertical and the wrists stacked under the bar.

MOVEMENT

- Contract your glutes and midline before you begin pressing the weight directly overhead.
- Keep your chin tucked and pull the head back slightly in order for the bar to clear the face, staying within a vertical bar path.
- Do not let your elbows flare out.
- After clearing the forehead, push the head forward and drive the armpits forward to lockout.
- Lower the bar while maintaining vertical forearms and a neutral spine.

Push (Horizontal) - Push-Up

SETUP

- Start by placing your hands between shoulder width apart and just outside of shoulder width, with your fingers pointing straight forward.
- Note that your feet should be hip width.
- Position your shoulders directly over your hands and keep your elbows at a 45-degree angle to your side.
- Keep a neutral spine, chin tucked; and engage your torso, keeping your feet within shoulder width.

MOVEMENT

- Squeeze your glutes and lower your chest to the floor, keeping your forearms parallel to your torso, along with your shoulders back and down.
- Keep the elbows within 45 degrees from your ribcage throughout the movement.
- Press through your hands, keeping the spine neutral, and return to the starting position.

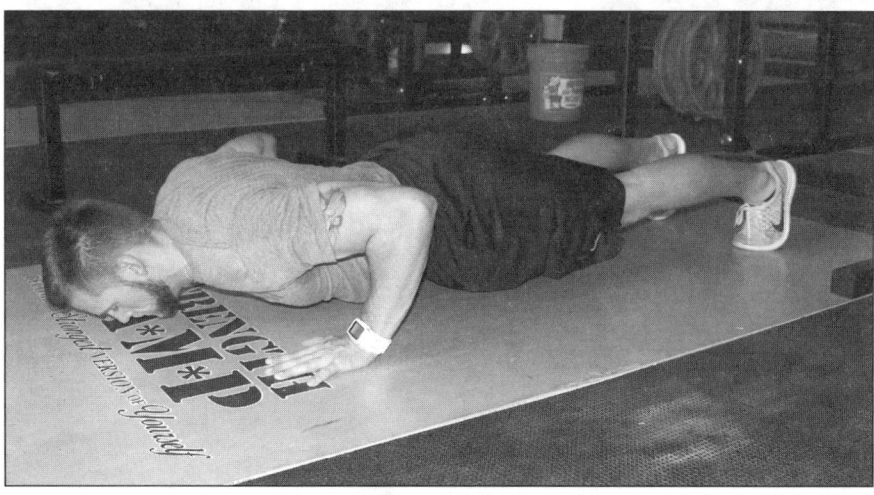

Pull (Horizontal) - Inverted Row

SETUP

- Lie underneath the bar with your knees bent. Adjusting your foot position will change the difficulty.
- Grip the bar just outside shoulder width with your hands pronated or supinated.
- Plant the feet into the ground and contract the glutes to create a straight line from your knees to the crown of your head.

MOVEMENT

- Retract your shoulder blades while driving your elbows down and behind you.
- Eliminating any downward movement in the hips draws the bar to your ribcage, just below your nipples. Keep the forearms perpendicular to the floor by pinning the shoulder blades together.
- Maintain a neutral spine and tight core throughout the movement, especially when returning to the starting position.

Pull (Vertical) - Pull-Up

SETUP

- Begin by gripping the bar at shoulder width apart with a pronated grip.
- Contract your midline and squeeze your glutes to stabilize your core. Pull your feet together and place them slightly out in front of your body.

MOVEMENT

- With your chin tucked and your head between your arms, pull yourself up with your forearms slightly in front of you and imagine driving your elbows into your ribcage.
- Drive up until the chin clears the bar without the head tilting back.
- Maintaining a neutral spine, you lower yourself in a controlled manner down into the original position.

Squat - Front Squat

SETUP

- With just the fingers, begin by grabbing the bar outside shoulder width (or wider).
- From here, step directly under the bar and drive the elbows forward and up from under the bar so that the upper arms are positioned parallel to the ground. The bar should be resting on the shoulders and upper chest, which help keep the bar steady and in place.
- The hands should not be supporting the bar.
- While maintaining thoracic extension, step back and lock the feet in place at shoulder width (or wider).

MOVEMENT

- Bracing the torso and keeping your elbows high allow your knees to bend first and lower your hips between your feet.
- Maintain a neutral, upright spine with the chin tucked. Then plant your feet into the ground and drive the weight up, squeezing the glutes at the top when you reach the original position.

BEND - DEADLIFT

SETUP

- Begin with your feet just wider than hip width.
- Position yourself so that the bar is about an inch away from your shins and your feet are facing forward.
- While keeping a neutral spine, hinge at the hips, pushing your butt back, and grip the bar outside your shins.
- Your hips should be slightly higher than your knees.
- From this position, maintain a neutral spine while bracing the torso to keep the upper back, glutes, and hamstrings contracted before you lift.

MOVEMENT

- While keeping your shins vertical and shoulders directly over-to-slightly-in-front of the bar, forcefully drive through the ground while lifting your chest.
- Keep the bar as close to your body as possible. The bar path should always remain constant.
- It is important that the spine remains neutral through the entire movement.
- After clearing the knees, forcefully contract the glutes, drive the hips forward, and pull the weight into the lock-out position. Stand tall with your spine still neutral and arms straight.
- Slightly bend the knees and hinge again, lowering the hips once the bar clears the knees, to return to the original position.

Twist - Standing Barbell Twist

SETUP

- Secure one side of the barbell into corner since you'll be moving only the other end of the barbell.
- Begin with your feet slightly outside shoulder width apart and the barbell positioned perpendicular between your feet, as if straddling it.
- Hinge and lift the barbell up, taking a step forward so that the top of the barbell is directly out front of you when the arms are extended.
- With a neutral spine, slightly bend the knees and elbows, then lock them in this position.

MOVEMENT

- Keep your feet planted, lower the barbell to one side of your hip without losing neutral spine and a tight core, and drive opposite shoulder towards the base of the barbell. This should result in a twist pattern.
- The top arm should straighten, as the lower arm bends slightly to move in a larger range of motion.
- Contract your torso, keep your feet flat, and drive the top of the barbell to the original position.
- Avoid pressing the barbell up with the lower arm.
- Repeat the same steps on the opposite side.

Lunge - Stationary Lunge

SETUP

- Stand tall with a neutral spine and your feet directly under your hips.
- Starting with the right side, take a large step forward by placing your right foot forward and flat on the ground while your left foot is propped on the ball of the foot.
- Both legs should create 90-degree angles.

MOVEMENT

- Slowly and in a controlled manner, lower your left knee towards the ground, making sure to lower your hips so they are even with your knee.
- Simultaneously bend the right knee and keep it directly above your right heel.
- Drive through the right heel and extend the hips to lift up.

Gait - Farmer Carry

SETUP

- Start by placing your feet within shoulder width apart and and aligning your ankles with the middle of the object's handles.
- Gripping the handles, pull your hips down to just above your knees while maintaining a neutral spine and keeping your shoulders back and down.

MOVEMENT

- Keeping your chest upright, push your feet through the ground while extending your hips as you stand up with the objects in your grasp.
- Remember to keep your torso tight, chin tucked, and shoulders back and down before you begin walking forward.
- As you walk, avoid swaying the hips by keeping your torso tight and a slight bend in your knees.
- To turn, drive the thumbs into each other to pin the front of the bars together (if using specialized farmers walk handles).
- Squeeze this position for the remainder of the turn to make sure that the torso does not rotate with the momentum of the handles.

Strength Mechanics

Push (Vertical) - Log Press

SETUP

- Approach the log with your feet directly underneath your hips and your shins positioned right against the log. You should be close enough that your toes are touching the log.
- Grip the handles while keeping a neutral spine.
- Push your hips and butt back, positioning the hips just above your knees as if you were preparing to deadlift the log off the ground.

MOVEMENT

- Extend your hips and lift your chest the same way you would in a deadlift to pick up the log and lift it past your knees.
- Immediately flex the hips again to push your chest into the log and your hips back, allowing the log to rest on your quads.
- From here, flare your elbows out to secure the log to your chest.
- With the upper body locked against the log, extend the hips and stand upright.
- Quickly flip the elbows around so that they go out in front of you and up simultaneously, allowing the log to be supported with your shoulders and your hands.
- Keeping your legs underneath your hips, quickly dip the hips and press the log straight up, making sure to clear the face. Once it does, quickly drive the head and armpits forward and lock out the elbows. Make sure that your shoulders are kept pinned back to stabilize the log overhead.
- Contract your glutes to stabilize your core and allow the log to return to your shoulders in a controlled manner. Then proceed to roll the log down your body and onto the floor.

Push (Horizontal) - Bench Press

SETUP

- Lay your back onto the bench and position the racked bar between the area above your nipples and below your chin.
- Grip the bar just outside of shoulder width apart. (Note that this can vary depending on the athlete.)
- Squeeze the bar as if you were trying to bend it apart.
- Squeeze your shoulder blades together and lock them in this retracted position.
- Position your feet below your knees. Your goal is create a small arch in your lower back by contracting your glutes, elevating your hips but keeping them on the bench, and using your feet to steady. Essentially, your shoulders and glutes will be the primary parts of you that will be in contact with the bench.

MOVEMENT

- Keep tight and unrack the bar. Align the bar over your chest, keeping your forearms and wrists stiff.
- Allow your shoulder blades to retract back and down.
- Lower your elbows to the floor at an approximately 45-degree angle from your ribs while maintaining rigid forearms.
- Squeeze the bar and your glutes and keep your feet planted on the ground as you drive the bar up by extending your elbows into the lock-out position.

Pull (Horizontal) - Bent-Over Row

SETUP

- Grip the bar just outside of shoulder width, with your hands pronated.
- Unrack the bar and stand tall with your feet spread out to shoulder width apart.
- While maintaining thoracic extension and a slight curve in your lower back, create a small bend in the knees by slightly dropping your hips.
- Hinge forward by driving your hips back until the arms are perpendicular to the floor, while keeping the torso parallel to the floor as much as possible.

MOVEMENT
- Retract your shoulder blades.
- Pull the bar to your ribcage while still keeping the forearms straight and pinning the shoulder blades together.
- Avoid any upward movement in the torso.
- Maintain a neutral spine while returning the bar to the original position.

Pull (Vertical) - Chin-Up

SETUP
- Grip the bar at shoulder width apart with a supinated grip.
- Contract your midline, squeeze your glutes, and stabilize your core. Next, pull your feet together and put them slightly out in front of your body.

MOVEMENT

- With your chin tucked and head between your arms, pull yourself up with your forearms slightly in front of you and imagine driving your elbows back into your ribcage.
- Pull up until the chin clears the bar, making sure not to tilt your head back.
- Maintaining that neutral spine the whole way through, you lower yourself down into the original position in a controlled manner.

Squat - Back Squat

SETUP

- Grip the bar at shoulder width apart with a supinated grip.
- Contract your midline, squeeze your glutes, and stabilize your core. Next, pull your feet together and put them slightly out in front of your body.

MOVEMENT

- With your chin tucked and head between your arms, pull yourself up with your forearms slightly in front of you and imagine driving your elbows back into your ribcage.
- Pull up until the chin clears the bar, making sure not to tilt your head back.
- Maintaining that neutral spine the whole way through, you lower yourself down into the original position in a controlled manner.

Bend - Stone Load

SETUP

- Begin by standing directly over the stone with your ankles directly in the middle.
- Lower your upper body and grip the stone by first placing your hands directly in the middle and reaching under the stone with your fingers.
- Your forearms should stay straight and squeeze the stone down the middle.
- Your hips should be higher than your knees.

MOVEMENT

- Lift the stone directly up by extending the hips and lifting your chest.
- Once the stone clears the knees, immediately place the stone on top of your quads.
- Move your feet closer together.
- From here, reach your hands over top of the stone as if you are reaching for your knees.
- After wrapping your arms fully around the top of the stone, statically secure the stone to your chest.
- Explosively extend your hips and push them forward, pulling the stone to your chin.
- Once the stone clears the platform, slightly shift your weight forward and place the stone over the bar, or lip of the platform.

Twist - Reverse Wood Chop

SETUP

- Start with a wide base, outside shoulder width apart and approximately 2-3 feet away from the cable's base. Keep your feet hips and shoulders directly square.
- The cable's height setting should be just above shoulder height.
- Grasp the handle with the outside hand, laying the other hand on top of it.

MOVEMENT

- With your arms slightly bent but locked, simultaneously push off the inside leg, shifting weight to the outside leg, and rotate the torso, reaching the cable down across the body toward the outside hip. This should all be one fluid movement.
- Throughout the movement, keep your hips and head square, and your feet planted as you rotate from one shoulder to the next.
- Then shift weight back into the inside leg as you return the cable to the original position.

Lunge - Step-Ups

SETUP

- Stand tall with a neutral spine and your feet directly under your hips.

MOVEMENT

- Starting with the right leg, lift the right leg up and forward, and place your right foot flat onto the elevated surface, creating a 90-degree angle in the right knee. (This angle can change depending on the height you are stepping up.)
- Drive through the right heel, extending the hips and keeping knees parallel to the ground. Maintain an upright torso and thoracic extension throughout the entire movement.
- After fully extending the hip, lift your left foot and plant it on the surface alongside your right foot.
- Brace the torso, and while keeping your movement under control, decelerate the left leg back down to the ground by placing all of your weight on the leg that remains on the platform.
- Once your left foot is in contact with the ground, step back with the remaining foot to return to the original position.

Gait - Yoke

SETUP

- Start by wrapping your hands around the bar outside of shoulder width. This can be adjusted for your comfort. Many athletes like to grip the vertical posts of the apparatus, but the key is to find a hand position that feels most stable for you.
- Place the bar on your traps by first pinning your shoulders back and

MOVEMENT

- While keeping a neutral spine and your feet directly under your hips, brace your torso and lift the apparatus directly up.
- Keep your midline and glutes tight, and begin walking forward.
- Never turn with the yoke on your back; always set it down first and then turn.

Speed Mechanics

Push (Vertical) - Barbell Jerk

SETUP
- Start by holding the bar in the front rack position (same as a front squat), in which the bar rests on your shoulders and upper chest instead of on your back.
- Unrack the weight, take a step back, and lock your feet underneath your hips.
- Pin your shoulders back and down, and brace your torso with a neutral spine.

MOVEMENT

- Quickly dip by driving the knees out and forward, pushing your glutes and hamstrings back slightly.
- Maintain an upright torso.
- Next, powerfully drive the bar up off of your shoulders by extending the hips and knees.
- As the bar travels vertically, move your head slightly back to allow the bar to clear your face.
- In the same fluid, simultaneous motion, flex the hips and knees to dip underneath the bar while keeping the feet underneath the hips.
- Once the bar clears the face, push your head forward while also driving your armpits forward and locking out your elbows overhead.
- After stabilizing the shoulders and torso, again extend the hips to stand up with the weight overhead.

Push (Horizontal) - Med Ball Chest Pass

SETUP

- Begin by evenly gripping the med ball with both hands and holding it directly under your chin.
- Keep the spine neutral and forearms parallel to your upright torso, and stand with your feet directly under your hips.

MOVEMENT

- Begin the movement by loading the hips, which is achieved by quickly lowering into a quarter squat while hinging slightly forward (and still maintaining a neutral spine).
- Drive through your legs by extending your hips, and simultaneously extend your elbows forward to produce equal force through both arms.
- Release the ball with as much force as possible once the body is fully extended.

Pull (Horizontal) – Single-Arm Cable Pull

SETUP

- Start approximately 2-3 feet away from the cable's base with your right arm extended and in a pronated grip on the cable's handle.
- Assume the stationary lunge position, starting with the left leg forward and the left knee at 90 degrees.
- The shoulders and hips should be square in relation to the cable's base; your spine should be neutral.

MOVEMENT

- Begin by driving the right elbow directly back.
- Simultaneously push off the left foot and rotate the hips so the left shoulder is pulled toward the cable's base.
- Fluidly shift into the right leg by planting your right heel into the ground and creating a 90-degree angle with your right foot and knee. As you shift the load from your front to back legs, your left elbow should be shooting toward the cable while the right elbow is pulling back across the chest in one fluid motion.
- To return, shift the weight back to the front leg by rotating the hips. Shift weight to the front leg as your shoulders move back to facing the cable's base, while reaching the right hand toward the base as well.

Pull (Vertical) - Single-Arm Lat Pulldown

SETUP

- Begin by sitting under the apparatus with the handle directly overhead.
- Sit tall with a neutral spine, keeping legs together and locked into the machine.
- Grip the handle with the right hand directly over the right shoulder. The arm should be fully extended.

MOVEMENT

- Maintaining a vertically positioned forearm, retract your shoulder blade and proceed to drive the elbow down and back toward the rib cage.
- Reach the elbow back until the upper arm--from the shoulder to elbow joint--becomes parallel to your upright torso.
- Avoid pulling the torso down by maintaining a strong core.
- Slowly let the handle return to starting position.

Squat - Vertical Jump

SETUP

- Begin by placing the feet directly under your hips, and stand tall with a neutral spine.

MOVEMENT

- Brace the torso and raise your hands up with your palms facing each other.
- With your elbows slightly bent and locked in place, forcefully drive your hands down and back, clearing the hips, while simultaneously bending at the ankles, knees, and hips.
- Keep the torso slightly upright, your shins stable, and your shoulders retracted.
- Once the hands clear the hips, forcefully extend your hips by shooting the hands directly vertical toward the intended target.
- In the air, reach the hand as high up as you can by extending your shoulders, and tap the vertical jump apparatus at your highest point. We want to avoid swiping at the apparatus.
- Allow your ankles, knees, and hips to decelerate properly when landing on the ground.

Bend - Broad Jump

SETUP
- Begin by placing the feet directly under your hips.
- Stand tall with a neutral spine.

MOVEMENT

- Brace the torso and raise your hands high with your palms facing each other.
- With your elbows slightly bent but rigid, forcefully drive your hands down and back, clearing the hips, while simultaneously bending at the ankles, knees, and hips.
- Hinge the torso forward until the shoulders align with the front of the toes. This loads the hamstrings and glutes.
- Once the hands clear the hips, powerfully extend the hips while driving your hands forward and pushing the belly button out and up into a 45-degree angle.
- Stay with your hips extended through the entire ascension.
- Once you near your descent, quickly flex your hips by pulling your knees out in front. This will allow you to "absorb" the ground and land in a low squat position to ensure maximum distance.

Twist - Tornado Ball

SETUP

- Start with your feet just outside of shoulder width and your toes slightly out. Open your hips and position your back approximately 3-5 inches from a wall.
- Grip the top of the rope with your thumb down.
- Wrap the rope twice over the top of the wrist and grab the base of the rope.
- Grip the base of the rope with your alternate hand as well.

MOVEMENT

- While keeping a neutral spine and your hips and shoulders directly square, quickly rotate by driving your hands across your belly button and allowing the ball to make contact with the wall behind you.
- Accelerate your hands back across your belly button to the opposite side.
- Once the hands clear your midline, quickly decelerate allowing the ball to strike the wall.
- Repeat back and forth as quickly as possible.

Lunge - Bulgarian Split Squat

SETUP

- Start approximately 3-4 feet in front of a bench or elevated surface.
- Hinge forward, placing all of the weight on your right leg. Place your left leg directly behind you and rest the top of the left foot directly on the bench.

MOVEMENT

- While keeping a neutral spine and the shoulders pinned back, flex your hips to lower them down and create a 90-degree angle in the right knee, while still keeping the shin perpendicular to the ground.
- Drive through the right heel, keeping the torso upright and extending the hips, to the original position.
- Alternate and do the same for left leg.

Gait - Sprint

SETUP

- Begin by finding your "power" leg. A quick test would be to attempt a layup on a basketball court. The leg you jump off of is typically your power leg. Keep in mind it may not always be your dominant leg. Usually right-handed people may use their left, and vice versa. For our purposes, let's say your power leg is your left leg.
- Start with your toes on the starting line. From here, position your feet so that your left toes align with your right heel. Now, with your right heel, create a 90-degree angle with your left heel. The distance from your right heel to your toes is the width of your hips, so lock that distance in place and point your toes forward.
- Stretch forward by reaching your upper body past the starting line.
- Shift your upper body back by loading your hips.
- Reach back with your right hand and place it on the line with your right shoulder directly over your right hand. Pull your left arm back to your left hip, elbow at 90 degrees.
- Tuck your chin and create a neutral spine, keeping your shins at a positive angle (basically, as close to the ground as possible) and your glutes above your knees.

MOVEMENT

- Explode through your feet by simultaneously extending your hips and powerfully pumping the left arm up.
- Swing the right knee out but keep the angles of your shins positive and as close to the ground as possible, while flexing the ankles.
- After fully extending the left hip, drive the right foot down and back into the ground and repeat on both legs for the remainder of the acceleration phase. Keep your chin tucked as well.
- Once you hit top speed, transfer out of the acceleration phase by maintaining a neutral spine and thoracic extension, and alternate driving the knees forward.
- Elbows should remain at 90-degree angles, and the hands should "pump", moving from the face to the glutes with each cycle.

SILENCE MECHANICS

For all Silence mechanics, please see Section III where we go in depth on the various techniques.

Section II
Physiological Strength

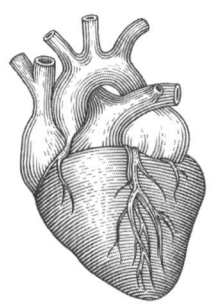

NUTRITION:
Biochemical Individuality, Macro Typing, Meal Prep, & Fine Tuning

BIOCHEMICAL INDIVIDUALITY

Biochemical individuality is a term that was coined by Dr. Roger J. Williams, a pioneering American biochemist who wrote a book by that same title.

In his studies, Williams discovered widespread anatomical and physiological variation among humans—from the different shapes, sizes, and locations of our organs to the distinct body constitutions we all possess.

Williams' theory of biochemical individuality stems from his research. Basically, this theory proposes that every human being is biochemically unique, and as such, responds uniquely to different foods.

Just like cars require specific types of fuel, we humans are affected by the "biological fuel" we consume. To help us run optimally, we would be wise to fill up our tanks with the right types of fuel for us and avoid the fuels that clog our engines.

Macro Typing

Macro Typing is a dietary system that has roots in the science of biochemical individuality. It was developed by researcher and nutrition expert William Wolcott, and you can learn more about it by reading Wolcott's book, The Metabolic Typing Diet.

In order to remain free from copyright concerns, I will use the term macro typing to describe the idea of basing your macronutrient ratios on genetic, as well as lifestyle differences.

With macro typing, the idea is that—because we are all metabolically and biochemically unique—the diet that works for me, or even for your relative, may be entirely unhealthy for you to adopt, and vice versa.

In other words, **there is no "one-size-fits-all" diet that works for everyone.**

Some people thrive when they eat more paleo foods, while others do better on diets that are high in raw foods. Many more perform and feel their best when they eat a combination of many different foods.

In determining an ideal nutrition plan, each of us must take into consideration our own biology and our environment.

A little history lesson: Thousands of years ago, our ancestors lived in a specific part of the world (perhaps in more than one area). Referred to as hunter-gatherers, early human groups were largely separated from one another throughout the world, so they developed within and adapted to their own particular habitats.

For over thousands of years, humans' digestive systems adapted to processing whatever foods were available in their respective regions and eaten in abundance. Since they ate the same types of food day in and day out, these humans also adapted to thriving on specific ratios of macronutrients (proteins, carbohydrates, and fats).

For instance, hunter-gatherers inhabiting polar and subpolar regions like northern Russia, Scandinavia, Greenland, Canada, and Alaska typically consumed lots of animal fat and ate relatively lower amounts of carbohydrates. Consumption of a high-fat, moderate-protein, and low-carbohydrate diet in those regions was necessary to survive the brutal Arctic winters.

Much further south, humans evolving in hot climates across Africa, Central and South America, Southeast Asia, and Oceania subsisted largely on carbohydrate-heavy diets that included some lean proteins and smaller amounts of vegetable-based fats.

Between the hottest and coldest places on Earth—across parts of North America, southern South America, Europe, North and South Africa, the Middle East, Asia, and southern Oceania—is a wide range of more moderate climates.

As you might expect, humans living in these regions had access to a wide spectrum of seasonal foods. Accordingly, they grew accustomed to eating more balanced proportions of fats, proteins, and carbohydrates. In some of these places, grains and raw dairy were consumed in addition to meat, nuts, seeds, fruits, vegetables, and other starches.

It is important to realize that despite eating *incredibly different diets*—ranging from paleo to nearly-vegetarian to everything in-between—primitive humans all maintained excellent health.

Of course, it wasn't just because of their diet. High levels of activity, exposure to the elements, adequate sleep patterns, and generally healthier lifestyles that were afforded by the natural environment also played significant roles in contributing to the robust health of early humans. Still, food was a big part of the equation.

Until recently, the one commonality shared by all of our ancestors' diets was an emphasis in **organic and minimally-processed, whole foods.**

Whether they were cooked or kept raw, meals were typically eaten fresh. Any foods that were preserved underwent natural processes, like drying, salting, and fermentation. Fermentation has been shown to provide further health benefits in the form of improved digestive health from increased enzymes and probiotics, or "good bacteria."

Clearly, there are many "best diet" plans out there.

So, how do you know which is right for you?

Well, wherever your ancestors lived, their digestive systems grew accustomed to thriving on the foods and macronutrient ratios that were available to them. In the process, they naturally developed intolerances to the foods they had no experience eating.

Many generations later, these genetic predispositions have been passed down to you.

Your ancestry is one of the biggest factors that influences your macro typing. But there are other factors that contribute to determining how your body processes food.

The climate in which you live, your daily activity level, and your stress levels, among various other factors, also impact your body's metabolic processes.

There are three macro types: heavy types, light types, and mixed types.

Heavy types are fast oxidizers, meaning they burn through calories rather quickly. I call them "heavy types" because of their typical need for foods heavier in proteins and fats.

Heavy types are typically (though not always) people whose ancestry goes back to areas in the far-Northern Hemisphere, where winters are long and harsh. Early humans living in these regions subsisted largely on animal flesh and seasonal fruits and vegetables.

If you frequently get very hungry—and even *"hangry,"* or hypoglycemic—between meals and often find yourself craving protein and fat-rich foods like steak, you may be a heavy type.

Heavy types thrive on diets that are rich in healthy proteins while being moderate in fat and carbohydrates.

Good sources of calories for a heavy type include meat (including dark and organ meats), fatty fish (like salmon), nuts, vegetables, seeds, healthy oils, whole eggs, raw dairy (if you can tolerate dairy), and low-glycemic carbohydrates.

When eaten by themselves, carbohydrates will typically not sustain heavy types for long, because they are metabolized much faster by the body than fat and protein are. Heavy types should accompany carbohydrates and any coffee consumption with fat and protein, in order to avoid crashing.

A heavy type whose diet is too carbohydrate-heavy—especially if those carbs are coming from high-glycemic foods, or sugary, fast-digesting carbs—may feel sluggish and "wired-tired." If you consume sweets, choose ones that contain fat and protein. For heavy types, the best time to eat higher-glycemic carbohydrates would be after your workout.

In addition, heavy types may find that eating a high-protein snack an hour before bed will help them sleep better at night. They will also function best by eating regularly throughout the day.

As a rough guideline, a heavy type might shoot for a diet composed of *45 percent protein, 35 percent carbohydrates, and 20 percent fats*. However, calorie-counting, or the methodical method of keeping track of calories, isn't for everyone, so these numbers can fluctuate from person to person.

Light types, on the other hand, are slow oxidizers, meaning they burn through calories more slowly and therefore thrive on a diet that is higher in carbohydrates. Unlike heavy types, light types can often go hours between meals without experiencing hunger or hypoglycemia.

I refer to them here as "light types" because of their typical tendency to feel, perform and look better with lighter choice foods such as fruits, veggies and light meats.

Light types often (again, not always) come from families whose ancestors lived in warm areas like Southeast Asia, Africa, and Central and South America, and had better access to an abundance of fresh fruits, vegetables, and starches.

If you are a light type, you may do well on a diet that is full of vegetables, fruits, starches, grains (if you tolerate them), lean protein, and a small amount of healthy fats. A baseline macronutrient ratio for a light type is: 20 percent protein, 70 percent carbohydrates, and 10 percent fat. However, this can vary from person to person.

Just like heavy types are best served by eating carbohydrates with their fat and protein, light types would be wise to accompany protein and fat intake with carbohydrates.

As a light type, you will likely find that you are able to tolerate sweets and lower quality sources of carbohydrates, such as white bread, pasta, and pizza, better than heavy types can. But this is no reason to consume these foods.

After all, you want to build your body with nutrients that will help you become the Strongest Version of Yourself, and if you are doing so with empty carbs, your body may not function as optimally as it could in the long-run.

As a light type, you may not be very hungry in the morning, and that is okay. You may be perfectly fine eating a big lunch with a smaller breakfast and dinner on a daily basis. Don't buy into the dogma that breakfast should be the biggest meal of the day for everyone. Trust your body.

Heavy and light types sit at opposite ends of the metabolic spectrum. In between them is the third metabolic type: **mixed types**. I'd say the majority of people fall into this category, so if the first two descriptions do not resonate with your experience, you might be a mixed type.

Mixed types are often (though not always) people whose ancestors lived in areas of moderate climates, or whose ancestry ranges across multiple regions of the world.

As you might expect, mixed types thrive on a well-rounded diet. Mixed types do best eating foods from both the heavy-type diet and the light-type diet.

There is no fixed macronutrient ratio for mixed types, but a ratio of *35 percent protein, 50 percent carbohydrates, and 15 percent fats* would be a good starting point to experiment with.

All this being said, your macro type fluctuates all the time, due to various factors like the current season, the time of day, and the amount of stress (including the neuromuscular stress of strength training) your body is being presented with.

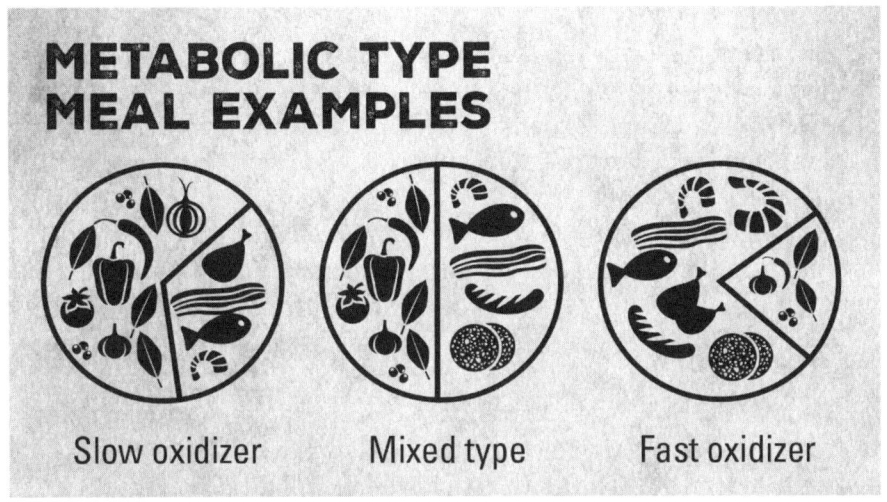

So, the most important thing to remember when eating according to your macro type is that *you must listen to your body.*

When it comes to nutrition, many of us fall into the trap of doing what looks good on paper, even when our own physical experience tells us it is not working. Rather than becoming attached to the label of any particular diet or macro type, I advise you to listen to your own body's signals.

Your body will tell you when you need to eat more protein, and it will also let you know when you should cut back on the fat and consume more raw fruits and vegetables.

For instance, I've found on days that I am not recovering from a heavy training session, I can get by with less meat and fewer calories, in general.

Of course, on the days when I do strongman training, I *crave* protein and fat to fuel my recovery. The same goes for when it's colder outside—my body just demands more calories and fat intake during the winter.

Here is a word of caution.

If you do score as a strong heavy type on the test, beware of consuming excessively high amounts of fat. The fats we eat today are more toxic than those to which our ancestors had access.

Furthermore—even if you are of, say, Inuit heritage (a good indicator for being a heavy type)—unless you are living outside 24/7 in extreme northern Canada and experiencing the same fat-burning cold that required your ancestors to eat so much fat to survive, then you likely do not need all the fat.

The truth is we are not living nearly as extremely as our ancestors did, with our central heating systems and comparatively inactive lifestyles. As such, we do not require the exact same nutrients our ancestors ate.

Meanwhile, carbohydrates tend to get a bad rap in the modern world of health and fitness, while protein and fat have skyrocketed to the status of superfoods. The truth is that we need all three macronutrients. Eat too much or too little of any one macronutrient, and you gain fat, lose energy, and grow weaker. Strive for balance.

The aforementioned descriptions should have given you some idea of which macro type you identify with. But to determine your macro type more accurately and begin fueling your body optimally, I encourage you to read William Wolcott's **The Metabolic Typing Diet** and take the test in it.

Paul Chek's "Primal Pattern Diet Typing Questionnaire" in How to Eat Move and Be Healthy will also give you a sense of your Metabolic Type®. However, Wolcott's test is more comprehensive.

Tracking

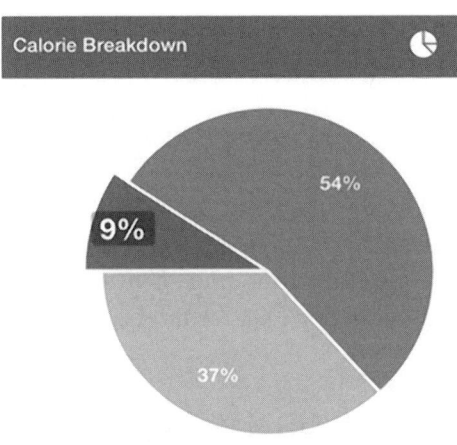

Once you've taken the test and determined your Metabolic Type® and the ideal macronutrient ratio you should be aiming for, it's time to put this knowledge to practice.

Two very helpful tools that I've used to keep me on track with eating based on my Metabolic Type® are the MyFitnessPal app and accompanying website. The MyFitnessPal app allows you to very easily log and track your daily calorie and macronutrient intake.

I understand that counting calories and tracking macros are not for everyone.

I personally find tracking useful because working with programming and parameters helps me achieve my goals more consistently, with less trial and error. But if you would rather eyeball your macros and caloric intake by eating intuitively and listening to feedback from your body, I encourage you to do that.

In my experience, **eating strictly according to your Metabolic Type® for 4-6 weeks** is a resourceful way to address any dietary concerns you may have, and optimize your digestion.

This means eating only the foods that agree with your Metabolic Type®, and eating them in roughly the right proportions for at least one month.

Generally speaking, if a food's ingredients were not made by nature, or if they are highly-processed, it is a good idea not to ingest it.

For anyone who is currently experiencing gastrointestinal distress, such as gas, constipation, and indigestion, I invite you to do the **full elimination** diet, or a variation of it, for one month of eating according to your macro type.

The elimination diet requires that you eliminate all potential problem foods from your diet. These typically include: sugar, alcohol, caffeine, gluten-containing "BROWS" (Barley, Rye, Oats, Wheat, and Spelt), pasteurized dairy, whey, casein, soy, refined foods and oils, and anything whose ingredients you cannot pronounce. You may also eliminate eggs, corn, peanuts, and nightshades (e.g. tomatoes, peppers, eggplant, white potatoes).

Generally speaking, the "cleaner" you eat for this one-month period, the more sensitive your body will become, and the better you will be able to determine, once the month is over, what foods work best for you.

Once you have finished your month of elimination, you may gradually reintroduce each of the foods you eliminated back into your diet. Start with sugar, then dairy, then grains, and so on, being careful to introduce one new food every two days, and observing how you feel after eating it.

When your digestive system has recuperated and become sensitive again, it will become very clear to you which foods serve you best. Your body will respond with indigestion to foods that do not contribute to your health; likewise, your body will respond with greater energy levels to foods that serve it well.

If you experience indigestion, gas, constipation, fatigue, foul body odor, or any noticeable decline in your overall vitality when reintroducing these foods, then you likely have a food intolerance to that particular food.

To cultivate your vitality and energy, limit your intake of the foods that your body has trouble handling. Eating these "junk foods" too often merely places unnecessary stress on your body.

At the same time, entirely eliminating problem foods often causes us to become *unhealthily* neurotic about our eating.

I have found that a good balance is to eat sweets, pizza, and other tasty foods you enjoy in moderation, and enjoy them when you do. Choosing higher quality "junk food," such as grass-fed ice cream, is a great way to minimize the toxic load on your digestive system.

Part of being healthy is not stressing over what you eat, and enjoying the food you eat.

Shopping for Food

Once you have determined your macro type and begun eating the foods that fulfill your unique needs, it is time to consider the types of quality foods you want to rebuild your cells with.

First, I want to preface this section with the following: *it is easy to become neurotic about nutrition, digestion, and diet, so beware of this trap and remember that diet is only one part of the equation.*

You become what you eat, yes, but food is not the only thing you "eat."

Your body is an open system, which means you are always "consuming" your surroundings. In turn, this voracious consumption contributes to the continuous building (and rebuilding) process that makes you who you are today.

The people with whom you surround yourself; the environment in which you live; the exercise you practice; the work you do; the music, books, movies, and images you feed your brain; the air you breathe; the water you drink; the thoughts you focus on—in addition to the literal food you eat, all of these "foods" become you.

Realize that although diet is important it is only one piece of the puzzle. Nutrition often gets worshipped as the golden key to achieving health, but improving vitality comes from more than just this single factor.

Unfortunately, many people are "unhealthy" despite eating all the right foods because, by focusing so much on a single aspect of health, they stress themselves out and inevitably neglect developing the other layers of strength.

In reality, there is no single key to strength—you've got to put everything into practice and stay balanced to grow stronger in all four layers.

The last thing you want to do is become so neurotic about the food you eat (or any other healthy practice) that merely thinking about food actually causes your body physical stress! It's also how varying degrees of eating disorders manifest themselves. What's more: this neurosis defeats the purpose of being conscious about what you eat.

Our bodies are more robust than we give them credit; humans, after all, are defined by their ability to rapidly adapt to change.

So a little gluten, dairy, or—heaven forbid—conventionally-grown food thrown into your diet here and there is not going to kill you. In fact, I believe small amounts may make your digestive system stronger and better adapted to the current ecosystem in which we live.

All that being said, there is no doubt about it—certain types of foods and dietary practices will serve you better than others, if your goal is to be as strong and vital as possible.

You are what you eat. The ingredients that become your cells (of which your body is entirely composed) come directly from the food your body metabolizes. And since all the cells in your body are regenerated every several years--some faster than others--*you literally become what you eat.*

So if you eat sugar and potato chips, or drink soda, your body will be regenerated accordingly. Your skin, your eyes, your organs—your very brain itself—will all be rebuilt with low-quality food.

While some athletes in their younger years can easily get away with this—at least for a while—over time this eating habit could lead to degeneration, disease, and injury. Remember: there are no shortcuts.

This same rule—you become what you eat—applies to consuming vibrant, organic, whole foods, too. Strong, healthy, and nourishing foods provide the building blocks for strong and healthy people.

About 90 percent of the time, I abide by this rule for feeding myself: **if the ingredients are man-made, I tend to avoid it, but if the food comes from the earth and agrees with my body, I will eat it.** Rather than worrying about avoiding "junk" foods, I strive to eat as much high-quality, organic food as I can.

The important takeaway from this section is that you should view **real food**—food that either grows wild or has been organically cultivated by farmers—as your most important sustenance for building *lasting* strength.

The research on the health benefits of eating organic foods is out there. Based on my own experiences, I've found organically-grown food to be better for health and more nutritious than conventionally-grown food. Plus, certified organic agricultural practices are healthier for the earth!

Organic foods are free of pesticides, chemical fertilizers, and all the other toxins that are found in many conventionally-grown, "natural" foods. They aren't genetically-modified (GMO) or irradiated either, which are two practices that I don't believe are healthy.

The point is that when you fuel your body with organic foods, you are using the strongest and most robust food materials to build a body that lasts.

However, not all organic foods are created equal. There are distinctions even among "organic" foods that we would be wise to consider.

For instance, organic *grain-fed* beef is different from organic grass-fed beef. Similarly, organic pasteurized milk is very different from organic raw, grass-fed milk. The differences lie in how the animals are raised: free-roaming and living as they are meant to versus being caged and sickly.

Grazing animals are meant to roam free and eat grass. When their diet and lifestyle stray from their natural ways and they are fed grains, antibiotics, and other supplements that are unnatural for them to eat, they become less healthy. Therefore, you become less healthy by eating them.

When milk is heated in the pasteurization process, the enzymes, vitamins, and amino acids that are naturally present in the milk are destroyed. Raw milk has a superior nutritional profile than pasteurized milk does, making the former easier to digest due to the enzymes in the raw milk.

Here are some guidelines for finding high-quality foods (I will discuss budget separately after).

When purchasing the best meat and dairy that you can get, aim to buy organic, free-range, and **grass-fed** (grass-*finished*) beef, bison, and lamb. If you can digest dairy (and if it is legal in your state), opt for raw (unpasteurized), organic, grass-fed, non-homogenized, and antibiotic- and-hormone-free dairy. And choose organic pasture-raised poultry (chicken, turkey, and eggs), as well as pastured pork.

If you enjoy seafood, it is a good idea to be moderate in its consumption, even if it is wild-caught. The reason is that our oceans and waterways have become polluted with sewage, industrial wastes, heavy metals, and other hazardous toxins that are absorbed in the foodchain and passed directly to us when we eat the fish.

Worse, farmed fish are not ideal to consume because they are fed grains, antibiotics, and soy, which are unnatural for them to ingest.

The best way to eat seafood is to get it wild-caught from uncontaminated water sources, and even then, eat it in moderation. If you insist on eating fish, vary the types of fish to minimize your chances of overloading on a particular toxin.

When buying fruits, vegetables, nuts, seeds, starches, and grains, aim to buy organic as well. Eat fruits and vegetables raw whenever you like. It is beneficial to eat a mixture of raw and cooked foods, since some nutrients are made more available when cooked while some fare better in a raw state.

If you tolerate grains, then buy organic whole grains. You may increase their nutritional value and make them easier to digest by soaking your grains in water overnight, before you cook them.

When choosing good fats, use organic, cold-pressed, unrefined oils and grass-fed ghee and butter. For seasoning, I use unrefined Celtic Sea Salt, Himalayan Salt, or Real Salt®, along with a variety of organic herbs and spices.

Finally, I limit my alcohol intake and drink 1.5 times my bodyweight in ounces of water per day. You can read more about how I keep myself hydrated in the section on water.

Now a word on expenses:

I understand that buying organic food is more expensive, and not everyone can afford it. As I said before, optimizing nutrition is just one aspect of growing stronger, and you can definitely grow stronger without eating organic food.

If you have the means to eat as I've described above, then I invite you to do that. Your body will thank you, and you will likely experience greater levels of energy and strength, if you aren't already eating this way.

But if you can't swing it, then that's cool, too. Just do the best that you can. Stick to eating **real, whole foods,** and aim to minimize toxins and maximize nutrients wherever possible.

While you don't have to buy *everything* organic, I do recommend at least buying antibiotic- and hormone-free meats and striving to get fresh produce from the EWG's "Clean Fifteen" list. This lists the conventionally-grown produce that typically contain much lower chemical residues than others, such as those dubbed the "Dirty Dozen."

A few other ways to save on food costs, especially when buying organic produce and free-range meats: buying and preparing your food in bulk, signing up for a local co-op, going in with a few friends on a local farm foods delivery service, and even buying directly from a local farmer.

With all that, I've offered you my insight on optimizing your food intake, but take it with a grain of salt, and more importantly, don't stress yourself out trying to get it perfect. If you want more information, read Chapter 4 in Paul Chek's ***How to Eat, Move and Be Healthy***.

Meal Preparation

Now that you have selected what foods you'll be eating, here are some tips for maximizing efficiency with meal preparation. If you are anything like me, you'll want to spend *as little time as possible in the kitchen!* Yet you also want your food to taste good. Here's what you do:

Cook fresh foods. Nutrients in foods can fade with time, as they grow older and more stale either in the market or in your fridge. Foods that are more fresh retain more nutrients that help provide you with more energy. For this reason, shop for groceries at least once per week.

Cook in bulk. Choose one or a couple of days a week to cook all of your meals for the week at once. That way, you can be done with it and just reheat your meals as needed throughout the week. This is probably the best way to save time cooking, and not to mention, reduce the stress of figuring out what to eat when you're hungry.

I prepare all of my meals at once and store them in glass Pyrex dishes, which I then reheat in a toaster oven throughout the week, when I am ready to eat them.

Stick to the basics. Unless you really enjoy cooking and have a lot of time during the week, you really need only a few good recipes.

Learn how to cook chicken breasts, ground beef, brown rice, sweet potatoes, broccoli, and a few other easy-to-make foods. Once you do, you've got all the skills you need to feed yourself well.

While you can branch out and experiment with cooking different things, I say that for simplicity's sake stick to the basics, at least for the first month of changing your diet.

And finally, cheat with caution.

It's been my experience that when doing an elimination diet, the short-term pain of saying "no" to that delicious-looking ice cream cone, or your favorite fried chicken that your mom makes, is worth it in the end. Resist the urge to relapse into your old eating habits, and know that at the end of the 4-6 weeks you can play around a bit with your nutrition plan.

In addition, you may find that in the initial days and weeks of eating according to your Metabolic Type®, you experience symptoms that seem to deviate from what the new diet intends. For instance, you may gain or lose weight at first, but you might also experience fatigue and strange bowel movements.

But I encourage you to stick to the diet even when that happens. These are just signs that your body is trying to adapt to your new dietary pattern. Eventually, things will stabilize, and you'll feel great.

Fine-Tuning

Once you've completed the 4-6 week period of adhering strictly to your macro type diet, you can begin fine-tuning your diet.

To do so, you must pay attention to how your body responds to the foods you eat.

Have you lost weight and fat? Have you gained strength? How are your energy levels? How do your eyes and skin look? How are you sleeping at night? Do you experience gastrointestinal distress (i.e. lots of gas or strange-looking poops)? Do you smell foul?

Ask yourself these questions and answer them honestly. You may want to keep a food journal to log your meals and jot down notes, thinking about how the foods make you feel after eating them and as the day goes on. It's important to keep a visual record because you may not be able to recall every detail with complete accuracy.

All of this data will help you determine the ideal foods and macronutrient percentages you should be aiming for to feel and perform at your best.

What's more: Your metabolism could change as a result of following your macro type, and you could develop intolerances to certain foods after eliminating them for a while. These are all helpful to note in your journal so that you can adjust your macros and foods accordingly.

After fine-tuning your diet extensively, you will eventually dial into what I call your "strength zone" and be able to hit it on a daily basis.

The strength zone indicates that you are in your optimal frequency: you feel strong, your libido and energy levels are high, you aren't hungry between meals, you don't have any cravings, you are able to focus, and you are generally ready to handle whatever the day brings.

If you aren't in your strength zone, then you have to take a look at your symptoms to determine what you need to change.

For instance, if you are hungry between meals, experience mood and energy swings, have nervous energy, feel wired-tired, experience headaches, and have difficulty focusing, then it's possible you may be eating too many carbohydrates.

More chronic signs of excessive carbohydrate consumption include constipation, acne, poor sleep, adrenal stress, neck and low-back pain, feelings of stress, a weakened immune system, and eventually, insulin resistance and diabetes.

However, these symptoms can also be caused by a number of other issues and do not necessarily mean you are consuming too many carbohydrates. But if you find these symptoms appearing alongside your dietary changes, then they may, in fact, suggest you are consuming too many carbohydrates.

As someone who is more on the heavy type end of the macro type spectrum, I've experienced the minor side effects of carbohydrate overconsumption many times.

For example, if I go out and eat a high-protein, high-carbohydrate, low-fat meal like sushi, I'll find myself starving merely an hour later, and craving fat and protein. Sure, I can fill my belly with all the rice and fish, but I'll still be hungry an hour later. I am sure many of you can relate.

A few ways to remedy these symptoms: eat more fat and protein; drink more water; avoid alcohol, caffeine, and other stimulants; and exercise, which helps you break down some of the sugars in your blood and lower your insulin. Doing these things will likely get you back in your strength zone and feeling much better.

On the other hand, if you experience any of the following: craving sweets or caffeine, feeling full but hungry, having a bloated and heavy feeling in your gut, feeling lethargic, depressed, or aggressive and annoyed; then you may be consuming too much fat and protein. Many of these short-term symptoms can be attributed to excessive fat and protein intake.

In the long run, signs that you are eating too much fat and protein include: fatigue and sweet cravings, joint and back pain, bad body odor, lack of motivation to exercise, hormonal dysfunction, obesity, and overall poor health.

As with the carbohydrate-related symptoms, these symptoms are not exclusive to excessive fat and protein intake. However, if you notice them cropping up after switching your diet, they could be indications that you need to lower your protein and fat intake.

To remedy this and put you back in your strength zone, I suggest: eating high-glycemic fruits and starches; taking digestive enzymes that contain protease (enzyme that breaks down protein) and lipase (enzyme that breaks down fat) to ease that "heavy gut" feeling; and even drinking some coffee or freshly-prepared juice for a pick-me-up.

Take note that it's important to take these measures only *after* you've stuck to your original diet for 4-6 weeks.

If you are feeling these symptoms before that period is over, it could very well be that you are consuming too many carbohydrates or fats and proteins, yes, but it might also be signs that your body is detoxing.

This is why it's so important to ride it out for those 4-6 weeks, unless you really don't feel well, of course.

Remember that the whole purpose of eating according to your macro type is to feel your best so that you can continue growing stronger. If it is really not working for you, then by all means change it up.

As you switch up your macronutrient percentages during this fine-tuning stage, be sure to log it all into your MyFitnessPal app (if you have chosen to use it) in order to track your progress and monitor the changes in your diet.

At the end of the day, whatever you do, nutrition is all about **listening to your body.**

Eat foods in moderation, and mix them up every now and then. Too much of a good thing—no matter how great it is—becomes poisonous.

You may also find that by rotating your foods—eating one type of meat and vegetable one day, switching to a different type of meat and vegetable the next day, and so on—your body could respond favorably. After all, keeping variety in your diet is important.

By consuming the foods that are suited for your genetics and lifestyle and *make you feel great*, and eating them in the right macronutrient ratio for your macro type, you will eliminate a large source of potential stress that your body would otherwise be forced to handle.

That's energy better spent on burning fat, regenerating your cells, producing muscle and sex hormones, and keeping you on the road to becoming the strongest *you* possible.

King

DIGESTION:
HEALTHY DIGESTION, ENZYMES, & PROBIOTICS

HEALTHY DIGESTION

You can have everything right—eating in accordance with your Metabolic Type®, as well as exercising and sleeping in the optimal amounts—but if your digestive system is compromised, it may be challenging for you to absorb all of the nutritional benefits from your food and continue growing stronger.

In the same way that filling up a car whose engine and internal guts are not up to par with premium gasoline will not magically make it run any more smoothly, simply eating good food and exercising without cleaning and "upgrading" your own "engine" will not be as effective.

There are a few signs to look out for when assessing the health of your digestive system.

Obviously, if you feel fantastic, chances are your digestive system is running strong.

Fantastic in this context means that you poop at least eight to twelve inches daily; your poop consistently passes easily and looks and smells normal; your skin, hair, and nails look healthy; your breath and body don't reek; you've got plenty of energy; your eyes are bright; and overall, you feel powerful and full of life.

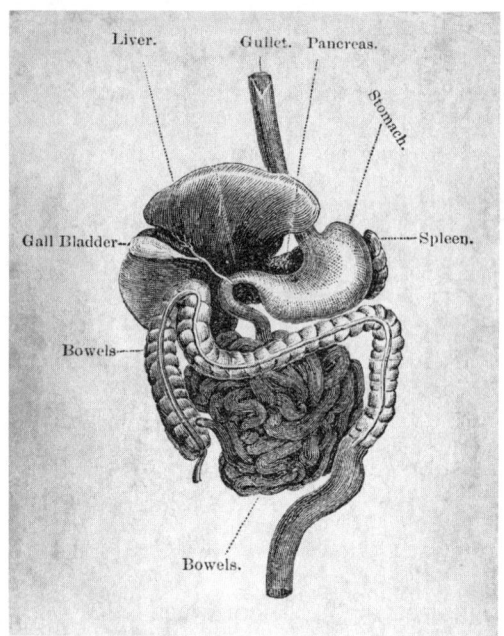

If, on the other hand, you experience indigestion in the form of frequent pungent gas, burping, bad breath, irregular bowel movements, foul-smelling and strange-looking poop, bloating, fatigue, acne, skin rashes, allergies, heartburn, headaches, asthma, short-term memory loss, pungent body odor, muscle and joint pains, and so on, then there is a good chance something has gone awry in your digestive system.

If you suspect you may be experiencing digestive issues, then take the steps to remedy it.

First, make sure you are drinking enough *clean* water.

Water is one of the best cleansing agents available to you. It will enable your body to produce enough enzyme-containing saliva to initiate the digestion process (in the mouth) and make the food easier to assimilate. When the body is dehydrated, it must draw water from its reserves in your organs and stool—not the best situation and is frequently the cause of constipation.

Avoid this issue by drinking plenty of purified water—about the equivalent of half your body weight (pounds) in ounces of water per day.

I drink most of my water between meals, so as not to dilute the digestive enzymes needed to break down my food when I am eating. (See my chapter on water for my recommendations on a filter.)

If you are experiencing indigestion, you may want to look to your diet.

Are you eating according to your Metabolic Type®? Are you consuming foods that your digestive system disagrees with? Are you eating processed foods (including pasteurized dairy, processed juices, and protein bars) and other junk that is backing up your digestive system?

Seriously, if you are not pooping at least once every single day, then take a look at what you are eating and how much water you are drinking.

Your body absorbs whatever you don't excrete, so if you are backed up, you are just recycling toxic waste that your organs already tried to pass through your system. Over time this could lead to a toxic internal environment that can have negative effects on your health and strength.

Think of it this way: If you don't take out the trash, what happens? Your home starts to stink; bugs, mice, and rats come into your kitchen to eat; no one wants to come to your house; and you feel miserable. Gross, right? So clean your inner house regularly.

Another question to consider: are you chewing your food thoroughly?

You may have heard this old Tibetan saying before: "Drink your food and chew your water."

When you thoroughly chew your food and other food substances (including water) before swallowing them, you activate many more enzymes in your saliva to help break them down into manageable pieces for your body to digest, and generally make the nutrient absorption process easier, too.

Next, look at your stress.

Stress can include diet-induced stressors of dehydration and poor nutrition, the neuromuscular demands of overtraining, the physiological stressors of antibiotics and other drugs, and the emotional and psycho-spiritual stressors inherent in everyday living—clearly, there are all kinds!

When you are stressed in any way, you activate the sympathetic branch of your autonomic nervous system (ANS), or your "fight or flight" response. This happens at the expense of your parasympathetic nervous system's functioning.

Since digestion is a function of the parasympathetic nervous system (the "rest and digest" aspect of the ANS), digestion is hindered by excess stress.

Having a certain amount of stress in your life is unavoidable, and, in reality, is a good thing. But it is important to remove stress from your life where you can, since we tend to run in catabolic--the process of muscle breakdown--overdrive. Slow down and learn to appreciate the small things in life; don't stress over everything.

For example, it is a good idea to eat in a relaxed, non-rushed environment. Take time to chew your food slowly as you listen to some good music or have an interesting conversation.

Alcohol, junk food, overtraining, poor sleep habits, unpurified water, antibiotics, and other drugs are all additional stressors that we should aim to at least minimize in our lives.

Of course, I am not a doctor, and there are times when antibiotics are indeed useful.

However, it is important to know that any time you take antibiotics you kill not only the "bad" bacteria in your system but also the "good" kind—the probiotics that help maintain a healthy gut and digestive system. If you must use antibiotics, be sure to follow it up with a probiotic supplement regimen to reintroduce the good bacteria to your digestive system.

Clearly, good digestive health is important for many reasons. If you do not address indigestion when you first notice it, it may develop into more serious issues like chronic inflammation and leaky gut syndrome, a condition that potentially causes your gut lining to allow substances into your bloodstream.

If you are having more serious digestive issues like these, it would be a good idea to consult with a naturopath or a doctor of your choosing.

ENZYMES AND PROBIOTICS

Before I begin this section, I must give credit to my good friend, Wade Lightheart, who provided me with much of the information that I'll share in the following pages. Other than being my friend, Wade is a three-time Canadian Natural Bodybuilding Champion and a sought-after expert on high-performance nutrition and digestion.

Now I've said it before, "You become what you eat." In actuality, this is only half-true.

To be more specific, *you become what you absorb*. This goes as much for what you are able to digest and assimilate as it does for what you do not *eliminate*.

Consider this hard truth for a moment. You could be eating the highest quality, free-range, organic food and doing so according to your Metabolic Type®, but unless your digestion is strong, you will not absorb all of the beneficial nutrients from your food.

In other words, if someone with a weak digestive system consumes 100 grams of protein over the course of a day, it is likely that he or she won't even digest and assimilate half that much protein. The same can be said of the fats, carbohydrates, and other micronutrients he or she eats--most of the nutritional value may go to waste!

Moreover, if your digestion is weak, not only will you not absorb all of the nutrients you consume, you also will not be able to *eliminate* all of the toxic waste that should evacuate your system in order for it to run more efficiently.

The bottom-line is that **your diet is only good insofar as you are able to thoroughly digest the foods you consume *and* eliminate their waste by-products from your body.**

Think of digestion as a three-part system: what is being consumed, what is being digested, and what is being eliminated. Whatever you consume, digest, and don't eliminate, your cells will use the remainders as building blocks and allow your physical body to continuously regenerate.

The question then becomes, "How can I increase the efficiency of my absorption and elimination?" This is where a proper understanding of enzymes, probiotics, and supplements comes in.

Digestive enzymes are proteins that are produced in the stomach, pancreas, small intestine, and salivary glands. They are also found in raw and fermented foods.

Enzymes break down macronutrients (proteins, fats, and carbohydrates) into their more useful constituents (amino acids, fatty acids, and simple sugars), which the body then converts to energy. Protease digests protein, lipase digests fat, and amylase digests carbohydrates.

Probiotics, which I've already alluded to earlier in this chapter, are beneficial bacteria that live in the gut and promote healthy digestion. They are the "good guys," if you will, that maintain a balanced intestinal flora.

You may think that it is unnatural, or perhaps a sneaky shortcut, to take enzymes and supplements to aid in your digestion and elimination. After all, our ancestors got by fine without them, right?

While that is true to some extent, that perspective overlooks the fact that our ancestors were eating far healthier and more nutritionally dense foods that even the best among modern diets can't match. Moreover, they were likely acquiring and eating these foods from healthier sources.

Sadly, our soils have been [depleted](#) of many vitamins and minerals that were once present just a century ago, let alone thousands of years ago when our ancestors still roamed the earth. As a result, our foods—even when grown organically—are by and large nutritionally inferior to the foods that our ancestors ate.

On top of that, even the healthiest among us still consume more processed and cooked foods than our hunter-gathering ancestors did.

Not so long ago, the majority of what the average human ate was raw, uncooked, and live. Our ancestors' diets were full of powerful digestive enzymes that would enable them to maintain very healthy digestion. Some native humans would even eat much of their meat raw!

To them, it was the law of nature to *take life in order to give life.*

Cooked food is, in a sense, dead. This means that your body has to draw from its own inner vitality to inject life into whatever "dead" food you eat. On the other hand, living food doesn't cost your body nearly as much, because it is already alive.

Of course, I am not recommending that you start eating a 100-percent raw food diet, complete with bloody steaks! In many ways, eating cooked food can be beneficial for your health, too.

Just know that cooking food destroys many of the digestive health-promoting enzymes already within the food. In essence, you'll need to strike a balance between eating a completely raw diet and an entirely cooked, over-processed one.

When you don't eat enough "live" foods, your body resorts to the enzymes from your limited reserves.

Imagine what will happen when you eat mostly cooked and processed foods for years. Over time the excessive "mining" of your body's enzyme reserves will take a heavy toll on your system. You might even say that your digestion "mine" could eventually break down and force the workers to go home.

In fact, my friend Wade believes that our eating insufficient amounts of enzyme-rich, live food is one of the reasons we tend to age and lose strength and muscle so rapidly as we grow older. Put simply, when the body exhausts its reserves of enzymes, bones and lean muscle mass are affected.

By contrast, eating enzyme-rich foods enables your body to conserve its digestive enzymes for other purposes, rather than secrete them into your system unnecessarily. You can think of eating live foods as a way of protecting and preserving your precious gold mine of enzymes.

Given this knowledge, I believe it is a good idea to consume—within the confines of your Metabolic Type®—plenty of fresh fruits and vegetables, as well as fermented foods, which contain large amounts of enzymes and probiotics. I eat raw and fermented foods *before* I eat the cooked food in a meal so that the enzymes can do their job in aiding digestion.

Now regarding the question of using supplements to aid digestion—yes, I believe you can certainly cultivate a strong and powerful digestive engine without the use of supplements. That is, by eating enzyme-rich foods. Adopting a mostly-raw food diet for a period of time may be a great way to strengthen a weakened digestive system and restore optimal digestive function.

However, this is challenging, especially when you are already changing around your diet in many other ways.

For a person who is in the process of revamping his diet and currently has a weakened digestive system, I believe that taking digestive enzymes and probiotics responsibly for a fixed amount of time is a resourceful "shortcut" for improving physiological strength.

If you would like to re-establish gut health without investing the time and resources that a raw food diet entails, these supplements may serve your needs.

As with any shortcut, it is important to be aware of the potential consequences of long-term use and not lean on the supplements forever. I do not currently endorse prolonged enzyme supplement use simply because I believe all supplements are tools that should be used in moderation, to catalyze rather than uphold vitality.

As with all of my recommendations, I encourage you to consult your body and make your own decision about supplement use.

HYDRATION: WATER & BATH & BODY PRODUCTS

WATER

As you may have heard, about 60 percent of our bodies are made up of water! In other words—similar to the mantra, "you become what you eat"—**you become what you drink.**

Today we in many parts of the world are fortunate enough to be able to drink clean water simply by turning on the faucet. I am grateful for this incredible blessing.

However, in striving to ensure that our water supplies are free of pathogens and bacteria, we have unfortunately poisoned them with chemicals like fluoride and chlorine.

On top of that, environmentally-unfriendly industrial and agricultural practices have further polluted our tap water with a number of neurotoxins: pesticides, heavy metals, and pharmaceutical drugs, to name a few.

None of these things contribute to developing a strong, healthy body. We may not yet fully realize the health implications, but just imagine what ingesting all of these pollutants on a daily basis may be doing to our bodies.

Knowing this, I have *always* ensured that my family and I drink the most nourishing and detoxified water that we can access—I did this even when I was broke.

For many years, we drank water that had been filtered through our reverse osmosis filtration system. Reverse osmosis is a filtration process that basically strips everything from the water—fluoride, heavy metals, pesticides, pharmaceuticals, and *minerals*.

While reverse osmosis (RO) purges water of all toxins, it unfortunately removes the beneficial minerals, too. In the same way that antibiotics wipe out both the "good" and the "bad" bacteria in your gut, reverse osmosis strips the water of *everything*, leaving you with very clean, albeit less nourishing, water. Fortunately, you can purchase additional remineralization devices to restore minerals to the RO water, but this gets expensive and is somewhat of a hassle.

There are other water filters on the market that purify water nearly as well as a reverse osmosis system does, while still preserving the water's mineral content.

Berkey Water Filters are portable water filters that—when used in combination with the PF2 Fluoride Filters—remove practically everything that RO does, but at a fraction of the price. These are great, easy-to-use filters for someone who is looking for a more affordable alternative to RO.

Still, there are other factors to consider when choosing a water filter, besides purity and mineral content. You also want to look at properties like water structure, pH, and charge.

Back in the chapter on digestion, remember how I explained that you really aren't what you eat but rather *what you absorb*? Well, it is the same for water. Your water is only as good as that which you are able to thoroughly absorb.

Water travels in groups of molecules, often referred to as clusters. Imagine a water cluster as a bundle of grapes, with each grape representing a water molecule.

There are some water filters, which I will get to in a moment, that change the composition of water in such a way that the clusters become smaller. In other words, the large bundle of grapes is broken up into smaller clusters of grapes. This is called micro-clustering.

Why would you want to do this?

Micro-clustering is kind of like water's version of masticating, or chewing, food, which works to preemptively break food down into smaller particles. And like chewing, micro-clustering makes it easier for your cells to absorb the water. By drinking micro-clustered water, your cells become "super-hydrated."

When water passes through the pipes in your home's plumbing system, the clusters of water molecules become very large—larger than those that naturally occur in moving rivers and springs, for example. Yet it is those smaller clusters that our bodies have become adapted to processing.

Water that moves through pipes tend to take on a right-angular pattern, whereas water moving through its natural element flows freely in a wavy pattern. This difference causes the clusters of water molecules to grow unnaturally large.

Keeping the grape-cluster analogy in mind, imagine that your cell walls are like fish nets. In order for your cells to become hydrated, the grapes must pass through the netting.

Now, if you try to pass a whole bushel of grapes through the net, it would be pretty difficult. But if you first break down the bushel into smaller parts, they can more easily pass through to hydrate your cells. This is how a micro-clustering filter works to help your cells achieve proper hydration.

Water pH, or the relative concentration of hydrogen ions in your water, is also something to consider when choosing a filter. Not to get into too much detail here, but you should at least know the basics. For starters, your blood is 7.365 pH. That's still neutral, albeit leaning a bit more on the basic (less acidic) side, but your blood pH can be affected by what you consume.

If you drink something acidic (like soda, sports drinks, and RO water), your body must extract bicarbonate buffers, like magnesium and calcium, from your connective tissues and bones in order to neutralize that acid and maintain that balance of 7.365 pH.

Don't forget that this is on top of the mineral-deficient diet we're eating. In other words, the body is already tapping into these mineral reserves more than it needs to.

If we were to follow this train of thought further, it is plausible that over time this over-extraction of the body's mineral resources—which is exacerbated by drinking acidic liquids—might lead to issues like connective tissue damage.

Drinking neutral to slightly alkaline-pH water, on the other hand, enables your body to keep its precious resources of minerals. In this case, there is no need for bicarbonate buffers to be extracted, because the water doesn't need to be neutralized.

Some people have expressed rational concerns that drinking slightly alkaline water will negatively influence digestion, based on the assumption that the alkalinity of the water might interfere with the acidic environment needed for the healthy digestion of food.

However, there is no need to worry because the body can differentiate food and water. The body releases stomach acid when *food* is ingested, but not when water is consumed.

Moreover, stomach acid is *highly* acidic, very low on the pH scale. In other words, even if stomach acid were released at the same time alkaline water was ingested, the alkalinity of the water would not be enough to counteract the acidity of your stomach acid.

The third important factor to take into account when choosing a water filter is water charge. I used to overlook this small detail, but I now pay attention.

To illustrate water charge, first think about this: whenever you are around the ocean, around waterfalls, or even hanging out after a lightning storm, you notice how you feel energized? Well, this surge of energy can be explained by the healing power of negatively-charged ions, which also happen to have antioxidant properties.

Basically, in these areas with moving water, the water picks up an electrical charge by simply flowing through, and as a result, kicks off negatively-charged ions. This is called an ionization effect.

When you breathe in these negative ions, your body uses the electrons, these negative ions, for energy and vitality. So, spend more time around natural bodies of water-- preferably moving water like oceans, rivers, and waterfalls—to take advantage of their cleansing and restorative effects on your body.

Luckily, there are some water filters that send an electrical, negative-ion-generating charge through the water following filtration. Filters like these are essentially re-creating the naturally-occurring, antioxidizing water that is found within waterfalls, springs, and oceans.

Drinking water that contains negatively-charged ions may aid in muscle recovery. The ions latch onto free radicals in your body and essentially flush from your system all the acidic waste and damage you incur from training, enabling you to recover faster and stronger.

I understand that these practices of making water particles smaller and more easily absorbable, altering pH levels, and inducing a negative charge may sound unnatural, perhaps like cheating.

And you may be right about that. But the reality is that the water we drink is *already unnatural*. It is filled with chemicals, grouped in abnormally large clusters, and unnaturally stripped of minerals.

Therefore, I would rather unnaturally strive to mimic the structure of the water that our ancestors drank than settle for drinking "unmanipulated" water from the tap or from an inferior filter. Either way, they would be unnatural for our bodies to consume.

If you think about it, water that has been micro-clustered, is slightly alkaline, and carries more negatively-charged ions is actually quite natural.

There are places around the world, like Lourdes, France and Tlacote, Mexico, that are known for having water with remarkable healing properties. The common characteristics of their water are in line with what we have been discussing. Their water contains: a raised pH (more alkaline), micro-clustering, and a negative charge—together they form "super water", similar to superfoods.

For all of these reasons, I now drink Kangen Water, which is water that has been purified, retains its minerals, and has the three "super water" characteristics described previously. In effect, Kangen Water is micro-clustered, offers various degrees of alkalinity, and is packed with negative ions.

Kangen Water Machines transform the composition of filtered tap water into that which resembles healing water found in high-elevation glacial streams and sacred water sites around the world.

It should be noted, however, that not all Kangen Water Machines remove fluoride.

I understand Kangen Water filtration systems are very expensive and may not be for you.

If that's the case, I recommend an RO filtration system in combination with a remineralizing system as another good (but also expensive) option.

Alternatively, Berkey Water Filters are still great and more affordable.

Finally, gravity-fed spring water is another excellent choice.

After all, it is the natural water that our ancestors drank. Spring water is pure living water that springs up from deep aquifers beneath the ground. In fact, spring water naturally accomplishes what Kangen Water does via technology, yet you reap all the benefits of naturally micro-clustered, ionized, and neutral-to-alkaline water, without its being manipulated through unnatural means. And often times, it is free!

If you feel up to the task, harvesting your own fresh spring water will provide you with the most nourishing, energizing water available. Daniel Vitalis' FindaSpring.com is a good resource for finding springs near you.

Obviously, collecting your own spring water has its downsides. It is more time-intensive, transporting it in large glass jugs can be a challenge, and you may not live near a good spring. But these barriers are minimal when compared to the benefits of drinking spring water.

If your budget is too tight for any of these filters, then do the best you can. Any filter is better than nothing. Even simply sticking to drinking water and cutting out all other drinks are steps in the right direction. As with all things, what matters is that you do the best you can.

Whichever filter you choose, **aim to drink half your bodyweight (lbs) in ounces of water per day.** Ideally, drink your water from glass containers, although stainless steel ones are good, too. I drink out of glass Mason Jars; you can get them for a couple of dollars per bottle.

What about bottled water? Bottled water is really not a great long-term option, aside from occasionally needing to travel with it. Both its impact on the environment and on your own health are not ideal, and can have negative effects on your body.

Most bottled water you drink are months—even years—old. That is to say, the water has been stored in plastic in all that time. Over time, chemicals from the plastic can leach into your water and create free radicals, which are positively-charged ions that damage the body by breaking down your cells and slowing recovery. These free radicals are attributed to accelerated aging and cell degeneration.

What's more: many of the compounds in plastics, called phytoestrogens, mimic a hormone called estrogen. When these phytoestrogens enter your system, they decrease testosterone levels and may even facilitate genetic mutations.

If you're interested in learning more, check out this documentary called The Disappearing Male to better understand the impacts that phytoestrogens and other hidden toxins have on our health.

BATH AND BODY PRODUCTS

The body is an open system. Just like how we become what we eat and what we drink, we become what we absorb through all of our organs, including our skin and lungs.

Commercial soaps, deodorants, and other body hygienic products contain numerous chemicals that can be absorbed through our skin.

When we put anything on our skin, our organs that are responsible for detoxification are forced into overdrive to remove those substances from our body. This places stress on the body's systems.

In my mind, it is a good idea to minimize these sorts of unnecessary and additional stressors on the body, especially since we live in a world that is already full of toxins.

There are many things we can do to minimize the toxic load on our bodies. One step we can take is to get a shower filter.

Your bath water comes from the plumbing pipes of your house and is often unfiltered. Bathing in unfiltered water, especially hot water, expels large amounts of chemicals like chlorine via water droplets into the air.

Because you are exposed, you then absorb these chemicals through your skin and lungs. If you are absorbing these chemicals this way, you are overriding your efforts to drink purified, filtered water. It is important that you invest in a shower filter as well.

As far as bathing products go, Dr. Bronner's makes excellent organic, biodegradable soap and bodywash and fluoride-free toothpaste. For a healthy conditioner, organic argan oil works well. Finally, Primal Pit Paste is an organic, entirely chemical-free deodorant that actually works and smells great.

At the time of writing this, I am not endorsed by any of these products. They are simply my recommendations because they have worked for me, and I know it can be difficult to find good go-to products.

King

BIOLOGICAL RHYTHMS: DAILY RHYTHMS, ANNUAL RHYTHMS, & SEASONS OF LIFE

DAILY RHYTHMS

If you want to maximize your strength and recovery, one of the most powerful tools you can implement in your life right now is to commit to getting enough sleep.

Ignore this section if you already feel well-rested and energized on a regular basis. I don't want to mess up what you already have going on.

For those of you who find that you are often tired—maybe you experience headaches, tiredness, eyelid twitching, yawning, low immunity, or just lower energy than you would like—these are all signs that your body is fatigued and needs more time to recover.

You might push past your body's natural warning signs for more sleep by stimulating your nervous system with sugar, caffeine, and other "pick-me-ups" throughout the day, but this causes chronic over-activation of the sympathetic branch of your nervous system.

That means it triggers the release of stress hormones from your adrenal glands, as well as the conversion of glycogen to glucose, which is released from your liver and into your bloodstream to aid you in "fighting," or "fleeing" from, the perceived threat your body believes it is being presented with.

In order to counter this massive spike in blood sugar levels, your pancreas releases insulin to deliver the glucose from your bloodstream to your cells. This effect also aids your muscles in fighting because the cells convert glucose into energy.

But if you are not expending much energy—like when you drink coffee or eat a cookie for your 3:00p.m. snack at work—whatever unused glucose gets stored as fat.

In addition, this insulin spike causes you to experience a dip in energy levels, so—unconscious of this process—you end up grabbing more sugar and caffeine to pick you up again.

You see? It's a negative spiral. Believe me, I've been there.

If you find yourself in this cycle and want to break out of it, then I invite you to try the following experiment.

For two weeks, go to bed every night by 10:00p.m., and wake up with the sun.

Your body's repair systems are designed to come into play during roughly the four-hour period of time between 10:00p.m. and 2:00a.m.

The recovery period for the nervous system and mental function happens during the next four-hour block: from 2:00a.m. to 6:00a.m.

If you are awake for a significant portion during either of these two 4-hour periods, you are missing out on a lot of the anabolic, recovery benefits that sleeping during these eight hours provides.

To maximize my own recovery and hormonal health, I aim to be asleep for a good chunk of this **10:00p.m. to 6:00a.m. window.**

Don't stress about being asleep for this entire period.

Just try to sleep during as many of these hours as you can. The more you sleep during these hours, the more muscle-promoting recovery effects you will experience.

In my experience, feeling well-rested is not so much about getting a particular number of hours of sleep per night. Instead, my experience has been that I feel most rested when I go to bed early and wake up early.

In fact, I believe getting 8 hours of sleep from 1:00a.m. to 9:00a.m. is not the same as sleeping from 10:00p.m. to 6:00a.m.

When you go to bed late, your body is thrown off of its natural circadian rhythm—essentially your body's internal biological clock of sorts—and will attempt to catch up on recovery during the day by releasing sleep-inducing hormones like melatonin while you are awake.

These hormones disrupt the whole hormonal cycle, and they're why you feel mentally and physically sluggish throughout the day.

Rather than releasing recovery hormones before bed, your body—still jacked up with daytime hormones, like cortisol, during the evening—keeps you awake when you want to be winding down.

Put simply, when you go to bed late, your whole hormonal rhythm is thrown off. You end up feeling tired during the day and wired at night.

When you allow your body to sleep during that optimal window for recovery between 10:00p.m. and 6:00a.m., you restore a healthy circadian rhythm, and everything falls into place. You feel tired when it is time to go to bed; and in the morning, you wake up, having all the energy you need to be strong and take care of business.

I know a lot of you may be used to going to bed well past midnight. Perhaps going to bed by 10:00p.m. sounds unrealistic.

If that is the case, then you must determine which is more important to you: your health or whatever it is you are doing late at night.

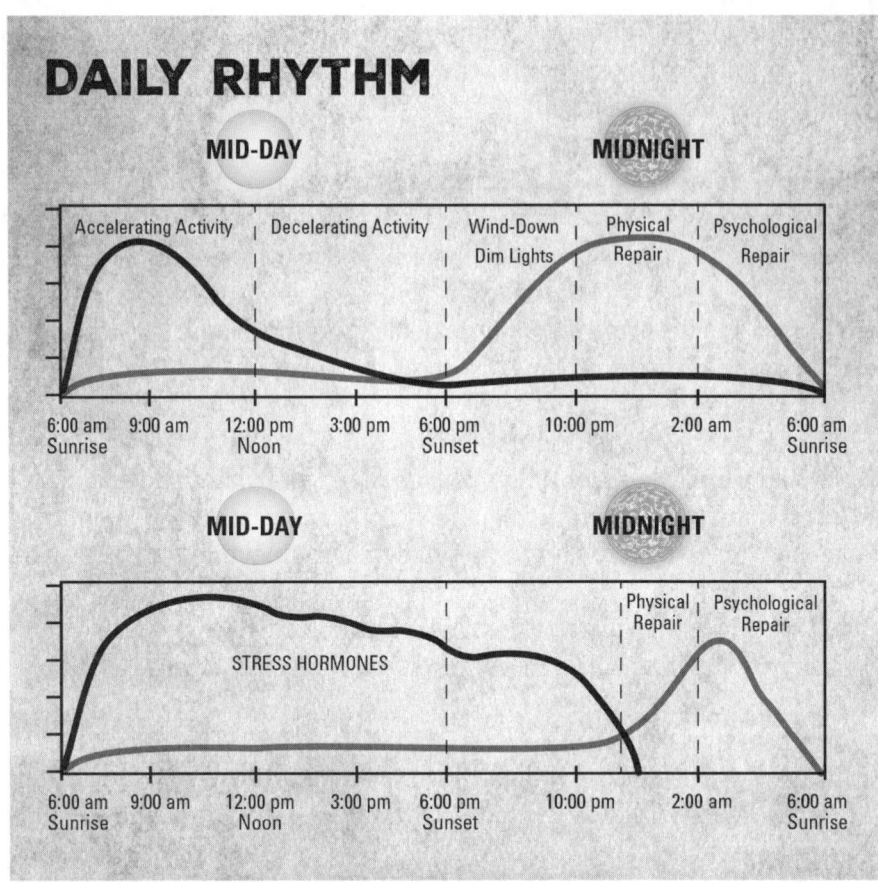

Source: Paul Chek http://chekinstitute.com

It may be a job; it may be partying; or it may be reading and writing. Whatever it is, ask yourself if what you are doing is worth the lack of energy you feel the next day, which also prevents you from being fully present with your training and other activities.

I am not here to tell you what the Strongest Version of Yourself looks like and does. **It may very well be worth staying up late.**

Perhaps staying up until 1:00a.m. every night allows you to socialize with your friends, make art, or build your business—all of which may be helping you grow stronger.

Decide what you value most.

If you value physiological health and strength above whatever it is you do late at night but, then, without getting neurotic about it, set yourself up to succeed by going to bed early. Help yourself have the energy required to be who you need, or want, to be.

Again, I recommend going to bed by 10:00p.m. But if that is too early, then pick a time that works for you and stick to it.

Tips for Better Quality Sleep

The first few days of going to bed earlier—especially if you are used to going to bed well after 10—may be difficult for you to fall asleep at first. If this is the case, resist the urge to sleep in the next morning.

Instead, commit to waking up with the sun, or setting an alarm for around 7:30a.m. every morning (if you'd like more sleep), and getting out of bed right away—no matter how tired you feel. Doing this will eventually reset your circadian rhythm and cause you to feel tired by 10:00p.m.

If you need an extra boost in the morning, skip the caffeine and sugar.

Instead, try a cold shower. Taking a cold shower first thing in the morning has a number of health benefits, and will provide you with a boost of energy without the side effects. Exposing yourself to sunlight and fresh air as soon as you wake up will also help to restart your natural circadian rhythm by triggering the release of daytime hormones.

And of course, make sure you eat well, drink lots of water, and exercise throughout the day.

They're healthy habits, but also because dehydration and the lack of exercise can prevent you from sleeping soundly. It has been my experience that the harder you work physically when the sun is up, the better you will rest at night.

Regardless of your Metabolic Type®, I suggest you avoid eating a carbohydrate-heavy meal without adequate fat and protein before bed, because doing so can spike blood sugar levels and keep you up at night.

It would also be wise to avoid consuming any stimulants in the evening and participating in stressful activities before going to bed. This includes consuming sugar and caffeine in the evening, as well as watching the news before bed.

Exposure to light is another important factor to consider when optimizing sleep.

Our bodies are not designed to tolerate bright lights at night. If you think about it, this makes sense.

For tens of thousands of years—up until the late 1800s—the only light source humans had access to past sunset was fire, in the form of campfires, torches, lanterns, and candles. Our eyes have not yet adapted to processing electric light very well.

Nowadays, we have computers, smartphones, and bright fluorescent lights all around us, available 24/7. These electronics emit a spectrum of light called blue light, which stimulates our body in the same way that sunlight does, activating catabolic hormones and delaying the secretion of sleep and recovery hormones like melatonin.

In order to minimize the release of sleep-disrupting stress hormones at night—and promote the secretion of melatonin—it is a good idea to dim the lights around your house and avoid electronics, including your computer and cell phone, before going to bed.

If you need to use light or electronics in the evening, try using dim lights and candles.

[F.lux®](#) is a free software you can download that automatically blocks out blue light on your computer screen after sunset. You may also want to check out [blue light-blocking glasses](#), which block out blue light from all sources when you wear them.

Once you go to bed, make sure your room is dark and free of artificial lights while you sleep. This includes lights from street lamps and car lights outside, as well as from electronic devices in your room.

Most people sleep best in a cool environment, so either crack the window open or set the air conditioning to a cool temperature.

A few other tips include: listening to some calm music before going to sleep, taking a bath with essential oils, creating a bedtime ritual, and not working where you sleep.

Annual Rhythms

Our bodies' natural rhythms are dictated by the movements of the earth and moon around the sun, as well as by the movements of the moon around the earth.

We have already discussed how the *daily* rhythms of the earth and moon affect our circadian rhythms. In a larger scale, the *annual* rhythms of the earth and moon, too, affect our physiological and energetic rhythms.

When early humans were developing and adapting to their particular environments, there was only nature in its disrupted state.

There were no artificial lights on at night, no room-darkening curtains to keep the sun out in the morning, no central heating during the winter, no air conditioning during the summer, no eight-hour flights across continents, and no pineapples in Alaska.

I am not saying these modern inventions are bad. I'm saying that for every shortcut we take in "outsmarting" nature, we pay a price. And the currency with which we choose to pay is stress on the body.

However advanced our technology has become, we have simply not adapted to handling it perfectly. Our bodies are still designed to operate in accordance with natural laws and cycles.

On a daily basis, we are affected by the rise and fall of the sun and moon.

On an annual basis, we are affected by the change in seasons—and the associated changes in weather and available resources—that are caused by the earth's position in relation to the sun.

Our lives tend to be somewhat out of touch with these rhythms of life because of our perceived separation from nature. Our technology creates boundaries between ourselves and the natural world in ways of which we are often unaware.

I am grateful for these technologies because they make life immensely easier.

At the same time, I believe there is a balance we must strike between living in the modern world—benefiting from all the amazing technology that is available to us—and living in accordance with the changing seasons, with which our bodily rhythms are inherently synchronized.

Using our gadgets without an awareness of, and respect for, the fact that our bodies are directly intertwined with the rest of nature inevitably costs us our health.

Elson Haas has written a wonderful book called Staying Healthy With the Seasons that is a helpful resource for guiding us back to living in ways that are more harmonious with the natural ebb and flow of our environment, and promote vitality.

I invite you to read his book to gain a practical understanding of how you might revitalize yourself by syncing up with nature's rhythms.

I invite you to read his book to gain a practical understanding of how you might revitalize yourself by syncing up with nature's rhythms.

Daniel Vitalis is a fellow YouTuber, entrepreneur, and Human Wildness Advocate. He is an expert on using various ancestral and modern methods to help you "ReWild" yourself, which you can learn more about by checking out his YouTube channel.

These two men will give you more information and resources than I could provide on this subject. But to give you something to work with in the meantime, here is my rough-and-ready guide to developing healthy, natural rhythms.

It starts with... spending more time outside.

This doesn't necessarily have to involve going camping, hiking, or performing any other outdoor activity that requires advanced skills, experience, and resources to do safely.

Spending time in nature can just as easily be going for a walk outside, swimming in a body of water, and getting outside in the sun on a regular basis. Simply immersing oneself in the natural world does wonders for rebalancing biological rhythms.

Whether you want to look at it from a spiritual perspective or a scientific worldview, nature has revitalizing properties.

All matter, according to physics, is condensed energy that is vibrating at unique frequencies. Energy manifests as various forms of matter due to differences in these vibrational frequencies.

In other words, earth is vibrating at a particular frequency—as is water, rock, glass, concrete, metal, wood, and plastic.

Generally speaking, unaltered nature—what we consider to be "wild"—vibrates at a frequency that is more conducive to *vibrance* and vitality. Human-altered nature—what we call "technology"—vibrates at a frequency that is less vital and may be more hospitable for disease.

Replace tap water with spring water; fluorescent lighting with sunlight; rubber and concrete with soil; stale office air with fresh oxygen; and air conditioning with sweat-drenching heat—and by matching your rhythms to the rhythms of nature—you switch yourself onto the vibration of vibrance and vitality.

When implemented well, barefoot walking is another excellent practice for restoring healthy vibrations in the body. Placing your bare feet upon grass, soil, sand, rock, and water grounds the roots of your nervous system to where they belong.

Don't take my word for it. Take your shoes and socks off right now and put your feet in some soil for a few minutes. Notice how grounded and calm you feel.

Simply spending time outside in the sun, and exposing as much of your body to its rays as your environment allows—in moderation—are more effective ways to reestablish healthy biological rhythms.

Sunlight especially is crucial. Everything from our immunity to our emotional state is strengthened by healthy exposure to sunshine.
Essentially, immerse your body in grounding and restorative natural environments safely and in a responsible manner to support healthy, hormonal rhythms.

Walk or run outdoors while sucking in fresh oxygen; eat local foods in season; try polar plunging; soak in hot springs; spend time around negative-ion generating waterfalls, rivers, and oceans; and exercise outside in weather that challenges our homeostatic regulation mechanisms, such as running in the rain, working out with no air conditioning, and spending time in cold weather.

With all of these practices, it is important that you use moderation and common sense.

Too much cold exposure gets you sick; too much sun exposure gets you sunburnt; you don't go swimming when there's lightning and thunder. Carelessly implementing these ancestral approaches to health defeats the purpose of using them.

But the more you begin to reinhabit the natural world in a responsible manner, the stronger and more vital you will become.

Spending time outside will also help you to notice seasonal cycles and how they affect your own biology.

The catabolic warmth and sunlight of summer signal to our bodies that it is a season for action. This is when we grow crops, hunt, and gather. Summer is a time to be active in work and in life.

Summertime also provides lots of cooling, enzyme-rich, raw foods that can help us sustain our increased activity. Depending on where you live, certain fresh fruits and vegetables abound. You'd be wise to take advantage and eat them!

In the fall, we reap from what we have sown in summer.

This is the harvest time. We continue to be active and eat lots of good food before the ground freezes up to prepare us for winter.

The sweet fruits and plentiful vegetables of summer and early fall give way to starchier produce. Nuts, seeds, and other sources of protein grow abundantly in the fall.

Winter is a time for rest and recovery. The abundance of cold and darkness in the wintertime allows for more time to sleep, to reflect, and to study new ideas and concepts.

Foods that grow in winter tend to be hearty, warming foods. I know that my body craves more hearty cooked meals during the winter to keep me warm.

And in the spring, we spring forth with life again and begin preparing for summer.

Just as nature comes to life, we come to life. We increase our exercise, and we eat more fresh produce.

Spring is the season of cleansing—greens, citrus, and herbs grow plentifully in spring, providing you with foods that will clean out your system. You may do a physiological cleanse, if you'd like. Or more simply, you might clean out your house.

A lot of this is intuitive.

As I mentioned earlier, spending time in the elements will naturally let you know what foods and activities you need more and less of.

If you exercise outdoors in the summer, you will crave cooling water and fresh fruits to replenish your cells. And if you spend time outside in the winter, you will want to sleep and eat more because of the cold.

Knowing what seasonal foods to eat is as simple as buying locally, or growing your own. Whatever is currently growing around you is what is in season. It is as simple as that.

I will be honest: I eat bananas in the winter and I use central heating. By no means do I live in perfect harmony with "unaltered nature," and I am okay with that.

I like wilderness, and I like technology. So, to fully inhabit my true habitat—and not a romanticized version of my ancestors' habitat—I believe that using both is to my advantage.

The purpose of implementing these nature-centered practices is not to return to living like a hunter-gatherer, but instead to become aware of these cycles, and respect them so that we can enjoy the great tools we have at our disposal while at the same time staying vital—as healthy, strong, 21st-century humans.

The human animal, after all, is meant to adapt.

SEASONS OF LIFE

Just as the earth experiences spring, then summer, then fall, and finally winter—your own life cycle has its seasons.

You, like winter, emerge into existence out of darkness.

For the first stage of your life, from the time you are born to about your mid-twenties, you grow and mature.

"The world is your oyster," as the saying goes. Naturally, you consume all of the nourishment that the spring of your life has to offer—in the form of mentorship, education, and other formative experiences—in order to prepare yourself for the heat of the next season.

When you've grown up, it is time to lay down your seeds and take action.

This is the summertime of your life, the time to be building businesses, developing relationships, and being a warrior out in the world. Usually, this season begins in your mid-twenties and ends in your mid-fifties, give or take a decade.

Who you become, the people you nurture, and the work you do in the summertime of your life all contribute to the making of your harvest, or your legacy. In the fall of your life, you reap what you sow.

And just as easily as you emerged, you eventually fall back into the cold of winter.

Do you see? There is a cycle to *everything*.

Now, what I just shared was a macro view of the seasons of life. But there are many more seasons within the course of a lifetime.

There will be times in your life when you must enter a fiery summer, and I am sure you have already experienced this. So long as you are active in the world, you will experience these summers.

The summer is an exciting time of your life. Seeds of action are planted and then come to fruition, benefiting the people you serve. This motivates you to work harder, to plant more, and to strive to be perennially generative.

But just as an endless summer would scorch the earth, leaving it infertile, living many summers in a row without taking breaks for you, too, will eventually burn you out.

It is not natural in nature, and it is not natural in life.

When you are in the heat of summer and you are "winning", it is easy to become blinded by the light of your success—so attached to working—that you fail to let go of the season and move with nature into fall and winter, and to cool off and chill out.

I did this, and it burned me out.

After a decade of never-ending summers, during which I simultaneously built a business and a family, I eventually got torched by the sun in the summer of 2014. Like Icarus, I came crashing down to earth.

I had paid little heed to my body's yearnings for winter and rest, so I was forced to "pay back my winters."

I did this by taking [eight months off](#) from making YouTube videos during the fall and winter seasons of 2014 to 2015. During this time, I also stopped lifting weights and remained physically active by doing yoga every day.

Paying back my winters was one of the most challenging things I've ever done. But it was just what I needed to spring back to life again.

We have a tendency in these times to favor the catabolic seasons—spring and summer—of outward action and growth, at the expense of pushing back our falls and winters.

As a culture, we celebrate youth, vitality, and aliveness.

We dye our hair, get plastic surgery, and take Viagra to attempt to artificially keep summer going, when we should really be experiencing fall. In going hard all the time, we tend to miss out on the harvests that fall and winter have to offer.

Tell me: if we appreciate the oranges, reds, and yellows of the autumn leaves, and we admire the snowy winter landscapes that the colder seasons bring us—why, then, do we dishonor the beauty that arises in us, in the forms of grey hair and wrinkled skin? Or on a micro level, why repress the fatigue and "lack of productivity" that occur from time to time?

I say—love your gray hair and wrinkled skin, love your tiredness. They are beautiful in the same way that the autumn leaves are. Fall and winter—while not *apparently* productive—are in fact the times when trees send their roots deeper into the soil, regenerating for the spring to come.

Realize now that fall and winter are as contributive to our growth as spring and summer—death and life are inseparable; they support each other.

Through the experience of burning out and being forced to rest, I learned the hard way that if I deny or ignore the urgings of the heart and gut to move into the next season, life will meet me with tremendous resistance.

You must be wise enough to honor the spontaneous, subconscious promptings of your body. When you listen in this way, life will take you exactly where you need to be with very little friction. There are times for action, and there are times for rest.

Ask yourself, "Which season am I in?" Whatever season you find yourself in, embrace it and appreciate the unique gifts it has to offer.

Is it springtime? If so, enjoy it. Eat up all the nourishment you can get. Read, study, travel, and experience life. You are being shaped into the person that will soon get his or her chance to go out in the world.

Don't rush the process. Enjoy this time now in incubation—for it's a wonderful season of budding and coming into your own. Pushing a flower to prematurely bloom, or rushing a caterpillar out of its cocoon, will hinder its growth. Hold on for a moment. Experience the wonder of being nurtured.

Or perhaps it is time for summer.

In this case, go hard. Build, create, and repeat. This is the time for creating your legacy. Who are you becoming? Who are you serving? What kind of harvest will you leave behind?

There is a wonderful saying by 'Abdu'l-Bahá that I often share. That is: "Be generous in prosperity, and thankful in adversity." Summer is a time of abundance and prosperity, so take time to celebrate and enjoy the fruits of your labor. Take a vacation.

But make sure also to share what overflows from your cup with others, in whatever way you deem fit. When you are filled with light, it will burn you unless you give it away. Plus, the world could use a little more light.

So, the key with summer is to work hard, but not too hard; share your success with others. Pay attention to the signs that warn you to chill out, and know that the summer sun always dims at some point.

Soon enough, fall comes.

This is where many of us fall into trouble. We want to reap the benefits of planting and harvesting in summer, but are then shocked that we have been broken down.

Remember, summer is great, but the time for that has passed. Now it is fall. Let us not miss out on what this great season has to offer by trying to return to summer. It won't work.

In the fall, the focus is less on doing and more on allowing and reaping the benefits of what you sowed during the summer. It is time to attend to yourself and the people in your life—to give them care. Enjoy your **relationships.** The people around us are the greatest gifts life has to offer.

And soon, it may be time for winter.

This is the most challenging season for most people. "Why me?" we ask, as we enter the darkness. "Why am I depressed and tired?" "Why am I not as productive as I was before?" "Why am I old?"

We must remember, as 'Abdu'l-Bahá says, to be "thankful in adversity" and see the good in resting. Winter is a time to reflect and meditate on your life. Rest easy and recover, so that we may come to life again in spring.

It has been said before that the only constant in life is change.

These seasons will come and go many times throughout your life. Learn to dance with them. Embrace each changing of the seasons in stride. It is our duty to honor the seasons when they come, and to fully experience and appreciate what they have to offer us.

All of our pain and suffering come from trying to paddle upstream against the current of life. We suffer when we try to attach ourselves to a particular season, the person we were during that season, and the things we thought we had.

The truth of the matter is that you never really possess anything—everything in nature is constantly in flux. Life is found in yielding to the river—yielding to the seasons—and allowing the Universe to take you on the adventure that it wants you to have.

When we embrace every season of our lives fully, and stop resisting, we become more alive.

Section III
Energetic Strength

YOUR BODY IS YOUR BRAIN:
THE THREE BRAINS, ELECTROMAGNETIC HEART, & CHAKRA SYSTEM

MIND AND BODY

These days the health, fitness, and personal development industries seem to be buzzing about the *mind-body* connection, a belief that thoughts, feelings, and attitude can influence biological functions within the body.

Now people who are serious about reaching their highest potential take this mind-body connection very seriously—and for good reason. As we've discussed in the chapter on Core Values, strengthening both the mind and body are necessary for evolving ourselves. It makes sense, then, that strengthening the *connection* between the two is just as equally as important.

I've heard the various discussions on the mind-body *connection*. For the most part, I agree with them and find them very useful. However, there is one detail that I feel is being overlooked:

The mind and body are one!

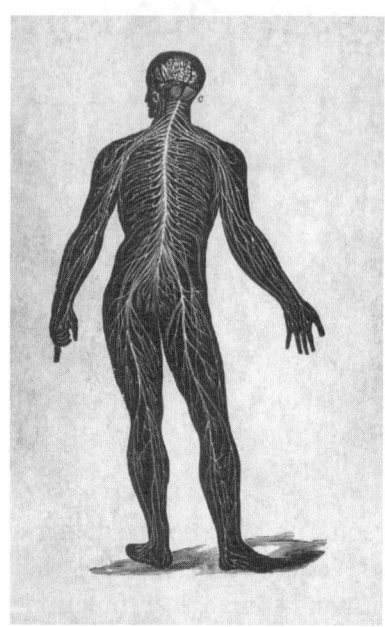

Let me explain what I mean. When we talk about a mind-body connection, it implies that the brain and the body are two separate entities that are somehow linked by a nebulous third party, a sort of "super-connector" that bridges the gap between the two.

Well, when I last checked, your brain and nervous system—from which thoughts and feelings emanate—were also physical parts of your body.

Imagine for a moment, if you will, your body's resembling a living flower. Your spinal cord serves as the stem, from which the root-like branches of your peripheral nervous system extend outward. At the very top of the stem sits your ever-blooming human brain, containing the petals of human consciousness.

Within this brain resides the "I," or what we often call the mind.

The mind doesn't just begin and stop at the head. It extends from your head all the way down to your toes, throughout your limbs, fingers, and every other portion of your body. Moreover, this "consciousness" communicates with itself. Whenever you feel pain or receive "information" from the external environment through your body, such as from touching a hot stove, that is its attempt at communication.

Our body is clearly affected by our thoughts. And vice versa. Yet in worshipping the petals, our conscious mind, we have forgotten the flower as a *whole*.

Visualize right now that you are holding a nice, succulent lemon in your hand.

Now imagine you cut it open and all the juices are running across your fingers. Next, imagine yourself biting into the lemon and feeling the lemon juices dribble down your chin as you eat it.

Did you start drooling just now? You see, just by having used our imagination and visualizing what we are familiar with—the taste of the lemon, in this case—we can trigger our salivary glands.

Conversely, just as we can stimulate our body by thinking we can stimulate our thoughts by adjusting our body.

To demonstrate what I mean, try carrying yourself with a sunken chest, a drooped neck, and a depressed look on your face for a day. You will likely feel like someone who is physically and psychologically depressed. Just like that, and without intending it, the chatter within your own mind will take on an unhappy tone.

Now if you do the opposite and walk around, while taking deep breaths, with an open chest, a wide smile, and bright eyes, you will feel energized and confident. Your thoughts themselves will become clearer, brighter, and more suitable for Becoming a Stronger Version of Yourself.

Truly, the body *is* the mind!

Your Three Brains

Right between your ears is the most sophisticated yet primitive piece of technology humankind has ever possessed: the human brain.

The brain can do miraculous things. It can: envision future realities, invent tools, communicate ideas through language and art, contemplate metaphysical ideas, and perform a host of other equally impressive tasks.

However, contrary to what most people will tell you, the "head brain" is not the only form of bodily intelligence to which we have access. In fact, there are three "brains."

You may have heard me speak before about the three intelligences within your body: **the Head, the Heart, and the Balls.** These are the terms I use to describe what certain scientists call your three "brains."

Dr. Paul D. MacLean, a neuroscientist and physician, wrote extensively about his **"triune brain"** theory. This model is a useful tool in helping us understand the different modes of consciousness that drive us.

Based upon his research on the brains of humans and other animals, MacLean asserted that the human brain was composed of three major neural centers that interact with one another, often competitively.

They are: **The reptilian complex,** which includes the brainstem, cerebellum, and basal ganglia; **the mammalian complex,** or the limbic system, which houses the amygdala, hypothalamus, hippocampus, and cingulate gyrus; and finally **the neomammalian complex,** or the neocortex.

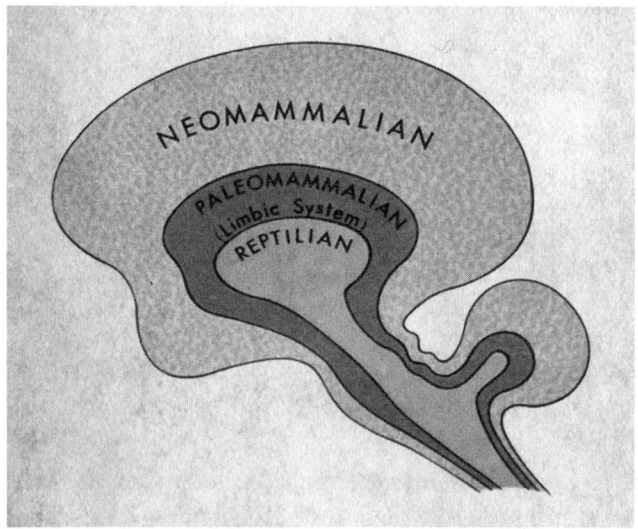

Triune Brain

According to MacLean, these three brains evolved on top of one another, throughout our evolution. The reptilian brain came first, then the mammalian brain, and finally, the neocortex.

He explained that, as reptiles evolved into mammals—and further yet, as simpler mammals evolved into humans—remnants of the earlier species' more primitive brain structures remained in the new species.

Each of these "brains" was responsible for a different mode of intelligence within the human animal. Each also had its own strengths and weaknesses.

To get a picture of how this triune brain was structured, *imagine that you had a one-room house that had been built underground.* You called this room: "I do."

In this underground "I do" studio, you could eat, sleep, exercise, go to the bathroom, fight, and have sex, but that was about it.

After a while, you got bored with just surviving and decided to add a couple of progressively more complex additions to your house, allowing you to do more things. The newer the addition, the more advanced its features.

You built the first addition—"I feel"—above the original room, still underground.

You wanted a space where you could socialize and experience a wider range of emotions. So you built a nice big room where you could hang out with friends and communicate with one another.

Soon enough, your curiosity grew, so you built yet another addition.

This room was built above ground and became a place for reading, writing, contemplating, and inventing new things. You kept all your gadgets—your computers, calculators, TVs, and video games—in this room. You called this room: "I think."

This whole strange house is analogous to MacLean's notion of how the human brain evolved.

Underground, or in your *subconscious,* comprises the first two stories of your intelligence, which are the reptilian and mammalian brains that house basic survival and emotional functions. Further aboveground is your neocortex, the brain that represents conscious, or higher thought.

In order to fully access the power of your brain, it is important to understand how each of these three brains functions and competes for your attention.

The reptilian brain—or what I refer to as the Balls—holds the power of ancestral wisdom and action.

The brainstem, cerebellum, and basal ganglia collectively form the reptilian brain and are associated with the most primal, rudimentary impulses that humans, other mammals, and reptiles all share.

You can think of this center of intelligence as your unconscious survival mechanism. It is responsible for regulating functions of the autonomic nervous system such as breathing, movement, heart rate, hunger, digestion, elimination, procreation, and the "fight or flight" response.

As a result of the reptilian brain's potential for destruction and indulgence, it is repressed by many cultures. After all, if we simply acted out of our lower consciousness, we would constantly fight, have sex, and defecate in public, so it would be hard to function socially.

This demonification of our reptilian nature has resulted in the castrated consciousness that most of us experience today, where our "head brain governs our actions and rules over our lower body.

On the other hand, I feel strongly that our inner reptile is not something to be denied nor repressed. In fact, the reptile brain is quite resourceful; its dark side only emerges when we repress it or act in a way that is unbalanced.

When accessed properly—in communication with the other two brains—the reptilian brain provides us with tremendous creative energy, animal-like intuition, and the ability to act quickly and instinctively. Your power for action comes from this primal instinct.

This is analogous to the "Jedi Force" that Obi-Wan and Yoda teach Luke how to harness in *Star Wars*. Use the Force, and "beware the Dark Side," they tell him.

The second room of your "brain house"—the "I feel"—is your mammalian cortex, or limbic brain. I refer to this center of wisdom as the Heart because it is the seat of emotion, memory, and social functioning.

To better understand how your mammalian brain functions, consider a dog.

A dog feels emotions like love, loyalty, anger, happiness, assertiveness, pride, and submission—emotions that are unavailable to an alligator, for instance, who operates only from the reptilian brain.

Dogs experience the reptilian drives of hunger, procreation, and basic survival mechanisms, but their capacity to care for their young and function socially distinguishes them and other mammals from lower-functioning reptiles.

The mammalian brain is the seat of spontaneity, emotion, and relations to others. "Following your heart," being in touch with your feelings, and developing an ability to be authentic and connect with others are all positive functions associated with this brain.

There is also a darker side to the Heart.

Spending too much time listening to the heart brain, at the expense of the others, turns a person into a soft, ungrounded pushover.

Tugged in every which way by his emotions and feelings of obligation to others, the man who is dominated by his mammalian instinct becomes ungrounded, losing the ability to take decisive action and think more objectively.

Thinking is a function the top floor of your "brain house": the neocortex, or what I call the Head.

Your neo-mammalian brain is a thick layer of tissue that encases the first two brains. It governs language, reason, calculation, rational thought, and all of the higher brain functions associated with thinking. The neocortex is the brain with which we are consciously most familiar.

Your head brain enables you to be self-conscious and aspire for more in life. This is your *thinking* mind.

When accessed properly, in conjunction with the lower two brains, a person can use this supercomputer to examine his life more objectively, setting goals and determining how best to use the power his body affords him.

But in the same way that we are tempted to remain in the other two rooms, we often spend too much time in the "I think" room.

Someone who is "stuck in their head" has trouble taking action.

Ungrounded in his convictions and out of touch with his feelings, a heady intellectual who chronically inhabits his head brain becomes an easy target for manipulation. He is led astray from his own inner convictions by those who are more grounded in their own convictions.

Like a tree without roots, this person is easy to topple over.

Most of us are way up in our Heads, and it is time we regained our body consciousness—the passion of our Hearts and the instinct of our Balls.

But in doing so, let's not forget the beauty of the head brain, the part of us that is responsible for all of culture: art, music, literature, knowledge, and the aspiration to Grow Stronger.

The flower of human consciousness becomes strongest when the roots, the stem, and the petals are all honored and accessed.

THE BRAIN IN YOUR GUT

Dr. Michael D. Gershon, a professor of Pathology and Cell Biology at Columbia University, has documented his findings on what he calls the second brain, or the brain in your gut, in his book called The Second Brain.

Throughout your gastrointestinal tract exists an extensive network of neurons called the enteric nervous system (ENS). The ENS contains the second largest concentration of neurons in the human body, behind only the brain in your skull.

Your "gut brain" has the ability to operate autonomously, or independently of your brain and spinal cord. In other words, your gut has an intelligence of its own, and it communicates with the head brain by sending what you might be familiar with as "gut feelings."

The enteric nervous system does more than run your digestion. It is also partially responsible for your emotional and mental state. Little known fact: your gut stores large amounts of two key neurotransmitters, dopamine and serotonin. Dopamine is associated with the regulation of impulse, movement, pleasure, reward, and motivation. Serotonin is responsible for feelings of happiness, as well as healthy sleep and appetite.

About 50 percent of the body's dopamine and 90 percent of the body's serotonin can be found in your gut!

Ancient systems of healing, such as Ayurveda and Chinese medicine, have always understood that a healthy gut is a healthy mind. What you eat has a direct impact on the levels of neurotransmitters that dictate moods like happiness, depression, discipline, and indulgence.

Imagine, then, what eating an unhealthy diet and taking large doses of antibiotics without a rigorous course of probiotics could do to *both* brains.

The body—just like the earth—is one system; what we do to one part of it will naturally affect the whole.

THE ELECTROMAGNETIC HEART

Religions have regarded the Heart as a sacred source of wisdom for thousands of years.

Science, on the other hand, has placed the Head on a pedestal, at least until now.

Founded in 1991, the HeartMath Institute studies the interactions between the human heart and the head brain, using a standard, scientific approach. They are making incredible headway in scientifically validating what religions have long understood.

Among their [findings](), HeartMath researchers have confirmed the existence of the heart's electromagnetic force field, using EEG, or electroencephalogram. This electromagnetic force field *permeates throughout every one of our cells and projects outward several feet from the body*, in all directions.

By contrast, the brain between our ears emits a much smaller—about 50 times that of the heart—electromagnetic field.

According to HeartMath scientists, this electromagnetic field of the heart changes frequency depending upon your emotional state. The energetic state of this "feeling force field," in turn, influences the feelings and thoughts of yourself and the people around you.

This sounds an awful lot like the Eastern concept of the "aura."

HeartMath has discovered that any emotion you experience significantly alters your heart rhythm, which is the regularity of your heartbeat over time.

Negative emotions like anger and frustration produce irregular heart rhythms, triggering a process called cortical inhibition, *which hinders our ability to think straight by partially cutting off higher brain function.*

This explains the phenomenon of people making poor decisions in the heat of their emotions and then saying something like, "I am sorry. My emotions got the best of me."

Positive emotions like gratitude, on the other hand, generate regular, healthy heart rhythms. The heart rhythms induced by positive emotions strengthen our immune system, and actually *activate our higher perception abilities within the brain through a process called cortical facilitation.*

This means that experiencing loving intentions and emotions in the heart enables us to think and make decisions more clearly.

Incredibly, your heart communicates with your head and the rest of the body, influencing your thinking and your health. This is science!

As I alluded to earlier, your heart also affects the people around you.

When you stand within a few feet of someone, the electromagnetic fields of your hearts interact, and depending upon each of your states, they either synchronize or clash.

If you and another person feel like you are "vibing," or are on the same page, it indicates that your heart fields are operating on harmonious electromagnetic wavelengths. If you are not on the same page—like if you are arguing, for example—that means that your magnetic fields are currently out of sync.

Another way of explaining this concept is to say that if you feel negative emotions such as hatred, fear, and envy, then the spectrum of electromagnetic energy that is projected through your heart field will be received as a dissonant, or unpleasant, vibration by someone who is operating on a more resourceful frequency. In social terms, you won't get along, and you'll get "bad vibes."

However, if you harbor in your heart positive emotions such as love, compassion, courage, and gratitude, people within close proximity to you—including yourself—will experience "good vibrations," or energetic harmony.

Generally speaking, the more powerful your electromagnetic field is, the more you will influence your environment and the people around you.

HeartMath has demonstrated that if a highly distressed individual is placed in the presence of someone who is grounded and in a state of calm, the electromagnetic field of the grounded person will overpower the anxious person's state, causing the anxious person's heart field to sync up to a frequency associated with calmness.

This says that, within your chest, you possess an almost magical tool that can change the way you and the people around you feel and think—almost at the flip of a switch!

I realize what I am saying may sound "woo woo," or even a bit crazy, but I am simply sharing with you the amazing science that a group of researchers has confirmed, and which humankind has long known intuitively.

More or less, HeartMath's research is confirming the scientific validity of the Law of Attraction, which states that you become what you surround yourself with, and you attract whatever is operating on the same frequency as you are.

Theoretically, this applies to your entire environment.

If you consider—in conjunction with the findings of the HeartMath Institute—the world of quantum physics and the idea that all of matter is really just subatomic vortices of energy vibrating at particular frequencies, then it is not all that big of a leap to presume that our electromagnetic fields interact not just with the people around us, but with everything.

Just from our experience, this makes intuitive sense.

I am sure that you have felt energetic connections to certain people, environments, animals, genres of music, and even ideas.

My theory, which science is beginning to confirm, is that we are shaped at the electromagnetic and cellular levels by internal and external environments that are interconnected.

It is time we pay more attention to the subtle intelligence of our hearts, for they can sense energetic harmony and discord in our environments before our brains even have a chance to attribute meaning to any of it.

Nerve Plexuses and The Chakras

So far, we've been exploring the concept that the body is the mind from a Western, *scientific* perspective.

In this section, I will consider consciousness through the *Eastern* framework of the chakra system, which emerged thousands of years ago among the yogis of India.

I realize not everyone is comfortable with exploring ideas about the mind and the body from a non-scientific perspective, and that is fine. You can skip this chapter if you'd like.

It is my belief that all of our modes of explanation and understanding —be they scientific or religious; true or false—are imperfect. Where science shows, metaphor points. This is why I use both methods to communicate ideas.

That being said, here is my condensed overview of the chakra system.

For further reference, I invite you to read Anodea Judith's Wheels of Life, which is a great introductory book on the subject and the source I used in my research. You can also check out the video series I made called "The Truth About Building Strength," in which I discussed these ideas visually.

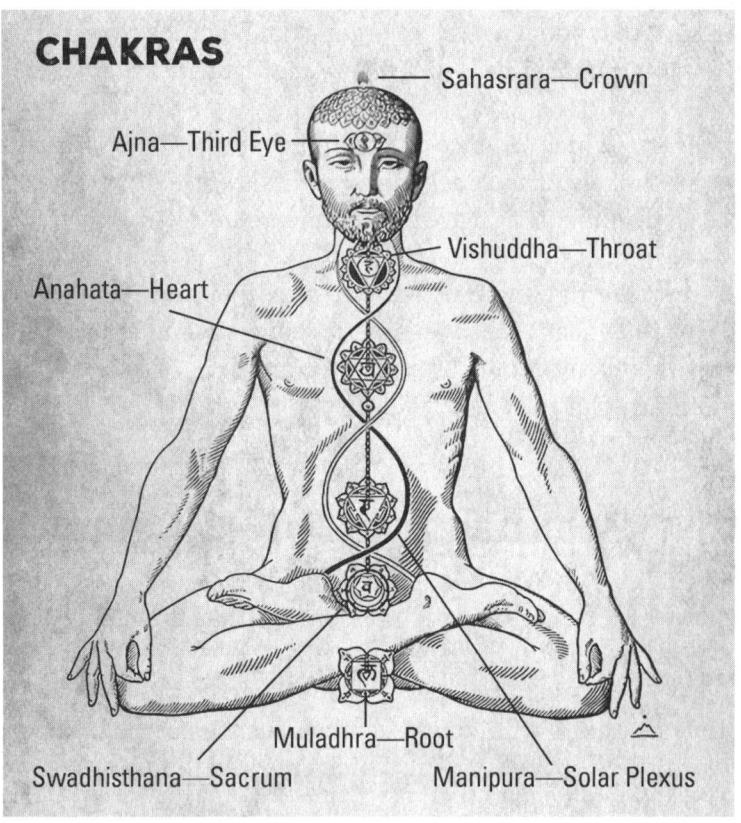

Source: madfuture.com

Yogis believe that a subtle, vital energy moves through our bodies, giving us strength and life. In India, this force is called *prana*. In China, it is called Qi, or chi.

This force goes by many different names in other cultures across the world, but for the sake of simplicity, I will call it "bioenergy."

Remember that energy, in and of itself, is neither good nor bad. How energy manifests in the world depends upon the frequency at which it vibrates.

With regard to bioenergy, the way it manifests depends upon where and how it is processed.

Just as the light of a rainbow appears to us as seven different colors (or seven different wavelengths), we experience various "spectrums" of bioenergy on account of its being processed through several different chakras.

Our strength is determined by how well we cultivate, access, and direct this bioenergy, or life force. The more plentiful and freer it is to flow through our body, the more powerful we become.

Cultivating life force is simply a matter of doing all of the practices I have shared with you so far in this book: eating well, drinking clean water, exercising, sleeping, spending time outdoors, etc.

Resourcefully channeling bioenergy, on the other hand, is directing it consciously to attract the thoughts, actions, and realities that we desire. But first, it necessitates an understanding of the chakras and how to balance them.

Stick with me here, as I delve into a topic that has often been misunderstood.

Traditionally, there are seven "chakras" that run from the base of your spine to the top of your head, and they are spread out fairly evenly.

Chakras are the energetic "antennae" of the body.

They are energetic processing centers, or gears, through which energy—from both your outer and inner environments—flows, exchanges, and likewise generates various forms of thought and action. The types of thoughts and actions a person produces depend on how each chakra is being accessed.

It is important to remember that the chakras are not one-way doors; they both *receive and transmit energy*. So, just as they serve as vehicles for manifesting outwardly, they also process your environment and affect you internally.

Here's what's really fascinating.

There are seven major nerve ganglia in the body that branch off of the spinal cord. Nerve ganglia are highly concentrated masses of nerve tissue in the peripheral nervous system that essentially function like mini-brains.

Sound familiar?

According to Anodea Judith, in her book Wheels of Life, **these seven major nerve ganglia in your body correspond to the seven major chakras.**

In order from bottom to top, the first through seventh chakras correlate with the following nerve ganglia: the coccygeal plexus, sacral plexus, celiac (solar) plexus, pulmonary and cardiac plexuses, pharyngeal plexus, carotid plexus, and the cerebral cortex.

(Notably, the chakras are also connected to the major endocrine glands in the body.)

You might say that the "head brain," the "heart brain," and the "gut brain" are just three of the seven major brains of the body, each having its own unique ways of processing and affecting our thoughts, actions, and environments.

For whatever reason, this amazing link often gets overlooked.

Those who do make the connection usually say that these nerve ganglia may be related to, but are not synonymous with, the chakras, and that the chakras themselves exist in an immaterial soul, often called the "subtle body," that overlaps with our physical bodies.

This is one interpretation. If it speaks to you, then I encourage you to proceed from that frame of mind.

But for those of you who are understandably skeptical of the existence of a soul or subtle body that only certain people claim to see, I still want to encourage you to receive the benefits of this metaphor of the chakras, saving the baby from the bathwater.

Consider, for a moment, the concept of the chakra-nervous system link in conjunction with what has already been said in this chapter. Remember, the body and the mind are one.

If there are seven major clusters of nerve ganglia (essentially "mini brains") that are connected to the CNS and head brain—is it that much of a leap to believe these centers in the body could be responsible for producing certain physiological, neuromuscular, and energetic states?

I invite you to adopt whatever perspective suits you—be it scientific, new age, or religious—because the concept of the chakra system is a powerful tool for self-discovery, even if it simply serves as a metaphor for the various modes of consciousness we humans experience.

If it helps, go forward with the mindset that these chakras and the seven nerve ganglia are *one and the same.*

THE CHAKRA SYSTEM

This understanding of the chakra-nerve ganglion connection will make the rest of this discussion on the chakras all the more lucid.

The goal is really to balance these energetic centers in a way that promotes energetic harmony throughout the body.

Like any electrical system, a chakra can be overcharged or undercharged.

If a chakra is charged too much or too little, unbalanced health will prevail in the corresponding aspects of body, mind, and character.

However, if a chakra is open and free, allowing the energy of the body to move powerfully through it, then balanced strength will naturally manifest.

The key is to get each chakra vibrating at an open, strong, harmonious, and balanced frequency.

In the next chapters, I will point you to various methods for balancing energetic activity.

For now, I want you to understand how each chakra functions, and what it looks like in balanced, undercharged, and overcharged states. This way, it will be easier for you to determine which exercises you may want to implement in order to achieve balance.

The first chakra, linked to the coccygeal plexus, is located at the base of the spine—around your tailbone, or coccyx—in the pelvic floor. Physiologically, this area is related to your perineum and adrenals. Neuromuscularly, the first chakra is associated with your "fight or flight" response.

Think about the first chakra as being linked predominantly with "earth" energy.

In a balanced state, this is your energetic center for grounded stability, instinct, and satisfaction. It is your "root system" for survival, and is really the foundation for all of your growth.

If you are tight, repressed, and undercharged in this area of the body, you will likely experience a sense of insecurity and generally have an overactive "flight" response. People who have an underactive first chakra are often those who have difficulty standing their ground and being rooted in their identity.

On the other end of the spectrum, an overactivated and loose first chakra manifests outwardly as an overly indulgent and lazy lifestyle. This person is too rooted, having little desire to aspire upward, get out, and do.

The second chakra, associated with the sacral plexus, is located in the sacrum, just above the coccygeal plexus. The sacral plexus is connected to your sex organs, sexual function, and reproduction.

It goes without saying that the second chakra is associated with water, libidinal flow, and creativity, all within a balanced state. At its core, the sacral plexus is your center for generativity and sensuality.

When the second chakra is underactivated, which is common in many cultures due to the repression of sexuality, a person could experience anything from low energy and sexual dysfunction to feelings of guilt and shame, particularly with regard to sex and relationships.

An overactivated sacral chakra is exhibited in a person who is supercharged with sexual energy. This person has a surplus of libido and does not know what to do with it.

He or she will appear scattered and ungrounded, jumping from relationship to relationship or job to job, without ever feeling the deep sensuality and satisfaction that a balanced sense of sexuality can provide.

The third chakra is related to the celiac (solar) plexus.

Also known as the "fire chakra," the third chakra is located in your upper abdomen and is connected to the "gut brain," the pancreas, and digestive function.

This is your power chakra, wherein the virtues of will, discipline, and self-worth are all housed.

In a balanced state, this chakra can provide a person with incredible amounts of determination and commitment. A powerful third chakra leads to lots of action and intuitive decisiveness.

When undercharged, however, the third chakra leads to weak willpower and inaction. Someone with an underpowered power chakra may research, read, and talk, but at the end of the day accomplishes nothing.

On the other hand, a person who is too charged with fire will likely burn out himself and the people around him.

The typical workaholic who strives to accomplish more and more may forget who he is and what is important to him. In an excessively charged state, this person ends up becoming neurotically power-hungry and aggressive.

Halfway between the first and seventh chakras lies *the fourth chakra,* the Heart Center.

This chakra is connected to the cardiac and pulmonary plexuses that located in the center of your chest, surrounding your heart and thymus. This is thought to be our center for compassion, related to the element of air.

With proper balance, this center gives us the ability to love and connect deeply with others, and also to devote ourselves to a cause.

Many religions speak of this region of the body as being our spiritual center, where the wisdom of the Head and the primal instinct of the Balls come together to form an energetic center of compassion that becomes both rooted and aspiring.

When one is closed off to this area, he or she will feel separated from others, resulting in a dull, cold personality and feelings of loneliness.

While finding time for solitude and journeying with purpose are important, we need to remember that journeying alone forever is *rarely* as fulfilling as journeying with others. We are social creatures, after all, so even the most stoic and hardened among us become all the more empowered by loving friendships and relationships.

If one is overcharged in the Heart, he or she becomes attached to people, things, and outcomes. No longer is love given freely and unconditionally without expectations. Now, one grows greedy for the return of affection, which can result in pain and sadness when things don't work out.

Moving on to *the fifth chakra*, it is located at the throat and the thyroid, and linked with the pharyngeal plexus and the element of sound.

Self-expression and communication are the major functions of this energetic center.

When a person is balanced in this area, he or she is a master communicator. This person draws from the passion of his heart and the insight of his mind to share his ideas and feelings in an expressive and lucid manner.

If this center is undercharged, the individual may not be very talkative, and may have trouble communicating with others. Perhaps he or she will blush or stutter in certain social situations. As a result, this person may develop resentment for feeling like his voice is not being heard.

An overactive throat chakra manifests as someone who can't stop talking.

This person dominates conversations, often interrupting and talking over people. It is very difficult for someone who has a supercharged throat chakra to listen to others.

The sixth chakra—also called the third eye—is located in the center of the forehead, right above the eyebrows. This center is associated with the carotid plexus and the pineal gland, as well as the element of light.

Clear insight, focused vision, and keen awareness are positive functions of this chakra, as long as it is accessed in a resourceful and balanced manner.

But when the third eye is closed and undercharged, a lack of awareness or blindness—the so-called "drunkenness" of illusion—prevails.

If overstimulated, the sixth chakra sends someone into imagination overdrive. This person becomes lost in the realm of thoughts and dreams, and loses his or her ability to remain grounded in reality.

Finally, the seventh chakra, or the crown chakra, is situated at the top of the head and accordingly associated with the element of thought.

This center involves the pituitary gland, which is the "king" of the endocrine system, governing its overall function. Also involved with the crown chakra is the cerebral cortex, which again rules over the rest of your brain and nervous system.

The crown chakra, when balanced, provides one with wisdom, order, understanding, clarity of one's life's mission, and transcendence. Your spiritual potentiality rests in this center.

Now consider what kings and queens do. Seated upon their thrones of deep wisdom, compassion, instinct, and power—in other words, the functions of the lower chakras—they empower their kingdoms, instilling in them order and generativity. This is healthy crown function.

An undercharged crown chakra will result in an uncentered and disorganized person. This individual does not know his purpose, and his life, as a result, becomes disordered.

An overcharged crown chakra will result in a very controlling, narcissistic, and tyrannical person. As if imprisoning the body, the unrooted mind restricts consciousness in all of the other energetic centers.

No matter how well the other chakras function, if a man's crown is dysfunctional, he will find it difficult to access the Strongest Version of Himself. The same can be said for any of the chakras.

It is important to observe yourself and become attuned to your inner bodily sensations.

Where are you tight? Where are you lax? In what ways is each chakra functioning in your life?

An excellent way to intuitively determine where you need more charge and where you could use a bit less is to ask yourself, "What character traits do I admire, and which ones do I detest?"

For instance, someone who admires a figure like the Rock likely seeks to charge the third, or power, chakra, though he may not be able to put this into words.

This person goes to the gym to build physical strength and muscle, but what he truly seeks is more energetic power.

How The Body Stores Trauma

So, back to the question I posed at the beginning of this chapter—why do we experience the mind and body as separate entities? And more importantly, how do we reunite what is already one?

First, let us tie together what we have already discussed.

Whether it is the ancient system of the chakras or modern neurology and psychology, there is a common theme when describing human consciousness.

We are bioelectric beings—living flowers of vast consciousness—whose intelligence resides as much in our roots as it does in our petals.

Whether we imagine our consciousness as residing in three brains, seven chakras, or both does not really matter. I use the Head, Heart, and Balls trinity to speak to all of these ideas.

The main point is that we have energetic centers within us that are responsible for animalistic drives, human drives, and angelic, God-like drives. And the key is to balance and integrate them.

I would like to return now to the metaphor of the human brain as a flower of consciousness.

As I alluded to earlier, the brain's strength and its ability to bloom depend upon how well-nourished its stem and roots—your nervous system—are by the soil of your physiology and the sunlight of your perspective.

We've already discussed ways of cultivating good "soil" in the chapters on physiological strength. And in the final section on Life Mastery, you will discover ways to shine some sunlight on yourself by adopting self-empowering perspectives.

I am sure many of you are already taking steps to develop physiological and mental health.

But there is one other key component to healthy growth whose importance often goes unrecognized: your roots must be able to *expand* freely.

If I had to take one issue within this sunlight + water + nourishing soil + root expansion equation for energetic blooming, that would be the suppression of body consciousness. I believe this one aspect to be responsible for stunting the development of fellow journeyers.

Anyone who has lived in modern society for a significant amount of time, which I imagine applies to most of us, has been energetically suppressed.

To speak in metaphorical terms: upon birth, we are placed into tiny flower pots that symbolize societal constrictions and rules, and ultimately prevent our roots from expanding as they naturally would, outside of civilization.

As we grow up, we are taught that some behaviors are "good" and others are "bad".

Unintentionally and intentionally, parents, teachers, and religious and cultural authorities teach us that we *should* do the "good" things and *should not* do the "bad" things.

We learn that throwing temper tantrums is bad.

Same with speaking up in class before it is our turn, touching our private parts and laughing when it is not "appropriate", crying when it isn't "cool", or showing pride when we accomplish something.

In effect, we are taught that to be human is bad. So we learn to suppress our wildness.

From very early on, we are trained to stifle our emotions—to restrict our roots. The cage is placed before us, and we—unaware that our consciousness is being damaged—obey and step inside. The girth is cinched.

Those children who rebel against the very rules that have been imposed upon them are met with punishment and disapproval, until they learn to submit. Wise children are labeled "class clowns" and "screw-ups".

"Stop doing that," they say, "It's not right."

Soon enough, even the wildest among the rebels becomes tamed.

Most likely, he or she is labeled with a disorder like ADHD, as I was. In a society that is caged and sick, being wild, vital, and free is diagnosed as a disease—something to tame and medicate.

There is no sense in blaming ourselves or others for this.

As children, questioning authorities and the subjective nature of morality was not something we were able to do. After all, we depended upon these very people for our survival, so we were forced to obey.

And the "oppressors" didn't know any better either. They were only trying to protect us.

The fact of the matter is that we accepted the cage and learned to restrain our natural impulses. We "sat down and shut up", and as a result, became nice, well-behaved, and rigid.

As we got older, all of this input from authority figures and our environment eventually became internalized.

We became the prison guards and the zookeepers, if you will. We began regulating our behavior on our own, making sure not to be rude, obnoxious, inappropriate, loud, embodied, and expressive.

Conditioned and contained by society, we unconsciously castrated our own consciousness, which, in turn, triggered the perceived mind-body separation that most of us experience today.

Many years later, many of us stand crippled and tense, like wildflowers who have rejected our roots. No longer identifying with the body, the "I" of our consciousness has become imprisoned by a head brain that rules over our lower portions, and keeps us rigid and not fully present.

Caging an organism as wild and expansive as the human animal is bound to have consequences.

Alexander Lowen, the western pioneer who popularized bioenergetics in the

Alexander Lowen

West, proposed that chronic suppression of emotions leads to the development of "muscular armoring," or *neurotic holding patterns.*

These "holding patterns" are habituated, faulty neuromuscular movement patterns that are brought on by energetic inhibition. I touched on this briefly back when I'd first introduced the Core Values, but now I can fully delve into it.

They significantly restrict our movement and sensation in certain areas of the body, cutting us off from the wellspring of vitality and richness that are available only to a person who inhabits and embodies his full self.

Most often, muscular holding patterns develop during childhood.

When we are young and experience a desire to act in a way that has been labeled "bad," our head brain initiates an inhibitory neuromuscular response, in order to hold us back from behaving badly.

For example, aggression is an emotion that is suppressed in most cultures.

A child who wants to fit into society will restrain his aggression by clenching his jaw, neck, shoulders, and even fists. These are all natural bodily responses associated with feelings of aggression.

If a child makes a habit of repressing these natural movements every time he experiences feelings of aggression, he will eventually develop muscular rigidity in the areas surrounding the jaw, neck, and shoulders, among others. This is an example of a neurotic holding pattern.

The same process can happen with any emotion that is suppressed.

If a child is bullied, he may look down and round his shoulders, which is a natural protection mechanism.

The brain that learns to submit to fear in this way, over time, evolves into a body that literally bows before life in submission. This person is unable to stand tall and erect, and he approaches life in the same way, bending to others' needs before his own.

To give another example, a person who repeatedly suppresses "inappropriate" feelings of joy—including laughter, smiling, sensuality, and the urge to sing and dance—may habituate neurotic holding patterns of nervous fidgeting, biting the tongue, and tightening the belly and hips.

Forty years later, this muscular armor may manifest as nervous ticks, stutters, tight hips, and a mediocre sex life.

Regardless of how they manifest in our lives, we all have neurotic holding patterns, which can affect the way we are and how we approach life.

Just to give you a visceral example of how your physical posture affects your character, I invite you to try the following exercise.

Try right now to sit completely slouched with your head bent down, your shoulders rounded forward, and your chest collapsed into your belly for one minute, and notice how you feel.

Let your head get heavy and your features droop.

Now, shake everything out for a few seconds and then get out of your chair and stand tall.

Spread your legs and arms wide, reach your spine to the ceiling, and keep your chest and head held high in a heroic, power pose. Smile a big proud smile, and hold that for one minute.

I am sure that, like everyone who experiences that exercise, you felt a remarkable change in your mental state when you changed your physical state.

So, imagine what years of neurotic physical posture could do to a person's character.

The body is the brain.

In terms of muscular armouring, the structure of a person's body reveals the state of his or her character. In general, the ways a person stands, walks, communicates, and expresses himself say a lot about who he is.

The most common areas of muscular tension I notice in my clients are the muscles along the front side of the body, including the face, jaw, neck, shoulders, chest, belly, hips, and pelvic floor.

This is because the neuromuscular holding patterns related to the emotions we often suppress—anger, fear, aggression, and sexuality—tend to involve the body's closing up and hunching over, which then shortens and tightens the normally supple and relaxed muscles across the face, chest, belly, and hips.

It does not help that sitting is a predominant activity within our culture. Unfortunately, sitting too often promotes a rounded back, stooped shoulders, and tight hips.

When the musculature along the front side of our bodies is tightened, it significantly reduces our ability to breathe deeply. I will get to this in a moment.

But for now, I invite you to examine yourself.

What would someone infer about your character just from looking at you?

What might that person learn about who you are and where you suppress emotion by watching you walk, play sports, dance, and socialize? Where are you tight? Where are you repressed? And how is this affecting who you are and how you approach life?

By learning to identify the neuromuscular patterns your body exhibits, you obtain a direct window into your character.

The great thing about this is that you do not need to remember a thing that has happened to you in order to make changes, because the problem is tangible; it is in your muscles.

It may be uncomfortable to admit to ourselves that we are damaged and weak in this way. But part of growing stronger is making peace with the shadow of our woundedness.

It is not vulnerability or fear that makes a person wounded and weak, but rather the muscular and emotional defenses he or she builds up so as to avoid experiencing life in all its pain and pleasure.

The strong man or woman accepts his or her injury, seeks to understand it, and moves forward to remedy it.

So how do we liberate ourselves from this muscular armor? How do we bust out of our tiny flower pot and access our full strength and vitality?

It may not surprise you that the answer to this question is found in our roots—way down the trunk of the evolutionary tree.

Dr. Peter Levine is a body-based psychotherapist and founder of the Somatic Experiencing® Trauma Institute. For several decades, he has been helping clients release neuromuscular armoring and emotional blockages through his Somatic Experiencing® approach.

In his book, In An Unspoken Voice: How the Body Releases Trauma and Restores Goodness, Levine shares a story about a very interesting phenomenon that he noticed when studying animals after they underwent stressful experiences.

Essentially, there are three responses an animal can have when under attack: fight, flight, or freeze.

Fighting and fleeing are two responses that immediately discharge the energy of the body and allow the animal to experience the emotions that are flooding its system.

Freezing, on the other hand, involves an *inhibitory* neuromuscular response. The emotions are temporarily restrained in order to allow the animal to be still, or to play dead, and to avoid being attacked by a predator.

Children experience this same freeze response when they suppress their emotions.

To a child, an angry, scolding authority figure is no different from an angry lion is to a gazelle: it is a predator that could hurt him. So, the child unconsciously executes a freeze response as a means of protection.

The difference between humans and other animals is that when an animal executes the freeze response, it actually *shakes* and *discharges* the energy afterwards, because it has no rational mind to reprimand itself for wild and irrational behavior.

Unfortunately, our primal instincts are repressed, and so by the time we are adults most of us have habituated *not* discharging the energy after we experience an incident during which we freeze and suppress ourselves.

We freeze, and then go about our lives as if nothing ever happened.

From childhood to adulthood, we hold back tears, yelling, stomping, laughing, sobbing, dancing, and a host of other expressions of our vitality, because it is not deemed appropriate at the time. And then we forget all about it.

Little do we know that all of this energy is still inside us, waiting to be released.

I think it's time we give ourselves permission to feel and be wild again—to expand our consciousness from the safe harbor of our heads and return to the great depths of our being.

We need to open the floodgates, break down the dams, and allow the power of our vitality to come rushing through us.

Let us shake, vibrate, sob, tap, tremble, laugh, breathe, and yell ourselves out of the cage!

BIOENERGETIC BREATHING:
THE BOW, BIOENERGETIC STOOL, & OPEN FRONT BREATHING

BIOENERGETIC BREATHING

When our bodies are rigid—particularly the front of the body—our breathing becomes restricted. And when our breathing is restricted, *everything about us* is restricted.

Breath is life, and I mean that literally.

We can go weeks without eating and days without drinking water, but we can't go without breathing for more than a few minutes.

Imagine what a person misses out on if he or she is not fully accessing the most primary form of nourishment that is available to animals: breath. We spend a lot of time worrying about how we eat and how we drink, but rarely do most of us consider how fully we breathe and what we breathe.

Yes, we do breathe oxygen, which also stimulates the electricity of our body.

But if our body is rigid and unable to expand to take deep breaths, then our ability to bring in the life force that enables us to express all that we have to offer is limited. Strength and breath are intrinsically linked together.

Take a moment now to observe your breathing.

Likely, you are like most of us and have not yet corrected the faulty breathing patterns that have developed from years of muscular armoring. You will notice that you tend to clench your stomach and pelvic floor as you breathe. Most of the expansion happens within your chest, and the breathing is somewhat fast and shallow.

Natural, deep breathing, on the other hand, is slow and steady, and it causes the belly to rise. The breath *expands* everything, including the belly, chest, and pelvic floor muscles.

A person who breathes deeply and powerfully in this way naturally develops a character that is as expansive as his or her breath.

The place to begin chipping away at the flower pot of neurotic holding patterns—and breaking free from the cage—is located on the musculature along the front side of the body. We will open this up to allow for more expansive breath.

The Bow

The Bow is the most effective exercise I have found for opening up the body and retraining proper breathing.

It was popularized in the 20th century by Alexander Lowen, the founding father of Bioenergetic Analysis. But it has been around for much longer than that; yogis and many other martial artists have been practicing variations of the Bow for thousands of years.

THE BOW, BIOENERGETIC STOOL, & OPEN FRONT BREATHING

The Bow targets those "vulnerable" soft areas that we long ago learned to tense up and armor in order to "protect" ourselves and others from our vitality.

Specifically, these are the muscles of the face, eyes, mouth, jaw, neck, chest, abdomen, hips, and pelvic basin.

Once you implement the Bow as a daily practice, it won't take long for you to feel these areas opening up again. Along with deeper breathing, you'll notice that your voice becomes fuller, your presence more grounded, and you will be less easily swayed by people and events.

Begin by standing with your feet no wider than shoulder width apart and with your knees slightly bent and relaxed. I recommend you do this without wearing any shoes or socks.

Take some time to orient yourself. Relax your shoulders, relax your face and jaw, and just breathe for a moment.

Now, pressing your fists firmly into your lower back and pinching your elbows in, I want you to lean back, *open your mouth and eyes as wide as possible,* and breathe. Feel the stretch across your entire body.

Continue to breathe deeply in this position, keeping your mouth wide open, for twenty slow breaths.

This exercise will feel uncomfortable the first few times you try it. If it is painful, then stop doing it.

If you experience mild discomfort in your back when performing the Bow, try to focus on expanding and stretching your lower abdomen, rather than attempt to lean back as far as possible, pushing your pelvis forward. This tends to take some of the load off of your back.

As long as your discomfort is not painful, keep breathing into the tight areas.

You may find that your body begins to shake and vibrate subtly.

These are good signs that indicate your body is opening back up and stored energy is being released. Stay with it, allowing yourself to *relax and let go into* the vibration and breathing deeply through the discomfort.

If you are really restricted, especially in the face and neck, those body parts may grow red with tension. You may even begin to cough and feel like you are choking.

If this is the case, a helpful, albeit uncomfortable, exercise you can use to break up the tension in your neck and throat is to stick your fingers down the back of your throat and force yourself to gag. Of course, make sure you have gone a couple hours without eating before trying this!

Over time, doing this will cause the muscular armor in your throat to relax and soften, opening up your breathing passages.

You may also want to yell, massaging your jaw and neck muscles as you do so. This also breaks up tension in this area of the body. You can watch me coach someone through these more advanced techniques in various videos on my Youtube channel.

Remember, the main focus here is to bring your breath DOWN, down to the region between your anus and your gonads—to the sex center.

When you perform the Bow correctly, you will feel everything, from your eyes to your belly and all the way down to your perineum, expanding with every breath.

This is what I mean when I often say you've got to "breathe into your BALLS," even though I realize that your lungs don't actually go down to your balls!

What I mean is that when you breathe completely, with your lungs and diaphragm expanding to their full capacities, you activate a cascading effect whereby your diaphragm pushes down on your organs, causing your abdominal and pelvic areas to expand.

As you progress with the Bow, you can experiment with different hand placements.

Hands behind the hips will help open up your hips more; hands clasped behind your head will place more of a stretch on your chest; and hands in the air and behind your head will increase the overall intensity of the exercise.

Depending on where you want to release tension, you can choose the hand placement that is most sufficient for your needs.

A note on mouth breathing: Most mind-body exercise traditions teach students to breathe through the nose, with a closed mouth. The reason we use an open-mouth approach when practicing the Bow is that it places a greater stretch on the tense musculature within the face, neck, and jaw. Breathing with mouth and eyes wide open reduces the facial tensions that promote shallow breathing.

Using the Bioenergetic Stool

The "Bioenergetic Stool" is a great addition to your bioenergetic breathing practice, once you've been performing the Bow regularly.

In videos on my Youtube I explain how to make one, and how to use it to maximize your breathing capacity.

It's pretty easy to make. All you need is a foam roller, a stool, a dowel rod, and a bungee cord to tie it all together.

The stool essentially provides you with a more intense version of the Bow, where you can use leverage to increase the stretch in key areas across the pelvis, belly, chest, and neck.

Lay down with your upper back against the foam roller while keeping your knees bent and with your feet placed firmly on the floor. Now stretch your arms overhead and behind you, drop your hips, open your mouth and eyes wide, and allow the stretch to happen. Breathe.

You can add more leverage to the stretch by reaching behind you to grab onto something, perhaps a table or a wall. Doing this while simultaneously dropping your hips will add to the stretch.

Placing different parts of your back on the stool will intensify the stretch in specific areas. This functions in the same way that using different hand placements does when performing the Bow.

You can add more leverage to the stretch by reaching behind you to grab onto something, perhaps a table or a wall. Doing this while simultaneously dropping your hips will add to the stretch.

Placing different parts of your back on the stool will intensify the stretch in specific areas. This functions in the same way that using different hand placements does when performing the Bow.

To emphasize the stretch across your throat and chest, lay down so that the backs of your shoulders and upper back come into contact with the stool.

For a stretch across your abdomen and solar plexus, place your lower back upon the stool.

And to open up your pelvic region, sit on the stool and lay back all the way, using another table or bed to support your arms and upper body.

Implementing the stool in your practice is an excellent way to really open up, once and for all, all of the tight areas that restrict your breathing.

You can lay on it for as long as you'd like. I recommend beginning with twenty full, deep breaths.

Supplementary Bioenergetic Exercises

The following practices are intended to supplement regular practice of the Bow and Bioenergetic Stool.

Tapping is one technique you can use to further facilitate the breakdown of muscular tension, allowing your muscles to return to their natural supple state. It's as easy as it sounds: it simply involves tapping wherever you happen to be tight repeatedly with your fingers.

I find this works particularly well on the chest, neck, and face.

Be aware that the intention with tapping is not to neurotically attack yourself but rather to gently, yet firmly, release areas of tension in your body. It is a gentle form of self-myofascial release, or self-massage. Remember to breathe and relax your facial muscles as you tap.

Chanting, or making sounds, is another method for opening up and mobilizing tense muscles, and is particularly effective when combined with tapping.

For thousands of years, chanting has been widely practiced across various religious traditions as a means of cultivating and channeling energetic strength.

A famous chant you may be familiar with is the sound *OM*, which is considered sacred by many. This is a fine place to start with chanting.

To begin, simply open your mouth and let out a deep *OMMMMMM*, feeling the sound vibrate deep within your pelvic floor. Relax your face and remember to breathe as you do this.

You can repeat this chant for a while, or you can experiment with different sounds by changing the shape of your mouth and the intensity of your projection. Allow whatever sounds arise to happen.

I've found that certain sounds tend to activate and break down tension in specific areas.

The key is in the pitch. Low, deep sounds will activate lower energetic centers, such as the pelvic floor and solar plexus. High-pitched sounds naturally target higher areas of the body. You will be able to feel where your voice resonates when you practice this.

If sound seems to be "stuck" in a particular area, that is where you should be making noise. Sing your way through the blockages!

The beauty of using your voice to stimulate your body is that you can do it anywhere.

Sometimes I chant while performing exercises like the Bow, or when I am using the Bioenergetic Stool. Other times, I will bounce up and down and shake while making deep, resonating sounds.

This combination of chanting with as deep a voice as possible and shaking and vibrating your body will bring you into a more grounded state.

As you become more experienced with these techniques, you can use the sound of your voice to induce episodes of bioenergetic catharsis, such as sobbing. I will explain how to do this in a later section.

Another technique I like to use, particularly with regard to opening up the belly, is to perform myofascial release using a ball of some kind. For my belly, I use a small kids-size basketball.

This can be a very painful exercise, especially for someone who is very tight in the belly, so proceed with caution.

To initiate this belly massage, all I do is place the ball on the floor and then lay on top of it, first orienting it right where my belly button is. Then I roll around—up and down and side to side—allowing the ball to press deep into my bowels.

This feels uncomfortable, almost like a soft continual punch to the gut. By all means, stop if you experience pain.

But as long as it is only discomfort that you experience, try your best to relax into the massage. Breathe through it. Notice where you are holding tension, and release it. Allow everything to relax.

Massage should not be limited to just the belly. While the belly is often one of the tightest and most neglected areas of tension in people, you are likely tight all over.

For one, the feet tend to be neglected.

Your feet are your roots, connecting you to the earth. In the same way restricted roots on a tree will prevent the tree from being nourished fully by the ground, constricted feet will make you less able to conduct the grounding energy of the earth so well.

So, take the time to massage the tension out of your feet, as well as any other areas you find are tight.

You can do this yourself by using various tools: foam rollers, lacrosse balls, and massage sticks like the Thera Cane. Or you may consult with a good massage practitioner.

As you experiment with massage, you may experience a rush of emotions that is triggered by massaging a certain area. You may laugh and giggle a bit, you may cry, or you may even experience feelings of anger and fear.

These are all great signs. You are opening up the gates to primal energy that has long been suppressed and must now be let go of.

Little by little, we are breaking down the cage.

Open Front Breathing

Open Front Breathing is usually what people talk about when they refer to diaphragmatic, or belly, breathing. This is a good starting point for most people to retrain their breathing.

The challenge with having people practice belly breathing right from the start, however, is that doing so does not address the roots of the issue--the neurotic holding patterns.

In my mind, having someone perform Open Front Breathing before practicing regularly with the Bow, the Bioenergetic Stool, and other somatic techniques is like instructing a caged zoo animal to break out of his cage by running straight through the bars. That just wouldn't work.

First, you have to break down the cage.

This is why I have my clients practice using the Bow and the Bioenergetic Stool in conjunction with Open Front Breathing.

Only after you have spent some time with the stool and the Bow are you opened up and ready to begin breathing deeply.

When performing Open Front Breathing, I recommend you wear loose-fitting clothes, including a loosened belt if you are wearing one. In fact, wearing *no* clothes for this exercise is even better because this allows for the full expansion of your breathing muscles.

To begin, lie down on the floor or on a bed.

With your knees bent, place your feet flat on the ground and allow your back and head to rest. Allow the ground to take all of your weight. You should feel heavy, as if you are sinking into the floor.

Once you are comfortable, open your mouth wide, placing your hands above your belly and groin and spreading your fingers out, as you see me do in the above photo.

You can place both hands above your chest, or one hand above your chest and one hand above your lower abdominal region.

The point is to draw your focus to the regions of your body that you are attempting to expand and activate with your breath.

Breathe deeply and slowly for as long as you'd like in this position. I recommend at least several minutes the first time you try this. Focus your attention on breathing into your pelvic floor. The key is to keep all of the muscles in your face, throat, chest, belly, and pelvic floor soft.

By maintaining the focus on your face, I have found that everything else falls into place. One cue that I use with myself and my clients when working with this type of breathing is: "Jaw open. Stretch the jaw."

The jaw seems to be the first place people close up and tighten when performing this exercise.

Again, you may experience strange new sensations when performing this breathing exercise, such as tingling, cramping, or a general "rush" of sensations.

If you do, don't be shocked. And if you don't, there is no need to be disappointed. You are still doing it right.

These sensations are just the body's natural response to opening up neuromuscular and energetic pathways that have been held rigid for so long.

If you'd like, you can get up and walk around in a circle when this happens. This will help ground your energy.

So, that's it. Want to breathe into your balls and grow stronger? This is how you do it.

After practicing these exercises regularly for a while—using the Bow, the Bioenergetic Stool, Open Front Breathing, and the various other techniques I discussed—you will begin to breathe deeply.

My intention is for you to discover a stronger and more grounded presence, a more embodied voice, greater physical and emotional motility, and a renewal of your vibrance. Breathing deeply will transform you into a Stronger Version of Yourself, no doubt about it.

For a comprehensive overview and demonstration of the breathing techniques I've discussed in the above sections, watch the video I created called "The Truth About Deep Breathing."

THE BIO-ENERGIZER WARM-UP

It is easy to miss a workout when you don't have a program, and especially so if you feel like your workouts are too long.

This is why I began implementing a Daily Bio-Energizer Warm-Up when I first got into bioenergetic breathing. It served as a way to hold me accountable to practicing all of the breathing exercises I have described to you.

I recommend performing the Daily Bio-Energizer Warm-Up Routine upon waking or before your workouts every day for a month. It takes all of ten minutes, and is a great way to charge yourself into an energized and grounded state for the day.

Rather than describe all of the steps in detail, I will direct you to my "Daily Bio-Energizer Warm-Up Routine" video, in which I explain everything you need to know.

This is a simple routine that you can shorten or lengthen to however long you would like it to be. For me, five to ten minutes gets the job done.

In the next section, I will discuss ways we can use the power of our newfound breath and vitality to perform cathartic exercises that allow us to discharge energy through movement and deep breathing.

King

MEDITATION:
Active Meditation, Bioenergetic Catharsis, & Anabolic Bioenergtics

Active Meditation

So far in this section, we've discussed ways of freeing our breath and restoring our vitality by stretching out and letting go of muscular armor.

Now that our bodies are more motile and our breath is freer, we can explore methods for initiating bioenergetic catharsis with movement and the power of our breath to further release tension.

If practicing with the Bow, the Bioenergetic Stool, self-massage, and Open Front Breathing is analogous to bending the bars that cage us within neurotic holding patterns, then Active Meditation and other forms of bioenergetic catharsis are akin to shaking the cage so that the nuts and bolts come loose.

Osho

Both processes facilitate liberation of the body.

Active Meditation is a system of rigorous, body-based meditations that was developed by a man named Osho.

I have been using various forms of Active Meditation to release tension and restore spontaneity in my body for over a decade. Doing these exercises may only look odd, but—as most who have tried it will tell you—the results speak for themselves.

The form of Active Meditation that I find myself practicing the most is [Dynamic Meditation](#).

Dynamic Meditation consists of five different exercises that are performed with your eyes closed and to music. They can be done alone or with others. In the full, hour-long meditation, each stage lasts between ten and fifteen minutes.

During the first stage, you charge the body with breath. The intention here is to essentially work yourself up into a "fit" and become supercharged with energy.

This is done by breathing rapidly and chaotically through the nose, focusing on the exhalation. Breathe deeply and exhale *powerfully*.

You may accompany your breathing with chaotic movement to help facilitate the charge. I like to pump my arms. The key here is to not develop any type of pattern with your breathing or movement.

After several minutes of performing this rapid breathing, you will likely feel tired and wired, like you are ready to pop.

As long as you aren't experiencing unpleasant symptoms such as excessive dizziness or breathing difficulties, I invite you to keep going. The more powerfully you charge your body during this stage, the stronger the release will be during the next exercise.

So try not to expend much energy in this stage, even with your movements. Conserve and continue building your charge. You'll get your chance to release soon enough.

After ten minutes of breathing, you will hear the music change, marked by the sound of a gong. This signals the beginning of the second stage.

By this point, the body is fully charged with breath. This is when we discharge the body through catharsis. In other words, this is your chance to throw a grown-up temper tantrum.

Anything goes for the next ten minutes. Use your full capacities for somatic expression to let it all out by moving and using your voice.

Whatever comes up—no matter how embarrassing it may be and as long as it doesn't hurt you or others—express it.

Cry, sob, laugh uncontrollably, yell violently, speak in tongues, roll on the floor like an angry toddler, slam your arms back and forth by your sides, shake your body, stomp, beat your chest, and allow whatever is trapped inside of you to be expressed. Shake the animal out of his cage.

Just go with it. There is no judgment. This energetic junk has been building up in your system over years of emotional constipation. It is time to let go and let it out.

After ten minutes of catharsis, you will hear another gong. This marks the beginning of the third stage.

So, we've charged and we've purged. Our system is clear.

The purpose of the third stage is to center and ground ourselves in our bodies.

In order to ground ourselves, we perform the "Ground Pound" exercise for the duration of this stage. This is the same exercise I use in my Bio-Energizer Warm-Up.

Stand flat-footed with your arms overhead. Now jump up just slightly and land heavily so that your whole body vibrates.

Each time you land, let out your deepest, most guttural and ape-like "HOOOOOOH!" You will feel the vibrations from your sounds and movement shake your pelvic floor.

You may have encountered this exercise before, perhaps in a documentary about ancient warrior cultures or while watching the New Zealand All Blacks perform their pregame "haka" ritual before a rugby match.

Wherever you witnessed this, variations of the "Ground Pound" have existed for thousands of years because ancient warriors have always known about the power that is generated through heavy stomping and booming chanting.

The vibrations caused by the deep sound of your own voice and the heavy landing of your feet upon the ground activate your lower energetic centers, which include your solar plexus and sex center. This is where your power, assertiveness, and your ability to remain grounded originate.

I make no guarantees, but based upon my own experience, I suspect that—after doing this with *full attention* for ten minutes—you will feel like the grounded and confident animal that you are.

The fourth stage is marked by silence.

The music abruptly stops, and you now have fifteen minutes to rest.

As soon as the music stops, remain as you are. Whether you're standing or collapsed on the floor, don't make any conscious effort to change your position. Any movement here interferes with the flow of energy through your body. So just relax wherever you are and pretend you've been shot with a tranquilizer.

Don't move a muscle; be still, and hibernate.

After about fifteen minutes, the music will come on again for the final stage.

It is now time for you to emerge from your deep relaxation as someone who has been reborn, grounded and pulsing with life.

Celebrate your vitality and rejoice in the music. Allow the music to resonate with you and feel all of the good emotions that arise. Dance and express yourself.

You may have to fake this at first, as you did with other exercises, but you will soon feel like swaying and flowing to the vibrations of your body and the music.

This concludes the meditation.

So, that's it.

I challenge you to try this meditation once. Grab hold of your courage and give yourself permission to look foolish. Who cares what you look like? This meditation isn't pretty, but it is indeed transformative.

Usually, I'll go for the full hour, using the recommended music that can be found on iTunes and on Spotify. I like using the music because the change in songs cues me to move onto the next phase. This way I don't have to think about it and take myself out of the meditation.

Now doing Dynamic Meditation for an hour is something to work up to. If you are just starting out, though, you can perform a shortened version of this meditation, perhaps going for one or two minutes per stage for a total of five to ten minutes.

I understand that it can be difficult to find a safe and quiet environment in which you feel comfortable letting loose and expressing yourself in the vulnerable ways Dynamic Meditation encourages. If that's the case, you may perform the meditation silently, without the music and without making sounds.

Of course, it won't be the same as doing it all the way, but it will still be effective.

Eventually, you will want to perform it for the whole hour, with the music, to get the most bang for your buck and fully experience Dynamic Meditation.

ADVANCED BIOENERGETIC CATHARSIS

Dynamic Meditation is a very resourceful and practical introduction to bioenergetic catharsis.

It is the first form of meditation that I recommend people start with because it has proven to be very effective for myself and so many others.

Implementing Dynamic Meditation into your routine is not so different from following a popular workout plan; the reps, sets, and exercises are all laid out for you. All you have to do is show up and do the work.

After having had some experience with Dynamic Meditation, you may want to explore more advanced and personalized techniques for inducing bioenergetic release, depending on where you find yourself holding tension.

I have already shared with you how to use the Bow, the Bioenergetic Stool, Open Front Breathing, tapping, myofascial release, the Bio-Energizing Warm-Up, and the sound of your own voice to reduce energetic and muscular tension throughout the body. You should continue working with these practices even as you begin exploring more advanced exercises.

Now I am going to give you four different exercises that my mentor, Robert Glazer, taught me.

Each of these exercises is designed to induce a specific form of emotional release. Experiment with whatever exercises you feel would be most helpful for you.

Again, just like with Dynamic Meditation, you will want to find a space where you can get loud and feel comfortable doing so.

The very <u>first exercise</u> is intended to trigger sobbing and the release of suppressed grief.

So many of us are swallowing our tears, holding ourselves back from experiencing the pain of sadness. It hurts to experience losing a loved one or going through a tough break-up.

But it is important to be with those emotions. There is something cleansing and restorative about experiencing grief and letting out a deep sob.

If you feel you may be currently suppressing grief, this exercise may help you open up those channels through which grief is released.

To perform this exercise, begin by either lying on the Bioenergetic Stool or standing in the Bow position. Breathe deeply for a good two minutes in whatever position you choose.

After a couple of minutes, continue breathing deeply in your current position and begin to sob.

Even if you're not actually sobbing, fake it until you make it. Let out deep sobbing sounds, wail, and mumble like a baby does before crying for as long as it takes until you experience the real thing.

It helps to call out the name of the person to whom your grief is related. This could be the name of a loved one or even your own name-- perhaps a younger version of yourself.

The <u>second exercise</u> is intended to help someone invoke in himself the spirit of confidence and assertiveness.

A lot of people these days suffer from feelings of timidness, suppressed aggression, lack of emotion, and social anxiety. So if you want to develop a more commanding and expressive presence, this is for you to allow your inner boss to come out.

Begin again with the Bow, or lie down on the stool. I want you to charge your body with breath for at least three minutes in this position. You can even go for five or ten minutes if you want. The longer you breathe in the Bow, the more charged you will become.

Once you are charged with energy, stand up from the Bow and get into a power pose with your legs and arms spread apart. Now, yell as loudly as you can from your pelvic floor. Bellow deeply and beat your chest as you do this. Roar like a LION.

After yelling like this for a while, I want you to use your voice in a different way.

This time, be just as loud as before, only now shout in short, powerful bursts with a slightly higher pitch. You should feel the vibration of your voice move from your abdomen and pelvic floor to your neck when switching from deep bellowing to this higher pitched battle cry.

To give you a better sense of what noise to make, shout as if you were intimidating an opponent on the battlefield, or scaring away a large animal.

When performing this "war cry," you may notice restrictions in your face, jaw, and neck muscles. A lot of us hold so much tension in the face because we're habituated to wearing masks of fake smiles and stoic, emotionless expressions.

A good technique you can use to further release tension in the muscles of the face is to massage these areas with your fists as you yell. Press your fists firmly into your jaw and neck muscles, and use your fingers to target specific areas of tension you find. If you want more techniques for reducing muscular tension in the face, check out my video titled, "Bioenergetics for Your Face."

This will be uncomfortable, but you will notice the muscles begin to soften.

Alternate between the deep bellow and battle cry shouts for several rounds.

The **third exercise** I am going to teach you will release neurotic holding patterns that are restricting your sexuality. Just as sadness and assertiveness are, sexuality is another commonly suppressed emotion. This exercise was actually my first introduction to bioenergetics. It was taught to me by the Neo-Reichian therapist who also introduced me to Dynamic Meditation.

Once again, begin by breathing in the Bow.

After breathing deeply in this position for a minimum of two to three minutes, head over to a bed or futon and start slamming your hips repeatedly into the mattress as hard as you can, without hurting yourself. That's right, I am telling you to hump the mattress.

I know you will probably feel resistant to doing this. After all, it's kind of ridiculous, but do it anyway. Thrust like you are having hard sex, but continue to breathe deeply and fully.

You may start to laugh. Enter this laughter. Allow your entire body to shake with each belly laugh. It is good to experience your sensuality.

This is opening you up to experience a greater range of pleasure. A person who laughs from the belly, rather than the face, will experience deeper and more powerful orgasms, and more pleasure in general.

A great follow-up to this exercise would be to put on your favorite music and dance to it. Shake your body, swing your hips, and dance!

The **final exercise** also involves a mattress. It will help release the emotions of anger and aggression.

Let us return to the idea of the reptilian brain: there's a warrior within us that wants to fight. He is savage, wild, and violent. Understandably, we keep him restrained because it is not resourceful to act on our violent tendencies.

But by holding him in, in turn, he takes out his aggression on us.

Now we need to express this violence out of us, in a resourceful way that doesn't harm ourselves or others.

I invite you to begin this exercise by charging your body with deep breathing in the Bow or on the Bioenergetic Stool for three minutes.

If you'd like, think back to a time when you felt very angry, yet had held yourself back. Breathe yourself into a fit of rage if that helps.

You will soon feel charged with anger. It is time to exorcise these demons.

There are multiple ways to do this. I like to use a tennis racket to strike a mattress over and over again. Yelling is another great way to release anger and one that we've already discussed.

Curse, yell, stomp, or strike—this is your chance to be violent and let the wild animal out of his cage.

If you are limited by your environment, you may yell into a pillow, or throw a temper tantrum on your bed.

As with all of these exercises, just make sure you aren't harming yourself or anyone in your environment. It is important not to direct your violence onto anyone, including yourself. That is what the mattress is for.

If you'd like to explore bioenergetics more—both in theory and in practice—I invite you to check out the work of Alexander Lowen and Wilhelm Reich. Lowen's Fear of Life is a great book to begin with.

Realize that there is no "right" and "wrong" when it comes to bioenergetics. How you express your energy is entirely dependent upon your issues.

Maybe you need to stomp, yell, shake, shout, and use a tennis racket to strike a pillow or mattress. Or perhaps you need to sob or chant deep, resonating sounds. Even still, you may just need to hump a mattress and laugh. It all depends on your history and what emotions need to be expressed and released.

In most cases, what comes out of you could resemble a three-year-old's tantrum. And that's perfectly cool.

Why?

Because most of us, even when we were three years old, weren't allowed to express our feelings. And ten, twenty, or seventy years later, these feelings are still energetically trapped inside of us, preventing the Strongest Version of Ourselves from emerging.

We all know the importance of defecating every day to clear out toxins from our physiological system. It is no different with our energetic system. We need to regularly take "energetic dumps" to free ourselves from emotional toxins.

How can you become the Strongest Version of Yourself when you continue to be constipated with emotional crap for years, decades even?

ANABOLIC BIOENERGETICS

In the past few sections, we have explored ways of discharging energy and muscular tension from the body, in order to free up the circulation of bioenergy within us.

In this section, I would like to share with you a couple of exercises for cultivating and circulating the body's energy. Now that we've opened up the body, having released tension and restored deep breathing, these energy-building exercises become more effective.

The way we build energy in the body is by coordinating our breath with movement.

If you look at any traditional practice for cultivating bioenergy—from tai chi to yoga—you will notice that the exercises always involve coordinating deep breathing with focused movement. Synchronizing these two forces enables a person to fully inhabit himself and channel his power.

"Hard" martial arts like Kung Fu and power-based forms of yoga emphasize quick, powerful movements coordinated with powerful breath. The focus is on generating force and directing it outward.

If you've ever watched Bruce Lee, you know what I am talking about. The greatest athletes are those who can harness the power of their breath and direct it explosively outward through movement.

Strength training is a form of this "hard" kind of martial art.

The other approach to channeling energy incorporates slow, non-linear movement with long, deep breathing. With these softer practices, such as certain forms of yoga and qigong, the idea is to move and breathe easily.

This is the approach that generates and builds energy, and is the style I want to teach you in this section.

The first exercise is called Scooping.

Begin by bending your knees slightly, feet about shoulder width apart. You can orient yourself, if you'd like to, by bringing your hands together at your heart's center in prayer position. This will help center you. Take a few deep and easy breaths here, focusing on the feelings in your heart.

Scooping

Now, open up your hands, with the palms facing out in front, and pretend as if you were waist-high in a river, scooping water.

As you inhale, squat down slightly and scoop the water up with your hands. As you exhale, circle your arms back overhead and allow the water to spill over your body. As you continue exhaling, lean back into a version of the Bow, with your hands at your sides, before coming back to standing position. Repeat this circular movement for ten slow repetitions to start.

Rather than try to power through the movements as we are used to doing with strength training, the focus here is to be fully present as we execute each repetition slowly.

The Wood Chop is another great energizing exercise.

Begin again with feet about shoulder width apart. Now clasp your hands together and pretend you are chopping wood with your arms.

Wood Chop

Inhale as you raise the axe and exhale as you swing through. Try twenty repetitions.

Experiment. There is really no "right" way to do these exercises. Do what feels right for you.

You can explore more of these energizing exercises in my <u>Anabolic Energizers</u> eBook, as well as in Paul Chek's <u>How to Eat, Move and Be Healthy</u>. He calls these Zone Exercises.

I invite you to explore on your own, too. Find a "working in" discipline—traditional or something you make up on your own—that uses synchronized breath and movement to fill you with energy.

The possibilities are endless. The most important thing is that you find a practice you enjoy.

Yoga and tai chi are two excellent disciplines that will introduce you to the benefits of "working in."

If you are not a fan of going to classes, there is a book written by B.K.S. Iyengar, Light on Yoga, that serves as a great guide to the many different yoga asanas, or poses.

Why Meditate?

Simply put, meditation is the art of chilling out.

The world in which we live is one of constant stimulation and affords many opportunities for distraction. Endlessly preoccupied with our gadgets, things to do, places to be, and people to meet, we often find ourselves feeling confused and uncentered—superconnected, yet still lacking.

"Who am I?" many of us wonder. "Where am I going? And what is my purpose?"

We tend to search for the answers to these big questions in books, conversations, internet forums, and our thoughts, but oftentimes doing so only further clouds the issue.

In my experience, the remedy to our confusion rests in being with ourselves through meditation. So rarely do we allow time for simply *being with ourselves* in this world of perpetual thinking and doing.

For the sake of another analogy: meditation enables us to step inside the eye of life's hurricane.

In life, we bear the downpour of our responsibilities, the gusty winds of our thoughts, the lightning strikes of our aspirations, the tidal waves of our emotional baggage, and the hailstones of our inner critic—all of these throw us amidst the tempest of our mind's chatter.

Swept up in this storm, we find that it is nearly impossible to stay centered and to be in touch with ourselves enough to know how we would like to proceed in life.

That is why we must come into the eye of the storm, where it is peaceful.

Here in the sunny center of the storm—out of the hail, wind, and rain—we discover our ability to observe our own lives from a detached and somewhat objective perspective. From being rooted and centered in our own silence, we proceed with decisions and actions that serve us.

Through meditation, our insight illuminates the way.

I am sure you have heard of the benefits of regularly meditating. There are so many different studies out there—just search PubMed to get a taste of the literature.

So, where do we begin?

As a practice, meditation does not require much effort, other than to let go and be. Theoretically, that makes sense, right?

In reality, getting out of our own way is one of the most challenging tasks of all.

Meditation Practices

My intention with this section is to provide you with a very basic outline of the meditation practices that I use, so that you can choose accordingly. You may also want to do your own research and find a practice—if you haven't already—that works for you.

Even now, many years after I first began meditating, these practices continue to support me on my journey of becoming the Strongest Version of Myself, and I am confident they will do the same for you.

My very first exposure to meditation came when I was in high school.

I had asked my uncle Elroy, who was my first strength coach, how I could recover faster from my workouts. He responded by teaching me this Body Scan Meditation.

This approach serves as a bridge between the active bioenergetic style of meditation we covered earlier and the more traditional approach to meditating that we are beginning to explore now.

I recommend doing this meditation before you go to sleep every night for thirty days. It is a good idea to stretch beforehand to bring your attention to your body. You may meditate standing or lying down with your back flat on the floor.

Close your eyes and take ten deep breaths.

Allow your weight to grow heavy, as if you were actually sinking into the ground deeper and deeper with each exhalation. This is called Savasana, or "Corpse Pose," in yoga. Allow everything to rest.

Now imagine there is a laser scanning your body very slowly, up and down, from the top of your head to your toes. Consciously observe how each part of your body feels as the laser passes over it. Notice where you are holding tension and allow it to release.

Rather than judge, we just want to bring some awareness to whatever areas in the body are tight.

Observe and feel your forehead muscles, eyes, nose, ears, cheeks, jaw, and tongue. Then slowly scan down to your neck, shoulders, chest, arms, fingers, and so on.

Again, we are not trying to fix anything. We are just bringing our awareness to the tension. Doing this will allow these areas to naturally relax.

Take about five minutes and use this body scan technique before you go to bed every night.

This scan brings conscious awareness to your body and will help you grow more familiar with the way energy moves through your body. You will likely also experience deeper sleep, allowing you to recover faster.

Another meditation technique I like to use is a simple meditation, during which I draw my attention to two sensations in my body simultaneously.

You can try this meditation by sitting down in a chair or on the ground, preferably outside.

Choose two sensations to focus all of your attention on. I often choose to focus on the sensations of my butt on the chair and the sun on my face, for instance.

If you do this exercise mindfully, deeply focusing on these two sensations, you will find that the mind has little time to enter into chatter mode. Instead, it is kept busy by observing these feelings.

When your mind's focus does slip, bring your attention back to the two sensations--perhaps the sun's warmth on your face and the pressure of your butt on the chair. Try this meditation for five minutes daily for a month.

Meditating on the breath is another common meditation technique that is a bit more challenging than the first two I have described.

With this method, you simply focus your attention on the breath moving through your body.

You may choose to pay attention to the expansion and decompression of your belly and pelvic floor with each inhalation and exhalation, or you might focus your awareness on the sensation of air entering your nostrils.

Whatever area of the body you choose to focus on, consciously feel the breath move through these areas, and bring your attention back to the sensation every time your mind wanders.

If you have a more visual mind and find yourself distracted, you might try imagining a ball of glowing white energy coming out of your belly, sitting halfway inside you. Picture this ball of energy expanding as you inhale and collapsing as you exhale.

With all of these techniques, we are giving our mind something to focus on within our body. This enables us to yoke together the mind and the body.

Mantra meditation is another form of meditation I've benefited from.

It is a staple in a lot of religious traditions, and for good reason.

You have the sacred *OM* of many Eastern religions; there is *OM Mani Padme Hum* in Buddhism; and in Christianity, you have the recitation of the Hail Mary, using rosary beads. Mantra is a great way to center and focus the mind.

Performing a mantra simply involves saying a particular phrase over and over and over again. You may choose a phrase that is personally meaningful, or it may be completely arbitrary.

The idea is that you are focusing the mind on something other than its own chatter.

I will share one more method with you, and that is **Focal Point Meditation**. I practiced this exercise when I was younger in order to help me fall asleep at night.

With this approach, choose any object to focus your attention on: a picture, an apple, your finger, or really anything you can think of. I practiced this meditation by lighting a candle and focusing deeply on the flame.

You may find your mind wandering away from the object, but just come back to the object when this happens. It takes practice.

The meditations I have shared with you all require you to focus your attention on something—be it your muscular tension, your breathing, a mantra, or an object. This approach has worked for me, but there are many other approaches out there that you may find useful.

Zazen, Transcendental Meditation, and Mindfulness Meditation all come highly recommended. I encourage you to experiment with different approaches until you find one that works for you.

Frequency Meditation

When starting out with more traditional approaches to meditation, you may experience—as I have—lots of mind chatter. In fact, most people experience this, and it can be quite frustrating.

After all, when many of these traditional meditation practices were being developed, there were no iPhones, traffic, news, and so on to stimulate the mind into overdrive.

People were less neurotic and in their heads then, so it was easier—though still not easy—for ancient people to enter these states of "no-mind" by simply focusing on their breath.

This is why I recommend starting out with bioenergetics and Dynamic Meditation, and continuing to use these approaches even as you explore other more traditional approaches.

The intense bioenergetic meditations help to ground our consciousness in the body, quieting the mind a bit.

Still, we are combatting years of restricted body consciousness and head brain overdrive.

Even with regular bioenergetics practice, you may still find yourself growing discouraged and questioning the effectiveness of meditation, especially when you first start out. Soon enough, you might even quit meditating.

It is important to understand that meditation requires patience. It may take months, and even years, of daily meditation practice for you to begin noticing significant results. Trust the process, and rest assured that it is working and gradually making changes to your brain.

That being said, different times call for different measures.

Many years ago, I decided that to get the most out of my meditation practice, I would need a little help "stepping into the eye of the storm". Given my lifestyle and the results I was seeking, it would have been very challenging for me to devote the hours that the traditional approach required per day.

So, I started using a binaural beats meditation audio program called Holosync®.

Holosync® uses different tones, or sound frequencies, which are played through each ear, to stimulate the brain so that it must integrate these dissonant frequencies and produce a perceived binaural beat.

This "brainwave entrainment" initiates a process called hemispheric synchronization, whereby the brain creates new neural pathways that increase communication between the right and left hemispheres of the brain.

Holosync® also slows down brainwave activity, inducing deeper alpha, theta, and delta states that are associated with sleeping and trance states.

All of these changes in the brain trigger the release of certain neurochemicals that enable you to enter deeply meditative states that would normally require many years of traditional meditation practice.

I know this sounds odd, and I cannot pretend to fully understand how the technology works. All I can say is that Holosync® has worked for me, helping me to quiet my mind and enter the eye of the storm for many years.

And the great thing about Holosync® is that you don't have to do anything. All you need to experience the effects of this powerful technology is put on a good pair of headphones and listen. You can meditate if you'd like, or you can just relax.

There are many other binaural beats meditation programs out there that are less expensive than Holosync®. The iTunes App Store has plenty of options for you. Brain Wave, developed by Banzai Labs, is a good one.

In my opinion, you would be hard-pressed to find a technology that matches Holosync® in terms of its effectiveness or the years of research and development behind it at Centerpointe Research Institute.

As with any supplement, I believe it is a good idea to know what you are getting into, as all shortcuts are bound to have some trade-offs. Plus, skepticism is good.

If your intuition advises you to go about meditation the traditional way, without using binaural beats, then I encourage you to proceed that way. I am sharing with you the path that has worked for me, but it is by no means the only way.

There are also other more traditional methods for inducing brainwave entrainment. They just require more effort.

These include chanting, drumming, using Tibetan Singing Bowls, and practicing other shamanic methods that have been helping spiritual seekers access meditative states for millennia. Since I am not very experienced with using these techniques, I encourage you to explore them further if they speak to you.

For more information on the neuroscience behind meditation and its effects on the brain, here are a couple of resources I have found helpful:

Buddha's Brain is a fascinating book for those of you who want to understand the biological process that meditation initiates. Author Rick Hanson discusses all the neurotransmitters, hormones, and changes in the brain that meditation promotes, from a scientific perspective.

For more on the philosophy of meditation, I recommend you read Osho. The Path of Meditation: A Step by Step Guide to Meditation is an excellent resource.

Solitude and Reflection

One of the best ways to step into the eye of the storm of your own life is to occasionally go outside of your everyday routine.

How you do this depends on who you are and which activities bring you the deepest feelings of peace, clarity, and fulfillment.

You may find that you like to implement shorter periods of solitude on a more regular daily or weekly basis.

For instance, I go for a peaceful hour-long walk by myself every morning. The silence enables me to reflect on the happenings of my life in a big-picture way.

Some people might enjoy treating themselves to a massage once a week, listening to music in a hammock, journaling, going for a run, or sweating their way to clarity at the sauna after a workout.

Others prefer to go out for longer bouts of solitude—perhaps a week or even several weeks—every few months or once a year.

Maybe you travel by yourself somewhere new. Oftentimes, placing yourself in an environment that is different from one you are used to can lead you to experience deep insights about your life.

Travel brings perspective. You may discover by experiencing a new culture and place that there are certain elements about your life back home that you would like to change, and other aspects of your life that you appreciate immensely.

While I do not advise "going into the wild", spending time outdoors and staying in a location that matches your experience level—a campground, cabin, or lodge somewhere—may appeal to you.

For those of you who seek an immersive experience in nature that allows for deep introspection and rugged physical challenge, [The National Outdoor Leadership School (NOLS)](#) offers exceptional courses for students of all types to experientially learn wilderness navigation and other backcountry skills in remote wilderness settings around the world—in a structured environment with expert instructors, of course..

Whatever form of "me time" appeals to you, choose one and incorporate it in your life.

All of us, no matter how extroverted we think we are, need time to reflect in private. Silence and solitude bring peace, balance, and clarity.

THE PSYCHE: THE QUEST OF MEANING & DEVELOPMENT OF THE PSYCHE

THE QUEST FOR MEANING

Wherever you look, creation stories from around the world speak of a remarkably similar pattern:

Adam eats the apple.

Bassari Man eats the fruit.

Enkidu eats the bread.

Hercules drinks from Hera's breast, Pangu bites the head of King Fang, Pandora's Box is opened...

And we god-like creatures fall from paradise into the world of pain and suffering.

In the beginning, it is said, humans lived in the realm of the gods and eternity.

At some point, we fell from this Garden and were born into time, space, and suffering. We became mortal and conscious. And for so long as we live, we aspire to return to paradise.

This is the universal Hero's Journey, and it manifests in tales wherever you look:

Hercules performs the Twelve Labours.

Gilgamesh slays beasts.

Jesus, Buddha, and Rama battle demons in the wilderness.

Parzival quests for the Grail. Odysseus and Ahab chart the seas.

Cúchulainn and Sundiata defeat whole armies.

Frodo journeys to Mordor...

And man searches for meaning—*as you are, reading this now*—journeying to the ends of the earth to find the elixir that might bring us back to paradise.

Regardless of your religious affiliation, I am sure the quest of the Hero resonates with your experience.

We are searching for something we feel we once had—call it Tao, God, happiness, Nirvana, or flow.

This is why we train, read books, live healthy lives, and grow stronger. We are seekers, all journeying towards—well, whatever you would like to call it.

I am not here to tell you that I have discovered the meaning of life. I haven't.

I cannot tell you the way to your own truth.

But I can share some tools that have shaped me on my journey of growing stronger. And perhaps they may serve you as well.

I invite you to experiment, as I have, and realize that there are many "flashlights" of insight that can serve to illuminate the metaphorical wilderness through which we journey in life—none of which are inherently better or worse.

On my journey, I have found the work of Carl Jung and a couple of his followers, namely Joseph Campbell and Robert Moore, to be quite helpful.

Individuation is the Jungian spiritual quest, and is the process of psychological integration.

In other words, conscious assimilation and acceptance of one's entire psyche, or mind, which includes those parts of oneself that one may not even be aware of.

Carl Jung

The way of individuation necessitates a journey inward to explore the unconscious.

It is within the dark and unexamined depths of our minds that we, whilst shining the flashlight of consciousness, discover the Strongest Versions of Ourselves.

The key is to not go overboard in this exploration and drown in the depths of our own psyche.

This is why we train and emphasize both body-based *and* "mind-based" approaches to growing stronger. If you neglect to exercise your body as intensely as you exercise your mind, you run the risk of going insane.

In the next section, I will provide you with a roadmap of the psyche that may assist you on your journey towards self-discovery.

THE FALL: DEVELOPMENT OF THE EGO

From a Neo-Jungian perspective, the creation stories from the beginning of this chapter symbolize the psychological stages of development.

As Adam and Eve did, we begin our lives in the Edenic womb. Nourishment, shelter, and love are all provided for us, and we—unaware of our nakedness—are content in the land of the unconscious.

Psychoanalytically, we still feel ourselves to be God's children in our earliest moments.

Before the birth of consciousness, there is no separation between ourselves, the natural world, and the gods; no distinction between "I" and "it"; no sense of space and time, right and wrong, or duality in general. We are at one with everything. We are at one with God.

Here, pain and suffering do not exist because we are living in eternity, where there is no basis for wanting.

And before we know it, we are pulled out, wailing into the world like falling gods.

Like Hercules, we are ripped from Hera's breast and cast down from Mount Olympus.

Hercules from Hera's Breast, by Jacopo Tintoretto

Like Adam, we eat the Apple of the Knowledge and are banished from Eden.

Just like that, the umbilical cord connecting us to paradise is snipped, and consciousness is born.

Forced into the world of opposites, we become aware of our nakedness; become awakened to our mortality and our suffering.

We quickly learn that we are no longer the gods we originally imagined ourselves to be.

Earth feels like a far cry from paradise.

Here, we must wear clothing, eat our vegetables, do as we are told, and develop boundaries between ourselves and the world around us.

The ego—or the "I"—is born, and along with it, the desire to return to the place from which we came and once stood in close proximity to God.

THE WINTER OF ALIENATION

The Fallen State of Man defines the consensus of human experience in the modern era. "God is dead," famously spoke Nietzsche.

Most of us today feel alienated, in a sense, from God, the Universe, or whatever you want to call It.

We identify with Adam and Eve, and with all the other heroes seeking the restorative boon.

In certain ways, we feel as though we have been "wronged" by some greater force. Our lives do not feel quite full.

We all experience suffering to some extent, and we all seek a remedy to our pain.

"If there is a God," we ask, "then why does suffering exist?"

This is the state of alienation.

I have been throwing around the term "God" rather loosely, so I feel it is time to explain what I mean when I use this word.

The imago Dei, or the image of God within the human psyche, is analogous to what Neo-Jungian thinker Robert Moore calls the "archetypal Self." When I use the word "God," I am talking about the archetypal Self.

What is the archetypal Self?

This Self is *not* you. The "you" I address is the ego.

The Self is the transpersonal force within and beyond us that is far greater and more complex than the "I" with which we identify.

It goes by as many different names as there are cultures: Zeus, The Father, Brahman, Tao, the Force, the inner Daimon, the Ring of Power, Richard Parker, Aslan, Moby Dick, and so on.

The Self is the Holy Grail of the unconscious—what we call the God within.

When one is in touch with it, one possesses power.

But when one is alienated from the Self, one's life lacks luster.

Many times, people who are in an alienated state ignore or reject their desire to reunite with the transpersonal.

They may experience suffering, but they may go about their business as usual. "That's life," they may tell themselves.

In order to numb his pain, the alienated individual might drink, party, and live an otherwise *worldly life*. He surrounds himself in the mundane, everyday activities of existence, including work, school, and all other duties. Maybe he becomes an atheist.

Mythologically, this man is trapped inside the "Matrix"—the constructed world that surrounds us —and wants to remain there, whether he knows it or not.

To put it another way, it is more comfortable for you to pretend that you are Joe S., who lives in New York City in the 21st century and works a 9-to-5, than it is for you to accept that you are actually an animal living on a tiny speck of rock that is hurtling 1,000 miles per hour around a blazing ball of plasma in a universe that is infinitely large—without having a clue as to what any of this means.

There is another type of ego that recognizes his dissatisfaction and confusion with ordinary existence and knows that another state of being exists.

This person is aware that he has fallen into a constructed perspective and wants to return to the reality he once knew.

As he realizes his alienation, the world around this man grows increasingly more barren and unappealing. What once carried meaning now seems entirely profane.

School, work, sports, certain relationships, etc.—his whole world and everything he has done up until this point—suddenly become meaninglessness for him.

"What is the point?" he asks. *"Who am I, and what on earth am I doing with my life? What is my purpose?"*

"What is the meaning of life?"

On the surface, this person may appear to have a great life.

He may have a good job, make a lot of money, or do well in school. He may be talented and live a life that seemingly brings happiness, at least from an outside perspective.

In light of his disillusionment, others may rebuke him for being irrational or ungrateful.

"Can't you just be happy with where you are and what you have?" they ask. "Come back to earth, let's go out and have a good time, have a few beers. Stop being so serious."

But there is no convincing this person. For him, life is becoming a wasteland and increasingly devoid of meaning.

Now to speak in terms of mythology, the alienated ego (or Adam) that is divorced from the unconscious (the Garden of Eden)—*and is now aware of having been fallen*—grows apathetic to life. With this realization and the subsequent crumbling of the imperfectly constructed world he has always known, suffering, despair, and oftentimes, an existential crisis ensue.

This ego is searching for the Grail that will redeem the world within and around him, whether or not he is conscious of it.

He knows a greater state of life is possible, but he just doesn't know where to begin.

If you find yourself in this position, I bring good news.

Life, in my experience, moves in cycles. And it is during our lowest points, right when we hit rock bottom and almost lose hope, that God-the-Universe-the-archetypal-Self reaches out to us.

SPRINGING INTO CONTACT WITH THE SELF

Psychological spring follows the winter of alienation and the bitter nights of existential turmoil.

During the spring season of the individuation journey, we come into contact with the Self and are, in a way, reborn through the experience.

Often it is only when the alienated ego lies in the very trenches of an existential crisis, finally gives up, and repents, *realizing its powerlessness,* that the Self knocks on his door.

Just when we acknowledge that we are unable to do it alone, unseen hands come to help.

Time and again, we see this theme manifest both in myths and in historical accounts of personal transformation.

On the brink of giving up hope, a scientist has a dream, and the next morning, he invents something.

A woman's life appears in shambles, and suddenly she experiences a miraculous breakthrough.

Viktor Frankl starves in Auschwitz.

Arjuna faces his fate on the battlefield.

Moses leads his people through the desert.

And so on.

Then *voila*, epiphany strikes!

The Self, moving from the depths of the unconscious, speaks to us not in words but through the language of *feelings, dreams, and synchronous events*. The voice of the Self, or the voice of God, is the voice of your _Heart and Balls_.

When you turn a deaf ear to the Self's knocking at your door—be it in the form of a gut feeling, a powerful dream, or a remarkable event that carries great meaning for you—the Self will contact you in progressively more severe ways.

In religious terms, when you push God out, God sends his wrath. You keeping up with the metaphor?

If not, it is illustrated in the story of _Jonah and the Whale_. In it, God tells Jonah to preach to the people of Nineveh, to which Jonah says, "No thanks," and flees.

Jonah and the Whale, by Pieter Lastman

Well, you could predict what happens. Jonah is tossed about in stormy seas and swallowed by a whale. The lesson here is that it is impossible to run from that which is within you.

It is only after going through an ordeal of humiliation and being faced with his smallness and lack of genuine power that the battered and alienated ego can accept his dharma, or what the Universe wants to do through him. Only then is the ego's existential turmoil eased.

Ignoring the promptings of the Self manifests in real life in the same way.

For instance, a woman feels that she is meant to be a personal trainer or an artist, but she tells herself, "Oh, it doesn't pay; it's not respectable, and I am not talented enough."

Instead, she gets a "respectable" job and ignores her true feelings.

And *what do you know*—she gets sick and depressed.

So long as we reject or ignore the voice of the body, we suffer. The more we resist, the more our suffering persists.

This may be controversial, or even insensitive of me, to say, but it is my belief that misfortune and suffering are merely devices the Self uses to bring us back into Its embrace and to guide us to our full potential.

In other words, adversity knocks us off our ego-constructed path in life and returns us to the road of our destiny.

"What about those who starve, those who are victims of abuse, or even those who have lost absolutely everything?"

Don't get me wrong. I do not pretend to have found the meaning for your suffering, and in no ways do I intend to trivialize anybody's pain.

We all suffer, and our pain is indeed real. To say someone is responsible for consciously "attracting" whatever suffering he or she experiences is insensitive and arrogant.

There is no fixed meaning to our suffering. I offer my empathy and compassion as a fellow sufferer.

But I invite you to consider that what looks like hell to the undiscerning eye might very well be pointing the way toward heaven.

God-the Universe-the Self-whatever-you-want-to-call-It contacts us in mysterious ways.

In my own experience with suffering, I've discovered that it is only when we stop seeing our challenges as cruel punishments and start recognizing our tests for what they are—wake-up calls and opportunities to evolve—that our relationship with the Self grows into a more resourceful alliance.

I challenge you to see that Zeus' throwing down lightning and God flooding the earth are not to batter us down but to wake us up.

Our struggles are simply barbells that have been placed before us as invitations to grow stronger.

There is a great Lakota-Sioux saying I once heard, and the translation goes something like: *"Whatever Great Spirit gives us—good or bad—is what we need."*

When we become grateful for our struggles and pains, seeing them as opportunities to evolve; when we give up control on "our" life the way we saw it planned, or the way our parents wanted it; when we finally listen and pay attention to the inner voice we have for so long tried to squash out of fear and pride—when we do these things, we open ourselves up to a conscious relationship with the Self.

No relationship in the universe is more important than your relationship with the Self—all others stem from it.

When the ego submits to the Self and gives up on the idea that he can control life, he is assisted.

By contrast, the ego that continues to disrespect the Self—by repressing its promptings (i.e. your passion) in favor of more "secure" paths to "success"—is thrown back inside the Belly of the Whale, where chaos, existential turmoil, and suffering ensue.

What the heck am I talking about? What is the practical takeaway here?

That is up to you.

If you want to keep running away, no one is going to stop you. You can keep attempting to exert your will over the Self, believing that you are smarter than that which created you, and that is fine.

Or, if you do recognize your powerlessness and genuinely seek to work with the Self, then you must do one thing:

Do the thing you are afraid to do.

If there was one lesson in this book—hell, in my entire life's work—that I want to empower you with, it is this.

You must do the thing you are afraid to do.

Follow that golden thread of intuition whenever it appears, because we only get occasional glimpses of our passion, after all.

A chance encounter; a riveting dream, or that time you found yourself losing track of time in the midst of an activity; those dreams that bring butterflies to your stomach and a nervous smile to your face. These and more are the frightening and wonderful aspirations the Self has for you, and you must act on them immediately.

As Joseph Campbell advised, **"Follow your Bliss."**

As Paulo Coelho has said in *The Alchemist*, pay attention to the omens and signs.

These promptings of the Self are pointing the way to your heaven on earth, peace, happiness, or whatever you want to call it. You know what you must do—it's just intimidating.

I often say that you have to "get out of your way."

Summer: Inflation

Once we spring into contact with the Self by respecting Its wishes for our life, we experience a psychological summer of illumination and radiance.

We are filled with light; powerful hands work in our lives; and the wasteland that was once the world around us transforms into a paradise.

Life is great. Everything is blooming around us. "This is it. I've got it!" we think to ourselves.

So long as we remember to attribute this newfound radiance to the Self, we continue to reap the benefits of this relationship.

Of course, that's easier said than done, especially the first time around.

Soon enough, we become drunk on the archetypal energy that fills us.

We then forget how small we once felt in the winter of our ego's alienation.

Blinded by what we begin to believe is our own brilliance, we think that we are "It".

This is the folly of ego inflation, or when the ego consciously identifies with the Self.

And just as the Self punishes those who reject It, the Self punishes those who commit identity theft, taking ownership for what is not ours.

Icarus, who flies too close to the sun, falls.

The hero, who arrogantly approaches the dragon, gets burned.

It is important to realize that you are not the greatness that shines through you. You are simply a vessel--as replaceable as the light bulb through which that light shines.

I speak these things from experience.

It would be wise during psychological summer to remind yourself of how powerless you are without the Self. This will help remind you that you are not It, nor did you create the success that surrounds you.

Indeed, in order for the individuation process to move smoothly, the ego must approach the Self from a place of humility and reverence.

You must approach the Self in the same way that you would approach a dragon or a lion.

Come in too hot and proud, and you get burned. Run away, and your life loses meaning.

But bow in respect, and you come into a relationship.

The journey to the Self requires patience and balance, as the ego navigates these seasons of development: inflation, deflation, alienation, and renewed contact.

In the summertime, it is a good idea to remember how deflated you felt in the winter.

And in the winter, remember that spring is around the corner—look out for the signs.

To not get too high on our highs or too low on our lows is to realize that each season contributes to our growth and facilitates smoother evolution.

With time, the hope of individuation is that the ego dances its way to equilibrium, finding a balance between the forces of alienation and inflation.

Ancient cultures recognized the danger of identifying with the Self.

This is why humans created gods, totems, and sacred mountains.

Projecting the Self onto external objects like these enables us to more easily relate to It without identifying with It.

Working with the archetypes facilitates this process.

Archetypes of Wholeness: King, Warrior, Magician, & Lover

Archetypes

Back in the section on our Strength Camp Core Values, I alluded to the archetypes and the principles herein, but now we will be delving into greater detail, starting with archetypes.

Archetypes are the projected instincts of the body.

They are analogous to the pantheon of gods found in most religions.

They are also related to the chakras and the alchemical elements.

In other words, from a Neo-Jungian perspective, all of the gods within a pantheon are psychological projections of the instinctual drives within us.

For example, Dionysus is a projection of our desire to indulge in pleasure. Poseidon is our rage personified, our impulse to exert excessive power. And Hades is a projection of our greed and selfishness.

So long as we are unaware of these forces and project them onto others, they continue to have power over us.

Once we recognize that every one of the angels and demons is within us, they stop controlling our behavior, and we are able direct our actions consciously in ways that serve our mission.

I condense all of the archetypes into the trinity of the Head, Heart, and Balls. But you can also look at each—the Head, Heart, and Balls—as containing several distinct gods.

Whereas gods, the chakras, and alchemical symbols are the projections of energies on the body, the mythological worlds from our stories are projections of our inner psyche.

Do you follow me so far?

That the hero journeying through the wilderness, or a modern protagonist fighting a battle in a movie, is a metaphor for the ego journeying through the psyche and his encounters with the archetypes.

Joseph Campbell shares the following, from *The Power of Myth*:

"All the gods, all the heavens, all the worlds are within us. They are magnified dreams, and what dreams are, are manifestations in image form of the energies of the body in conflict with each other. And that's all myth is. Myth is a manifestation in symbolic images, metaphorical images, of the energies within us, moved by the organs of the body, in conflict with each other. This organ wants this, this organ wants this: the brain is one of the organs."

Joseph Campbell

Our myths and dreams serve as the fingers that point toward integrating these clashing, energetic drives within us, leading us to wholeness.

To take these stories *literally* is to miss the point.

As Bruce Lee says in *Enter the Dragon*, "Don't concentrate on the finger, or you will miss all the heavenly glory."

From Jesus, in Luke 17:21, "Neither shall they say, Lo here! or, lo there! for, behold, the kingdom of God is within you."

God, or the Self, is the Archetype that lies at the center of all these deities, clashing within the psyche.

The goal of the hero is to discover the buried treasure, or the Self, as he maneuvers between the poles of inflation and alienation. Along the way, he encounters various mythological creatures, angel helpers, and demons—all of which represent the unconscious instincts of the body.

In tales of successful heroes, we find examples of egos that have found the Self and became successfully individuated.

To name a few: Jesus on the Cross, Shiva's Cosmic Dance, and Buddha beneath the Bodhi tree are all mythological depictions of the ego that has become individuated and is in conscious communion with the Self.

Note: this does not necessarily imply that these men were not historical figures. The wise men who wrote about these heroes understood the dynamics of psychological growth, and therefore, framed their stories to fit the archetypal heroic journey.

These images suggest that the Self is encountered at the Center: of the cosmos, of the Cross, of the Tree, of the mandala, of the Lakota Medicine Wheel, and in the wavy line that dances between yin and yang.

In many of these images is the idea of a quaternity, or four quadrants. This suggests that the hero's journey to the Self consists of four parts.

Neo-Jungian thinker Robert Moore has explored the tetradic nature of the journey to the Center extensively.

Robert Moore

His book, *King, Warrior, Magician, Lover: Rediscovering the Archetypes of the Mature Masculine*, is one that I highly recommend everyone read, women included, because these ideas apply to all of us.

In his book, Moore proposes that four primary archetypes—the King (or Queen), the Warrior, the Magician, and the Lover—are the four central portals, if you will, through which the powerful energy of the Self becomes available to the ego.

In the same way that Kundalini energy manifests through the seven chakras, the power of the Self is transmitted to us through these four archetypes. You'll notice that the metaphors for both the archetypes and the chakras use different language to essentially describe the same process.

And so in the same way that energy can manifest in unresourceful ways within an unbalanced chakra system, archetypal energy will present itself in unresourceful ways to the ego, assuming the ego fails to access these four energies in a balanced and respectful manner.

Further, the successful journey to the Self requires that the ego balance and integrate the functions of the King, Warrior, Magician, and Lover by neither rejecting nor identifying with any of them but rather, serving each as a hose serves water.

Truly, each of these four powers is but one facet of the Self.

The King, Warrior, Magician, and Lover can be summed up, respectively, as the Being, Doing, Thinking, and Feeling principles of the Self.

To help illustrate what this means, you may visualize each archetype as being positioned on each end of a cross' vertical and horizontal axes.

The King and the Magician are opposing functions that balance each other, just as the Lover and the Warrior are.

Hence, the King stands at the crown of the cross, on the northern axis and opposite the Magician, who is positioned beneath the King on the southern axis.

On the horizontal east-west axis stand the Lover and the Warrior, at opposite ends.

The point where the Lover and the Warrior intersect is the same place where the King and Magician meet. It is also where the "Lord of the Four Quarters", the individuated ego, dances his cosmic dance of transcendence.

The creative tension that is caused from the intersection of the Lover and the Warrior generates what I often call **"tender aggression."** This is the combination of the Warrior's stoic action with the Lover's warm passion.

In a similar way, the King and the Magician also complement each other: the King's power is informed by his Magician's wisdom. The alchemical virtue of **"contemplated force"** is produced by the combination of the two's energies on the vertical axis.

Together, these wonderful virtues of tender aggression and contemplated force are the "alchemical gold" that becomes available to the ego when it accesses these four archetypes more or less equally.

Unfortunately, the ego that does not access these functions in a balanced way experiences the "shadow forms" of the archetypes.

Each archetype has two shadows. Both are extremes, lying on one end of the spectrum. The goal is to find the spot that is "just right."

As you read about each of the archetypes in the following sections, you will notice that you may resonate with some more than others. Moreover, you will notice that you are currently relating— in varying degrees—to the shadow elements as well.

This is good. The more you understand how you relate to these archetypes in your life, the better equipped you will be for the journey inward.

We will discuss techniques for developing stronger relationships with these archetypes in a later section. For now, let's explore how they function.

Lover

The Lover is the archetype of passion, sensuality, feeling, joy, connection, support, empathy, and embodiment. The Lover corresponds to the second and fourth chakras.

Within the psyche, it is the Lover that awakens in a person a zest for life and all of its beauty.

The Lover has a strong emotional sense that all things are connected. He wants to experience *everything*, delighting all five of his senses in all that he does.

The Lover feels his way through life—he feels for the world. When others are in pain, it is his pain also; and when they are happy, he is happy.

"The Kiss" by Gustav Klimt

Accessing the Lover in a balanced way enables a person to connect deeply with himself, others, and the world around him.

When the ego is relating to the energies of this archetype in unbalanced ways, the Lover's shadow manifests in one of two forms: the Addicted Lover or the Impotent Lover.

The Addicted Lover is the grown-up version of the typical "momma's boy." This is the Lover in overdrive, and results when the ego is inflated and identifies with the Lover.

The person with this archetype's shadow form is too "in love" with everything, forever indulging his senses and being unable to get down to business. Jumping from romantic partner to romantic partner and job to job, he imagines himself to be a sex symbol, Eros, as well as a Dionysus.

This man is ungrounded, deriving his happiness from external sources. He is dependent on others, and the thought of eating alone or being alone for too long makes him cringe.

On the other side of the coin is the Impotent Lover, the archetype of the fantasizer, the hopeless dreamer. This archetype manifests when a person is out of touch with, or suppresses, the Lover energies.

A person who is accessing the Lover in this unbalanced way never gets anything done either. But it is not because he is busy indulging in his vices as the Addicted Lover does.

The Impotent Lover is unfruitful on account of his living in the world of make-believe. He vicariously experiences the thrill of accomplishment by indulging in his own fantasies and in the lives of others.

The man who accesses this shadow form of the Lover will will talk about all that he wants to do without any execution. He fantasizes about his crushes, but never asks them out; he would rather watch porn and masturbate in secrecy. He has grand visions for an entrepreneurial business, but never follows through. In simple terms, he is unreliable.

Accessing the Impotent Lover causes a person to overvalue others while undervaluing himself. As he idealizes other people, he disavows responsibility and gives away his power. He will say yes, even if it means saying no to himself, and even if he knows he is unable to follow through on his word.

This person could use a bit more self-love, impetus, and a zest for living his life amongst the world.

When a person moves beyond these shadow poles and develops a conscious relationship with the Lover in his full radiance, he will undoubtedly experience an influx of libido, enthusiasm, and a sense of compassion and connectedness with all things.

He who accesses the mature Lover experiences his body and life fully.

Psychological, emotional, and sexual intimacy come naturally to this person, as do feelings of joy, pleasure, and ecstasy.

He has a masterful ability to appreciate the subtle flavors of life through art, people, music, food, the natural world, and all other things that are beautiful. It is as if he sees God in everything.

The mature Lover is orientated toward love, not fear, and is emotionally available and balanced. He accepts himself and others unconditionally, and listens to the instincts of his heart.

In relation to the other archetypes, the Lover serves as the connecting function, keeping the group in harmony. Checked by the mature Warrior's ability to act and remain detached, disciplined, and grounded, the sensitive Lover becomes ever more resourceful.

The Lover serves the King by providing him with the compassion necessary to be nurturing. The Lover also balances the Magician's cognitive abilities with his sensuality.

As an example, look no further than Zorba, from *Zorba the Greek*, who is an exemplary model of the Lover in his mature form.

Warrior

The Warrior is the archetype of aggressive action, courage, discipline, commitment, loyalty, and honor in the psyche.

The Warrior gets the job done. He is skillful, purposeful, efficient, and emotionally detached from the work he does. Once the King decides what must be done, the Warrior executes his command thoroughly. The Warrior corresponds to the first and third chakras.

The shadow forms of the Warrior manifest as the Sadist and the Masochist. The former is born from ego inflation with Warrior energy, whereas the latter is the result of ego alienation from the Warrior.

The Sadist is the bully. He is too aggressive, using the power of his sword to berate and abuse others.

He slashes out, hurting his relationships. "I don't need anyone!" exclaims the person who is in Warrior overdrive. "It's my way or the highway, so get out of my way," he might say.

The man who unconsciously identifies with the Warrior in this way imagines himself as an Achilles.

He allows his emotions to get the best of him—anger, violence, and intimidation dominate his life. He finds it very challenging to respect authorities of any kind, even those who are fair and just.

In reality, this person acts out of his own insecurity of feeling small.

On the other end of the spectrum is the Masochist, or coward.

This man is afraid of his power and suppresses it by turning his sword onto himself. Rather than berate and abuse others, he bullies *himself*.

"Achilles" by Franz Matsch

The Masochist is ungrounded, lacks a sense of purpose, and is limited by his passivity.

Others step over him and bully him because he fails to set up boundaries in his relationships and dealings with others.

Milton, a character from the movie *Office Space*, wonderful depicts this shadow side of the Warrior. In the movie, he is harassed by his coworkers and manager, and simply allows it to happen.

As we witness these behaviors unfold in myths and in real life, the man who denies his Warrior for too long eventually ends up swinging to the other extreme of bullying.

On the other hand, the mature Warrior stands at the center of the Sadist and the Masochist.

Accessing the Warrior in his fullness, the mature Warrior, endows a person with focus and discipline.

The mature Warrior sets up necessary boundaries in his relationships—something the Masochist has trouble doing. However, unlike the Sadist, the Warrior exerts his force with grace and compassion.

No one will step on the Warrior or push him off course, although not because he threatens and intimidates by force but because he is grounded in himself. He is so immersed in working on himself and carrying out the King's orders that no outside event or person can distract him from his missions.

When necessary, the Warrior deals the blow of creative destruction.

This may mean ending a relationship that is not resourceful, quitting a job that is not in line with our core values, getting rid of bad habits, or standing up to injustice—even if it means the initial pain of ripping off the band-aid, so to speak.

When the Warrior clears out the old, he makes way for the new. His use of his sword is always motivated by love, not hatred or apathy.

In relation to the other archetypes, the Warrior's stoicism is tempered by the Lover's warmth.

This combination produces the alchemical quality of tender aggression, creating a compassionate Warrior who fights for love and not against evil.

The Warrior in his full power serves the King wholeheartedly, for a warrior without a cause is dangerous to himself and to others. As well, the Magician employs the Warrior with the skills and street sense needed to execute his mission carefully.

The movies *Gladiator* and *Braveheart* represent modern archetypes of the mature Warrior.

Magician

Moving onto the vertical axis of the cross, the Magician archetype inhabits its southern end.

Clever, wise, skillful, reflective, and insightful, the Magician aids the ego that relates to it by providing his magic. This magic is the force that drives us to read, to acquire skills and knowledge, and to master our vocation. This archetype corresponds to the fifth and sixth chakras.

When a person is inflated with Magician energy, he exhibits traits from the shadow form known as the Detached Manipulator. By contrast, a person who has a weak link to the Magician experiences the other shadow form, the Denying "Innocent" One.

Shaman

The former shadow form, the Detached Manipulator, abuses his power of cleverness, using it to wreak havoc on himself and the world around him. He is a cold, intellectual, and arrogant prick, who is quick to poke holes in theories and belittle others with grand displays of his knowledge. He loves nothing more than to see other people suffer on account of his "cleverness".

The Manipulator has a knack for deflating the joy and pride of those around him.

As a kid, he tells you that Santa isn't real, and as an adult, he often becomes a heady, diehard atheist who makes fun of religious people, while being unaware that he, in his fundamentalism, has much in common with his shadow.

He pretends that no one could possibly be smarter than he, but this arrogance stems from his deep-rooted discomfort with not knowing, as well as a lack of self-worth.

He plays practical jokes, tells lies, gossips, and makes fun of others. He dominates discussions, combatively deconstructs opinions that differ from his own, and thinks he is above the world and all the "dumb" people around him.

Unlike the other shadow, the Denying "Innocent" One, the Manipulator actually does have the skills to back up his talk in some ways, but he does things like withholding information from others—even when he feels it could help them—because he'd rather feel "special" and maintain his status of "guru". He would rather ridicule others, who are using their magic, than make a "fool" of himself.

Inwardly, the Manipulator is the cold, passive-aggressive, and sadistic inner critic of self-sabotage.

He is perhaps the lowest among the shadow archetypes, and is often identified with Satan and other villainous figures in mythology.

The other shadow pole of the Magician, the Denying "Innocent" One, is the archetype of the "armchair adventurer".

This person experiences the power of the Magician vicariously.

He plays video games, reads, and researches endlessly—yet rarely takes action on account of his perfectionism and his fear of looking "stupid" or making "wrong" decisions.

So, he becomes a "keyboard warrior," who undermines the efforts of people who are actually doing things in the world.

He can write your ear off with a YouTube comment correcting your form on a deadlift, but when the time comes for his skills to be tested, he chokes because he has no experience. This person chuckles to himself when those whom he trolls become angry.

The Denying "Innocent" One pretends to knows things, but he really does not understand them.

Behind his mask of feigned mastery sits a man who is insecure with his incompetence, and is subsequently envious of those who access the Magician in productive ways. He lacks the compassion of the Lover, the drive of the Warrior, and the decisiveness and vision that the King has to offer.

When a person accesses the Magician in a balanced way, though, he acquires an inner genius and shaman. The mature Magician has access to the knowledge that the Detached Manipulator possesses, but rather than hold onto it greedily, he shares this knowledge with the world.

He has mastered the arts of communication and insight. He has also achieved mastery in his vocation through the time he has spent reflecting, learning, and practicing his craft.

Because of this, the man who accesses the mature Magician is able to skillfully proffer his gifts in the service of others.

The mature Magician is an alchemist. He uses his wisdom, embodied skills, and ability to tread the waters of the unconscious to help the ego navigate the journey to the Self.

The Magician serves as the wise sage, or the spiritual counselor, among the archetypes.

He provides the King with insight, so that he may make informed decisions. He provides the Warrior with technical proficiency, so that he may carry out the King's orders. And he provides the Lover with useful intuition, so that he may relate to the world around him.

Without the King, the Magician has no direction and authority; without the Warrior, he gets nothing done; and without the Lover, he fails to use his services for good.

The character Gandalf from *Lord of the Rings* and Nikola Tesla, an inventor who is best recognized for his contributions to modern electricity, are examples of mature Magicians.

KING AND QUEEN

The archetype of the King, or Queen, sits in his throne at top of the cross.

If there was ever an archetype that is severely lacking in ourselves and in our world, it is this royal energy. We crave the Return of the King.

The King is the principle of authority, vision, and empowerment in the psyche. His very presence affirms, protects, and nurtures the individual who accesses him in a balanced way, as well as all those who surround him.

Centered, intuitive, and calm, the King instills order, justice, and his blessing in the kingdom of the psyche. He has a clear vision and endows a man with the quality of decisiveness. The archetype of the King corresponds to the seventh chakra.

The ego that is inflated with King energy experiences the shadow of the Tyrant. The ego that is alienated from the King accesses the shadow of the Weakling.

Where the mature King commands respect, the Tyrant *demands* it. He is consumed by the Ring of Power and wants to control everything around him.

Born from his own insecurity and lack of centeredness, the Tyrant seeks to intimidate and dominate others, including the ego. He's the inner perfectionist or the Type-A personality that drives the body to perform better and better—until it collapses.

Where the King empowers, the Tyrant disempowers, squashing any displays of strength or greatness that are not his own.

The person who accesses the King in his Tyrant shadow form simply cannot take orders from others. He also can never relax, and *always* has to call the shots and lead from the front.

He is compulsively dominant, doesn't take kindly to constructive criticism or advice, despises weakness, and grows angry when the people around him do not submit to his demands and serve him.

The Tyrant is narcissistic and wants to be worshipped and bowed to. He thinks that he is God and forgets that he is just a conduit.

A perfect embodiment of this archetype is the ruthless German dictator Hitler, along with domineering fathers, egocentric bosses, and corrupt politicians that abuse their positions of power.

The Tyrant believes himself to be the center of the universe—everything around him belongs to him and exists solely to serve him.

On the contrary, the shadow of the Weakling is the other extreme: flat, submissive, and indecisive.

The person who accesses the Weakling projects his royal authority onto others, thus disavowing power and responsibility.

He blames his circumstances. "The teacher gave me a bad grade because he's racist," says the Weakling. Or says, "My genetics suck. I'm a hardgainer [or an endomorph], so it's impossible for me to look like that guy with great genetics."

The Weakling is the disempowering and complaining voice within an individual's psyche.

The ego possessed by the Weakling takes forever to make decisions; yet when he does decide, he can't commit. He will go back and forth between all the different options before (and after) declaring what must be done. He is not a conscious actor in his reality, but rather, a passive recipient of what he calls "fate".

The character of Commodus in *Gladiator* embodies the archetype of the Weakling. Another great example is Cameron from *Ferris Bueller's Day Off*.

Accessing the King in his mature form is a matter of coming to peace with the shadows of the Tyrant and the Weakling, and moving on.

The good King is a steward and servant of the realm. He is objective, centered, and fair.

The mature King serves the kingdom of the psyche through his vital, nourishing, and affirming presence. He is the mentor that pats you on the back and gives you a fist pound. He is the father, or mother, who makes sacrifices to provide for his, or her, family. He is the boss that encourages an employee to run with his great idea.

The King respects all, affirming life itself.

Seeing both dark and light—shadow and strength—in everything, the King showers all in his presence with empowerment, striving to bless and cultivate the life—the Strongest Version—within all things.

He has dealt with his narcissism and is secure in his own being, enough so that he encourages, rather than squashes, the greatness that exists outside of him.

Inwardly, the King provides an individual with an objective center, from which he can manage and organize his life. He blesses the ego that accesses him with integrity, creativity, vision, and decisiveness.

The man who accesses the mature King manages his energy for the good of the whole.

Rather than hoard his vitality as the Tyrant does—or, on the other extreme, empty his "cup" for others, thus exhausting himself and laying waste to the entire kingdom—he cultivates enough virility that his "cup" may overflow, so that he may optimally benefit himself and the kingdom.

Sourcing himself in the vital energies of life, he serves only insofar as he is not depleted.

The person who is inflated with unbalanced King and Lover energy—who sees himself as the sacrificial messiah—ends up sabotaging his heroic efforts to serve others beyond his means.

This inflated "messiah" ego is like a farmer who feeds his animals the last of his food before feeding himself, and then starves to death. He has killed himself and all of the animals in his overwhelming "righteousness."

The mature King feeds himself first, but unlike the Tyrant, he remembers to feed everyone else afterwards.

In conjunction with the Lover's compassion, the King remembers that his role is to serve, rather than be served. In relation to the other archetypes:

The Warrior provides the King with the impetus to carry out his mission.

The Magician counsels the King, informing his decision-making process so that he is able to use his power resourcefully and responsibly.

By resisting the temptation to shirk the Self's orders, or identify with the Self, the mature King leaves a lion's legacy.

Jesus, Sundiata, Aragorn, and Rama are examples of mature Kings.

THE INNER JOURNEY:
Dancing the Four Quarters, Eating Your Shadow, & Finding the Center

Dancing the Four Quarters

I've mentioned it before, but I again encourage you to read Robert Moore's King, Warrior, Magician, Lover, along with the other books I have included in the resources section, in order to understand these archetypes in more detail.

Before we dive further into the section, a quick note: I will be frequently referencing Christianity, not because I believe it to be better or worse than any other path to the Self, but simply because it is the tradition that I have been exposed to since childhood, and am thus more familiar with it.

From having read my condensed descriptions of the archetypes, though, I am sure you now have a better sense of how you relate to the King, the Warrior, the Magician, and the Lover in your psyche, in both their mature and shadow functions.

To a large extent, the culture and environment in which you grew up can have an impact on determining the degree to which you relate to a particular archetype, regardless of your natural disposition.

For example, if you grew up in a home where the King, Warrior, and Lover energies appeared to be already occupied by your family members, then you likely took on a dominant Magician function, even if you tended toward a different archetype.

Today, you will likely still play the role of the Magician wherever you go, affecting your relationships with friends, romantic partners, teachers, bosses, coworkers, and strangers.

There is no sense in blaming your parents, yourself, or any other circumstances for the lack of balance in your psyche, as that is part of the journey. *Now* that you are conscious of these forces, however, there are no excuses.

As you examine yourself, it is always important to take the empowered position, rather than play the victim.

Instead of thinking, "My parents didn't show me enough affection, so now I'm screwed up," ask yourself:

"How is this shadow currently manifesting itself in my life? How might I access this archetype in a more balanced way?"

Before you do anything else, I invite you to go again through each of the eight shadows and four mature archetypes, and answer these two questions.

Once you have answered these questions honestly, it is time to begin putting your understanding to practice.

I am no expert in relating to these energies, so I invite you to explore additional resources to help you further your development along this path inward.

As of right now, I will share some methods that I have found helpful for consciously relating to the four mature forces within the psyche.

It begins with finding objects in your external environment upon which you can **project** the different archetypes.

Projecting the contents of your psyche outwardly enables you to relate to them more effectively than attempting to do so while they remain inside your head.

This may be somewhat easier for the religious because they may already be familiar with having sacred images that carry power for them.

For others, it is important to find gods, but these do not have to be religious figures.

Why do I recommend working with material gods, or objects that offer meaning to you?

Without projecting the archetypes onto personally meaningful objects, you end up unconsciously projecting them onto other people. These energies are simply too powerful for you to contain inside.

If you observe yourself, you will likely notice that you have projected the gods in certain places.

For instance, we may already project our greatness onto a person whom we admire, perhaps a great athlete, artist, or celebrity.

Why else would we want to get autographs, shake hands, and elbow our way up to the front of the stage, but to simply be blessed and affirmed by the King, Warrior, Magician, and Lover in their physical forms? But be careful.

When you project onto other people, they might disappoint you. No person can ever fully be an archetype—we are too flawed, imperfect.

That said, it would be a wise move to retract the projections you have placed upon other people. You can do so by asking yourself who

KING

in your life serves each function and finding somewhere else to project these forces.

My suggestion is that you **choose five totems:** one for each of the four mature archetypes, as well as an additional one for the archetype of the opposite sex. So a man would choose a Goddess, and a woman would select a God.

Projecting your Anima or Animus—the feminine and masculine inner personality, respectively—onto a totem is important for the same reason that projecting each of the others is helpful. Doing so saves you from projecting your God or Goddess onto another person, which often creates dependency in a relationship.

For this practice, you may use small statues, pictures, posters, and other objects.

As I mentioned, it is important that you spend some time and effort searching for images that mean something to you and trigger a sense of reverence.

King, Warrior, Magician, Lover

If you are religiously inclined, you may use images from the specific tradition that you practice.

A Christian, for instance, might use the symbols of the four evangelists: Matthew the Angel (Magician), Mark the Lion (King), Luke the Ox (Warrior), and John the Eagle (Lover). Virgin Mary would be his Goddess.

As yet another example, someone might use the following Hindu deities: Kamadeva (Lover), Hanuman (Warrior), Ganesha (Magician), Vishnu (King), and Lakshmi (Goddess)—or Shiva as your King, and Parvati as your Goddess.

For a less traditional approach, you might choose images that carry less religious meaning in the modern era, such as from the Greek or Egyptian pantheons; or even animals and characters from movies, books, and other mythologies.

As an alternative to using posters and statues, you may wish to use ritualized objects, such as a sword for the Warrior, a crown for the King, a shamanic drum for the Magician, and a flute for the Lover.

These are all just ideas, and I invite you to choose your own. The most important thing is that it must carry power for *you*.

Once you've found the five totems—one for the Goddess and one each for the mature King, Warrior, Magician, and Lover—the next step is to place them strategically around a room, where you will see them often.

Choose a room that is private and serves as your inner sanctum or temple, like a bedroom or private office. Ideally, this is a room that you spend time in, alone.

Position these totems in ways that honor them and bring them to life.

Now, let's be honest.

If you don't consider yourself to be particularly spiritual or religious, what I am about to describe might sound odd (if it doesn't already).

But if you have read this far, then I trust that you are serious about growing stronger. Trust your heart and gut on this—if it speaks to you, then I encourage you to try the following practice:

Once you have placed these sacred totems around your temple, it is a good idea to **ritually honor them in some way**.

This might look like prayer. It might involve lighting incense. Perhaps you meditate on these figures, or simply take time at the end of your day to look at them and thank them for their presence in your life.

Whatever the case, you must treat them as you would a god (because that is what they represent). If you are not religious, then at least pretend, and do so sincerely.

Even if it feels odd at first, the way you treat these images—once they carry your psychological projection—directly influences how these energies manifest in your life.

In reality, you are practicing what the truly religious have known and done throughout the ages.

This is deep, reverent meditation on the Self. The benefits from this practice will vary based on the degree to which you approach it with **reverence and humility**.

However, this is not idol worship.

The difference is that you are worshipping the powers they represent, not the objects themselves. The totems are not God, but merely fingers that point the way. Idol worship is praising an image that contains no meaning.

From a certain perspective, God can be just as potently present in a photograph of a grizzly bear as It can in a crucifix.

If the feeling arises in you, you may pray to these archetypes.

Bow before the King and request His blessing; ask the Magician for His counseling; ask the Warrior for His commitment; and ask the Lover for His enthusiasm.

Ask the archetypes to forgive you for running away, or for being inflated.

When you make a conscious effort to relate to the archetypes through devotional practice, you open the gates to the power of the Self.

In metaphorical terms, you turn on the spigot, and the water comes gushing out and onto the world. Similarly, if you turn on the light switch, light pours into the room.

Without a doubt, you will shine when you access the Self, and the people around you will notice.

But heed this caveat.

When you do open up the channels for the archetypes to move through you, **you must not take credit for the work they do**.

Exercise your humility—"All glory and honor are yours, Almighty Father [King, Warrior, Magician, Lover, Goddess], forever and ever."

Remember not to fly too close to the sun. Dance with the seasons of life. Learn to not take yourself too seriously. Et cetera.

In his audio series, The Ego-Archetypal Self Axis, Robert Moore shares a wonderful interpretation of The Lord's Prayer.

He likens the phrase, "Give us this day our daily bread...", to the ego's asking the archetypal Self to fill it with the energy needed to accomplish its tasks and in service to the Self.

Essentially, if you make an effort to relate to the archetypes but instead use their energy for your own ego satisfaction—greed, pride, laziness, and all the other "sins"—the Self will cut you off.

This goes to say that remaining humble and in good relations with the archetypes is to honor their grace; to use their energy to carry out what the Self wants to do through you, rather than to squander it for your own enjoyment and "power."

Remind yourself of this fact—that the energy you are afforded is not yours but theirs—by dedicating ritualistic acts to the archetypes.

Sacrificing "your" time and energy, in addition to living the life the Self intends for you, demonstrates that you work not for yourself but for the Self.

There are many ways to do this. Perhaps you make a pilgrimage, go for a hike, or train as a way to offer your honor and gratitude. You could also donate money anonymously, or do a kind favor for someone else. It must involve having skin in the game, having great meaning, and sacrificing "your" resources.

As Abdul Baha says, "Be generous in prosperity."

When your cup is overflowing, give it away freely and expect nothing in return. Your power is not yours, and the moment you pretend it is and waste it away in indulgence, you lose it.

Also, it is important to be private about your devotional practice.

By drawing attention to yourself when you act kindly and generously, you fall into inflation. And still, the Self will cut you off from the flow of creativity.

Performing charitable works without calling attention to ourselves is the way we remain in conscious relationship with the Self, without getting inflated.

As long as these totems contain your projections, treat them with the utmost care.

Make sure you position them securely and give them their own spaces in the room. These objects are no longer profane—you have infused them with the sacred.

They carry powerful psychological projections, so the way you treat them physically will naturally affect the way they treat you psychologically.

The more we grow to treat the archetypes with integrity— for they witness everything we think and do—and the more we remember to not take ownership for their glory, the stronger we become.

Bonus:

Another practice for bringing balance into our relations with the archetypes is to consciously choose to listen to the music *that carries the energy of which we find ourselves lacking.*

Music is a manifestation of energy. Music carries the archetypes in its rhythms, its melodies, and its timbre.

If you are strongly infused with imbalanced Warrior energy, experiment by listening to more reggae, Motown, and Spanish guitar. This will bring the Lover back into your life.

If you identify with the Addicted Lover, on the other hand, listening to tribal music, or any music with a driving beat such as A Tribe Called Red, will aid in bringing out the Warrior.

Shamanic drumming and other forms of meditative music will aid the Magician function. The King's music is classical and silence.

Finding role models or personal heroes to model yourself after, and learning everything you can about them, is another resourceful practice for bringing these energies into balance.

This might mean reading myths, watching videos and movies, or listening to biographies about people you admire.

Flooding your mind with stories about heroes inspires and gives life to your own individuation journey.

You can read about more ways of accessing the archetypes in the back of [King, Warrior, Magician, Lover](.).

Eating Your Shadow

As you progress in dealing with the archetypes, you may find it helpful to engage with their shadow forms. We all have shadow issues, despite thinking we don't.

I advise you to proceed with caution when interacting with these darker forces.

"Shadow work" is a serious practice, so you may want to consult with a reputable Jungian psychoanalyst that is familiar with this type of practice.

If you are worried that bringing your shadow into the light of consciousness will invite evil forces to move through you, don't worry. People commit bad deeds when they suppress their shadow, not when they accept it.

The more someone suppresses his shadow, the more powerfully he projects it onto others. For example, Hitler had a monstrous shadow in his closet, and he sought to eradicate it from the world.

The same could be said for extremists and terrorists of all kinds. Ugliness is seen as "out there," not a potentiality lurking within us.

The person who becomes conscious of his shadow and accepts the ugliness—his potential for evil—that resides within him moves beyond it. He realizes that just because the shadow is inside of him does not mean it can dominate him.

Just as Jesus faced Satan in the desert, and as Buddha and Rama battled the demons of the forest, the individuating ego is strong enough to resist the temptation to merge with the "dark side."

So, becoming conscious of the shadow does not mean that you become it, just as shining a flashlight into a closet does not make you become what you see in there.

Rather, it enables you to recognize all of the monsters and angels—your spectrum of potential for good and bad—that reside in your metaphorical closet. With this liberating recognition, you stop projecting them onto others.

When you begin to realize that the junk you see in other people is really just a speck of dust in your own eye; and when you understand that the gold you see in others is really the radiance that is also within you—your relationships with your surroundings grow more harmonious.

There is no getting around it. If you are committed to becoming the Strongest Version of Yourself, your shadow must be dealt with at some point.

Of course, this is an ongoing process. It will take time. Now may not even be the time, but just trust your intuition.

I recommend that you explore the resources I provide at the end of the book to better familiarize yourself with these practices.

One effective practice for bringing the shadow into light is to **interpret your dreams**.

Dreams can be incredibly illuminating. If you think about it, it is as if the Self produces a personalized movie for us every night, trying to point the way to the light, if only we'd pay attention.

This is the hard part: interpreting your dreams begins with remembering them.

You can't always recall them, but it takes practice. If you have trouble recalling your dreams, try writing down whatever you can remember immediately upon waking for a couple of weeks.

It may also help to consciously set an intention every night before you go to bed by telling yourself that you *will* remember your dream in the morning. Perhaps eventually, you will start remembering them.

Once you do, you can begin decrypting the language of the Self.

There are a number of resources out there to help you interpret the symbols and events of your dreams. But the best tool you can use is your own brain, and those of your friends and family.

You already know—perhaps better than any book or outside person can tell you—what a particular image means to you if you consider it long enough.

Active imagination is another Jungian technique that can be used to initiate dialogue between you and the shadows of your unconscious.

You can do this by performing a free-flow handwriting exercise, during which you write out a question and see what voice answers on paper.

You might ask about a particular self-sabotaging pattern that is invading your life. Perhaps you encountered a mysterious figure in a dream, and you want to know what it is trying to convey.

Write, *"Who are you, and what do you want to tell me?"*

You will always get an answer. Write as quickly as your hand can go for as long as you feel inspired, without stopping or editing the words that come up.

It might feel like you are talking to yourself, but you aren't.

You are actually conversing with a shadow aspect of the Self. If you muster up the courage and confidence to try this exercise, you may be surprised at what insight is revealed to you.

A third tool I have found to be resourceful is to view the world around you as a mirror.

Just like dreams, what you see in the world and in others is a direct reflection of what is happening inside of you.

Pay attention to synchronistic events. Perhaps you have been seeing a certain number all of the time. Perhaps you run into a mentor-type figure just when you needed one the most.

Determine the meaning behind seemingly unrelated events that are mysteriously coinciding in your life. As Paulo Coelho writes in The *Alchemist*, pay attention to the omens.

The Self is contacting you. As much as you seek the Self, the Self, too, wishes to come into relation with you.

The people that show up in your life serve as mirrors, also. Performing shadow work from this frame of mind can have powerful effects.

Ask yourself, **"Which person in my life can I absolutely not stand? Who disgusts me? Whom do I hate?"** Right there is a shadow projection for you to deal with.

You must discern, just as you would a character in your dreams, what this person's presence in your life is revealing about your own unconscious.

What dragons have you been too afraid to face in yourself that are now showing themselves, in projected form, in the outer world?

And in a similar light, upon whom are you projecting your angels?

Whom do you admire, agree with, and want to be friends with? Look in the mirror. All that you hate and all that you admire are inside of you.

The shadow will be inside of us forever. But we can integrate it and decide not to act on its impulses by bringing it into conscious light and choosing not to indulge. Remember: this is a never-ending journey.

FINDING THE CENTER

So, back to the original question I presented at the beginning of this chapter: "Where is God?"

The simple answer is that God is within you but is not you.

This presence is the source of all life. How It appears to you depends entirely on how you relate to It.

If you run away from the Self, you experience Its shadow. If you identify with the Self, you also experience Its shadow.

The dragon breathes its fire upon the inflated and alienated egos.

But pain and suffering are merely God's balancing mechanisms that He uses to bring us back to Him.

As Krishna reveals Himself to Arjuna in *The Bhagavad Gita*, the Self reveals Itself to us gradually, in the forms that we are ready for, and that will catalyze our evolution.

If life is knocking you down, I challenge you to resist the temptation to curse fate, yourself, or anyone else.

Instead, listen to the message—you are off course, and the Self is knocking on your door. What does the Universe want to do through you? *Will you surrender?*

What is your bliss? Where is your *en-theosiasm*? Look at the etymology of that word—Theos is the Greek word for God.

What are you being *in-spir[it]ed* to do?

Coming into communion with the Self is an arduous and heroic process that takes a lifetime.

The journey to the Center is paradoxical.

The way in is the way out, and the way out is the way in. And the way is to get out of the way and keep getting out of the way.

We come into relationship with the Self as we would a wild animal, with courage, reverence, respect, and vigilance.

And we do this by dancing with the archetypes, and by paying attention to our dreams, our feelings, and the world around us.

We say prayers and perform devotional acts as enthusiastically as monks—all the while knowing that all that we sacrifice is within us and is not us and transcends us.

Stepping aside when the powers of the Self move through us, we say, "It's not me. I am just a vessel. The Self is doing Its work, and I just happen to be standing here."

We know the Self is wiser than I, stronger than I, more compassionate than I, and more powerful than I.

King

Section IV
Life
Mastery

King

YOUR VISION: Establishing Your Vision & Core Values

Why Have a Vision?

Determining your mission, or your vision for the future, is less a matter of creating a dream than it is of *discovering that calling that you have always had and which it is your duty, or dharma, to respond to.*

What are you being called to do? Who are you being called to become?

Your fate is not unchangeable.

Your destiny is there already, but you must meet it halfway by first aligning yourself with your calling and moving from there.

The practice of vision-setting I would like to share with you was first introduced to me over a decade ago by Brian Tracy, in a program called <u>The Luck Factor</u>.

As soon as I heard him describe the following process, I immediately wrote in my journal my vision for the life I felt inclined to live. I encourage you to do the same.

Today, I eat the fruits that grew from those tiny little "vision seeds" that I planted many years ago.

Of course, the seeds of my dreams were not mine; they had been given to me well before I realized them. But it was up to me to place them in nourishing soil and water them with action.

Without my planting and caring for those seeds, they would have remained unrealized potentialities. Wonderful, yes. But worthless.

Mind you, the visions I set down on paper came to fruition in ways I could not have possibly intended.

You do not totally control life, but you do play a role in fulfilling your own destiny.

It is up to you to determine your vision and to take action that moves you toward your dreams, but you cannot try to control how they happen.

In my life, I have allowed my visions to manifest in their own due time. I think that was key.

There have been moments when I forgot about a seed I had planted and then—all of the sudden—a tree bearing fruit was there!

As with all things, it is a good idea not to [rush growth](), or try to force your dreams to happen. After all, too much sun here or too much water there will leave you with a dead sapling.

Trust that by setting your intention, going to work, and allowing the Self to take care of the rest—your dreams will surely manifest when it is time.

Establishing Your Vision and Core Values

I envision my life in four areas: **health, vocation, relationships, and legend.**

For each of these four categories, I write down the vision I have on a single sheet of paper.

Envisioning my life in this way helps me balance my focus and my life, but it can take some conscious effort for you.

I use two triggers to spark my imagination when drafting up a vision.

First, I use the **"lying on my deathbed"** perspective.

I imagine that at the end of my life, when it is all said and done, what kind of relationships, health, and vocation would I have wanted? And what legacy did I leave behind?

I then ask myself what my **perfect day** would look like with regard to each category. For instance, what does a perfect day of health look like, or a perfect day of work?

Once I have developed a clear vision for one of these four categories, I choose four **core values** that I will adopt to support my fulfilling that particular vision.

Rather than focusing on values that are associated with doing, I encourage you to adopt virtues of *being*.

In order to manifest any visions you may have, you will have to become the type of person who is capable of doing it.

Who do you have to become to fulfill your vision? What core values must you strengthen in yourself in order to live your perfect day of health on a daily basis, have the relationships you would like, and do work that serves to fulfill your legend?

This is the time to dream irrationally.

Carry no doubts or uncertainty about how realistic your vision is. If it is truly aligned with your deepest aspirations, you hold the power to realize it.

Legend

You may begin by envisioning your **legend,** or the legacy you will leave behind.

Alluding to Carl Jung, Joseph Campbell referred to this as *"Living Your Myth."*

Determining your legend comes first, because the other three categories—health, vocation, and relationships—all *support* your ultimate purpose here on earth.

When you discover your personal legend, everything else—the kind of health, relationships, and career you want in life—becomes clear.

I invite you now to **imagine your last day on earth.**

There you lie, on your deathbed, surrounded by your loved ones, the life slowly fading from your eyes.

You are looking back on your life—*now what do you see?*

Do you have regrets? Is there a moment in your life you look back on and think to yourself, "If only I'd done that differently then…?"

If you could do it over again—if you had but another 5 years of life—what would you do? Is there something you must do before you die? Someone you must become?

What do you think people will say about you after you are gone? How did you make the people in your life feel when you were still living? Whom did you serve?

At your funeral, what will your loved ones, friends, colleagues, and strangers say—and believe in their hearts—about your character?

Your legend depends on every action you make this day, and going forward.

Accordingly, you must ask yourself with every decision that you make, *"What if this were compounded?"*

For example, if I stole this thing or cheated in this particular way today—and if everyone did this—what kind of world would we live in?

Or, "If I generously support this person—and if everyone in the world supported one another in this way—what kind of world would we live in?"

Every action, whether seen and "unseen," adds to your legacy.

Looking back on your life from the deathbed perspective, with all these other questions floating around in your mind, ask yourself the following question:

What would it mean for me to not just life a full life but live the fullest life imaginable... ? **Whom must I become in order to die with a big, peaceful smile in my heart?**

Discover the reason you are alive today. If you are unable to find a reason, then create one.

Your visions and core values can change, so don't worry about getting them perfect. Just choose the ones that give you the most excitement and currently speak truest to you. After all, you can always make changes down the road.

Record your answers to these prompts now.

Once you have written down your vision, it is time for you to select the core values that will support the legend you wish to embody.

Imagine yourself as your fully-realized self, who has attained your dreams.

Looking back from this perspective, **which values did the Strongest Version of Yourself adopt to succeed on your journey?** These are the core values you would be wise to adopt.

To give you an example, the core values that I have chosen with respect to living my legend are: **philanthropy, faithfulness, art, and love.**

Living a life of **philanthropy** means serving my cause and my people with integrity.

It means that by the time death comes around, I have held nothing back and used every last ounce of my strength to empower myself and the people around me to grow stronger.

Faithfulness relates to my loyalty, my degree of accountability, and my trustworthiness.

Will I be remembered as a man of his word? Do I follow through on the things I say I will do?

With **art** and **love** come the tangible results of my existence—what did I leave behind? My legacy can come in many forms.

Did I build a business that empowered my community? Did I raise healthy children as best I could? And did I fully love the people in my life?

These are my values, but I invite you to choose your own. These are your actions, *your* relationships, and *your* legacy that you will have to face before you leave this world.

Choose four core values right now that support the fulfillment of your legend.

After writing down your vision and your core values, put them up somewhere where you will see them every single day, multiple times per day. Try taping them to your bathroom mirror or beside your bed.

Ideally, this space is also somewhat private.

Because your vision is personal, so I suggest that you do not share it in full detail with others.

I say this not necessarily to help you avoid having your ideas stolen, but more because it has been my experience that **the more you share what big dreams you have before you actually manifest them, the less likely you are to fulfill them.**

It might sound counterintuitive, but by talking about your grand visions with others, you tend to experience some of the perceived joy of having accomplished them in your imagination, without their actually happening. This can take away your motivation.

Avoid the temptation of mental masturbation. Focus your energy toward making your vision become real.

HEALTH

The success of your mission depends on how healthy you are. It does not matter how amazing your dream is if you are too dead to fulfill it.

Take some time now to establish your vision for the health you would like to cultivate and maintain.

Fast-forwarding to the end of your life, you should ask how healthy and vital was the Strongest Version of Yourself?

And what did you do to support and develop your body to ensure that it'd become the *most resourceful vehicle possible* to carry you toward fulfilling your unique legacy?

Imagine the Strongest Version of Yourself standing before you now.

Notice how deeply he breathes, how grounded he is, and how fully he accepts and loves all aspects of himself.

Feel the life force he radiates—how empowered you feel standing in his presence.

Now, ask this Strongest Version of Yourself what you did to develop such robust health.

What did you eat, and when did you eat it? How much time did you set aside to enjoy your meals in a relaxed environment?

When did you go to bed and wake up?

What form of movement did you practice?

What was your meditative practice of choice?

Did your legend call you to develop strength, agility, flexibility, quickness, or a combination of these skills?

There are no right answers—it is up to you to decide.

The key here is to choose the practices that you both enjoy and intuitively feel work best for you, as opposed to choosing based on what you think you should do.

Be honest with yourself about your own genetic and environmental strengths and weaknesses. Play to your strengths!

For instance, with regard to training, there are many ways to develop strength and athleticism.

Find the form of movement that you enjoy, and are thus most likely to commit to, and do that. It does not have to be lifting weights or even strength training for that matter.

Working against what comes naturally is tiring. Go with the natural strengths you have been given, and cultivate them to the fullest.

The theme that I am alluding to throughout this book is that we are all unique, and so what works for one person may not work for you.

Some people are better built to run than to lift, while others may be better off doing yoga.

Some people thrive when they lift Atlas stones and perform heavy squats and deadlifts, and others discover their strength through bodyweight movements or through a chosen sport.

Just do whatever it is that you enjoy doing. Experiment.

Now, once you have considered these questions thoughtfully, I invite you to write down your answer to the following question:

"What would my perfect day of health look like?"

A perfect day for me begins with getting up early and going for a walk.

Then I go about my business, making sure I train and eat well throughout the day, before returning home to rest.

For you, it might be a little bit different.

Maybe you like to sleep in. If you want to wake up at noon, then do that.

The more deliberate and detailed you are in your answers, the clearer the vision becomes.

Remember, promoting vitality involves balancing the forces of anabolism and catabolism in your life and in your body.

Working hard on achieving your goals while ignoring the fact that your body is breaking down is counterproductive.

So, it is important that you choose practices now, both for relaxing and working hard.

Ask yourself, "How can I have fun and relaxation—even if only for 10 minutes—on a daily basis?

Write down your vision for your health now.

After crafting this vision, I recommend you establish four core values that will support you in becoming vital and strong.

The values I have adopted for my health are: **ambition, discipline, knowledge, and balance.**

Are you **ambitious** enough to achieve the level of health you seek to maintain?

Whatever you want to achieve—whether it is greater strength, fat loss, flexibility, or something else—you should be able to set that goal down on paper and have enough ambition to make it happen.

Do you have the **discipline** to—as I often say, quoting Elbert Hubbard—do what you have to do to succeed—in becoming vital and strong—whether you feel like it or not?

Do you have the knowledge to develop habits that support your health? This has a lot to do with self-knowledge, too, and awareness of your own body's needs.

And do you **balance** the forces of anabolism and catabolism in your life?

Of course, these values are not limited to health and can be applied to many other aspects of your life.

I invite you to adopt mine, or choose your own.

VOCATION

The German language uses different terms to distinguish between work, vocation, and mission.

The word *arbeit* translates roughly to work, or job.

The word *beruf* refers more to the career, or profession, that you are called to perform.

But there is another word, *berufung*, which literally means your "appointment," or your "calling," in life.

When your *beruf* is aligned with your *berufung*—when your vocation and your mission are in harmony—your life is set on a powerful track.

So, when I ask you what your dream job is, I am not talking about a romantic daydream you might attempt to realize, or some convenient job that just so happens to simultaneously pay the bills and be something you enjoy doing.

What I am really asking is—

What work are you being appointed to do in this life?

It is not just, "What do I want out of life?" And neither is it only, "What is life asking of me?"

Perhaps it is a combination of the two: what type of work do you feel called to do *and want to pursue?*

Many people have expressed that they have trouble determining their own calling, but they misunderstand.

Your calling is a constantly evolving *feeling*—not a particular job itself, but the journey that interweaves all of the different hobbies and occupations that you find yourself doing along the way.

Knowing your calling is less a matter of figuring something out in your head, and more a matter of growing sensitive enough and courageous enough to trust the subtle inclinations of your body and acting on them.

In my experience, it is not until later in life—looking back and connecting the dots of all the things you did—that you can really know what your calling was.

But you must start somewhere, right?

The place to begin is to tune into the voice of the body—the voice of the Self—and determine for yourself what life is asking of you.

Where are your current sources of energy, or which activities bring you to life? Where do you find yourself spending your resources: your time, money, and energy? That is likely a good place to start.

It does not have to be perfect.

As long as you start somewhere, and as long as you continue to honor the evolution of your passions as you journey on through life, it has been my experience that your passions will funnel you into your true calling.

I invite you now to once again imagine yourself on your deathbed, this time focusing on the work you did. Consider the following questions:

How did you make use of your unique combination of talents and strengths in serving others in some form?

How did your career assist you in living out your personal legend?

And finally, How did your work enable you to uphold your commitments to your health and relationships?

Remember, all four of these aspects of your life—legend, health, vocation, and relationships—support and balance all others.

Now, having asked yourself these questions, I invite you to describe what your ideal day of work would look like.

What type of work do you do, and whom do you serve by doing it?

Where do you work? What climate do you live in? Do you work in an urban environment or a natural setting with mountains, or the ocean perhaps? Be specific.

Do you work alone or with people? Which do you prefer?

If you do work with others, with whom do you work? What would your ideal coworker look like?

Do you prefer working with people who are more introverted and get the job done in solitude, or would you rather be in a louder, more collaborative working environment? How about your boss...do you like working for someone, or would you rather be your own boss?

What is your working environment like? Are you standing, sitting, or moving around all day? Do you work remotely, online? Or would you prefer to go to the office every day? How often do you work? How often and where do you vacation?

These are some questions to spark your imagination.

If you already do have a job, ask yourself, "Is the work I am doing aligned with my core values and my legend?"

As Steve Jobs once famously advised in his [Stanford commencement speech](), ask yourself, "If today were the last day of my life, would I want to do what I am about to do today?"

If the answer is "no" for too many days in a row, you know you are not living in harmony with your core values. And if you are serious about growing stronger, then either that must change or your *perspective* must change.

Here is a sneaky trick for if you are working a job (or going to a school) that you don't enjoy but do not necessarily want to quit:

If you are struggling with your current situation, I challenge you to find a way to reframe the story you tell yourself about into something more constructive.

For instance, whatever it is that you are doing—be it work, school, or a relationship—if you reframe it as something that contributes to the fulfillment of your legend, you may find that it is easier to continue doing.

The core values I've adopted to support my vision for my vocation are: d**evotion, compassion, creativity, and enthusiasm.** Again, feel free to choose mine, or craft your own.

I guarantee you that no matter how much you love the work you choose to do, there will be days when you don't feel like doing it. This is where **devotion** comes in.

Ask yourself, *"Is the work I am doing truly in line with my core values for my health and relationships, and will it enable me to live out my legend? Do I have a good enough reason to be doing what I am doing to remain committed, even on the days I don't feel like doing it?"*

You must be able to keep your "big picture" mission prioritized so that even on days when you don't feel like doing the mundane stuff (that even the most fulfilling of work entails), you do it anyway, because you are *that* devoted to your cause.

Developing **compassion** is another key to the success of your vocation. Your vocation is an act of service in that you are serving someone in some way through your work.

Working from a place of compassion—or proceeding from a place of thinking, *"What can I give?"*—will serve you and your clients far more effectively in the long run. The heart is always a good place to come from.

Creativity is very important because we all have this innate desire to create something. And we live in a magical age in which we are given an amazing number of resources to open an infinite number of creative doorways and possibilities.

With the internet, anyone can be an author, a poet, or a motivational speaker--you can be anything you want to be. *What creative process do you most enjoy doing?*

I like to write, teach, and make videos. Some of my friends are magnificent musicians, app developers, and graphic designers. Other friends are incredible athletes, coaches, speakers, and teachers.

Whatever it is that makes you feel good—that allows you create, to turn a bunch of parts into a whole—is something you would be wise to pursue and do.

This lends itself to **enthusiasm**. According to Emerson, "Nothing great was ever achieved without enthusiasm."

I'd touched on this in the previous chapter: look at the root of word *enthusiasm,* notice that *en-thus* comes from the Greek *en-theos,* where *en* means "in" and *theos* means "god". So the word enthusiasm roughly translates into "possessed by god(s)" or "divinely inspired."

I challenge you to come into contact with that divine inspiration and follow where it leads you.

If you wish to become a master at what you do, you must enjoy the creative process your work entails.

I often say to choose a vocation you love doing (no matter how "crazy" or "odd" it may look to others).

Doing work you love is the easiest way towards mastery and finding fulfillment in your work, because it provides you with abundant energy. This will allow you to develop your craft much further than if you were to try to develop in a "secure" job that you did not like.

That being said, doing work you love is not the only way to find fulfilling work.

If you can create a compelling enough reason for why you do what you do, it does not matter what your work is. If your mind sees what you do as a component to the fulfillment of your personal myth, then you will begin to love whatever it is that you do.

Relationships

Good **relationships** are the foundation for success in all areas of your life.

This begins with your relationship with yourself. If you do not love yourself entirely and actively ensure your own needs are met, you will find it difficult to do the same for others.

Know this: however you treat yourself is how you will treat others. This is why, ironically, the most selfless thing you can do is to be self-*centered* (albeit *not* selfish).

Once you love and accept all aspects of yourself completely and treat yourself that way, once you become grounded and centered in your being, serving and empowering others will come naturally.

Imagining and looking back at yourself from the end of your life, ask yourself right now, *"How well did I love myself? Was I my own best friend? Was I completely honest with myself?"*

You see, it is easy—without realizing it—to neglect the one person in your life who is your partner in everything that you do and are: you.

Establishing Your Vision & Core Values

Back when I played football and was a professional Strongman—and even at various stages of my entrepreneurial career—I subconsciously developed a masochistic relationship with myself. I had been so focused on pushing and grinding my way toward my goals that I battered myself to the ground. Eventually, I wore myself out.

I am now conscious of this tendency in myself and have learned that the best way to balance my ambition is to set aside time throughout the day and week just for relaxation.

Practicing self-love not only involves making sure your needs are met; it also means not subjecting yourself to environments, perspectives, relationships, and other commitments that disempower you.

Don't worry so much about being rude. It is more detrimental to both yourself and the other person to keep commitments that you are unable to uphold, than it is to cut the tie and be free, if you feel you are being anchored down.

Ask yourself: *"What kinds of people did I surround myself with? Who supported me in fulfilling my destiny, and how did I support others in realizing theirs?"*

In life, you can either unconditionally accept the relationships that are handed to you, or you can create connections that you find mutually fulfilling.

Ask yourself: *"If I could do it over again, what values would I look for in a friend, life partner, mentor, and business partner? What kind of brother, sister, son, husband, wife, father, mother, friend, teacher, and student would I have been?"*

Which relationships suit you best? Are you a man or woman who enjoys a committed relationship, or do you prefer to "play the field"? Do you want to get married, have kids, and start a family? Or would you rather become a monk?

There are no right or wrong answers to these questions.

If we are not deliberate about answering, we tend to repeat the relationship-based habits that we have inherited subconsciously from our parents.

For instance, our parents were a certain way with us, and so, if we are blind to it, we will treat our own children that way. Your mother was a certain way with your father, and so you will be that way with your spouse, if you don't shed conscious light on it.

But those of us who create visions for our life can avoid that trap by deciding specifically the type of relationships we would like to foster: romantically, familially, with friends, with teachers, and of course, with Self.

Based on your answers to these questions, you can design your perfect day, this time focusing on your relationships.

For instance, set aside certain times of the day for yourself, for spending time with your wife, as well as with your children, your friends, and what have you.

You will also want to adopt a strong set of values to support your relationships. The ones I have chosen are: **generosity, assertiveness, discernment, and forgiveness.**

There is no such thing as a stingy lover. It is good to give freely—with no strings attached. You will find that by being generous, others tend to respond favorably to you. What you give comes back to you in different ways. Generosity is one of the greatest virtues a person can embody, in my opinion.

It is also crucial that you **assert** yourself in your relationships with others. Ask yourself, *"Does the person with whom I am in a relationship share my vision for our relationship, whether it become romance, friendship, or business?"*

Do you have the strength to set up boundaries and to say "no" in your relationships? *What are those boundaries?* Are you honest and transparent with yourself and others, and are you able to assert your wishes clearly and respectfully?

Don't allow people to tread on you, bring you down, or take from you without your permission. Knowing how to say "no" in relationships is as important as understanding how to say "yes."

Discernment is the ability to take a step back and assess whether your current relationships are resourceful to you or not.

Looking somewhat objectively at your life, you will realize which relationships are not resourceful for your greater vision. Maybe those friends who play video games every waking hour are not your crowd. Perhaps that woman, as beautiful as she is, might not be the best one for you to marry.

Whatever the case may be, you have to be discerning enough to examine your relationships.

Are the people in your life those whom you want to be surrounding yourself with, and are they supporting you on your mission?

The people with whom you associate have tremendous impacts on your character and on your legend. As Jim Rohn said, "You are the average of the five people you spend the most time with." That is to say, if the five people you associate with are lazy, then you yourself may adopt that tendency.

And finally, **forgiveness** is key.

Don't throw stones, because we all live in glass houses. The understanding that you yourself are imperfect—just like everyone else—is a prerequisite for being able to forgive. Give people the benefit of the doubt, without being naive.

Oftentimes, forgiving the other person is better than "winning" an argument. It does not mean that they are justified in their error, but reprimanding them for their actions usually does not accomplish anything.

Forgiving someone else is as much for you, if not more, than it is for the other person.

Setting the Intention: Visualization & Affirmation

VISUALIZATION AND AFFIRMATION

Reprogram your mind to align with your visions and core values, and you will become a more conscious co-creator of your reality.

John Assaraf, a spiritual philanthropist and teacher, calls this neural reconditioning.

It has been said many times before that we become what we think about most. My experience confirms this.

Our character automatically changes to meet, or to come into accordance with, our most dominant thoughts and beliefs.

Thousands of years before positive self-talk became popularized in the self-development community, our ancestors were using various affirmation, visualization, and self-talk practices in their daily lives to empower themselves.

They referred to these mind-strengthening practices as prayer, mantra, and meditation.

Realize that by changing our mental conversation—the way we talk to ourselves—we literally change the structure of our brain, by creating new neural pathways and overriding old ones.

Altering our brains in this way changes our thoughts, our words, our deeds, our habits, and ultimately, our character and our actions.

Who you are today is a product of your neural patterning, up until now.

In other words, you have been practicing affirmations your entire life—you have just been doing so subconsciously.

Whenever you peer into the mirror, you are looking at all the thoughts that you have ever experienced, become emotionally invested in, and believed were true—whether they were told to you by yourself, your parents, culture, religion, teachers, or the TV.

You are being brainwashed, whether you consciously choose to do so yourself or unconsciously allow others to do for you.

But *how* do you want to be brainwashed?

Do you want to be a slave to the mental programming that others inflict upon you, or would you rather choose your own "software"?

When you deeply imprint into your mind the visions, character traits, goals, and beliefs you wish to make manifest on a daily basis, it is only natural that they eventually become your reality.

When I first started out in business in 2006, I met a man named Bob at an internet marketing seminar.

Bob taught me a number of things, the most important of which were how to meditate and how to reprogram my mind using the process I describe in this chapter.

He did not provide me with a lot of information. All Bob said was, "Elliott, trust me on this one. Give this a try for 60 days."

I did, and guess what? It worked.

I extend to you the same invitation. Practice the visualization and affirmation techniques that are described below for sixty days, multiple times a day.

It is time for you to take responsibility for the thoughts, beliefs, values, and actions that influence your reality.

VISUALIZE

Find a quiet place where you will not be disturbed. You can do this exercise while standing, seated, or lying down.

Once you have found your place, close your eyes and take twenty deep breaths.

Begin to relax all of the muscles in your body, starting from the top of your head and working down. Release the tension in these areas: forehead, eyes, jaw, lips, neck, shoulders, chest, arms, hands, belly, back, legs, feet, and toes.

Keeping your eyes closed, you should focus your concentration at the center of your brow, right above and between your eyebrows. Now I would like you to think back to a moment in your life when you experienced a spectacular success.

When I do this exercise, I revisit the time in college when I ran a ninety-yard touchdown through walls of defense, including one of the D-backs, and spiked the ball in the endzone—what a great feeling to return to.

The memory you choose should be among your proudest moments. You should be able to recall it vividly in your body—that is, you want to choose a memory that charges you with emotion. Perhaps you made the game-winning play; had the courage to talk to an attractive woman; or maybe you climbed a mountain.

Whatever it is, once you have chosen this memory, return to the series of events that led up to your moment of victory. Call upon your imagination and replay these events in your mind as vividly as possible. It is important to also feel the memory, pretending as if it were physically happening all over again.

I know this sounds silly, but I want you to physically repeat the actual movements you performed during your peak experience, as well. Feel the emotions involved with what is happening to you, breathe faster, and move dynamically.

Remember, your body is your mind. So the more powerfully you recreate the memory physically by **emoting**, the more strongly this visualization practice will affect your subconscious mind.

When I go back to my memory of the touchdown, I visualize myself getting ready, standing behind the quarterback.

I can hear the cadence. I can see and feel myself running and juking the defenders. I am breathing faster, my heart is pumping, and the adrenaline is rushing through my veins.

When you practice this enough, it will almost feel like you are there again.

You will soon approach the climax of this memory—your moment of victory. It is here that you will want to create an **emotional anchor**.

For me, this looks like the following:

I am running down the field, breaking tackles, running past defenders and spinning around them, with the D-back nipping at my heels. The D-back grabs hold of my ankle just as I cross the endzone. Then I get up, spike the ball, and shout out: "YES!"

My emotional anchor here is my spiking the imaginary ball and exclaiming, "YES!"

Your emotional anchor should be whatever physical expression you feel that defines your moment of victory. You will feel great when you do this.

Additionally, make it as powerfully emotive as you can, because you will use this anchor in the next exercise to further "anchor" you into the vibration of attracting what you desire.

AFFIRM

Once you have reenacted your mental movie through *visualization*—and have ended it by expressing your enlivening emotional anchor—the next step is to immediately perform a positive, ***present-tense*** **affirmation**.

With this, you are effectively training your body to associate the feelings of joy, pleasure, and accomplishment with what you would like to have happen in your life.

As you firmly declare your gratitude for "having" what you actually seek to obtain in the future—via these good feelings flooding through your system—your body will be inclined to actualize that which you have germinated in your mind.

Here is the framework of the present-tense affirmation of gratitude that I follow: **"I am so happy and grateful now that...X."**

As an example of how this is used, let's say your goal is to make $50,000 per month.

First, go through your visualization of victory and express your emotional anchor, experiencing all the good feelings associated with "winning."

Then immediately say to yourself with conviction, **"I am so happy and grateful now that...** *I am earning $50,000 every month!"*

You can then **visualize** what it would be like to earn $50,000 per month. Imagine yourself logging into your bank account and seeing all of those zeroes next to your statement.

That example is for the sake of simplicity, but perhaps your goal is to find the life partner of your dreams.

In that case, you would again go through the visualization and express your emotional anchor before saying, with eyes closed, **"I am so happy and grateful now that** *I spend my life with the woman (or man) of my dreams."*

Visualize your life with this person: *What color is her hair? How does she smile? How does she feel and smell? What is she wearing?*

Whatever your goal is, you want to emote throughout your visualization and feel the same emotions you would feel as if you'd already had what you wanted.

This is an act of embedding your vision—the seed—deeper and deeper into your nervous system—the soil—so that your subconscious mind can work on making the flower bloom.

Let's review.

First, you go through your mental victory and create an emotional anchor of your choice.

Get excited and feel alive, doing whatever it takes to make your whole body smile with joy, accomplishment, and pride. If your heart rate and breathing are not high, then you are not anchoring powerfully enough.

Once you are flooded with feelings of achievement and happiness, imagine vividly what it is that you want. Give gratitude for it in the form of: **"I am so happy and grateful now that..."**

It takes about forty to sixty days to reprogram your brain. So, don't feel bad if you've done this for a month and you still see no tangible results.

"Dammit, I still have bills," you may think to yourself.

Don't worry about it. Just focus on cultivating those good feelings within you. If you are doing this correctly, the roots of your "vision flower" are surely spreading themselves deeper into the soil, but it takes time for flowers to manifest outwardly.

As with everything in this book, be patient. It is your commitment to the process that enables you to change.

You are a magnet for all the people, circumstances, ideas, and resources that you need in life. Rather than look outside for results, turn inward and ask for discipline, commitment, patience, and trust in the process.

Try this visualization and affirmation exercise at least **twice per day for sixty days.**

Back when I was first building Strength Camp, I'd become so hooked on this practice that I was at one point visualizing and affirming every hour of my waking day. Every hour on the hour, in-between clients, I would go into the back of the gym somewhere and take about five minutes to go through my little victory dance.

This only works if you bring massive, creative intensity. I keep repeating this for a reason.

A big reason why people quit doing affirmations is that they are not doing it big enough.

You have to truly work yourself up into a charged state for anything to happen. Going through the motions with a bland performance won't do you any good.

Transmuting Negative Thoughts

During this journey of growing stronger, especially as you begin implementing positive visualization and affirmation practices, you will encounter negative voices. Sure, some of these critics are external, but oftentimes, the loudest are those within us.

We all have self-sabotaging "inner critics" that attempt to undermine our efforts to grow stronger. John Assaraf calls these "automatic negative thoughts."

They tell us things like, "*Oh, that's impossible. There's no way you can do that.*" Or, "*She doesn't want you to ask her out on a date—you're an ugly loser.*" Or, "*You don't deserve that.*"

Unrecognized and uninhibited, thoughts like these will squash your dreams before they ever have a chance to rise. Negative thoughts beget and reinforce negative neural pathways, which will hinder your success. These are the pests within, if you will, that prevent us from fully blooming.

The first step in freeing yourself from these limiting beliefs is to recognize them when they pop up.

"*Hey, let's start a business,*" says your trustworthy and capable friend. And you think, "*Oh, I could never do that.*"

Or someone invites you to a party you would like to attend, and you hear: *"Oh, man, I'm too fat right now."* Or, *"I am too awkward. Maybe years from now when I have found a way to beat fear."*

Catching these negative thoughts when they appear, you will realize that they sound like a four-year-old's thoughts and make little sense. Well, that is because they are, and they don't!

As a child, you formed these negative thought patterns that were based on disparaging remarks from insecure adults and peers and that you later internalized. Because you accepted these thoughts at a subconscious level, they are still "limiting" you, even after ten, twenty, and fifty years down the road.

The first step in becoming less swayed by this negative neural programming is to realize that you are subconsciously giving credence to the thoughts of insecure children, and thus holding yourself back from doing what is necessary to Become the Strongest Version of Yourself.

Once you have recognized this fact, you must decide what to do with the thoughts.

Rather than fight, repress, or ignore—all of which get you nowhere—I recommend that you transmute, or *transform*, these negative, limiting thoughts into positive, supportive ones.

Here is how you do it:

The next time an automatic negative thought arises, take a brief moment to observe it. No need to analyze the thought or pay it any great deal of attention; just notice it, so that it is no longer in the dark.

Now grab your emotional anchor and ground yourself in a state of pride, joy, and confidence. Feel the emotions of empowerment and love.

Then state one of your positive, present-tense affirmations, allowing the negative thought to pass on by like a cloud overhead when the sunshine returns.

Here's an example: say that you are currently broke, and your friend invites you out to dinner. You have only $10 to your name, but you know dinner costs $25. So, the first thought that comes to mind is: "Man, I hate being broke. Being broke sucks."

Recognizing this negative thought, you grab your emotional anchor and say to yourself with conviction: **"I am so happy and grateful now that** I am making $50,000 a month."

Once you make a regular habit of replacing negative thoughts with positive affirmations, you will begin to strengthen the positive neural pathways that will help you grow stronger.

Take note that you will likely experience a lot of cognitive dissonance when you first begin practicing.

It is going to feel silly. You might think, "Why am I talking to myself?"

But you are not talking to yourself. You are reprogramming your mind, much in the same way that you must reprogram a computer if the software is not up to par.

Bonus: **Using vision boards** *is another exercise I have used to augment my visualization and affirmation practice.*

This is a fancy way of saying "to surround yourself with images of your goals and dreams." Doing this is yet another way of planting into your subconscious your vision for the future.

This can be anything from the types of relationships you want to have, to the neighborhood or home you want to inhabit, to the part of the world in which you would like to travel or live.

Place pictures—drawings, posters, or print-outs from the internet—strategically in your home or office such that you will constantly see them.

THE HERO'S JOURNEY

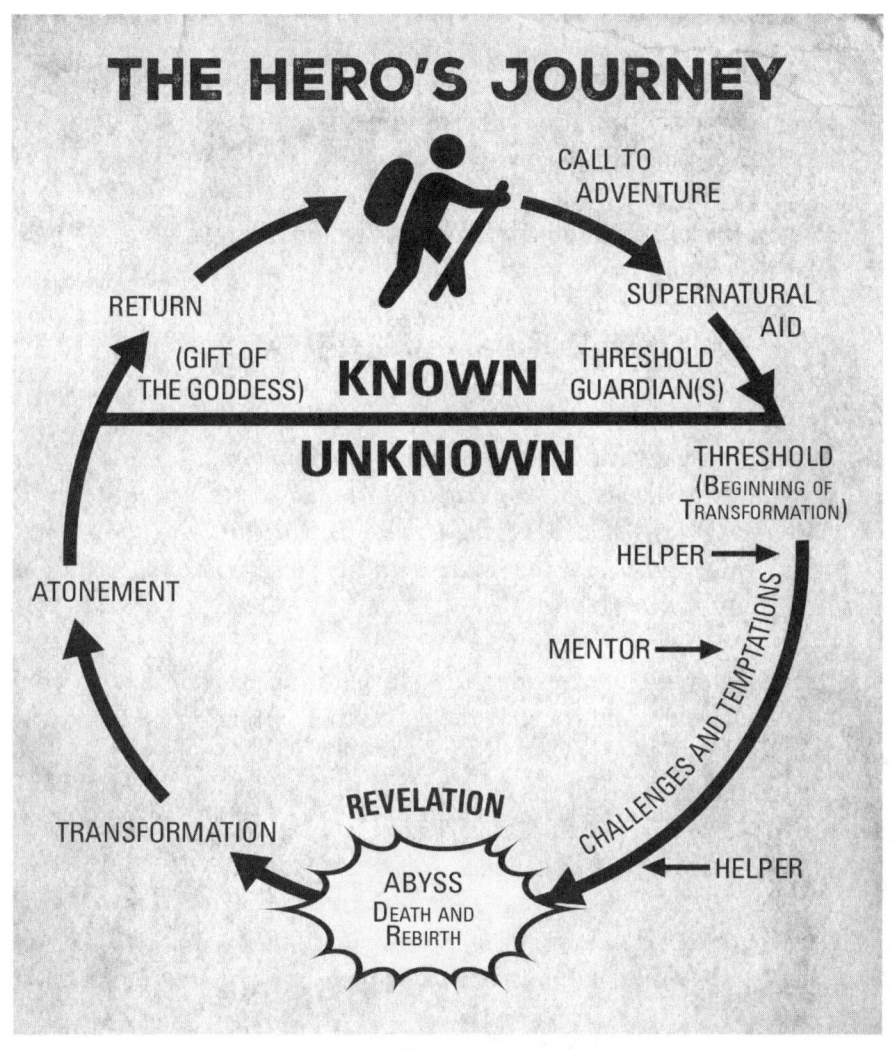

Separation, Initiation, Return

The Hero's Journey, or the monomyth, is a universal narrative that Joseph Campbell encountered in his comparative study of world mythology during the 20th century.

At the heart of all of our stories—be it ancient, modern, and personal—is a common, recognizable theme. And while the characters change, the stages do not.

According to Campbell, this theme is composed of three primary phases: separation, initiation, and return. They expand into a total of seventeen more specific stages.

Before I explain these stages in detail, I would like to give you a sense of the overall theme.

This quotation from Campbell's The Hero With a Thousand Faces sums up the journey in a few words—

*"A hero ventures forth from the world of common day into a region of supernatural wonder **[separation]**: fabulous forces are there encountered and a decisive victory is won **[initiation]**: the hero comes back from this mysterious adventure with the power to bestow boons on his fellow man **[return]**."*

Take a moment to consider the stories that are familiar to you, including your own, and you may recognize this pattern.

Luke Skywalker leaves his uncle's ranch and learns how to use the Force from Obi-Wan Kenobi and Yoda, before facing off with Darth Vader and returning a Jedi Knight.

Frodo leaves the Shire, fights off Sauron and the Orcs with his friends and mentors, and returns home—transformed.

Separation, Initiation, Return

Simba journeys into the savannah, and with the help of some animal friends, metamorphoses into a Lion King, returning to battle Scar and protect the Pride Lands.

Prefiguring Simba by thousands of years, Sundiata and Rama are likewise driven from their kingdoms into the wilderness, where they defeat evil tyrants and finally return as Kings to their respective thrones in Mali and Ayodhya.

In one of the oldest myths of humankind, King Gilgamesh leaves Uruk; slays demons with his sidekick Enkidu; finds the flower of immortality; and—upon returning—restores peace, order, and generativity to the Kingdom of Uruk.

Hercules, who fell from paradise as a child, successfully executes the Twelve Labors, which involved slaying beasts and plucking the fruit of immortality, in order to ascend to his home on Mount Olympus.

And so on and so forth.

There is a reason these stories are so similar.

And it has nothing to do with ancient alien conspiracy theories.

We witness the same Hero, wearing thousands of different cultural masks, appear throughout the millennia because the authors of these stories inherently understood that there are certain stages in the journey toward personal transformation and self-discovery.

These men hoped that creating heroic mirrors that point the way through myth might inspire our own Hero's Journey, the most important one of them all.

You see, the Hero's Journey and the Journey to Becoming the Strongest Version of Yourself are one and the same.

The beauty of any mythology is that it is written all about and for you, me, and all of us.

My intention with this chapter is to provide a condensed overview of the Hero's Journey— Campbell's "road atlas" for life—so that you may be able to determine which stage you currently face, and be able to proceed heroically.

I have included examples of both modern and ancient heroes to give you a tangible sense of the theme.

After reading this book, I invite you to explore the myths that I have referenced in the resources section—in particular, those that are of interest to you. By reading about the heroes who came before us, our own journeys are invigorated.

For further reference, read Joseph Campbell's The Power of Myth, followed by The Hero With a Thousand Faces, which explains each stage of the Hero's Journey in detail.

The Ordinary World

The "Ordinary World" is where the hero begins his or her adventure.

This is the realm of the profane and the familiar. It is the world of dependency on one's parents and other authorities, where life is comfortable, respectable, and—ultimately—vanilla.

The Ordinary World is where we find Luke Skywalker on his aunt's and uncle's farm; Frodo in the Shire; Harry Potter on Privet Drive; Dorothy in Kansas; and Neo in his office.

In ancient myths, Buddha lives within the safe walls of his father's palace; Gilgamesh indulges his senses in his kingdom of Uruk; and Parzival lives in the safety of his mother's home in the forest.

At some point in his life, the hero begins to question his everyday existence in this womb of safety, security, and normalcy.

In a way, he does not quite fit into the world around him anymore, or at least he feels this way. Many of his relationships and activities no longer excite him.

"Is this it?" he wonders. There is a sense of longing for something beyond the ordinary.

The hero knows he is searching for something, but he just cannot quite put his finger on what it is. Whatever it is, he knows that life in the Ordinary World has lost meaning.

In Jungian terms, this is the state of ego alienation. Truly, what the hero unconsciously seeks is to "know thy Self"—to answer the perennial question, *"Who am I?"*

If you find yourself in this stage, hold on. Do not attempt to rush the process. You will get your opportunity for adventure very soon. In the meantime, listen to your feelings, and pay attention to the signs.

THE CALL TO ADVENTURE

Soon enough, the hero gets his or her wake-up call.

It is as if the Universe knows when we are ready for adventure and sends us a herald.

Depending on how long we have been ignoring it, the Call could present itself either "sublimely" or "painfully." Chances are, it will be somewhat painful.

The Call to Adventure is a wonderful, albeit frightening, invitation to leave the Ordinary World and journey into the unknown.

It might manifest in the form of finding out you have cancer, getting dumped, losing your job, or graduating from college and having to leave your parents' home.

Or perhaps a friend invites you to travel the world with him, or you get a job offer that thrills you—except you are forced to leave your home if you accept it.

If you are in touch with your body and pay attention to the subtle language of your Heart and Balls, the Call could arise as a gut feeling. In other words, you can catalyze your own adventure.

Maybe you want to "drop out" of the world for a while and travel.

Maybe you want to start a business, or join forces with someone who already has.

Maybe you want to change careers.

Or perhaps you come across an inspirational book or YouTube video that invites you to embark on The Dangerous Journey of Following Your Heart, and it sparks an idea.

You know deep down that whatever this is you got to do this thing. It's just that…"It's risky."

Regardless of how we are called, the Call is *always* nerve-racking.

It's not scary in the sense of thinking: "jumping off that bridge is probably not such a great idea."

It's different from that. First, there is a resourceful kind of fear that protects us from truly harming ourselves; then, there is the type that represents the ego's, or our own, fear of leaving the comfortable and what we know.

This second fear is the one that gives us that the feeling of numerous "butterflies in our stomachs."

It is the fear of aliveness and excitement that are born from imagining doing the things we are afraid to do; the things that make us nervously smile and giggle. You know what I am talking about.

It is this fear that we must confront and barrel through when answering the Call to Adventure.

Mythologically, we witness the Call in Gandalf's knocking on Frodo's door in the Shire; in Odysseus' and Achilles' being called to battle the Trojans; in God's asking Noah to build an ark; and in the banishment of Sundiata, Simba, and Rama from their kingdoms.

We see it also in the story of Siddhartha Gautama. In it, the future Buddha leaves his father's kingdom for the first time and is confronted by the suffering within existence in the form of an old man, a sick man, and a dead man. He is then enlightened to the fact that there is a world beyond the palace walls of conformity and security.

I imagine many of you reading this now have felt the Call to Adventure at some point in your life. Or perhaps you are experiencing it right now.

If you are serious about growing stronger, there is no getting around it—you will have to face and accept the Call at some point.

I am not here to say that you have to do it now. Perhaps you are not yet ready, and that is fine.

But know that the Call will continue to come back to you in progressively more painful ways the longer you ignore it. This, I guarantee.

If you reject the Call to Adventure in your twenties, it will show up again and again. If left ignored, it will arrive in the form of a midlife crisis many years later.

The Self is knocking at your door. Will you answer, or will you run away?

REFUSAL OF THE CALL

Accepting the Call is often the easier path in the long run.

Of course, choosing the journey of your Heart's and Gut's inclinations has its challenges, but they are exhilarating, transformative challenges.

Opting out of the journey, on the other hand, signs you up for a life of miserable challenges.

So long as you ignore the Call, the Universe will continue to knock you around, trying to get your attention.

As violently as God smites Jonah and as aggressively as fate curses Phil in the movie *Groundhog Day*, the Self shakes your life with mishap after mishap until you finally wake up and say, "OK. I accept the journey."

Unfortunately, it may be too late for those who've refused the Call long enough and never moved beyond the ordinary world of childhood. Read Franz Kafka's short parable, Before the Law, for a wonderful depiction of this.

Though we may have dreams, we soon enough let go of them.

Other people who have grown unconsciously angry with themselves for not accepting their own Calls to Adventure might say things that make us reconsider rising to the Call as a worthwhile endeavor.

Regardless, people will call you irrational and arrogant for wanting to pursue the Call. "Who are you to...(*fill in the blank*)?"

Many of us are prone to give in to these external voices of cowardly logic and our own legitimate fears, so we give in and call the journey off.

After all, it is scary to leave the familiar and venture out into the unknown.

In a way, it is also irrational, foolish, and against head brain logic.

Pursuing your dreams and following your heart are always leaps of faith. There are risks involved, and success is never guaranteed.

When we refuse the Call and turn back inside the cozy womb of conformity and "respectability", comforting ourselves with cautious self-talk and not wishing to *"let down"* those whom we value, we experience a new kind of anxiety.

Only this anxiety is different from the invigorating nervousness we'd experience had we accepted the Call to Adventure.

This new anxiety after refusing the Call stems from the recognition that we have chosen to become dead to our very nature.

In striving to make the people around us feel more comfortable with their own decisions, we squash our extraordinariness and lapse into mediocrity to play it safe.

Worse yet, in order to numb the pain, we distract ourselves with "worldly" activities.

We binge on substances; on sex and porn; on TV, social media, and online "research." We throw ourselves into workaholism, working respectable jobs we don't like, taking classes we don't like, dating people we don't like... all to distract us from our own frustration and anxiety with living lives that go against who we are.

The myth of King Midas is a story about someone who has refused his Call.

The man with the "Midas touch" worked hard and made lots of money, only to discover that his life had been a desolate wasteland, wherein even all the gold in the world could not satisfy him. Having chased the *trappings* of success, he failed to find fulfillment.

In the process of denying himself, he rejected his true riches, which were actually the unique set of interests, values, talents, and relationships he'd once had. Having been blinded by the golden illusion of "security," he overlooked his true riches.

A person might want to be an artist, travel the world, or be a personal trainer, a teacher, or a monk, but instead he forces himself into a more secure and respectable life.

That is merely procrastination, self-sabotage, and delaying the inevitable.

We are the heroes of the myths that are also our lives.

We can choose to allow the hand of the Author to carry out our story, or we can turn against the pen and attempt to write it ourselves.

The reality is that we cannot stop the inevitability of the journey. We can only make it more comfortable by allowing it to happen, or make it more painful by resisting.

SUPERNATURAL AID

When the Hero accepts the Call, he is always given help.

Batman has Robin; Frodo has Samwise; Simba has Timon and Pumbaa; Buzz has Woody; Luke has Obi-Wan, Han Solo, Yoda, and the others; Harry has Ron, Hermione, Dumbledore, and Hagrid; Rama has Lakshmana; Gilgamesh has Enkidu; Achilles has Athena...the list goes on!

In your own life, help will come in the form of mentors and friends.

Perhaps you interact with this mentor in person, as one would do with a teacher or a coach. Mentorship can also be provided remotely or through books, YouTube videos, and other outlets.

Regardless of how the mentor appears, he or she will provide you with ideas and skills, helping you hone your craft, so that you can succeed in fighting your battles down the road.

Friends are also agents of Supernatural Aid.

They make the journey more enjoyable, and oftentimes, can save us from sinking into the quicksand of our own hubris.

As you can see, the Hero's Journey cannot be done alone.

If you have accepted the Call and feel you have not yet found your "people," then look harder.

I promise you that they are there. You just may not yet recognize them.

Crossing the First Threshold and Entering the Belly of the Whale

Blessed with Supernatural Aid, the Hero leaves the Ordinary World and enters the field of adventure.

Examples include Alice's falling down the rabbit hole into Wonderland, and Neo's accepting Morpheus' invitation to take the red pill.

Once the Hero passes the guardian standing by the threshold of his own fear—personified as the gatekeeper in Kafka's "Before The Law"—there is no turning back.

In life, Crossing the Threshold is moving out of your parents' house, selling your possessions, quitting your job, and buying a one-way ticket to adventure. Sink or swim--you have committed to the journey.

This can be a humbling experience.

Here in the Belly of the Whale, the Hero realizes that the realm of adventure is altogether different from the romantic and mystical world he had imagined it would be.

There are many challenges to be overcome; home is a long way away.

Faced with his predicament, the Hero may begin to experience some remorse. *"Man, that was foolish,"* he may think to himself.

To put it in real life situations: Perhaps after quitting your job, you realize that you are broke and have no money for food and gas. Perhaps after flying across the world, you realize you are homesick. Or perhaps you get a gym membership to lose weight, but you get burned by your first workout in years and realize how hard this journey will be.

No matter the form it takes, this is a difficult threshold to cross. For a time, you may even get "swallowed up" by your disillusionment. You might become depressed and begin daydreaming about going back to the Ordinary World.

But eventually, the Hero emerges—somehow, you find a way to make end's meet.

This requires slaying your first monster, toxic, lingering habits that hold you back.

You must put down the old habit, once and for all. Stop looking at pictures of your ex and finally move on. Show up again to the gym the next day, even though you feel like quitting. Only then will you move to the next phase of your journey.

In so making it through the Belly of the Whale, metaphorically speaking, the ego experiences a small rebirth. The ego has taken a hit. And having tasted your own blood, you realize your imperfection and vulnerability.

This makes you stronger for the battles down the road.

THE ROAD OF TRIALS

Before Hercules became a true hero, he skillfully executed the Twelve Labors. Before Gladiator found Elysium, he had to fight in the Colosseum.

In a similar manner, you must master your own challenges and successfully navigate your own Road of Trials to Become the Strongest Version of Yourself.

Adversity is the Universe's way of testing us to see if we are truly strong enough to handle what treasure may come to us.

We see this in The Bhagavad Gita, in which Krishna withheld Himself in His full radiance until He knew Arjuna was ready and capable of beholding Him—the power of the Self.

Only those heroes who have "gone the distance" and successfully "resisted the dark side," so to speak, are trusted with the Holy Grail, the Ring of Power, the Force, and other symbolic mementos of the journey's treasure.

Overcoming the obstacles that life throws at you during your Road of Trials inevitably transforms you into a Stronger Version of Yourself. And with greater strength comes greater responsibility.

Building Strength Camp has been a Road of Trials for me.

The Road was long and involved: gaining clients, building a team, finding a gym, waking up at 4am to train before I coached, moving gyms, and starting over again—twice—making videos, dealing with criticism, building an online tribe, managing money, and balancing work, health, and family life.

All of these trials symbolized the mythological monsters that I've had to slay in my journey.

I continue to grow from these challenges even now. But thankfully, I have all the help I need.

The Hero's Journey of Growing Stronger is an endless succession of ascents and descents.

You climb one mountain and are awarded with new strengths and a new perspective. For a brief moment, you get a breath of fresh air—a chance to enjoy the fruits of your labor and celebrate.

Just as soon as you revel in your victory, you must go back down into the valley and start all over again.

Temptation and the Final Ordeal

Eventually, the Hero must face his biggest monster alone.

Siddhartha Gautama endured Mara's temptations in the forest, just as Jesus was presented with Satan's Three Temptations in the desert.

The great Luke Skywalker was tempted to run away from battle. Gladiator, Harry Potter, Achilles, Arjuna, and every other hero who made it this far were no different.

In actual life, the Temptation to retire from the journey prematurely manifests similarly.

Separation, Initiation, Return

Take an entrepreneur, for example. While facing the giant task of building the business he has always held in his Heart's vision, he hears the siren's call of a life spent free from work on warm, sunny beaches. He is tempted to forget about it all and retire.

Or there's the example of a former addict, who is presented with a convenient opportunity to be lured back into relapse.

Bruised and battered from having already passed many trials and tribulations, the Hero who faces the Final Ordeal is tempted to call the journey off so that he may settle down and finally rest.

After all, a part of him says, "I have worked hard enough."

But so long as we heroes live in this world, I believe we must continue journeying. To quit at this point, in my mind, would be a mistake.

If Steve Jobs had indulged in his temptation to accept defeat when his own company fired him, we would not have MacBooks, iPhones, and iPads.

If Martin Luther King had quit after receiving any one of the countless death threats that were sent his way, segregation may have stuck around much longer.

If Joseph Campbell had told himself, "You know, I really don't have to write this book," then the millions of people whose lives have been revitalized by the Hero's Journey may never have followed their dreams, myself included. And you would not be reading this book.

For the Hero who comes to the brink of transformation, there is always the temptation of quitting the journey.

The inner self-saboteur deals us his most powerful blow to see if we are strong enough to transcend. And it is the Hero who transcends his own egoic wish to retire from the journey and summons up the courage to fight the greatest battle yet that will step that much closer towards Becoming the Strongest Version of Himself.

Just like how Luke faces his father, Darth Vader; Harry Potter faces Voldemort; and Rama faces the dark lord, Ravana.

Buddha overcomes Mara, and Jesus overcomes Satan. These Heroes never tire and move on to confront their greatest challenge.

Atonement and Apotheosis

The approach to the Self is metaphorically portrayed in myth as the Hero's confrontation with the dragon or demon. To be sure, it is a frightening experience for the Hero because it necessitates his being wounded.

When the Hero faces the Final Ordeal, he is confronted by his own smallness.

In order to succeed, the Hero realizes he must surrender. This act of letting go transforms him.

Hercules becomes a God. Jesus rises into Heaven. Buddha awakens. Luke becomes a Jedi Knight. And Rama, Gladiator, Gilgamesh, Sundiata, and Simba all become Kings.

When the inflated ego moves beyond his vices of desire, fear, and control, he overcomes temptation, letting the infantile part of him mature.

The paradox of being transformed is that the ego wins by losing—ultimately, he comes to life through being wounded.

The encounter with the shadow transforms the ego from being a proud, independent, inflated Hero into a genuinely humble servant of the Self.

This Hero has found the Jewel in the Lotus, Jivan Mukti. He has plucked the fruit of Eternal Life and eaten from it. He has found Nirvana in Samsara, Heaven on Earth, and Bliss in Suffering.

Return With the Elixir

Through the encounter with the Self, the individuated ego gains its ultimate treasure, the Holy Grail, or the Force.

But the journey does not stop here.

In fact, the state of individuation is never accomplished. *Communion with the Self is a never-ending dance.*

So, the question now is: will the ego continue to dance the dance of individuation, allowing the Elixir to be given freely through him to his community, or will he hoard the power for himself?

Just as there is a Refusal of the Call, there is also a Refusal to Return.

It would be easy for Moses to stay on Mount Sinai, for the monk to stay in his cave of "enlightenment," for Jesus to remain in Heaven, and for Gilgamesh to live alone at the end of the world with his Flower of Immortality.

After all, for the Hero who has tasted Paradise, returning to live in an imperfect world has its challenges, and is—in a certain sense—not very appealing.

But the true Hero realizes that to remain in Paradise alone would be to destroy its beauty. His selfishness would sever his connection to the Self. This leaves him with one choice:

The redemption of the Hero's Journey is found in the Hero's returning to the ordinary world of pain and suffering to serve others.

Jesus, Buddha, Muhammad, and all the other prophets all come back to spread the message of freedom from suffering. King Sundiata comes back to his homeland, where he restores peace and order in the Kingdom of Mali. And Gilgamesh does the same in his own Kingdom of Uruk.

In the end, the Hero's most heroic virtue is compassion and the commitment to serving others. He does not see himself as a sacrificial messiah—for that would be an inflated view—but as a servant to his community.

Freedom to Live

And that is the Hero's Journey in a nutshell.

I have given you the map for the journey of Becoming the Strongest Version of Yourself, but it is only a map, not a guidebook. And only you can do the walking.

I am not here to tell you what to do. I am simply here to surface and bring to light what you already know deep within.

That is, if you ignore the Call and always do what you are told, you will eventually die an unfulfilled person. People will still love you, and you will have some beautiful moments, but your last experience will be a dying breath of regret, and not bliss.

Now if you do "follow your bliss," as Joseph Campbell advised his students, *and you allow that strange thing that is happening inside of you to unfold,* then you will at least know what it means to be alive. That is your only guarantee.

You will be challenged, you will stumble, you will fall, and when life gets hectic, you may wonder why you ever took the "road less traveled" in the first place.

But through all those trials and tribulations, all the sleepless nights, and painful battles, you will be filled with excitement and enthusiasm. You will be at peace with yourself.

You will smile, you will laugh, you will dance, and you will love yourself, your life, and the world. The people around you will gravitate towards you—your own empowerment empowers them, and they empower others.

When you ignore rationality and respectability, and *just follow the intuitive promptings of your Heart and Balls,* you will enjoy this life infinitely more than if you were to live the life that everyone else tells you to live.

I tell you: there is no greater feeling than getting out of the way and experiencing the life that has already been written for you. It won't always be easy, but it will be *your myth.*

Where do you begin? **You begin by "following your bliss."**

What are you afraid to do? Again, not afraid in the sense of "I shouldn't jump off this bridge," but scared in the sense of exhilaration—of being uncomfortable with leaving the known, the secure.

What irresponsible dream sends the butterflies in your stomach into a raging storm of flapping wings? What spreads a nervous smile of excitement across your cheeks at the thought of finally being alive?

You know what to do.

King

INITIATION:
THE OUTER JOURNEY, RITUAL PROCESS, & INITIATION IN THE MODERN ERA

THE OUTER JOURNEY

Ever since the dawn of humankind, we humans have observed that there are certain transitions that take place within a lifetime.

First, we are born. Then we enter adolescence and become adults, followed by middle age, old age, and finally death.

These major life stages are certainly traumatic for the ego.

Transitioning from a child to a 22-year-old adult in the real world is scary, but so is being a healthy grown man, who wakes up the next morning, wondering what his life has become.

Ancient cultures recognized this, so they created rites of passage.

These "initiations" were designed by the elders within a community to help individuals transition from one life stage to another as smoothly as possible.

Ancient societies realized that if they had not created spaces for people to transition into the next life stage, they'd have ended up with a community of grown men and women who still acted like teenagers, and young adults who acted like children—as we have in our culture.

Today, rites of passage still exist, but unfortunately the vast majority of these rituals have lost their potency.

I would venture to say that you would be hard-pressed to find a legitimate initiation process in this day and age that is actually effective and not destructive. Yes, they are out there, but they are few and far between. We all suffer because of this.

For women, their first menstruation biologically marks the beginning of adulthood, thereby providing women with at least a sense of mature identity. By contrast, young men lack any sort of experience—biological or otherwise—that marks their manhood.

You get a wet dream, sure, but it does not carry the same weight as a woman discovering her true powers for procreation.

Young men, especially in today's era, crave to be initiated.

You see this with many men joining the military, college fraternities, sports teams, and street gangs, all of which offer their own initiation rituals.

Unfortunately, many of these rituals are led by broken men—men who have been beaten down by their own misguided initiation experiences, or lack thereof—who, in turn, initiate boys into an immature form of manhood through sadistic humiliation and tribalism.

Rituals like these initiate men not into mature, nurturing, and generative vessels of masculine power, but into agents of false machismo that are driven by insecurity. These men feel a need to prove themselves "man enough" by drinking more, fighting more, winning more, and having more sex. *"Am I a man yet?"* they wonder.

This is not true initiation, but a sorry form of bullying. And it results from the chaos in which we find ourselves today, amongst broken men, broken women, and broken systems.

You don't make a man out of someone by telling him he is a "pussy" and demanding that he prove himself worthy of your respect.

You teach a young man his worth by showing him his strength.

The reality of our current world is that its inhabitants are desperately confused. People are earnestly seeking transformation, but they don't know where to find it.

We mistake our early-life, midlife, and old-age crises for signs that something is wrong with us, not understanding that they are the natural and normal wake-up Calls to Initiation to point us towards maturity.

In attempts to remedy what we deem are our "disorders," we turn to perverted forms of initiation.

Aging men are confused by the influx of their Lover energy and miss their virility, so they act like they are in college again.

At the same time their husbands are becoming softened, aging women become hardened with Warrior energy, or want to be "pretty" again, so they die their hair, get boob jobs, and inject Botox.

As a result of this confusion, extramarital affairs and divorce rates run rampant in our society.

And these behaviors are passed down. Because their parents' and grandparents' give a lack of affirmation, nurturance, and presence—caused by their own preoccupation with life—young men and women today are deeply insecure.

So, to find the acceptance they so desperately seek outside of themselves, they turn to binging on promiscuity, drinking, drug abuse, violence, eating disorders, body mutilation, danger, and other forms of self-abasement.

My heart goes out to the confused men and women of today, young and old, who have been denied our proper rites of initiation. That is because I know how it feels.

Unconsciously, the self-sabotaging acts we see young men and women doing today are attempts at self-initiation.

With no rites in place or elders to offer guidance, young adults subject themselves to excessive drinking, hooking up, and fighting in attempts to prove to themselves and others that they are mature adults that are worthy of respect.

In other words, the immature forms of masculinity and femininity that have become the norm in the modern era are a direct consequence of the lack of authentic mentorship and initiatory experiences in today's world.

We must once again establish genuine ritual processes, if we are ever to *succeed as a species.*

That may sound like an overstatement, but the truth is that the health of an individual's psyche—let alone that of the broader society—depends on legitimate rituals. Without some form of ritual, humans are lost.

So, what needs to be done?

I believe the place to begin is to explore the mechanisms behind successful rites of passage.

Ritual Process

Victor Turner was a cultural anthropologist who had a passion for studying initiation rites. He wrote a book, *The Ritual Process,* in which he documented his findings and established his central theory.

Every rite of passage that Turner encountered followed the same basic process. They involved three stages: the pre-liminal, liminal, and post-liminal phases.

The initiate is separated from his community and his current identity (pre-liminal), and is thrown into the initiatory experience, in which he experiences a humbling challenge and puts an end to his old identity (liminal). He is then re-incorporated into the community as a more mature, psychologically-integrated individual (post-liminal).

I am sure you recognize the similarities.

The tripartite nature of Turner's initiation process—separation, initiation, and return—is the same underlying structure in Joseph Campbell's Hero's Journey model. It is also the same transformational death-and-rebirth process through which all heroes pass.

These three phases of initiation transport an individual from his everyday life in the ordinary world into a liminal space, in which his values and self-image are challenged, causing him to undergo a metamorphosis of character.

Through the experience of being ritually broken down and built back up into a stronger and more integrated version of himself, the initiate is sent back into the ordinary world, where he now functions with a new, more mature identity.

Today, Robert Moore picks up where Victor Turner left off in the public discourse on initiation. I encourage you to read Moore's excellent book, *The Archetype of Initiation*, if you are intrigued by these ideas.

Moore has proposed that there are three components that must be present in a successful rite of passage.

While it is impossible to guarantee the success of a ritual in transforming an initiate, a facilitator can do his best to make it conducive to success by establishing these three elements.

First, you need a **ritual elder.**

The elder designs and guides new initiates through the transition by providing nurturance and support.

A good ritual elder has been initiated himself and is secure enough in his own masculinity not to abuse his power by humiliating initiates in a sadistic way. He is compassionate and trustworthy, motivated by an impulse to empower his community.

Second, you need a **sacred space.**

A properly framed ritual space is safe, contained, and isolated from the ordinary world.

In order for a space to be made sacred, initiates and elders must regard it with a deeply reverential attitude, respecting its limits and boundaries.

In manufacturing sacred space, the ritual elder facilitates a process by which a sense of communitas is experienced by initiates. This is the sense of brotherhood, equality, and—in a sense—the temporary loss of individual status and identity that is necessary to facilitate a transformation of character.

And finally, you need an effective ritual process to which the initiates must voluntarily submit.

A good ritual elder understands the importance of creating a challenging trial that, when overcome, can reveal to a man his manhood.

This challenge must involve some form of ritual humiliation, by which the inflated ego is humbled, causing the initiate to replace his old identity with a new, more mature one.

The ritual wound is dealt not to the person's character or body, as is often the case with most failed attempts at initiation, *but to his own infantile grandiosity.* That is the part of him that is preventing his Strongest Self from emerging.

These are the components of a successful initiation.

INITIATION IN THE MODERN ERA

Our ancestors had a few key elements in their initiation rites.

From the sweat lodges and vision quests of the Native Americans, to the stone-lifting rites of the Highlanders, to the lion-killing tests of the Maasai—traditional initiations always involved a supporting cast of ritual elders, a strategically developed and challenging process that the initiates respected, and a sacred space that was formally framed and contained.

Unfortunately, trying to mimic ancient rites of initiation today is often not practical, except for a few legitimate practices that still exist and are rooted in ancestral wisdom.

Rites must be resourceful to the time, people, and culture that they serve.

Killing a lion with your bare hands (or with a gun) is no longer a resourceful rite of passage. Neither is physically maiming anyone, let alone yourself. The wound must be dealt to that immature aspect of the *psyche* that needs to "die", NOT to the body.

Though we often tend to romanticize times past, ancient cultures were not perfect nor were their initiation ceremonies. In fact, many of them were destructive.

While the infantile egos of those ancient men and women were meant to be wounded *during* the process of initiation, oftentimes their egos were permanently injured! Many of these ancient rites of initiation required initiates to hurt, or even kill, others to demonstrate their manhood.

From my frame of mind, these initiation rituals are not resourceful for our times. Perhaps they were then, but they have gone way out of fashion.

So, where does that leave us?

If you understand the framework of initiation, the possibilities for modern rites of initiation are endless.

Living the Hero's Journey is one means of ritual initiation, and doing so undoubtedly carries the potential for powerful transformation.

Here, the sacred space is the world, and Life itself serves as the ritual elder.

In this case, the ritual process is as simple as going through the journey. You experience a major life transition or a challenging life experience. And so there begins your initiation into a Stronger You.

Your ritual process today might be paying off your college loans, building a NonJob™, healing yourself back to health, playing a sport, crawling your way out of depression, overcoming a bad habit, or Growing Stronger in any other way.

Moreover, there is a key difference between ancient rites and modern rites that I haven't yet addressed.

Where traditional rituals initiated *groups* into functioning members of small tribes, successful initiation in the modern era should focus on initiating *individuals* through **personal challenges** that turn them into compassionate and contributing members of a **global community**.

The times are changing. Tribal exclusivity will not initiate humankind into a stronger species in the future any more than it has in the past (and it has not).

We are living today with the consequences of tribal initiations. Things like religions, nations, political systems, and social cliques that fight one another will inevitably destroy us if we continue down this path.

No.

We are done with exclusive tribes that make shadows of one another.

What we need today are rites of passage that *value* rather than suppress uniqueness, and that empower the greatness within individuals rather than seek to squash it.

What we need are seasoned and nurturing ritual elders, mentors who see themselves not as gurus or as leaders but as servants, beacons who are secure enough in themselves to get out of the way and allow the initiation process to unfold.

We need elders who understand how to invoke sacred space and how to restore mystery and divinity to the wasteland of a world that we've created, where science has rightfully demystified our old mythologies.

And we need ritual processes that neither promote nor repress our aggression—or any other single aspect of ourselves, for that matter. Instead, they must initiate us into an integrated experience of being fully alive and embodied in all that we are.

We need rites of initiation that have the power to transform, are inclusive of everyone, and initiate all of us into a global humanity.

King

GROW STRONGER & EMPOWER OTHERS

Our Mission

From the beginning, our mission at Strength Camp has been to Grow Stronger and Empower Others.

This had been my intention when I first started training clients out of the back of my van in local parks, and this has remained my intention for Strength Camp, now and forever.

It is my belief that you teach a man his worth by showing him his Strength. This applies to all men and women, young and old.

By now, you are familiar with my conviction that "Your Body Is Your Mind." Several chapters back, I discussed that our nervous system is rooted in our physiology, and our physiology flowers into our thoughts and our character. Strengthen one, and you strengthen the other.

Given the proper space, mentorship, and process, a person who trains his body is also simultaneously training his mind and character.

It has been my experience that strength training with the support of a coach can be a powerful means for establishing containment (sacred space), programming (ritual), and coaching (elder support) to empower and facilitate the growth of an individual from boyhood to manhood—or any life transition, for that matter.

I truly believe that strength training holds the power to initiate boys into men and girls into women, when given the right conditions. This has already been happening at Strength Camp for many years, and it is only now that I have the language to explain it.

It is from this perspective that Strength Camp continues to operate as we expand into larger arenas—not just as a gym—but as a sacred space for transformation, with a ritual process that is facilitated by supportive coaches and an empowering community of journeyers.

For the past few years, every Monday between 4:00 p.m. and 6:00 p.m., I have witnessed dozens of individuals from around the world come to my gym for the following: to feel the power of this sacred space, to experience a sense of fellowship, and to be supported by mentors in the ritual of strength training.

At every Open Gym, for two hours, we lift barbells, flip tires, push sleds, carry kegs, and load Atlas stones. Upon celebrating with the initiates, I see men and women who have become slightly stronger than when they were first seen coming through my door.

If nothing else, the ritual process we offer at Strength Camp reveals to people of all backgrounds the Strength that dwells inside of them. This strength gives them the courage to take action in the direction of their dreams, and provides them with the self-confidence to trust that it will all work out in the end.

For far too long, we have been without rituals of initiation. And all too often, young people have suffered because of this.

Strength Camp seeks to provide the mentorship, containment, and challenging yet supportive processes that are needed for conscious and deliberate transformation—for all those who walk through our doors.

I won't pretend that we have a perfect process, or that it is the only one that is out there, but in a world that is lacking of authentic rites of initiation, I feel confident in offering the services we provide.

A Global Community of Strong Men and Women

Dear Fellow King,

It is my conviction that we all possess a deep sense of wanting to see the world heal from our fragmented personal and collective unity.

That yearning for order and wholeness arises from our Inner Kings and Queens.

Our ancestors believed that when the King's inner life is out of order, so will be his kingdom.

As opposed to our segregated, tribal ancestors... today our tribe is global.

With the spread of the Internet, humankind has become a collective kingdom.

No longer are we segregated by geography or race. We live in a world wide community.

The only forms of segregation that still exist are those created by our imbalanced egos.

I firmly state that we, humankind, are One.

As a single family, if one of us has suffered injustice, we have all suffered injustice.

For "thy kingdom come" to be a reality we must work tirelessly to reintegrate our personal King, Warrior, Magician and Lover energies; but we must also devote ourselves to something bigger than ourselves.

Unless we focus the powerful energies within us upon something other than our own egoic wishes, there will be no personal or collective kingdom available for any of us to nurture. Our world is in chronic disarray because men have taken to only think of themselves, in absence of one another and the Earth which birthed us.

Our first problem is alienation from our higher Selves. We are deeply disconnected from our physical bodies and the subtle language of our souls.

To be the Strongest Versions of OurSelves goes far beyond the attainment of outer victories and goals, and into the realm of self-love, trust and integration.

When we look inwards with a desire to become fully integrated ourselves, we will find that the outer world will soon follow.

Your call to adventure is an inner journey.

And as with any journey there is need for process, community and coaching.

This is your invitation to become The Strongest YOU, in the powerful way you've always sensed inside.

I would like to introduce you to a process of "ritual initiation" where you take full accountability for devoting yourself to daily rituals which offer to transform your character and guide you towards the Strongest You.

Unlike the primitive initiation processes of our ancestors or the pseudo-initiation found in gangs and hazing activities, I would like to teach you how to initiate yourself into Kinghood through simple daily rituals I have personally used for over a decade in order to organize my life to receive and give more abundance to the world.

Also, I would like to welcome you to our community of like-minded Kings and Queens whom I refer to as our King Squad.

Here you will find all kinds of powerful new friends, each on his or her own journey, but always available to offer a kind word or helping hand.

We love and support one another, because that is what Kings do.

Finally, I lovingly refer to myself and all of you on this journey with me as kings. And I am very aware of the position I hold as teacher, mentor and coach to many of you.

I take my role very seriously, and my greatest aim in life is to see each one of you blossom into the magnificent, generative kings you really are.

But in reality only a handful of us are ready dig deep into our souls and do the critical work necessary to heal our personal wounds and restore the Earth to its divine beauty.

The first step in growing stronger is to acknowledge that we don't know everything (none of us do), and that we can't travel this journey alone; humility is required.

So, I humbly invite you allow your inner King to come forth, for yourself and the world, by joining our free "VIP King Coaching" video course where we will begin with **a single daily ritual, that takes less than five minutes to do, which you can implement right now to get you started on your journey.**

Also you will receive my **"Grow Stronger Daily Letter,"** which has been read by hundreds of thousands of our people for almost ten years now.

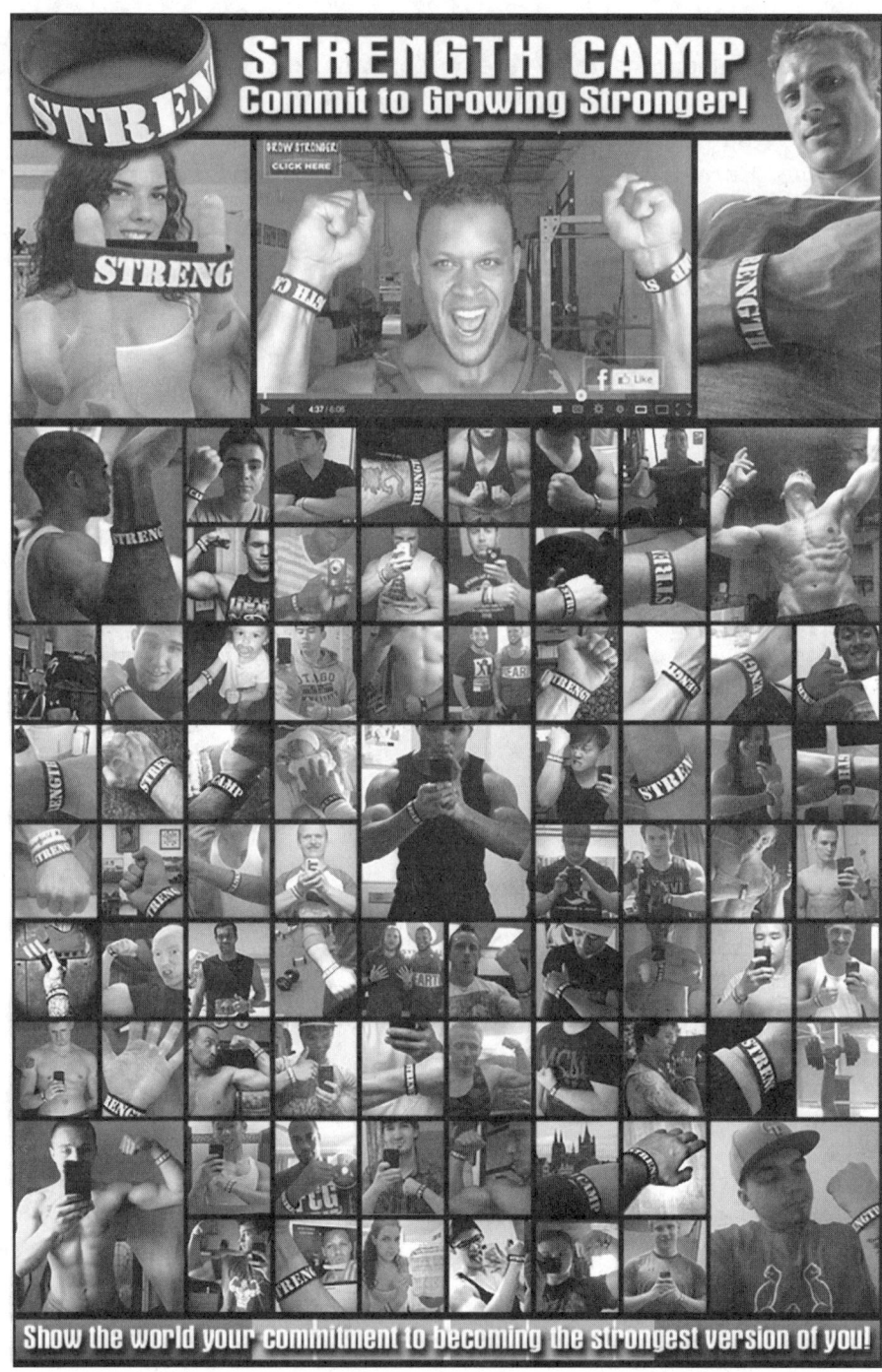

GROW STRONGER AND EMPOWER OTHERS

Visit www.StrengthCampCore.com to sign up now.

You will also get access to our free online resource Rolodex, to dig deeper into the ideas mentioned in this book, and several other downloadable worksheets and mindmaps for you to use right now.

Elliott Hulse

www.elliotthulse.com

King

REFERENCES

SECTION 1

1. Chek, Paul. *How to Eat, Move, and Be Healthy*. San Diego, CA: C.H.E.K. Institute, 2004.
2. Csikszentmihalyi, Mihaly. *Flow*, Harper Perennial Modern Classics, New York, 1990.
3. Diane Lee, *The Pelvic Girdle: An Approach to the Examination and Treatment of the Lumbopelvic Hip Region*, Philadelphia, PA: 2004
4. Paramore, Lee. *Power Posture: The Foundations of Strength*, Apple Publishing: 2001.
5. Ross, Barry. *Underground Secrets of Running*, Lulu Enterprises Incorporated, 2005.
6. Siff, Mel. *Supertraining*, Denver, CO, Supertraining Institute, 2004.

SECTION 2.1

1. Chek, Paul. *How to Eat, Move, and Be Healthy*. San Diego, CA: C.H.E.K. Institute, 2004.
2. Price, Weston A. *Nutrition and Physical Degeneration*. Lemon Grove, CA: Price-Pottenger Nutrition Foundation, 2008.
3. Williams, Roger J. *Biochemical Individuality*. Austin, TX: University of Texas Press, 1998.
4. Wolcott, William L. *The Metabolic Typing Diet*. New York: Random House, 2000.

SECTION 2.2

1. Chek, Paul. *How to Eat, Move, and Be Healthy*. San Diego, CA: C.H.E.K. Institute, 2004.
2. Howell, Edward. *Enzyme Nutrition*. Wayne, NJ: Avery Pub. Group, 1985.
3. Kaufman, Doug A., and David Holland. *The Fungus Link*. Rockwall, TX: MediaTrition, 2003.
4. Lightheart, Wade T. *Hydration Breakthrough For Athletes*. Reno, NV: Alliance Press, 2014.

SECTION 2.3

1. Batmanghelidj, Fereydoon. *Your Body's Many Cries For Water*. Falls Church, VA: Global Health Solutions, 1995.
2. Lightheart, Wade T. *Hydration Breakthrough For Athletes*. Reno, NV: Alliance Press, 2014.

SECTION 2.4

1. Chek, Paul. *How to Eat, Move, and Be Healthy*. San Diego, CA: C.H.E.K. Institute, 2004.
2. Haas, Elson. *Staying Healthy With the Seasons*. Berkeley, CA: Celestial Arts, 2003.
3. Vitalis, Daniel. "Home." Daniel Vitalis. N.p., n.d. Web. 02 Dec. 2015. <DanielVitalis.com>.

SECTION 3.1

1. Gershon, Michael D. *The Second Brain*. New York: HarperCollins Publishers, 1998.
2. "HeartMath." *HeartMath*. The HeartMath Institute, n.d. Web. 02 Dec. 2015. <HeartMath.org>.
3. Judith, Anodea. *Wheels of Life*. St. Paul, MN: Llewellyn Publications, 1987.
4. Levine, Peter A. *In An Unspoken Voice*. Berkeley, CA: North Atlantic Books, 2010.
5. Lowen, Alexander. *The Language of the Body*. New York: Collier Books, 1971.
6. Lowen, Alexander. *The Way to Vibrant Health*. New York: Harper & Row, 1977.
7. MacLean, Paul D. *The Triune Brain in Evolution*. New York: Plenum Press, 1990.
8. Martin, Howard. *"TEDxSantaCruz: Engaging the Intelligence of the Heart."* Online video clip. YouTube. YouTube, 14 Jan. 2012. Web. 02 Dec. 2015.
9. Reich, Wilhelm. *Character Analysis*. New York: Farrar, Straus and Giroux, 1980.
10. Scaer, Robert. *The Body Bears the Burden*. New York: Routledge, 2014.

SECTION 3.2

1. Reich, Wilhelm. *Character Analysis*. New York: Farrar, Straus and Giroux, 1980.
2. Lowen, Alexander. *The Language of the Body*. New York: Collier Books, 1971.
3. Hulse, Elliott. *"Bioenergetics for Social Confidence."* Online video clip. YouTube. YouTube, 23 Apr. 2014. Web 04 Dec. 2015.
4. Hulse, Elliott. *"Daily Bio-Energizer Warm Up."* Online video clip. YouTube. YouTube, 19 May 2012. Web 04 Dec. 2015.
5. Hulse, Elliott. *"How to Breathe Into Your Balls."* Online video clip. YouTube. YouTube, 22 Mar. 2013. Web 04 Dec. 2015.
6. Hulse, Elliott. *"The Truth About Deep Breathing."* Online video clip. YouTube. YouTube, 12 Sept. 2012. Web 04 Dec. 2015.

SECTION 3.3

1. Chek, Paul. *How to Eat, Move, and Be Healthy*. San Diego, CA: C.H.E.K. Institute, 2004.
2. Harris, Bill. "Scientific Research Validates Holosync's Benefits." Centerpointe Research Institute. Centerpointe Research Institute, n.d. Web. 4 Dec. 2015. <http://www.centerpointe.com/articles/articles-research>.

REFERENCES

3. Hulse, Elliott. *"Bioenergetics for Your Face."* Online video clip. YouTube. YouTube, 1 Aug. 2013. Web 04 Dec. 2015.
4. Hulse, Elliott. *"Exercise for Building Confidence."* Online video clip. YouTube. YouTube, 2 Mar. 2012. Web 04 Dec. 2015.
5. Hulse, Elliott. *"Grief Release Exercise."* Online video clip. YouTube. YouTube, 18 Oct. 2012. Web 04 Dec. 2015.
6. Hulse, Elliott. *"1 Easy Method to Meditate and Balance Your Nervous System."* Online video clip. YouTube. YouTube, 4 Jun. 2014. Web 04 Dec. 2015.

SECTION 3.4

1. Edinger, Edward. *Ego and Archetype.* Boston, MA: Shambhala Publications, 1972.
2. Hulse, Elliott. *"The Voice of Your Heart and Balls."* Online video clip. YouTube. YouTube, 28 Jan. 2014. Web 04 Dec. 2015.
3. Moore, Robert. *"A Neo-Jungian Mapping of The Psyche."* The C.G. Jung Association of Central Ohio. Chicago, IL: IS Productions, 2009. MP3. Bollingen Lecture Series.
4. Moore, Robert, and Max Havlick. *Facing the Dragon.* Wilmette, IL: ChironPublications, 2003.
5. Moore, Robert. *"The Ego and Its Relations With The Unconscious."* Chicago, IL: The C.G. Jung Institute of Chicago. 16 Apr. 1991. MP3.
6. Moore, Robert. *"The Great Self Within."* Chicago, IL: The C.G. Jung Institute of Chicago. 27 Feb. 1993. MP3.

SECTION 3.5

1. Moore, Robert, and Douglas Gillette. *King, Warrior, Magician, Lover.* New York: HarperCollins Publishers, 1990.
2. Moore, Robert, and Douglas Gillette. 1992. Narr. David Dukes. *The King Within.* Audible Audiobook Download. Phoenix Books, 2009. MP3.
3. Moore, Robert, and Douglas Gillette. *"The Lover Within."* Chicago, IL: The C.G. Jung Institute of Chicago. 22 Jan. 1990. MP3.
4. Moore, Robert, and Douglas Gillette. *"The Magician Within."* Chicago, IL: The C.G. Jung Institute of Chicago. 2 Apr. 1990. MP3.
5. Moore, Robert, and Douglas Gillette. *"The Warrior Within."* Chicago, IL: The C.G. Jung Institute of Chicago. 18 Jan. 1989. MP3.

SECTION 3.6

1. Edinger, Edward. *Ego and Archetype.* Boston, MA: Shambhala Publications, 1972.
2. Hulse, Elliott. *"3 Kinds of People In Your Life."* Online video clip. YouTube. YouTube, 12 May 2014. Web 04 Dec. 2015.

3. Moore, Robert. "*A Neo-Jungian Mapping of The Psyche.*" The C.G. Jung Association of Central Ohio. Chicago, IL: IS Productions, 2009. MP3. Bollingen Lecture Series.
4. Moore, Robert, and Max Havlick. *Facing the Dragon*. Wilmette, IL: Chiron Publications, 2003.
5. Moore, Robert. "*Practicing The Presence of The Other Within.*" Chicago, IL: The C.G. Jung Institute of Chicago. 8 Nov. 2003. MP3.
6. Moore, Robert. "*The Ego and Its Relations With The Unconscious.*" Chicago, IL: The C.G. Jung Institute of Chicago. 16 Apr. 1991. MP3.
7. Moore, Robert. "*The Great Self Within.*" Chicago, IL: The C.G. Jung Institute of Chicago. 27 Feb. 1993. MP3.

SECTION 4.1

1. Greene, Robert. *Mastery*. New York: Penguin Books, 2012.
2. Hulse, Elliott. "*How Do I Know My Calling?*" Online video clip. *YouTube*. YouTube, 30 May 2013. Web 04 Dec. 2015.
3. Tracy, Brian. 1996. Narr. Brian Tracy. *The Luck Factor*. Audible Audiobook Download. Nightingale Conant, 2014. MP3.

SECTION 4.2

1. Assaraf, John. "Daily Neural Reconditioning." *Johnassaraf.com*. P4d, n.d. Web. 04 Dec. 2015. <http://johnassaraf.com/daily-neural-reconditioning>.
2. Assaraf, John. "*Automatic Negative Thoughts.*" Online video clip. *YouTube*. YouTube, 21 Jan 2015. Web 04 Dec. 2015.
3. Hulse, Elliott. "*Transform Negative Thoughts.*" Online video clip. *YouTube*. YouTube, 2 Jun 2014. Web 04 Dec. 2015.
4. Tracy, Brian. 1996. Narr. Brian Tracy. *The Luck Factor*. Audible Audiobook Download. Nightingale Conant, 2014. MP3.

SECTION 4.3

1. *Braveheart*. Dir. Mel Gibson. Prod. Mel Gibson. By Randall Wallace. Perf. Mel Gibson, Sophie Marceau, and Patrick McGoohan. Paramount Pictures, 1995. DVD.
2. Campbell, Joseph. *The Hero with A Thousand Faces*. Novato, CA: New World Library, 2008.
3. Campbell, Joseph, and Bill Moyers. 1988. Narr. Joseph Campbell and Bill Moyers. *The Power of Myth*. Audible Audiobook Download. Highbridge, 2007. MP3.
4. Campbell, Joseph. *Myths to Live By*. New York: Viking Press, 1972.
5. Coelho, Paulo. 1988. Narr. Jeremey Irons. *The Alchemist*. Audible Audiobook Download. HarperAudio, 2005. MP3.

REFERENCES

6. *Gladiator*. Dir. Ridley Scott. Perf. Russell Crowe and Joaquin Phoenix. Dreamworks L.L.C and Universal Studios, 2000. DVD.
7. *Groundhog Day*. Dir. Harold Ramis. Prod. Harold Ramis. By Harold Ramis and Danny Rubin. Perf. Harold Ramis, Bill Murray, and Andie MacDowell. Columbia Pictures, 1993.DVD.
8. *Hercules*. Dir. Ron Clements and John Musker. Walt Disney Home Video, 1998. DVD.
9. Hesse, Hermann. *Siddhartha*. New York: New Directions, 1951.
10. Homer, Robert Fagles, and Bernard Knox. *The Iliad*. New York, NY, U.S.A.: Viking,1990. Print.
11. Hulse, Elliott. *"How to Become a Lion Amongst Sheep."* Online video clip. YouTube. YouTube, 31 Oct. 2013. Web 04 Dec. 2015.
12. Hulse, Elliott. *"Dangerous Journey of Following Your Heart."* Online video clip. *YouTube*. YouTube, 30 Oct. 2013. Web 04 Dec. 2015.
13. Hulse, Elliott. "Hero's Journey (Becoming a Real Man)." Online video clip. *YouTube*. YouTube, 19 Oct. 2013. Web 04 Dec. 2015.
14. Hulse, Elliott. *"Call To Adventure."* Online video clip. *YouTube*. YouTube, 30 Jan. 2014. Web 04 Dec. 2015.
15. Kafka, Franz. "Franz Kafka Online." *Before the Law*. Trans. Ian Johnston. Franz Kafka Online, n.d. Web. 04 Dec. 2015. <http://www.kafka-online.info/before-the-law.html>.
16. Kinsella, Thomas. *The Tain*. New York: Oxford University Press, 2002.
17. Mitchell, Stephen. *Gilgamesh*. New York: Free Press, 2004.
18. Narayan, R. K. *The Ramayana*. New York: Penguin Books, 2006.
19. *Niane*, D. T., David W. Chappell, and Jim Jones. Sundiata. Harlow, England: PearsonLongman, 2006.
20. *Patton*, Laurie L. The Bhagavad Gita. New York: Penguin Books, 2008.
21. Rowling, J. K., and Mary GrandPré. *Harry Potter: The Complete Series*. New York: Scholastic, 2009.
22. *Star Wars Trilogy*. Dir. George Lucas. Perf. Harrison Ford and Mark Hamill. Twentieth-Century Fox Corp., 1977. DVD.
23. *The Lion King*. Dir. Roger Allers and Rob Minkoff. By Irene Mecchi, Jonathan Roberts, Linda Woolverton, Tim Rice, Elton John, Matthew Broderick, James Earl Jones, and Jeremy Irons. Buena Vista Pictures Distribution, Inc., 1994. DVD.
24. *The Matrix*. Dir. The Wachowski Brothers. Perf. Keanu Reeves and Laurence Fishburne. Warner Home Video, 1999. DVD.
25. *The Wizard of Oz*. Dir. Victor Fleming. Perf. Judy Garland and Frank Morgan. MGM, 1939. Videocassette.
26. Tolkien, J. R. R. *The Lord of the Rings*. Boston, MA: Houghton Mifflin, 1967.
27. *300*. Dir. Zack Snyder. By Zack Snyder, Kurt Johnstad, and Michael B. Gordon. Prod. Gianni Nunnari, Mark Canton, Bernie Goldmann, and Jeffrey Silver. Perf. Gerard Butler and Lena Headey. Warner Bros. Pictures, 2007. DVD.

SECTION 4.5

1. Bly, Robert. 1990. Narr. Richard Ferrone. *Iron John*. Audible Audiobook Download. Recorded Books, 2012. MP3.
2. Gennep, Arnold Van. *The Rites of Passage*. Chicago, IL: U of Chicago, 1960.
3. Hulse, Elliott. "*How Strength Saved My Life.*" Online video clip. *YouTube*. YouTube, 24 Oct. 2013. Web 04 Dec. 2015.
4. Levinson, Daniel J. *The Seasons of a Man's Life*. New York: Random House, 1978.
5. Michaels, William. *The Sacred and The Profane*. New York: St. Martin's, 1989.
6. Moore, Robert L., and Max J. Havlick. *The Archetype of Initiation*. Philadelphia:Xlibris, 2001.
7. Turner, Victor W. *The Ritual Process*. Chicago, IL: Aldine Pub., 1969.